D0207639

THE VIEW FROM THE HELM

THE VIEW FROM THE HELM

Leading the American University during an Era of Change

JAMES J. DUDERSTADT

The University of Michigan Press ⁂ *Ann Arbor*

Published in the United States of America by
The University of Michigan Press
Manufactured in the United States of America
⊗ Printed on acid-free paper

2010 2009 2008 2007 4 3 2 1

A CIP catalog record for this book is available from the British Library.

Library of Congress Cataloging-in-Publication Data

Duderstadt, James J., 1942–
The view from the helm : leading the American university during an era of change / James J. Duderstadt.
p. cm.
Includes bibliographical references and index.
ISBN-13: 978-0-472-11590-7 (cloth : alk. paper)
ISBN-10: 0-472-11590-1 (cloth : alk. paper)
1. Universities and colleges—United States—Administration.
2. College presidents—United States. 3. Educational leadership—United States. 4. Duderstadt, James J., 1942– I. Title.

LB2341.A357 1997
378.1'01—dc22 2006103238

To Anne, Susan, and Kathy
with appreciation and admiration
for their roles as Michigan's first family

CONTENTS

PREFACE

The American university presidency is one of those highly respected yet generally misunderstood roles in contemporary society. Most outside the academy view leading a major university as a prestigious and significant assignment, comparable to a corporate chief executive officer or senior public official, such as a governor. Certainly the size, complexity, and social impact of the contemporary university demand considerable skill as a leader, manager, politician, and, of course, fund-raiser extraordinaire. Yet, despite the importance of the presidential role, many students and faculty on the campus view university presidents as one of the lower life-forms of academic administration, and their respect for presidential authority is accordingly limited. The public visibility and responsibility of presidency, its rather anemic authority, and its accountability to lay governing boards demand both a very thick skin and a tolerance for high risk. The late Yale president A. Bartlett Giamatti once put it: "Being president of a university is no way for an adult to make a living. Which is why so few adults actually attempt to do it. It is to hold a mid-nineteenth-century ecclesiastical position on top of a late-twentieth-century corporation."[1]

At the University of Michigan, the Office of the President is located in the Fleming Administration Building,[2] a formidable block-house-shaped structure with a Mondrian pattern of narrow slits for windows. This fortresslike building, constructed during the days of campus protest in the 1960s, suggests power and authority—and perhaps as well isolation from the surrounding campus. Yet in reality this building is the helm of the university ship of state, where the president must chart a course and then navigate the institution from its traditions, achievements, and obligations of the past, through the turbulent seas of social change, toward an uncertain—indeed, unknowable—future.

My own tenure at this helm of the university—as provost, acting president, and president—lasted almost a decade, sandwiched between other academic roles as a professor, research director, and dean, all at the University of Michigan and together spanning almost four decades. I regarded serving as president of the university as both a privilege and a high calling. But I must admit that there were times when it also seemed to be just another one of those onerous assignments a faculty member is asked to assume, more akin to chairing the curriculum committee or a task force on budget cuts than to being elected as a powerful chief executive officer of the university. Hence, it was not particularly surprising to most of my colleagues at Michigan when, following my 10 years at the helm of the university, I returned to the faculty to resume my activities as a teacher and a scholar, although such a decision was certainly counter to the current tendencies of many university presidents to migrate from one institution to the next.

Recently, several of my colleagues have reminded me that one of my presidential duties remained unfulfilled. Most presidents of major universities, such as the University of Michigan, are expected to write their memoirs of the experience. In some cases, these efforts turn into autobiographies that are both amusing and therapeutic. Others instead draw on their experiences as university presidents to focus on issues related to higher education and its role in society, a path I have followed in past tomes concerning an array of topics, such as the future of the public university, technology, and—perhaps against my better judgment—intercollegiate athletics.

In response to the reminders, I decided to kill several birds with one stone, by writing such a memoir but, rather than organizing it as the traditional chronological narrative, instead using my tenure as president of the University of Michigan to animate a commentary on the state of the contemporary university presidency. In this effort, I have also introduced a historical perspective by drawing on the experiences and achievements of earlier presidents of my university. This synthesis of memoir, history, and commentary was stimulated by my strong belief that successful university presidents are usually those who build on the history, traditions, and culture of their institutions, learning well from the experiences of their predecessors. To illustrate this important principle, part I of this book begins in chapter 1 with a brief summary of the history of the University of Michigan, identifying what Burton Clark defines as its *institutional saga*—those longstanding characteristics that determine its distinctiveness. Here I have devoted particular attention to how earlier Michigan presidents have both shaped and been shaped by the Michigan saga in their efforts to face the challenges and opportunities of their eras.

With this historical background, the book then moves in chapter 2 to discuss the various paths to a university presidency, drawn heavily from my personal experience and later roles as counsel and confidant to both those seeking university presidencies and those responsible for selecting university leadership. Chapter 3 then turns to the selection and evaluation of university leaders, with the aim of providing guidance to both the hunters (governing boards) and the hunted (candidates) in the presidential search process. Again this chapter draws on my experience, as a quarry of the presidential hunt.

The diverse roles and responsibilities of the contemporary university presidency are the subject of part II of this book. Academic institutions are, in reality, very complex social communities. Their leadership involves not simply managing a complex array of activities but, more significant, providing intellectual, moral, pastoral, and, on occasion, even spiritual leadership for large, diverse communities. After a brief review of the general aspects of university leadership in chapter 4, chapters 5–9 consider in some depth particular presidential roles, including executive responsibilities, academic leadership, political roles, moral leadership, pastoral care for the university community, and strategic leadership.

Part III of this book concerns the personal and professional life of the university president. Chapter 10 provides a perspective of the wear and tear of public leadership, its rewards and challenges, and the role of and impact on the presidential family. Chapter 11 illustrates the degree to which both risk and failure are important elements of all presidencies. The final chapter concerns the endgame, the decision to step down, and the afterlife of the university presidency. It concludes with a brief assessment of whether the contemporary university presidency, at least as it is currently structured and perceived, is a realistic assignment, capable of attracting talented individuals and enabling their successful leadership of these important social institutions.

It seems appropriate to mention here an important caveat. Although I have had the good fortune to have experienced essentially all of the academic leadership roles in the university—from my early years as a rank-and-file faculty member involved in teaching, research, grant hustling, supervision of PhD students, and faculty governance, to various administrative assignments as dean, provost, and president—I have done so at a single institution, the University of Michigan. This happens to be an anomaly in higher education, since these days it is quite rare for a university president to be selected from an institution's own faculty and rarer still for a university faculty member to spend an entire career at a single institution. To some, my mobility impairment may suggest a personal character flaw, perhaps a lack of imagination or marketing skill. However, I used to rationalize this dogged determination to remain in Ann Arbor by recalling an observation made by a former dean colleague that there were very few institutions in our society today worthy of total loyalty and commitment and that fortunately the University of Michigan was one of them. Actually, I do not remember just which of our deans said this, since he or she has probably long since left the university for greener pastures. In any event, it was a belief I shared.

Furthermore, the University of Michigan has played an important role in both defining and transforming the nature of higher education in America in the past, and it continues to do so today, in such areas as social inclusion (e.g., the 2003 Supreme Court cases defending the importance of diversity), technology (e.g., the 1980s development of the Internet), and public character (e.g., the "Michigan model" of transforming an institution of higher education into a privately supported public university more capable of balancing the vicissitudes of tax support with success in the competitive marketplace for private support). Hence, what better place could there be to use as a springboard for a career-long effort to lead change. Or at least, so I have believed.

Clearly the issues and perspectives discussed in this book are heavily influenced by the particular characteristics of the University of Michigan. Since Michigan is one of the largest and most complex universities in the world, the scope and complexity of that institution sometimes can magnify issues to levels far beyond those experienced by most other institutions. Yet, while perhaps different in magnitude, my experiences as president at Michigan are, for the most part, quite similar in character to those faced by the presidents of most colleges and universities.

The task of leading a university can be complex, confusing, and frustrating at times. The wear and tear of being on call 24 hours a day, 365 days a year; of defending the institution against its foes and sometimes even its friends; of conveying a sense of optimism and hope amid the doom and gloom that pervades a campus during hard times—all take their toll. Most presidents of the University of Michigan (myself included) have wondered at times, in personal papers or intimate conversations, whether they made the wrong decision to accept the position. On my last day in office, I took my e-mail pager, long cursed for its frequent emergency messages that drove my Pavlovian responses to crisis, and tossed it into a nearby lake as a symbol of cutting the cord and returning to the freedom of faculty life once again.

Together, my wife, Anne, and I began our years in Ann Arbor in university family housing in 1968, returning 20 years later for another decade in university housing in the presidential mansion. After 10 years at the helm of the university, serving together in my assignments as provost and president (which for us, as with many other colleagues in university leadership positions, were two-person roles), we decided to return to the faculty and the community where we began our Michigan odyssey. We have continued to serve on the faculty and within the campus community, if sometimes only as ghosts of the university past, since invisibility is an absolute requirement for has-been presidents. We both regarded the opportunity to serve in the presidency of the University of Michigan as not only a calling of great responsibility but a privilege of leadership and service on behalf of a truly remarkable institution. It is my hope that this book will convey such a sense of both the challenges and the rewards that accompany the role of leading the American university.

Ann Arbor, Michigan
Fall 2006

ACKNOWLEDGMENTS

The arcane skills required to lead a major university are best learned from other accomplished academic leaders. In this regard, I must acknowledge the extraordinary impact that earlier Michigan presidents have had on my own career: Harlan Hatcher, Robben Fleming, and Harold Shapiro served as mentors, friends, and confidants. Beyond this, other Michigan leaders, several of whom went on to major university presidencies themselves, have been important role models, including Frank Rhodes, Billy Frye, and Chuck Vest. So, too, my friends and colleagues serving on the Michigan faculty and as deans and executive officers have similarly had great influence on my role as an academic leader.

Beyond the privilege of serving a great university, perhaps the most rewarding and satisfying aspect of my presidency was the ability to join with many remarkably talented and dedicated people in the task of keeping Michigan among "the leaders and best." The size, complexity, and aspirations for excellence of the university both require and attract great leadership at all levels, among its faculty, students, staff, administrators, regents, and alumni. Whatever success was achieved during my years at the helm of the university was due to a very considerable extent to the effort, talent, wisdom, and courage of the Michigan leadership team, defined in the broadest sense.

During the decade covered by this book, the University of Michigan was particularly fortunate to have a truly remarkable team of executive officers, many of whom continued on to other significant leadership roles in higher education, all of whom had extensive experience with higher education, and all of whom are owed a deep debt of gratitude. This team consisted of the following people in the following positions:

Provost: Chuck Vest, Gil Whitaker, Bernie Machen

Executive Vice President and Chief Financial Officer: Farris Womack

Vice President for Research: Linda Wilson, Bill Kelly, Homer Neal

Graduate Dean: John D'Arms (d.), Bob Weisbuch

Vice President for Student Affairs: Henry Johnson, Mary Ann Swain, Maureen Hartford

Vice President for University Affairs: Walt Harrison

Vice President for Development: Jon Cosovich (d.), Joe Roberson, Tom Kinnear

Secretary: Dick Kennedy (d.), Harold Johnson, Roberta Palmer

Associate Vice President: Doug Van Houweling, George Zuidema, Charles Moody, Lester Monts, Rhetaugh Dumas, Harold Jacobson (d.), John Jackson, Robert Holbrook

Chancellor: Blenda Wilson, Clint Jones, Jim Renick, Charlie Nelms

Athletic Director: Bo Schembechler (d.), Jack Weidenbach, Joe Roberson

Assistant: Robin Jacoby, Shirley Clarkson, Connie Cook, Ejner Jensen, Susan Lipschutz (d.)

During my tenure, Michigan was truly a deans' university, providing the deans of our schools and colleges with unusual authority and opportunity, depending heavily on their leadership, and attracting some truly remarkable academic leaders. And, of course, the progress achieved by a university of the size and complexity of the University of Michigan depends on the efforts of talented and committed faculty, staff, and student leaders. Hence, in a very real sense, the progress documented in this book should also be regarded as a summary and a tribute to all of their extraordinary achievements.

Revisiting the personal experiences of leading one of the nation's leading public research universities and capturing those experiences in accurate, balanced, and engaging prose a decade later is no small feat. It required the assistance and wise counsel of many former colleagues, too numerous to mention here. But of particular help in the development of the book was the critical analysis of Lisa Baker, who, as my former media relations officer, had learned well the difficult task of telling me what I sometimes did not want to hear; Julie Steiff, a particularly skilled and thoughtful editor, who has worked with me on several earlier book projects; and James Reische, who, as the assigned editor at the University of Michigan Press, provided strong and constructive feedback on various drafts of the manuscript.

However, most significant in this effort has been the role of Anne Duderstadt. Without her ability (not to mention her memory) to capture the spirit, excitement, and satisfaction of those years—tempered, of course, by occasional frustration and disappointment—this book would have been quite impossible. The two of us stood side by side at the helm during this decade of university leadership, experiencing the trials and tribulations of university leadership together. It was her contribution to our university leadership that frequently steered the institution through stormy seas and away from the doldrums, as it prepared to enter a new century.

PART I

The Path to the Presidency

I

THE LEADERS AND BEST

The beginning of a new university presidency is usually associated with the pomp and circumstance of an academic inauguration ceremony. The colorful robes of an academic procession, the familiar strains of ritualistic music, and the presence of distinguished guests and visitors all make for an impressive ceremony, designed to symbolize the crowning of a new university leader. Of course, like most senior leadership positions, the university presidency takes many forms depending on the person; the institution; and, perhaps most significant, the needs of the times. Clearly, as the chief executive officer of an institution with thousands of employees (faculty and staff) and clients (students, patients, sports fans), an annual budget in the billions of dollars, a physical plant the size of a small city, and an influence that is frequently global in extent, the management responsibilities of the university president are considerable, comparable to those of the CEO of a large, multinational corporation.

A university president is also a public leader, with important symbolic, political, pastoral, and at times even moral leadership roles, particularly when it comes to representing the institution to a diverse array of external constituencies, such as government, business and industry, prospective donors, the media, and the public at large. The contemporary university is a political tempest in which all the contentious issues swirling about our society churn together: for example, civil rights versus racial preference, freedom of speech versus conflicting political ideologies, social purpose versus market-driven cost-effectiveness. It is of little wonder that today's university president is frequently caught in the cross fire from opposing political points of view, making the presidency of a major university both considerably more difficult and less attractive now than in earlier eras.

My service on various advisory committees and as understudy to two earlier Michigan presidents had provided a rigorous education on the nature of the contemporary university presidency prior to my ascent—or perhaps descent, in the minds of some—to this leadership role. It was therefore perhaps not surprising that on that beautiful fall day in October 1988, my wife, Anne, and I approached my inauguration as Michigan's eleventh president with considerable apprehension. We viewed even the terminology used to describe the inauguration event, the "installation" of a new president, as suggestive more of bolting one into the complex machinery of the university administration than of coronating a new leader. Yet we also viewed this opportunity to serve our university as both a great privilege and a very considerable responsibility. Fortunately, after two decades at Michigan, we were well steeped in the legend and lore of the university, a very key requirement for a successful university presidency.

INSTITUTIONAL SAGA

Successful university presidents must be well informed (acclimated or indoctrinated) to the history, traditions, and cultures of the institutions they are leading. The way that academic institutions respond to changes in leadership is very different than, for example, the way that the federal government adapts to a new president or the way that a corporation is reshaped to accommodate a new CEO. Universities are based on long-standing traditions and continuity, evolving over many generations (in some cases, even centuries), with very particular sets of values, traditions, and practices.

Burton R. Clark, a noted sociologist and scholar of higher education, introduced the concept of "organizational legend," or "institutional saga," to refer to those long-standing characteristics that determine the distinctiveness of a college or university.[1] Clark's view is that "[a]n organizational legend (or saga), located between ideology and religion, partakes of an appealing logic on one hand and sentiments similar to the spiritual on the other"; that universities "develop over time such an intentionality about institutional life, a saga, which then results in unifying the institution and shaping its purpose." Clark notes: "An institutional saga may be found in many forms, through mottoes, traditions, and ethos. It might consist of long-standing practices or unique roles played by an institution, or even in the images held in the minds (and hearts) of students, faculty, and alumni. Sagas can provide a sense of romance and even mystery that turn a cold organization into a beloved social institution, capturing the allegiance of its members and even defining the identity of its communities."[2]

All colleges and universities have a social purpose, but for some, these responsibilities and roles have actually shaped their evolution and determined their character. The appearance of a distinct institutional saga involves many elements—visionary leadership; strong faculty and student cultures; unique programs; ideologies; and, of course, the time to accumulate the events, achievements, legends, and mythology that characterize long-standing institutions. For example, the saga of my alma mater, Yale University, was shaped over the centuries by old-boy traditions, such as secret societies (e.g., Skull and Bones); literature (from dime-novel heroes, such as Frank Merriwell and Dink Stover, to Buckley's *God and Man at Yale*); and national leadership (William H. Taft, George H. Bush, Bill Clinton, George W. Bush, and Gerald R. Ford—although the latter was first and foremost a Michigan man).[3] Harvard's saga is perhaps best captured by the response of a former Harvard president who, when asked what it takes to build a great institution like Harvard, responded simply, "Three hundred years!" Notre Dame draws its saga from the legends of the gridiron, that is, Knute Rockne, the Four Horsemen, and the Subway Alumni. Big Ten universities also have their symbols: fraternity and sorority life, campus protests, and gigantic football stadiums.

While institutional sagas are easy to identify for older universities (e.g., North Carolina, Virginia, and Michigan among the publics; Harvard, Yale, and Princeton among the privates), they can sometimes be problematic to institutions rising rapidly to prominence.

During the controversy over inappropriate use of government research funds at Stanford during the 1990s, the late Roger Heyns—former Michigan dean; chancellor at the University of California, Berkeley; and then president of the Hewlett Foundation, adjacent to the Stanford campus—once observed to me that Stanford faced a particular challenge in becoming too good too fast.[4] Prior to World War II, its reputation as "the farm" was well deserved. Stanford was peaceful, pastoral, and conservative. The extraordinary reputation it achieved first in the sciences and then across all the disciplines in the latter half of the twentieth century came on so abruptly that the institution sometimes found it difficult to live with its newfound prestige and visibility, as its inquisition by a congressional inquiry into misuse of research funds in the 1990s demonstrated.

Again I quote Burton Clark: "The institutional saga is a historically based, somewhat embellished understanding of a unique organization development. Colleges are prone to a remembrance of things past and a symbolism of uniqueness. The more special the history or the more forceful the claim to a place in history, the more intensively cultivated are the ways of sharing memory and symbolizing the institution."[5] A visit to the campuses of one of our distinguished private universities conveys just such an impression of history and tradition. Their ancient ivy-covered buildings and their statues, plaques, and monuments attesting to important people and events of the past convey a sense that these institutions have evolved slowly over the centuries—in careful and methodical ways—to achieve their present forms and define their institutional saga. In contrast, a visit to the campus of one of our great state universities conveys more of a sense of dynamism and impermanence. Most of the buildings look new, even hastily constructed to accommodate rapid growth. The icons of the public university tend to be their football stadiums or the smokestacks of their central power plants, rather than ivy-covered buildings or monuments. In talking with campus leaders at public universities, one gets little sense that the history of these institutions is valued or recognized. Perhaps this is due to their egalitarian nature or, conversely, to the political (and politicized) process that structures their governance and all too frequently informs their choice of leadership. The consequence is that the public university evolves through geological layers, each generation paving over or obliterating the artifacts and achievements of its predecessors with a new layer of structures, programs, and practices. Hence, the first task of a new president of such an institution is that of unearthing and understanding its institutional saga.

THE MICHIGAN SAGA

To illustrate, let me adopt the perspective of a university archaeologist by sifting through the layers of the University of Michigan's history to uncover its institutional saga. Actually, this exercise is necessary both to explain my particular experience as a university president and to set the stage for a more in-depth analysis of the various elements of university leadership. So what might be suggested as the institutional saga of the University of Michigan? What are the first images of Michigan that come to mind? Academic activities such as students listening attentively to brilliant faculty in the lecture hall or studying in the library? Scientists toiling away late in the evenings in the laboratory, striving to understand the universe; or scholars poring over ancient manuscripts, rediscovering our human heritage? Not likely.

The University of Michigan is many things to many people, but its images are rarely stimulated by its core missions of teaching and scholarship. To some, the university's image is its football team, the Michigan Wolverines, decked out in those ferocious winged helmets as it stampedes into Michigan Stadium before a crowd of 110,000, rising to sing the Michigan fight song, *Hail to the Victors.* Others think first of a Michigan of the arts, where the world's leading orchestras and artists come to perform in Hill Auditorium, one of the great concert halls of the world.

For some, Michigan represents the youthful conscience of a nation—the birthplace of the teach-in protests against an unpopular war in Vietnam, site of the first Earth Day, and home of the century-old *Michigan Daily,* with student engagement in so many of the critical issues of the day. There is also the caring Michigan, as experienced by millions of patients who have been treated by the University of Michigan Medical Center, one of the nation's great centers of medical research, teaching, and clinical care.

Then there is the Michigan of the cutting-edge research that so improves the quality of our lives. For example, it was at Michigan fifty years ago that the clinical trials were conducted for the Salk polio vaccine. It was at Michigan that the gene responsible for cystic fibrosis was identified and cloned in the 1990s. And although others may have "invented" the Internet, it was Michigan (together with another "big blue" partner, IBM) that built and managed the Internet backbone for the nation during the 1980s and early 1990s.

Michigan can also be seen as a university of the world, long renowned as a truly international center of learning. If you walk down the streets of any capital city in the world, you will encounter Michigan graduates, often in positions of leadership. Indeed, Michigan is even a university of the universe, with the establishment of the first lunar chapter of the UM Alumni Association by the all-Michigan crew of Apollo 15.

These activities may serve as images of the university for many. I would suggest, however, that they are less a conveyance of the nature of Michigan's institutional saga than a consequence of its more fundamental traditions and character. To truly understand Michigan's saga, one must go back in time almost two centuries ago, to the university's founding in frontier America.

It can be argued that it was in the Midwest, in such towns as Ann Arbor and Madison, that the early paradigm for the true public university in America first evolved, a paradigm that was capable of responding to the needs of a rapidly changing nation in the nineteenth century and that still dominates higher education today. In many ways, the University of Michigan has been, throughout its history, the flagship of public higher education in America. Although the University of Michigan was not the first of the state universities, it was the first to be free of sectarian control, created as a true public institution, and responsive to the people of its state.

The University of Michigan (or, more accurately, the Catholepistemead or University of Michigania) was established in the village of Detroit in 1817 (two decades before Michigan entered the Union), by an act of the Northwest Territorial government. It was financed through the sale of Indian lands granted by the U.S. Congress. The founding principle for the university can be found in the familiar words of the Northwest Ordinance, chiseled on the frieze of the most prominent building on today's campus, Angell Hall: "Religion, morality, and knowledge being necessary to good government and the happiness of mankind, schools and the means of education shall forever be encouraged."[6] This precept clearly echoes the Jeffersonian ideal of education for all—to the extent of an individual's capacity—as the key to creating the educated citizenry necessary for a democracy to flourish.

Actually, the first incarnation of the University of Michigan (the Catholepistemiad) was not a university but, rather, a centralized system of schools, borrowing a model from the imperial University of France founded by Napoleon a decade earlier. It was only after the state of Michigan entered the Union in 1837 that a new plan was adopted to shift the university beyond secondary education, establishing it as a "state" university after the Prussian system, with programs in literature, science, and arts; medicine; and law—the first three academic departments of the new university.

Both because the university had already been in existence for two decades before the state of Michigan entered the Union in 1837 and because of the frontier society's deep distrust of politics and politicians, the new state's early constitution (1851) granted the university an unusual degree of autonomy as a "coordinate branch of state government," with full powers over all university matters granted to its governing board of regents (although, surprisingly enough, it did not state the purpose of the university). This constitutional autonomy, together with the fact that the university was actually established by the territorial government and supported through a land grant from the U.S. Congress, has shaped an important feature of the university's character. In financial terms, the University of Michigan was actually a U.S. land-grant university—supported entirely by the sale of its federal lands and student fees (rather than state resources)—until after the Civil War.[7] Hence, throughout its history, the university has regarded itself as much as a national university as a state university, albeit with some discretion when dealing with the Michigan state legislature. This broader heritage has also been reflected in the university's student enrollment, which has always been characterized by an unusually high percentage of out-of-state and international students.[8]

Furthermore, Michigan's constitutional autonomy, periodically reaffirmed through court tests and constitutional convention, has enabled the university to have much more control over its own destiny than have most other public universities.

Implicit in the new constitution was also a provision that the university's regents be determined by statewide popular election, again reflecting public dissatisfaction with the selection and performance of the early, appointed regents. (The last appointed board retaliated by firing the professors at the university.) The first assignment of the newly elected board was to select a president for the university (after inviting back the fired professors). After an extensive search, they elected Henry Philip Tappan, a broadly educated professor of philosophy from New York, as the first president of the reconfigured university.

Tappan arrived in Ann Arbor in 1852, determined to build a university very different from those characterizing the colonial colleges of nineteenth-century America. He was strongly influenced by such European leaders as von Humboldt, who stressed the importance of combining specialized research with humanistic teaching to define the intellectual structure of the university. Tappan articulated a vision of the university as a capstone of civilization, a repository for the accumulated knowledge of humankind, and a home for scholars dedicated to the expansion of human understanding. He maintained: "[A] university is the highest possible form of an institution of learning. It embraces every branch of knowledge and all possible means of making new investigations and thus advancing knowledge."[9]

In Tappan's view, the United States had no true universities, at least in the European sense. With the University of Michigan's founding heritage from both the French and Prussian systems, he believed he could build such an institution in the frontier state of Michigan. And build it, he did, attracting distinguished scholars to the faculty, such as Andrew D. White and Charles Kendall Adams,[10] and placing an emphasis on graduate study and research and on investing in major research facilities.

Of course, in many other ways, the university was still a frontier institution, as the early images of the campus suggest. Yet even at this early stage, the University of Michigan already exhibited many of the characteristics we see in today's universities. One might even make the claim that the University of Michigan was not only the first truly public university in America and one of its first land-grant universities but also possibly even its first true university, at least in the sense that we would understand it today. To be sure, the early colonial colleges, such as Harvard and Yale, were established much earlier by the states (or colonies), as were several institutions in the south, such as the University of North Carolina, the University of South Carolina, and the University of Georgia. But all were governed by clergymen, with the mission of preparing young men for leadership in church or state. The University of Michigan, predating Thomas Jefferson's University of Virginia by two years, was firmly established as a public university with no religious affiliation. Michigan's status as a land-grant university, provided through congressional action, predates by almost half a century the Land-Grant Acts establishing the great state universities (e.g., the Morrill Act of 1862). And Henry Tappan's vision of Michigan as a true university, stressing scholarship and scientific research along with instruction, predates by two decades other early American universities, such as Cornell University (founded by Andrew D. White, one of Tappan's faculty members at Michigan) and Johns Hopkins University.

From its founding, Michigan has always been identified with the most progressive forces in American higher education. The early colonial colleges served the aristocracy of colonial society, stressing moral development over a liberal education, much as did the English public schools, which were based on a classical curriculum in such subjects as Greek, Latin, and rhetoric. In contrast, Michigan blended the classical curriculum with the European model that stressed faculty involvement in research and dedication to the preparation of future scholars. Michigan hired as its first professors not classicists but a zoologist and a geologist. Unlike other institutions of the time, Michigan added instruction in the sciences to the humanistic curriculum, creating a hybrid that drew on the best of both a "liberal" and a "utilitarian" education.[11]

Throughout its early years, Michigan was the site of many firsts in higher education. Michigan was the first university in the West to pursue professional education, establishing its medical school in 1850, engineering courses in 1854, and a law school in 1859. The university was among the first to introduce instruction in fields as diverse as zoology and botany, modern languages, modern history, American literature, pharmacy, dentistry, speech, journalism, teacher education, forestry, bacteriology, and naval architecture. It provided leadership in scientific research by building one of the first university observatories in the world in 1854, followed in 1856 with the nation's first chemistry laboratory building. In 1869, it opened the first university-owned hospital, which today has evolved into one of the nation's largest university medical centers.

Michigan continued as a source of new academic programs in higher education into the twentieth century. It created the first aeronautical engineering program in 1913, then followed, soon after World War II, with the first nuclear engineering (1952) and computer engineering (1955) programs. The formation of the Survey Research Center and associated Institute of Social Research in the 1950s stimulated the quantitative approach that underpins today's social sciences. Michigan was a pioneer in atomic energy (with the first nuclear reactor on a university campus), then later developed time-sharing computing in the 1960s. In the 1980s, it played a leadership role in building and managing the Internet, the electronic superhighway that is now revolutionizing our society. Michigan's influence as an intellectual center today is evidenced by the fact that it has long been one of the nation's leaders in its capacity to attract research grants and contracts from the public and private sector, attracting over $800 million a year in such sponsored research support today.

Throughout its history, the University of Michigan has also been one of the nation's largest universities, vying with the largest private universities, such as Harvard and Columbia, during the nineteenth and early twentieth centuries, then holding this position of national leadership until the emergence of the statewide public university systems (including, e.g., the University of California and the University of Texas) in the post–World War II years. It continues to benefit from one of the largest alumni bodies in higher education, with over 450,000 living alumni. Michigan graduates are well represented in leadership roles in both the public and private sectors and in such learned professions as law, medicine, and engineering. Michigan sends more of its graduates on to professional study in such fields as law, medicine, engineering, and business than any other university in the nation. The university's influence on the nation has been profound through the achievements of its graduates.

What can be said of the role of sports, such as football, in Michigan's saga? The Michigan Wolverines play before hundreds of thousands of spectators in Michigan Stadium and millions of viewers across the nation. Michigan leads the nation in football victories, ironically passing Yale (on whose team I played in my college years) during my presidency in the 1990s. Standing tall in the history of sports are such Michigan gridiron legends as Fielding Yost, Tom Harmon, Bo Schembechler, and Gerald R. Ford. Yet as difficult as it may be for many fans to accept, football and other Michigan athletics have always been more of an asterisk to the list of the university's most important contributions to the nation. Michigan's sports are entertaining, to be sure, providing students, alumni, and fans with the thrill of victory and the agony of defeat—and always a topic of conversation at reunions. But in the grander scheme of higher education, they have proven neither substantive nor enduring in terms of true impact on the state, the nation, or the world.

Michigan students have often stimulated change in our society, but they have done so through their social activism and academic achievements rather than their athletic exploits. From the teach-ins against the Vietnam War in the 1960s to Earth Day in the 1970s to the Michigan Mandate in the 1980s, Michigan student activism has often been the catalyst for national movements. In a similar fashion, Michigan played a leadership role in public service, from John Kennedy's announcement of the Peace Corps on the steps of the Michigan Union in 1960 to the university's involvement in launching the AmeriCorps in 1994. Its classrooms have often been battlegrounds over what colleges will teach, from challenges to the Great Books canon to more recent confrontations over political correctness. Over a century ago, *Harper's Weekly* noted that the university's "most striking feature . . . is the broad and liberal spirit in which it does its work."[12] This spirit of democracy and tolerance for diverse views among its students and faculty continues today.

Nothing could be more natural to the University of Michigan

than challenging the status quo. Change has always been an important part of the university's tradition. Michigan has long defined the model of the large, comprehensive, public research university, with a serious commitment to scholarship and progress. It has been distinguished by unusual breadth, a rich diversity of academic disciplines, professional schools, social and cultural activities, and intellectual pluralism. The late Clark Kerr, the president of the University of California, once referred to the University of Michigan as "the mother of state universities," noting it as the first to prove that a high-quality education could be delivered at a publicly funded institution of higher learning.[13]

Interestingly enough, the university's success in achieving such quality had little to do with the generosity of state support. From its founding in 1817 until the state legislature made its first appropriation to the institution in 1867, the university was supported entirely from its federal land-grant endowment and the fees derived from students. During its early years, state government actually mismanaged and then misappropriated the funds from the congressional land grants intended to support the university. The university did not receive direct state appropriations until 1867, and for most of its history, Michigan's state support for its university has actually been quite modest relative to many other states. Rather, many people (including myself) believe that the real key to the University of Michigan's quality and impact has been the very unusual autonomy granted to the institution by the state constitution. The university has always been able to set its own goals for the quality of its programs, rather than allowing these to be determined by the vicissitudes of state policy, support, or public opinion. Put another way, although the university is legally "owned" by the people of the state, it has never felt obligated to adhere to the priorities or whims of a particular generation of Michigan citizens. Rather, it viewed itself as an enduring social institution with a duty of stewardship to generations past and a compelling obligation to take whatever actions were necessary to build and protect its capacity to serve future generations. Even though these actions might conflict from time to time with public opinion or the prevailing political winds of state government, the university's constitutional autonomy clearly gave it the ability to set its own course. The university has always viewed such objectives as program quality or access to educational opportunity as institutional decisions, rather than succumbing to public or political pressures.

This unrelenting commitment to academic excellence, broad student access, and public service continues today. In virtually all national and international surveys, the University of Michigan's programs rank among the very best, with most of its schools, colleges, and departments ranking in quality among the top 10 nationally and with several regarded as the leading programs in the nation. Other state universities have had far more generous state support than the University of Michigan. Others have had a more favorable geographical location than good, gray Michigan. Yet it was Michigan that made the unusual commitment to provide a college education of the highest possible quality to an increasingly diverse society—regardless of state support, policy, or politics. The rapid expansion and growth of the nation during the late nineteenth and early twentieth centuries demanded colleges and universities capable of serving all of its population (rather than simply the elite) as the key to a democratic society. Here, Michigan led the way both in its commitment to wide access and equality and in the leadership it provided for higher education in America.

Particularly notable here was the role of Michigan president James Angell in articulating the importance of Michigan's commitment to provide "an uncommon education for the common man." Angell challenged the aristocratic notions of leaders of the colonial colleges, such as Charles Eliot of Harvard. Angell argued that Americans should be given opportunities to develop talent and character to the fullest. He portrayed the state university as the bulwark against the aristocracy of wealth. Angell went further to claim that "the overwhelming majority of students at Michigan were the children of parents who are poor, or of very moderate means: that a very large portion have earned by hard toil and by heroic self-denial the amount needed to maintain themselves in the most frugal manner during their university course, and that so far from being an aristocratic institution, there is no more truly democratic institution in the world." To make a university education available to all economic classes, Michigan kept tuition and fees minimal for many years. President

Angell put it, "The whole policy of the administration of the university has been to make life here simple and inexpensive so that a large portion of our students can support themselves."[14] This commitment continues today, when even in an era of severe fiscal constraints, the university still meets the full financial need of every Michigan student enrolling in its programs.

As historian Frederick Rudolph suggests, it was through the leadership of the University of Michigan after the Civil War, joined by the University of Minnesota and the University of Wisconsin, that the state universities in the Midwest and West would evolve into the inevitable and necessary expression of a democratic society.[15] Frontier democracy and frontier materialism combined to create a new type of institution, capable of serving all of the people of a rapidly changing America through education, research, and public service. As Rudolph notes, these institutions attempted to "marry the practical and the theoretical, attempting to attract farm boys to their classrooms and scholars to their faculties."[16]

The university has long placed high value on the diversity of its student body, both because of its commitment to serve all of society and because of its perception that such diversity enhanced the quality of its educational programs. From its earliest years, Michigan sought to attract students from a broad range of ethnic and geographic backgrounds. By 1860, the regents referred "with partiality" to the "list of foreign students drawn thither from every section of our country."[17] Forty-six percent of the university's students then came from other states and foreign countries. Michigan awarded the first U.S. doctorate to a Japanese citizen, who later was instrumental in founding the University of Tokyo. President Angell's service in 1880–81 as U.S. envoy to China established further the university's great influence in Asia, when he later persuaded the United States to allow China to invest the reparations from the Boxer Rebellion in a new university, Tsinghua University.

The first African American students arrived on campus in 1868. Michigan was one of the first large universities in America to admit women in 1870. At the time, the rest of the nation looked on with a critical eye, certain that the experiment of coeducation would fail. Although the first women students were true pioneers (the objects of intense scrutiny and some resentment), the enrollment of women had increased by 1898 to the point where they received 53 percent of Michigan's undergraduate degrees, roughly the same percentage they represent today.

One of Michigan's most important contributions to the nation may be its commitment to providing an education of exceptional quality to students from all backgrounds. In many ways, it was at the University of Michigan that Thomas Jefferson's enlightened dreams for the public university were most faithfully realized. The university has always taken great pride in the diversity of its students, faculty, and programs, whether that diversity is characterized by gender, race, socioeconomic background, ethnicity, or nationality—not to mention academic interests or political persuasion. The university's constitutional autonomy enabled it to defend this commitment in the face of considerable political resistance to challenging the status quo, eventually taking the battle for diversity and equality of opportunity all the way to the U.S. Supreme Court in landmark cases in 2003. In more contemporary terms, it seems clear that an important facet of the institutional saga of the University of Michigan would be its achievement of excellence through diversity.

A HERITAGE OF LEADERSHIP

Of course, while university presidents are most successful when they understand and respect the institutional saga of their university, they are also capable of shaping it to some extent. Perhaps more significant, the long history and unusually strong traditions characterizing some universities, such as the University of Michigan, inform, define, and shape their leadership. It has sometimes been suggested that the regents of the University of Michigan have been fortunate to have always selected the right leader for the times. Yet history suggests that the achievements of Michigan's presidents have been due less to good fortune or wisdom in their selection than to the ability of this remarkable institution to mold its leadership. For this tradition, all should be grateful, since change inevitably happens in both rapid and unexpected ways in higher education, as evidenced by the diverse roles that the university's presidents have played over time.

Henry Philip Tappan (1852–63)

Henry Philip Tappan, Michigan's first president,[18] brought to Ann Arbor a vision of building a true university that would not only conduct instruction and advanced scholarship but also respond to popular needs. He aimed to develop an institution that would cultivate the originality and genius of the talented few seeking knowledge beyond the traditional curriculum, along with a graduate school in which diligent and responsible students could pursue their studies and research under the eye of learned scholars in an environment of enormous resources in books, laboratories, and museums. Although his expectation that university professors should engage in research as well as teaching disturbed some, it also allowed him to attract leading scholars and take the first steps toward building a "true university" in the European sense.

Yet Tappan also had an elitist streak. His vision, personality, and European pretensions eventually began to rub the frontier culture of Michigan the wrong way, with one newspaper describing him as "the most completely foreignized specimen of an abnormal Yankee we have ever seen."[19] Although Tappan's first board of regents strongly supported his vision, they were replaced in 1856 by a new board that, almost immediately after its election, began to undermine Tappan's leadership, by using a committee structure to weaken his executive powers. The board's opposition to Tappan was joined by several faculty members strongly resistant to change, along with the powerful editor of a Detroit newspaper. Eventually, the convergence of these hostile forces emboldened the regents to fire Tappan in 1863, ironically during a secret session soon after the regents' defeat in the statewide election. The lame-duck board named as his successor Erastus Haven, a former faculty member who had long sought the position.

Despite this ignominious end to his tenure by a hostile board of regents, Tappan is viewed today as one of the most important early

American university leaders, not only shaping the University of Michigan, but influencing all of higher education and defining the early nature of the American research university. Years later, President James Angell was to have the last word on the sordid incident: "Tappan was the largest figure of a man that ever appeared on the Michigan campus. And he was stung to death by gnats!"[20]

Erastus Otis Haven (1863–69)

A professor of Latin language and literature from 1852 to 1856, Erastus Haven had been among those seeking Henry Tappan's dismissal and viewed himself as a possible successor. Although the newly elected regents were lukewarm to Haven, they quickly concluded that it would be too disruptive to bring back Tappan, particularly after, following his departure from Ann Arbor, he had lashed out publicly at those who had undermined him at Michigan. Although Haven had no personal agenda, he was able to win over elements from both campus and community and succeeded in consolidating some of the reforms Tappan instituted. He secured a modest annual appropriation from the state legislature. He defended Michigan's unusually large out-of-state enrollments (then two-thirds) by reminding the legislature that the university had been funded through the sale of lands granted by the U.S. Congress rather than through state tax dollars and hence had national obligations, an argument subsequent presidents would frequently repeat.

However, Haven broke no new ground in moving further toward Tappan's vision of a university. He sided with the regents to deny admission to women. The unusual nature of his appointment in the wake of Tappan's firing would continue to deprive Haven of strong faculty and regental support. He soon became frustrated with faculty criticism and left in 1869 for the presidency of Northwestern University.

Henry Simmons Frieze (1869–71)

The regents asked Henry Frieze, professor of Latin language and literature, to serve as president pro tempore until Erastus Haven's successor could be selected. Frieze would later serve in the interim role on two other occasions, when his successor, James Angell, went on overseas assignments. Despite his brief tenure, Frieze accomplished much, quietly moving to admit women; obtaining the funds to build University Hall, the dominant academic building of the nineteenth-century campus; and establishing the University Musical Society, the center of cultural life in the university and Ann Arbor to this day.

Perhaps most significant, Frieze created the American secondary school systems, the high schools, as we know them today. Prior to the Civil War, most public education occurred at the primary level, and colleges and universities were obliged to create associated academies to prepare students for college work. Frieze began the practice of certifying select Michigan public schools as capable of offering respectable college preparation, thereby freeing the university from preparatory commitments and stimulating the schools of the state to extend their responsibilities into secondary education. This device unleashed the high school movement in the Midwest and later the nation, not only enabling the state universities to cultivate scholarly aspirations, but reshaping public education into clearly differentiated elementary and secondary schools.[21] James Angell put Frieze's contributions well: "No man except President Tappan has done so much to give to the university its present form and character. No one was ever more devoted to the interests of this institution or cherished a more abiding hope for its permanent prosperity and usefulness."[22]

James Burrill Angell (1871–1909)

Michigan's longest-serving president (38 years), James Angell, had served as president of the University of Vermont and on the faculty of Brown University before coming to Ann Arbor. He presided over Michigan's growth into the largest university in the nation. He was persuasive with both the regents and the state legislature. He managed to convince the state to fund the university through a mill tax (a fixed percentage of the state property tax), thereby avoiding the politics of having to beg the legislature each year for an operating appropriation (as is the practice today).

Although Angell himself was not an educational visionary, he recruited many faculty members such as John Dewey who strongly influenced the direction of American education. It is during Angell's long tenure that we can mark the first appearance of many of the University of Michigan's present characteristics, such as the academic organization of schools and colleges, the four-year BA/BS curriculum of 120 semester hours, the *Michigan Daily,* the Michigan Marching Band, and the Michigan football team. When Angell arrived, the university had 33 faculty and 1,100 students, and the university administration consisted of only three people: a president, treasurer, and secretary. By the time Angell retired in 1909, the university had grown to over 400 faculty and 5,400 students.

As noted earlier, Angell was an articulate and forceful advocate for the role of the public university in a democracy. He continued Frieze's efforts to shape coherent systems of public elementary and secondary education and replaced the classical curriculum with a more pragmatic course of study with wider utility and public accountability. With other public university leaders of the era, such as Charles R. Van Hise at Wisconsin, he established the state universities of the Midwest in a central role in the life of their states.

Yet Angell also embraced much of Tappan's original vision for a true university in Ann Arbor. He favored eliminating the freshman and sophomore years and focusing the university on upper-division and graduate education. Interestingly, Angell joined Andrew White of Cornell in attempting to slow the professionalism of college football. When Michigan students invited Cornell to play its football team in 1873, White replied to Angell: "I will not permit thirty men to travel 400 miles merely to agitate a bag of wind!"[23] Thirty years later, in 1906, Angell called the formative meeting in Chicago of the Western Conference (later to become the Big Ten Conference), with the intention of reforming the sport. But he suffered an embarrassing end run when Michigan's famous coach Fielding Yost persuaded the regents to withdraw Michigan from the new athletic conference in 1908, because the conference would restrict the outside income of coaches. (Walter Byers observes that it took a decade—and a new board of regents—for Michigan to end this "flirtation with foolishness," restore faculty control of intercollegiate athletics, and rejoin the Western Conference.)[24]

Perhaps most indicative of Angell's vision was the advice that he gave a visiting committee of trustees from the newly formed Johns Hopkins University. He convinced them that the time was right for the development of a great graduate university on the German model. Very much in the Michigan spirit, he argued that whatever they did ought to be something new and different,[25] that a rapidly changing nation required new colleges and universities that could change with it. Angell was the last among Michigan's "headmaster" presidents, men who fostered an intimate relationship with students and faculty. The large, complex university of the twentieth century would require a far different type of leadership.

Harry Burns Hutchins (1909–20)

At the age of 63, Harry Hutchins, dean of the University of Michigan Law School, was named interim president in 1909, to succeed James Angell. After several candidates, including Woodrow Wilson, declined to accept the Michigan presidency, the regents decided to appoint Hutchins president for a 3-year term, which was later

extended to 5 and then 10 years. Hutchins largely continued the Angell agenda, with the first significant additions to the campus from private gifts: a large concert hall (Hill Auditorium) and a women's residence hall (Martha Cook Hall). Hutchins made the first concerted effort to pull together Michigan's growing alumni body, with such major projects as the Michigan Union (the nation's first student union). However, he also faced the difficult challenge of leading the university through World War I, which rapidly exhausted his remaining energy and led to his retirement in 1920.

Marion Leroy Burton (1920–25)

Marion Burton was attracted to Michigan from the presidency of the University of Minnesota (and, before that, Smith College). Tall, with a commanding presence and a persuasive voice, he captivated students and legislators alike. His talent for organization and his vision of an expanding university precisely fit the needs and spirit of the post–World War I years. He understood that following the Great War, the demand for a college education would be enormous. It would be a time for the university "to spend boldly rather than conserve expediently," as Hutchins had done. Burton recognized: "A state university must accept happily the conclusion that it is destined to be large. If the state grows and prospers, it will naturally reflect these conditions."[26] Propelled by the prosperous economy of the Roaring Twenties, construction on the campus boomed, and enrollments increased. Burton was also an academic innovator. He restructured the board of regents to give the deans more authority; created faculty executive committees as a form of shared governance at the school and department level; instituted faculty sabbaticals; and attracted visiting faculty in the arts, such as Robert Frost. Unfortunately, Burton suffered a serious heart attack in 1924, and he died at the age of 49, after only five years as president.

Clarence Cook Little (1925–29)

In the aftermath of Marion Burton's tragic death, the regents searched for a young man in vigorous health. They turned to the 36-year-old president of the University of Maine, Clarence Cook "Pete" Little, as Michigan's next president. A cancer researcher with all of his degrees from Harvard, C. C. Little favored the Michigan focus on research, but he clung to the New England collegiate ideal of a selective student body, with an emphasis on character development rather than preparation for a career. In effect, he pushed the Harvard educational model (complete with the Harvard "houses," instead of students living independently in boarding houses and fraternities), along with a common curriculum for the first two years through a "university college"—much to the dismay and determined resistance of the Michigan faculty. These educational objectives, coupled with his controversial stand on such social issues as Prohibition and birth control, soon created strained relations both on the campus and across the state. Although Fielding Yost, now athletic director, managed to build Michigan Stadium during Little's tenure, other accomplishments were modest, and after only four years, Little submitted his resignation in 1929, to become director of the Jackson Memorial Laboratory in Maine. The regents were faced once again with finding a new president, for the third time in a decade.

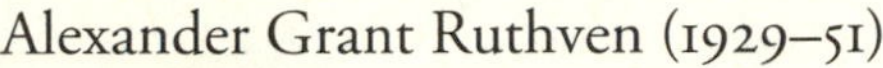

Alexander Grant Ruthven (1929–51)

Alexander Ruthven received his PhD in zoology from Michigan in 1906 and served as a faculty member and later as director of the University Museum. He became the dean of administration, the university's second-ranking administrator under C. C. Little, and was selected as president by the regents after a perfunctory search just weeks before the stock market crash of 1929. He was already very experienced in both university administration and state relations, and he understood well that it is "absurd to think that a lay board can handle the details of the modern university, or that the president is a headmaster, capable of directing all financial, academic, and public relations activities." Instead, he created a corporate administration, in which the regents served as "guardians of the public trust and . . . functioned as custodians of the property and income of the university," while the president was viewed as the chairman of the faculties, just as the deans were chairmen of their faculties and administrative heads of their schools.[27]

Ruthven led the university for two decades, through the traumas of the Great Depression and World War II. He managed to protect the university from serious cuts in state appropriations during the Depression, although the mill tax was eventually replaced by the process of annual appropriations from general state revenues in 1935. He understood well the dangers of wartime priorities, and he was skillful in protecting the core education and research missions of the university, even as it served the nation in exemplary fashion during World War II. In 1951, when Ruthven finally retired, the university had grown to over 21,000 students, including 7,700 veterans enrolled under the GI Bill.

Harlan Henthorne Hatcher (1951–67)

For Alexander Ruthven's successor, the regents selected Harlan Hatcher, former vice president for faculty and curriculum, dean, English professor, and student (BA, MA, and PhD) all at Ohio State University. Hatcher was noted for his teaching, writing, and administrative talents. He moved rapidly to restructure the university's administration to take advantage of the postwar economic boom. Hatcher's 17-year tenure saw dramatic expansion in enrollment and the physical campus, including the acquisition and development of the North Campus in Ann Arbor and establishment of regional campuses in Flint and Dearborn to accommodate the doubling of student enrollments from 21,000 to 41,000. Under Hatcher's leadership, Michigan continued its reputation as one of the world's leading research universities, with major activities in nuclear energy (the Michigan Memorial Phoenix Project), the space program (including the nation's leading programs for astronaut training), biomedical research (the clinical trials of the Salk vaccine), and the physical sciences (Donald Glaser's invention of the bubble chamber), as well as the development of the quantitative social sciences (the establishment of the Institute for Social Research and the Survey Research Center). During Hatcher's tenure, student high jinks (the first panty raids occurred in 1952) were balanced by serious social issues: for example, during the Red Scare years, two faculty members were dismissed for refusing to testify before the House Un-American Activities Committee. The university benefited from generous state support during this era, enabling such important educational innovations as the Residential College, the Pilot Program, and the Inteflex Program (a novel combined BS/MD program).

Although Hatcher's skillful approach as a gentleman scholar provided effective leadership during the 1950s, it was challenged by the emerging student activism of the 1960s: the formation of the Students for a Democratic Society by Michigan students, such as Tom Hayden, in the 1960s, as well as growing student protests over such issues as civil rights and the Vietnam War. It was clear that times were changing, and a new style of leadership would be necessary as student activism against "the establishment" escalated during the 1960s. Hatcher retired in 1967, at the age of 70.

Robben Wright Fleming (1968–79)

The regents turned to Robben Fleming, chancellor of the University of Wisconsin, to lead the University of Michigan during a time of protest and disruption. Fleming's background as a professor of labor relations specializing in arbitration and mediation served him well during the tumultuous years when Ann Arbor was a center of student activism. His patience, negotiating skills, and genuine sympathy for the concerns of students and faculty helped Michigan weather the decade without the destructive confrontations that struck some other universities. Despite pressure from conservative groups, Fleming was careful both to respect the freedom to protest and to avoid inflexible stands on nonessential matters, believing that most protesters would soon wear themselves out if not provoked. Fleming's background as a labor negotiator also served him in good stead with the increasing unionization of the university; as numerous employee groups unionized, strikes became a familiar routine in campus life. In 1971, even student groups (e.g., the University Hospital interns and residents and then the graduate teaching assistants) successfully unionized.

Fleming believed that the most important role of the president in a successful university was to keep things running smoothly and that this could best be done by recruiting a team of outstanding administrators. He once noted, "If you start out as president with a provost and a chief financial officer who are superb people, you are about three-quarters of the way down the path of success, because these are your critical areas."[28] Fleming had an abundance of such administrative talent in the provosts Allan Smith, Frank Rhodes, and Harold Shapiro and in the chief financial officers Wilbur Pierpont and James Brinkerhoff.

The cutback in federal research funding associated with the burden of the Vietnam War and with a state economy weakened by the OPEC oil embargo and the energy crisis limited both campus expansion and new initiatives, although Fleming did manage to launch the planning for the most ambitious project in university history, the Replacement Hospital Project. Student activism continued over such issues as minority enrollments (the Black Action Movement demanded in 1970 that the university commit itself to the achievement of 10 percent enrollment of African American students); the debate over recombinant DNA research in 1974; the university's continued involvement in classified research (which eventually led to the severing of its relationship with the Willow Run Laboratories in 1972); and the growth of the environmental movement, culminating in Earth Day in 1970 (when the students hacked a Ford vehicle to death on the Diag). Fleming handled each of these issues with skill and effectiveness. Yet it became clear that the continuing erosion of state support was not likely to recover and that a new financial strategy involving significant private fund-raising and tuition revenue would be necessary. Hence, after a decade of leadership, Fleming stepped down in 1977 and was succeeded by Allan Smith, the former provost, as interim president for a year.

Harold Tafler Shapiro (1980–87)

After an extensive nationwide search, the regents turned inside to select the university's provost, Harold Shapiro, as the next president. A Canadian by birth and educated at McGill and Princeton universities, Shapiro had served as chair of the University of Michigan's Department of Economics and led the economic forecasting project that analyzed the Michigan economy. He understood well that the state's economy would likely drop in prosperity to the national aver-

age and below in the years ahead. As it happened, during the 1970s and 1980s, state support would fall from 60 percent of the university's general and education budget to 30 percent (and it declined still further, to 15 percent, during the 1990s). Together with his provost, Billy Frye, Shapiro started the university down the long road toward becoming a privately supported public university, since he had little faith that generous state support would ever return. Despite the weak state economy, the university moved ahead on such important projects as the completion of the Replacement Hospital Project, the successful move of the College of Engineering to a new North Campus complex, a major private fund-raising campaign for $180 million, and a rebuilding of the quality of the physical sciences at Michigan.

Yet Shapiro's most important impact as president lay not in his financial acumen but, rather, in the high standards he set for the quality of the university's academic programs. Both as provost and as president, he raised the bar of expectations for faculty hiring, promotion, and tenure. He understood well that the reputation of a research university is determined by the quality of its research, graduate, and professional programs and that quality in these programs is in turn determined by faculty achievement and reputation. He realized that only by being recognized as a leader among its peers would the university acquire the financial strength and independence to afford and achieve excellence in undergraduate education.

MICHIGAN'S CHARACTER AS A TRAILBLAZER

What might be suggested for the Michigan institutional saga in view of the university's history, its traditions and roles, and its leadership over the years? Among the possible candidates from Michigan's history are the following characteristics:

1. The Catholepistemead or University of Michigania (the capstone of a system of public education)
2. The flagship of public universities or "mother of state universities"
3. A commitment to providing "an uncommon education for the common man"
4. The "broad and liberal spirit" of its students and faculty
5. The university's control of its own destiny, due to its constitutional autonomy providing political independence as a state university and to an unusually well-balanced portfolio of assets providing independence from the usual financial constraints on a public university
6. An institution diverse in character yet unified in values
7. A relish for innovation and excitement
8. A center of critical inquiry and learning
9. A tradition of student and faculty activism
10. A heritage of leadership
11. "The leaders and best" (to borrow a phrase from Michigan's fight song, *The Victors*)

But one more element of the Michigan saga seems particularly appropriate during these times of challenge and change in higher education.

Shortly after my appointment as provost of the university, Harold Shapiro arranged several visits to the campuses of peer institutions to help me learn more about their practices and perceptions. During a visit to Harvard, I had the opportunity to spend some time with its president, Derek Bok. As it happened, Bok knew a good deal about Michigan, since, in a sense, Michigan and Harvard have long provided a key communication channel between public and private higher education in America.

Bok acknowledged that Harvard's vast wealth allowed it to focus investments in particular academic areas far beyond anything that Michigan—or almost any other university in the nation—could achieve. But he added that Michigan had one asset that Harvard would never be able to match: its unique combination of quality, breadth, and capacity. He suggested that this combination enabled Michigan to take risks far beyond anything that could be matched by a private university. Because of its relatively modest size, Harvard tended to take a rather conservative approach to academic programs and appointments, since a mistake could seriously damage an academic unit. Michigan's vast size and breadth allowed it to experiment and innovate on a scale far beyond that tolerated by most institutions, as evidenced by its long history of leadership in higher education. It could easily recover from any failures it encountered on its journeys along high-risk paths. Bok suggested that this ability to take risks, to experiment and innovate, to explore various new directions in teaching, research, and service, might be Michigan's unique role in American higher education. He persuaded me that during a time of great change in society, Michigan's most important saga might be that of a pathfinder, a trailblazer, building on its tradition of leadership and relying on its unusual combination of quality, capacity, and breadth, to reinvent the university, again and again, for new times, new needs, and new worlds.[29]

This perception of Michigan as a trailblazer appears again and again in its history, as the university explored possible paths into new territory and blazed a trail for others to follow. Actually, Michigan has been both a trailblazer, exploring possible new paths, and a pioneer, building roads that others could follow. Whether in academic innovation (e.g., the quantitative social sciences), social responsiveness (e.g., its early admission of women, minorities, and international students), or its willingness to challenge the status quo (e.g., teach-ins, Earth Day, and the Michigan Mandate), Michigan's history reveals this trailblazing character time and time again. Recently, when Michigan won the 2003 Supreme Court case concerning the use of race in college admissions, the general reaction of other colleges and universities was "Well, that's what we expect of Michigan. They carry the water for us on these issues." When Michigan, together with IBM and MCI, built NSFnet during the 1980s and expanded it into the Internet, again that was the type of leadership the nation expected from the university.

Continuing with the frontier analogy, while Michigan has a long history of success as a trailblazer and pioneer, it has usually stumbled as a "settler," that is, in attempting to follow the paths blazed by others.[30] All too often this leads to complacency and even stagnation at an institution like Michigan. The university almost never makes progress by simply trying to catch up with others.

My travels in Europe and Asia always encounter great interest in what is happening in Ann Arbor, in part because universities around the world see the University of Michigan as a possible model for their own future. Certainly they respect—indeed, envy—distinguished private universities, such as Harvard and Stanford. But as public institutions themselves, they realize that they will never be able to amass the wealth of these elite private institutions. Instead, they see Michigan as the model of an innovative university, straddling the characteristics of leading public and private universities.

Time and time again I get asked questions about the "Michigan model" or the "Michigan mystique." Of course, people mean many different things by these phrases: the university's unusually strong and successful commitment to diversity; its hybrid funding model combining the best of both public and private universities; its strong autonomy from government interference; or perhaps the unusual combination of quality, breadth, and capacity that gives Michigan the capacity to be innovative, to take risks. Of course, all these multiple perspectives illustrate particular facets of what it means to be "the leaders and best."

I believe that the institutional saga of the University of Michigan involves a combination of quality, size, breadth, innovation, and pioneering spirit. The university has never aspired to be Harvard or the University of California, although it greatly admires these institutions. Rather, Michigan possesses a unique combination of characteristics, particularly well suited to exploring and charting the course for higher education as it evolves to serve a changing world.

THE ROLE OF INSTITUTIONAL SAGA IN PRESIDENTIAL LEADERSHIP

University presidents can play important roles in creating and defining institutional sagas. Clearly, early Michigan presidents, such as Henry Tappan, James Angell, and Marion Burton, were important in this regard. Other Michigan presidents have been successful in defining, shaping, and strengthening the trailblazing character of the university. Most Michigan presidents were sufficiently aware of the institution's history and accomplishments that they were able to utilize its saga to address the challenges and opportunities of their era.

History also suggests that the tenure of those who chose to ignore the Michigan saga was brief and inconsequential. This is an important point. Although university presidents can influence the saga of their university, they also must recognize that these characteristics provide the framework for their role, capable both of enhancing and constraining their actions. Successful presidents are attentive to an institution's saga, respecting its power and influence over the long term and carefully aligning their own tenure of leadership with its elements. Presidents who are either ignorant or dismissive of the institutional saga of their university have little impact and rarely last more than a few short years.

Leading a university involves much more than raising money, building the campus, recruiting faculty, and designing academic programs. Universities are social institutions based on ideas, values, and traditions. While they function in the present, they draw strength from the past as they prepare to invent the future. Only by embracing, building on, and perhaps helping to shape the institutional saga of a university can a president span successfully the full range of presidential roles.

So how did a perspective of Michigan's institutional saga—at least as I understood and interpreted it—shape my own presidency? At the outset, let me caution that a president should not become overfocused on the ethereal tasks of developing and achieving visions for the future based on the institutional saga from the past, so that the realities of the present are ignored. This was certainly true in the mid-1980s, when I began my assignments first as provost and then as president of the University of Michigan, which had been through a very difficult decade. State support had deteriorated to the point where it provided less than 20 percent of the university's resource base. The Ann Arbor campus, ranking as the nation's largest (with over 26 million square feet of space), was in desperate need of extensive renovation or replacement of inadequate facilities. Although the fund-raising efforts of the 1980s had been impressive, the university still lagged far behind most of its peers, with an endowment of only $250 million, clearly inadequate for the size and scope of the institution. There were other concerns, including the representation and role of minorities and women in the university community, campus safety, and student disciplinary policies. So, too, the relationships between the university and its various external constituencies—state government, federal government, the Ann Arbor community, the media, and the public at large—needed strengthening. Moreover, all of these challenges would have to be met while addressing an unusually broad and deep turnover in university leadership. Yet I refused to let these challenges of the moment dictate the university's agenda. Instead, I was determined to build on the Michigan saga—at least as I understood it.

At the top of my list was sustaining Michigan's long tradition of leadership by enhancing the academic quality of the institution. This was a natural priority for a former dean and provost, with extensive experience in raising expectations for faculty quality through recruiting, promotion, and tenure review; in using regular reviews to assess and strengthen academic program quality; and in recruiting and admitting students of the highest quality. To be sure, building the environment necessary for excellence would require both creativity and persistent determination (not to mention a good deal of luck), since it would require restructuring the financing of the university to become essentially a privately supported public university. Private support would have to be increased substantially, resources managed far more effectively; cost cutting and productivity enhancement would have to become priorities if we were to be successful. The challenge would also require a leadership team of great talent—executive officers, deans, chairs, and administrative managers.

But leadership required something more. As president, it was my task to raise the bar, to encourage aspirations to become the very best, rather than to settle for what some of our faculty termed "the complacency of fifth-ism," the tendency to be satisfied with a national ranking always somewhere in the top 10 but rarely first. We needed to challenge the institution to pick up the pace, to be more demanding in our expectations for student and faculty achievement. This, in turn, would require outstanding facilities for instruction and research; highly competitive salary programs to attract and retain the best faculty; and strong student financial aid programs to attract the best and brightest, regardless of socioeconomic circumstances.

Equally important, however, was honoring the university's long-standing commitment to provide, in Angell's words, "an uncommon education for the common man," to embrace diversity as a critical element of our institutional saga. The key here was to realize that in an increasingly diverse nation and world, diversity and academic excellence were no longer trade-offs. They were intimately connected and mutually reinforcing. To this end, it was essential to launch a far more strategic effort to strengthen the representation of people of color and women among our students, faculty, staff, and leadership, if we were to retain the university's reputation for national leadership in equal opportunity and diversity.

Michigan's long-standing tradition of student and faculty activism was a characteristic to be both respected and embraced. There might even be times when we might intentionally stimulate such activism. Yet, at the same time, we needed to transform our all-too-frequently adversarial relationship with the student body with a new spirit of mutual respect and cooperation, by stimulating a generation of student leaders who would infuse their challenges to the institution with a sense of loyalty and responsibility.

A sense of history and purpose also determined my external agenda. Top priority was given to actions that would enable the university to protect its traditional autonomy, its capacity to control its own destiny. Although we would try to work through persuasion and building political alliances, there would be times when reason and influence were simply not sufficient. I realized from the experience of my predecessors that it would occasionally be necessary for me, in my role as president, to take a stand—against the governor, the state legislature, Congress, even our own board of regents—on issues I believed to be essential to the university's future.

Finally, and perhaps most important, I embraced Michigan's history as a trailblazer by attempting to encourage a greater sense of excitement and adventure, risk taking and commitment, throughout the institution. To some degree, this required breaking down barriers and bureaucracy, decentralizing authority and resources. But it also involved recruiting both faculty and academic and administrative leaders who relished Michigan's go-for-it culture. I was determined to launch initiatives that were driven by the grass-roots interests, abilities, and enthusiasm of faculty and students. While such a high-risk approach was disconcerting to some and frustrating to others, there were fortunately many on our campus and beyond who viewed this environment as an exciting adventure.

My approach as president of the university was to encourage strongly the philosophy to "let every flower bloom," to respond to faculty and student proposals with "Wow! That sounds great! Let's see if we can work together to make it happen! And don't worry about the risk. If you don't fail from time to time, it is because you aren't aiming high enough!" We tried to ban the word *no* from our administrators—with one notable exception. I made it a cardinal rule never to accept an argument that Michigan had to do something simply because everybody else was doing it. Such an approach was about the only way a faculty or staff member was almost certain to receive an immediate "No!" (if not a serious reappraisal of the proposer's competency). My understanding of our institutional saga had convinced me that while Michigan was a great pathfinder, a leader, it was usually a lousy follower. As I mentioned in the preceding section of this chapter, the university almost never made progress by simply trying to catch up with others.

In assessing the decade of leadership from 1986 to 1996, it is clear that this approach to leadership—building on Michigan's institutional saga—enabled the university to make remarkable progress. But I sought something beyond excellence. I embraced the university's heritage as a pathfinder, first as Michigan defined the nature of the public university in the late nineteenth century, then again as it evolved into a comprehensive research university to serve the latter twentieth century. I had become convinced that to pursue a destiny of leadership for the twenty-first century, academic excellence in traditional terms, while necessary, was not sufficient. True leadership would demand that the university transform itself once again, to serve a rapidly changing society and a dramatically changed world. It was this combination of leadership and excellence that I placed as a vision and challenge to the university.

In countless talks before the university's extended family (students and faculty on campus, alumni, legislators in Lansing, and the citizens of Michigan), I described a future in which three crucial elements—knowledge, globalization, and diversity—would dominate. Knowledge was becoming increasingly important as the key to prosperity and social well-being. Rapidly evolving computing and communication technologies were quickly breaking down barriers between nations and economies, producing an increasingly interdependent global community where people had to live, work, and learn together. As barriers disappeared and new groups entered the mainstream of life (particularly in America), isolation, intolerance, and separation had to give way to diversity and community. A new, dynamic world was emerging. If the university wanted to maintain the leadership position it had enjoyed for two centuries, it not only had to adapt to life in that world; it had to lead the effort to redefine the very nature of the university for the century ahead.

THE "WHAT," "HOW," AND "WHO" OF THE UNIVERSITY PRESIDENCY

This chapter has drawn on the experience of the University of Michigan to illustrate how a university president needs to discover, respect, and build on the saga of an institution—its history, traditions, and values—both in developing a vision for the future of the university and in leading it toward these goals. In this sense, the institutional saga of the university is key in shaping the "what" of presidential leadership. Unless one understands the saga that shapes the values, cultures, and achievements of an institution over the years, effective leadership is well-nigh impossible—although history certainly provides many examples of the devastation that can occur when a leader tramples over the saga of an institution.

The next challenge is the "how," that is, how university presidents provide the leadership necessary to guide their institution in the direction of their vision. For a university, the "how" is comprised of many elements: executive leadership and management, academic leadership, political leadership, moral leadership, and strategic leadership (the "vision thing"). Since no leader has a range of attributes and skills to span the full range of leadership needed for a university, team building becomes key to success. The first line on the president's to-do list should be to recruit talented individuals into the key academic and administrative leadership roles of the university (e.g., executive officers, deans, key directors) and to form them into effective teams dedicated to the welfare of the institution.

However, before tackling the many aspects of university leadership, it first seems appropriate to address the "who" of the presidency. How are university presidents selected? What is their background? How do they prepare for this leadership role? In chapter 2, I illustrate the process by again using my personal experience as a case study, since my own progress through the academic ranks as professor, dean, and provost was quite typical of the experience of many university presidents—although both my opportunity to lead the institution where I had served as a faculty member and my decision to return later to a faculty role in that same institution, after serving as president, were highly unusual.

2

THE PATH TO THE PRESIDENCY

The brief history of the University of Michigan provided in chapter 1 is intended in part to illustrate the evolution of the role of the university presidency over time as the nature of the American university has changed. Tappan and Angell were analogous to headmasters, providing both intellectual and moral leadership, with strong religious backgrounds. Ruthven and Hatcher assumed broader management and executive responsibilities, as the university grew into a large, complex community. Fleming and Shapiro accepted even broader responsibilities, functioning very much on the national and even international stage, as the university became a global enterprise.

Although today's university presidents no longer play the direct role in the lives of university students that they once did in the early colonial colleges, their roles are far more complex, requiring leadership along many fronts: executive, academic, financial, political, strategic, and even (on occasion) moral. The American university president is clearly a role of great importance to both higher education and broader society. It would therefore seem logical that the preparation for this role should be rigorous and that the selection of a university president would involve a careful, thoughtful, and rational process.

In reality, however, the early careers of most university presidents resemble more of a random walk process, careening from one assignment—and institution—to the next, driven more by chance and opportunity than by any careful design or training. Moreover, the search for and selection of a university president is a complex and all-too-frequently confusing process, conducted by the governing board of the institution according to a Byzantine process more akin to the selection of a pope than a corporate chief executive officer. Leaving aside for the moment the more logical question (raised by the musings of Giamatti quoted in the preface) of why any sane person would want to become a university president, this chapter considers the various paths to such a position. First, we need to understand just what university presidents do and how they fit into the complex organizational structure of the university.

TINKER, TAILOR, SOLDIER, SAILOR; RICH MAN, POOR MAN, BEGGAR MAN, THIEF; . . . AND UNIVERSITY PRESIDENT

Universities, like other institutions, depend on strong leadership and effective management to face the challenges and opportunities posed by an ever-changing world. Yet in many universities, the tasks of management and even leadership are held in very low regard, particularly by the faculty. To both students and faculty alike, the term *university administration* has a sinister connotation, like *federal government* or *bureaucracy* or *corporate organization.* Although many outside academe view a university president as the top rung in the academic ladder, many faculty members would rank it near the bottom, suggesting that anyone aspiring to such a position is surely lacking in intellectual ability, good judgment, and perhaps even moral integrity. In fact, one occasionally hears the suggestion—usually from one of the more outspoken members of the faculty—that any strong academic, chosen at random, could become an adequate university president. The argument is that if one can be a strong teacher and scholar, these skills should be easily transferable to other areas, such as institutional leadership. Yet, in reality, talent in leadership is probably as rare a human attribute as the ability to contribute to original scholarship.

There is little reason to suspect that talent in one characteristic implies the presence of talent in another.

There are actually several decidedly different flavors of university president. Most commonly, we think of the role as that of the leader of a university campus. But such a campus may be a component of a larger university system, in which case the campus executive is usually entitled a "chancellor" and reports to a system chief executive officer known as the "president."[1] The campus president/chancellor has a complex array of roles, involving not only executive responsibilities for the academic programs, business, and service activities (e.g., hospitals and football teams) of the campus but also important external roles, such as private fund-raising and public relations. In contrast, the president of the university system usually focuses on managing the relationship with political bodies (e.g., state government and the university governing board), along, of course, with bearing the responsibility for hiring and firing campus chancellors.

Michigan is a bit of an oddity here, since the president is both leader of the Ann Arbor campus and head of a small system including campuses at Flint and Dearborn, both of which also have chancellors. While this dual role as president of the UM system and chancellor of the Ann Arbor campus greatly enhances the authority of the position, it also doubles the headaches, because the president is responsible for national, state, community, and regent politics; fund-raising; student and faculty concerns; and intercollegiate athletics.

University presidents are expected to develop, articulate, and implement visions that sustain and enhance their institutions' academic quality and reputation, an activity that involves a broad array of academic, social, financial, and political issues that envelope a university. Through their roles as the chief executive officers of their institutions, university presidents have significant managerial responsibilities for a diverse collection of activities, ranging from education to student housing to health care to public entertainment (e.g., intercollegiate athletics). Since these generally require the expertise and experience of talented professionals, the president is the university's chief recruiter, identifying talented people, recruiting them into key university positions, and directing and supporting their activities. In fact, one of the most common causes of a failed presidency arises from an inability to build a strong leadership team or an unwillingness to delegate adequate authority and responsibility to those more capable of handling the myriad details of university management. Unlike most corporate chief executive officers, however, the president is expected also to play an active marketing role in generating the resources needed by the university, whether by lobbying state and federal governments, seeking gifts and bequests from alumni and friends, or launching clever entrepreneurial efforts. There is an implicit expectation on most campuses that the president's job is to raise money for the provost and deans to spend, while the chief financial officer and administrative staff watch over their shoulders to make certain this is done wisely and prudently.

The university president also has a broad range of important responsibilities that might best be termed symbolic leadership. In a sense, the president and spouse are the first family of the university community, in many ways serving as the mayor of a small city of thousands of students, faculty, and staff. This public leadership role is particularly important when the university is very large. As the university's most visible leader, the president must continually grapple with the diverse array of political and social issues and interests of concern to the many stakeholders of higher education.

Moral leadership is also an important responsibility. Although it is sometimes suggested that the moral voice of the president died with the giants of the past—Angell (Michigan), Eliot (Harvard), and Wayland (Brown)—it is clear that the contemporary university continues to need leadership capable and willing to address moral issues, such as integrity, social purpose, and the primacy of academic values.[2] Moreover, as I stressed in chapter 1, presidents must understand and respect the history of their university, its long-standing values and traditions, if they are to be successful.

Finally, the president is expected to be a defender of the university and its fundamental qualities of knowledge and wisdom, truth and freedom, academic excellence and public purpose—an advocate for the immense importance of higher education to society. The forces of darkness threatening the university are many, both on and off the campus. Whether dealing with an attack launched by an opportunistic politician, the personal agenda of a trustee, a student disruption, or a scandal in intercollegiate athletics, the president is expected to take up arms and defend the integrity of the institution. Needless to say, this knightly role carries with it certain hazards. The buck always stops at the president's desk.

So where does one find candidates with the skills to fit such an unusual position? Although the early leaders of American colleges were drawn primarily from teaching or religious vocations, one finds today's university presidents drawn from almost every discipline, profession, and career. They include not only academics but also leaders from government and business. Law professors were popular in the 1960s, with the need to mediate student disruptions and handle the complex relationships with state and federal government. Economists are particularly in vogue these days, perhaps because universities are once again under considerable financial stress. In these times of technological change and a knowledge-driven economy, one also finds an increasing number of university presidents drawn from the ranks of scientists and engineers.[3] University presidents from professional disciplines, such as business and medicine, are less common, perhaps because these professional schools are usually so wealthy and powerful in contemporary research universities that the faculty is afraid to "put a cat into the canary cage" by supporting the appointment of a dean of a medical or business school as university leader. Presidents of major universities are also rarely selected from education schools, because these programs are generally viewed as focused primarily on primary and secondary education.

As one looks more broadly across the landscape of American higher education, it is increasingly common to find governing boards selecting presidents with nonacademic backgrounds, such as business, government, or politics. This might be explained, in part, by the increasing financial and management complexity of the contemporary university or, in the case of public universities, by complex relationships with state and federal government. But cynics could also suggest that the selection of presidents from beyond the academy may reflect the increasing discomfort of many governing boards with "academic types" who stress academic values, such as academic freedom and tenure, rather than cost-effectiveness and productivity.

Generally, however, the most distinguished institutions still demand that those considered for presidential leadership have demonstrated achievement within academic circles. Otherwise, the university faculty is unlikely to take their leadership seriously. Since this was my own experience, I begin my discussion of the various paths to university presidency by considering the traditional academic path.

THE ACADEMIC LEADERSHIP LADDER

To better explain both the nature of the university presidency and its leadership responsibility, it is useful to begin with a brief discussion of the layers of academic leadership within the university and the career ladders leading to various leadership positions. In reality, the university administration is simply a leadership network—primarily comprised of members of the faculty themselves, sometimes on temporary assignment—that extends throughout the university and within academic and administrative units. At the most fundamental organizational level are academic departments, such as history, surgery, and accounting. Most faculty identify first with their academic departments, since these departments relate most closely to the faculty's primary activities of teaching and research. Departments are led by chairs, usually appointed by deans for a fixed term (three to five years), albeit with input from the senior faculty members in the department.

At the next organizational level are clusters of academic departments organized into schools or colleges—such as law, medicine, engineering, and the liberal arts—and led by deans who are selected by the executive officers of the university (e.g., the provost or president). In most universities, deans are the key academic leaders responsible for academic quality. They select department chairs; recruit and evaluate faculty; and seek resources for their school, both within the university (arguing for their share of university resources) and beyond the campus (through private fund-raising or research grantsmanship). As the key line managers of the faculty of the university, they have rather considerable authority that usually aligns well with their great responsibilities.

At the highest organizational level of the university is the central administration, consisting of the president, provost, and various vice presidents (or vice-chancellors), denoted generically as the "executive officers" of the university, with broad administrative responsibilities for specific university functions, such as academic programs, student services, and business and finance. Although the executive officers report directly to the president, they are also more directly responsive to the governing board than are other academic leaders, such as deans or department chairs. The career background of executive officers is generally correlated with their functional responsibility. For example, while vice presidents for academic affairs (or provosts) and vice presidents for research generally come from faculty ranks with experience as department chairs or deans, vice presidents for business and finance usually come with solid management and financial credentials, frequently with MBAs and business experience.

It is important to understand the random nature of the careers of most academic administrators. After all, few faculty members begin their careers with aspirations to become academic leaders. Most have chosen their professions because of interests in teaching and research as well as a yearning for the independent lifestyle characterizing academe. They abhor administrative roles and look on faculty colleagues attracted (or sentenced) to administrative assignments as unfortunate souls with fundamental character flaws. Very few faculty members are willing to accept administrative appointments, and those who aggressively seek such roles are just the leaders that universities probably want to avoid.

There are many drawbacks to academic leadership roles such as department chairs or deans. These positions rarely open up at a convenient point in one's career, since most productive faculty members usually have ongoing obligations—for teaching or research grants—that are difficult to suspend for administrative assignments. Although an energetic faculty member can sometimes take on the additional burdens of chairing a major academic committee or even leading a small department or research institute, the time requirements of a major administrative assignment, such as department chair or dean, will inevitably come at the expense of scholarly activity and the ability to attract research grants. The higher administrators climb on the academic leadership ladder, from project director to department chair to dean to executive officer, the more likely it is that the rungs of the ladder will burn out below them, as they lose the necessary scholarly momentum (at least in the opinion of their colleagues) to return to active roles in teaching and research or to attract research grants. The pressures on department chairs and deans are a microcosm of the pressures on today's university presidents—budgets, regulations, personnel, fund-raising, and faculty politics. The consequences, too, are similar. Beyond a certain level, typically that of a dean, there is little turning back to the role of a professor once again.

This raises yet another dilemma. As one moves up the academic leadership ladder, burning the rungs below that lead back to the faculty, one sometimes bumps into a ceiling, which leaves no choice but to jump to a ladder at another institution. The pyramid of available academic administrative posts narrows rapidly in a university, and these positions rarely open at the time when academic leaders seek (or need) to move to the next rung of the ladder. Frequently, the only alternative is to look beyond the current institution, at the possibility of jumping to an administrative assignment at another university—sometimes a rung up the ladder, sometimes laterally. Many senior academic leaders have a résumé that looks almost like that of a corporate executive. They drift from institution to institution as they jump from one leadership ladder to another, leaving both their scholarly activity and institutional loyalty far behind.

These features of careers in academic leadership raise an obvious question: why would anyone attracted to a university faculty position intentionally wade into the swamp of academic administration? Academic administration is usually the furthest thing from the mind of those faculty members with the most leadership potential and the strongest credentials in teaching and scholarship. Rather, the most able academic leaders have to be cajoled, seduced, or bribed into assuming such roles.

As one who has lured many dozens of faculty members into administrative positions and has launched them on—or, rather, doomed them to—academic leadership careers, let me share with you some insider tricks of the trade. The first place to look for prospective academic leaders is among the chairs of faculty committees. Service on these committees is generally a voluntary activity, reflecting the willingness and interests of a faculty member to serve the institution beyond their customary roles of teaching and research (i.e., to accept duties above and beyond the call). Furthermore, such committee chairs are generally selected by faculty colleagues based on respect and leadership ability. Another productive approach is to find faculty members whom colleagues generally turn to for advice on important issues—although these are generally not the most outspoken people at faculty meetings. Those with leadership potential are usually characterized by broad scholarly and teaching interests, capable of seeing the big picture. They are also those who usually say no to offers of administrative appointments, at least when first approached.

My own experience as a dean and provost hunting through the groves of academe for academic leaders suggests that most are captured when they are in the wrong place at the wrong time. For example, they may be caught in a search with few other qualified candidates. Sometimes, the key personality trait is a chronic inability to say no to a request to take on a new assignment, whether because of institutional loyalty or because of fear of the consequences if a known colleague is selected for the role.

The positive aspect of the search process is the recognition that at the level of an academic department or school, the selection of academic leaders (chairs, deans, and even provosts) is usually made by knowledgeable academics who will be their immediate supervisors (e.g., a dean, provost, or president). Usually, these are seasoned academic leaders, with extensive personal experience as teachers and scholars. Because these searches are highly confidential in nature, the assessment of the credentials of possible candidates can be relatively free from political factors. Although a faculty search committee may be used to assist in the screening and vetting of candidates, the final decision is decidedly not democratic and usually will be made by a single individual. Perhaps more significant, most able academic leaders realize quickly that their own success—and fate—will be determined by the quality of their appointments. Hence, they have strong motivation to go after the very best. As will soon become apparent, the contrast between searches at the departmental or school level, on the one hand, and presidential searches and selections, on the other, could not be greater.

THE PATH TO THE MICHIGAN WHITE HOUSE

Perhaps the best way for me to illustrate the meandering path that leads to a university presidency is to describe my own experience. Like the appointments of my predecessors, my selection as the eleventh president of the University of Michigan was highly dependent on politics, personalities, and chance. My path to Ann Arbor led from a small farm town in Missouri to Yale University in the East, then to a top secret nuclear research laboratory in the mountains of New Mexico, then to Pasadena, and finally back across the country again to Michigan.

Both my wife, Anne, and I had grown up in Carrollton, Missouri, a small farm town (population about 5,000 and falling) located about 70 miles northeast of Kansas City. As was typical of such farming communities, most of the boys were expected to become farmers, while the girls were expected to become housewives. Of those high school graduates fortunate enough to attend college, most chose professional majors (e.g., engineering or agriculture) at the local public colleges and universities. Yet, in a strange twist of fate, rather than following in the University of Missouri traditions of my family, I headed east for college, to Yale University. This requires a brief explanation.

When I attended high school in the late 1950s, few in my town had ever considered going out of state to college; I was only the second student from Carrollton ever to take the SAT. Largely at the encouragement of my family, I decided to apply to several of the more popular national universities. During the applications process, I learned that the elite schools of Yale and Harvard were located in New England rather than England (where I had always thought they were, along with Oxford and Cambridge), so I decided on a whim to apply to Yale, knowing absolutely nothing about it. Beyond my surprise in receiving a letter of acceptance to Yale was my awe over a telegram (the first I had ever seen) sent by the Yale football coach, encouraging me to attend Yale and play on his football team. The die was cast.

So, with Yale sight unseen, I headed off in the fall of 1960, experiencing my first airplane flight, my first trip to New York, my first adventure finding my way to Grand Central Station and taking the train up to New Haven, and my first Yale experience: freshman football practice. At the time, almost two-thirds of Yale students were from highly competitive preparatory schools, such as Andover, Exeter, and Choate. These students were already well prepared for both the academic rigors and the social graces of a blue-blood institution. In contrast, when I arrived at Yale, I was quite unprepared for its academic rigor—having never done any homework in my life—and equally unprepared for the pace of its extracurricular life.

Although I was successful on the football field (my team won the Ivy League Championship), my early academic performance was lackluster, with a B average and a realization that there was no way I was prepared to major in my chosen field, chemical engineering. (I kept cutting chemistry laboratory to attend football practice.) Fortunately, by the end of my first year, I began to figure out the Yale academic system, elevating my grades to an A average and switching to electrical engineering. I knew nothing about this field, but everyone said it was the hardest engineering major, so I reasoned that it had to be worthwhile.

My academic interests also began to broaden considerably, moving first into physics and later into an array of courses in the humanities and social sciences. My growing academic success and academic interests soon outpaced my football career, and I gave up varsity football for intramural competition during my junior year. In 1964, I graduated summa cum laude in electrical engineering and accepted a fellowship to attend graduate school at Caltech.

A further bit of explanation about my undergraduate education and degree is appropriate here. All undergraduates at Yale were required to select one of the usual disciplinary majors, but they were also required to select a minor area of concentration. Since the minor and major concentrations had to be in different areas, I selected psychology as my minor area, with a specialization in child psychology. Many years later, I would realize the fortuitous nature of this minor concentration, since this training was of critical importance in my various roles in academic administration—not so much for understanding students as for understanding faculty (in terms of stimulus, response, reward, reinforcement, etc.).

Meanwhile, an even more important development was occurring back in Missouri during my last years at Yale, with my courtship of a former high school classmate (and head cheerleader) then at the University of Missouri. As will become apparent later, this was a stroke of almost miraculous good fortune for higher education, since Anne's skills and wisdom were very key elements of our (and it was always *our*) leadership role at Michigan. We reached a decision during our last year in college that a long-distance relationship left much to be desired, and immediately after our graduations, we were married.

So, leaving Yale, the Ivy League, and the East Coast behind, I headed west, stopping in Missouri, where Anne and I were married following her graduation from the University of Missouri and then headed on toward California. But first we stopped off in New Mexico, where I had a summer appointment as a visiting research physicist at the Los Alamos Scientific Laboratory. In the mid-1960s, atomic energy was still shrouded in top secret security. I was required to qualify for Q-level security clearance from the Atomic Energy Commission (AEC) even to receive an AEC fellowship to study at Caltech. Needless to say, security was an even higher priority at Los Alamos, where the town that stood adjacent to the laboratory and housed the families of lab employees had only been opened to the public a few years earlier. Families of visiting scientists lived in barracks of World War II vintage, dating from the days of the Manhattan Project.

Even though we spent only a summer at Los Alamos, it proved to be a formative experience with important consequences. I worked in a technical group supporting the Rover nuclear rocket program, a top secret program intended to develop and test rocket engines powered by nuclear fission reactors. During the mid-1960s, it was planned that after the successful completion of the Apollo program to land a man on the moon, a manned mission to the planet Mars would follow rapidly, perhaps as early as 1980. Many scientists believed that chemical rockets were inadequate for manned planetary missions because of the radiation exposure associated with extended spaceflight. Hence, the nation had launched a major program at Los Alamos, Project Rover, to develop nuclear rockets for future interplanetary missions. The project was quite successful in designing, building, and static testing a sequence of nuclear rocket engines at their Nevada test site. I worked on the test programs for these nuclear rocket engines, acquiring in the process a strong interest in both nuclear power and spaceflight.

Since nuclear rocket development was classified as a secret project, I was required to record all of my work in bound notebooks, which were then locked in a safe each evening when I left the secure area of the laboratory. This routine of recording my work—and my thoughts—in bound notebooks became a habit that continued throughout my research as a faculty member and my work as an academic administrator. Today, our bookshelves are filled with these notebooks, which are still accumulating at a rate of several each year.

After our summer experience at Los Alamos, Anne and I continued on across the country to Pasadena and Caltech. Not uncommonly, our image of Pasadena and Caltech had been formed by the television broadcasts of the Tournament of Roses Parade and the Rose Bowl, when the skies were blue and the San Gabriel Mountains ringing the city stood out sharp and clear.[4] It was quite a contrast when we arrived in late August in the midst of a smog alert that continued for weeks, blotting out the mountains and trapping the heat.

Although Pasadena was an important chapter in our family history—Anne's career; my MS and PhD degrees; and the birth of our daughters, Susan and Kathy—it was a remarkably short period, lasting only four years. Part of the reason for the brevity was the Vietnam War; with the threat of the draft always lurking in the background, there was strong motivation for graduate students to complete their degrees as rapidly as possible. It was also a time of ample job opportunities: the space and defense programs were in high gear, and universities were continuing to expand their faculties to respond to the baby boomers. I took advantage of Caltech's highly interdisciplinary character by earning my degrees in subjects spanning a range of topics in physics and mathematics. Since I had managed to complete my MS and PhD in three years, my dissertation advisors suggested that I might want to spend an additional year as an AEC postdoctoral fellow, broadening my research interests and possibly joining the Caltech faculty.

Although I was most interested in remaining at Caltech, I agreed to two job interviews at the suggestion of my faculty advisors: one at the University of California, Berkeley, and one at the University of Michigan. The Berkeley interview was hosted by the chair of the Department of Nuclear Engineering, Hans Mark, who was later to become secretary of the U.S. Air Force and then president of the University of Texas. The Michigan interview was the more problematic of the two. Michigan's Department of Nuclear Engineering was not only the first such program established in this country; it also ranked among the top such programs in the world. Despite this, I was not particularly enthusiastic about visiting Michigan to explore a job opportunity, particularly in the late winter cold. I agreed to do so as a favor to my thesis advisor, who portrayed Ann Arbor as nirvana, although it was a gray, drizzling day in March when I visited. However, Anne had grown weary of the smog and traffic of Southern California and longed to return to the Midwest. While I was flying back to Los Angeles after the interview, the department chair called Anne and told her they were going to make an offer. Since Anne had already made up her mind that California was not in our future, she accepted on the spot. Hence, I arrived back in Pasadena only to learn that the Duderstadts were headed to Michigan.

ON TO MICHIGAN

In December 1968, we loaded our furniture and our VW onto a moving van in the 90-degree heat in Pasadena (a Santa Ana condition) and boarded a plane for Michigan. We arrived in a subzero blizzard and moved into the Northwood IV housing complex on the University of Michigan's North Campus. Despite the climatic shock, we found ourselves very much at home, both in Ann Arbor and at the University of Michigan—so much so, in fact, that we have resisted occasional opportunities to move back to California and chosen to remain in Ann Arbor ever since.

For the next several years, I climbed the usual academic ladder, progressing through the ranks as assistant, associate, and then full professor of nuclear engineering. Michigan's Department of Nuclear Engineering was ideally suited to the generalist approach of a Caltech education. It was small, research-intensive, highly interdisciplinary, and almost totally focused on graduate education. Its reputation attracted outstanding faculty and graduate students of unusual breadth and ability. Hence, it was well suited to my roving intellectual interests, first in nuclear reactor physics, then in nonequilibrium statistical mechanics, then in laser-driven thermonuclear fusion, then in supercomputers, and so on. In the early stages, most of my work was highly theoretical, requiring only a blackboard and chalk. However, my interests later evolved into using very large computers (so-called supercomputers) to simulate highly complex phenomena, such as nuclear fission and thermonuclear fusion systems.

As a theoretician, I had developed a good knack for reducing complicated problems to the simplest possible level of abstraction and for explaining complex concepts in terms that my students—and even an occasional lay audience—could understand. While many university faculty members focus on teaching only a few courses closely related to their area of expertise, I rarely taught the same course twice. As a result, I not only ended up teaching most of the undergraduate and graduate courses offered by our department, but I designed and developed many of them. Since I usually produced copious lecture notes for each of these courses, I soon shifted to writing textbooks to expand my pedagogical efforts. Although several of the textbooks written during the late 1970s continue to be used today (admittedly in very specialized fields of nuclear energy), I always viewed textbook writing as an avocation rather than as a profession.

Both the quality and quantity of my research and teaching were sufficient to propel me rapidly through the academic ranks, with promotion to associate professor in 1972 and to full professor in 1975. I soon began to realize, however, that the traditional faculty role, while enjoyable for the moment, would probably not hold my attention for the longer term. I always had great envy and admiration for my more senior faculty colleagues who had been able to maintain both scholarly interest and momentum through the several decades of their academic careers. But whatever the reason, I soon found my concentration and attention beginning to wander to other activities in the university, as I began to be drawn into faculty service and eventually administrative activities.

Several key features of this first phase of my career would have an impact later on my role as an academic leader. First, and perhaps most significant, both my educational experiences and my faculty career had been associated with institutions that were clearly among the very best in the world—Yale, Caltech, and the UM Department of Nuclear Engineering. I had developed a keen sense for not only being able to recognize excellence but also knowing firsthand the commitment it takes to achieve it. Second, both my education and my scholarly career had been in environments characterized by unusual intellectual breadth and creativity, with an exceptionally strong scientific foundation. Although I would later hear occasional grumbling that "Duderstadt is a physicist, not an engineer," I was, in truth, able to span both pure and applied scientific fields. Finally, my career had been spent in institutions with exceptionally strong programs in research and graduate education. All of these experiences would serve me well as I moved into academic leadership roles during the 1980s.

All too frequently, scholars in my particular areas of theoretical physics and mathematics have relatively short productive careers—typically only a decade or two—before they lose the fresh creativity that frequently accompanies youth and fall into the same scholarly ruts that trap their colleagues in unproductive directions. After a decade of research, I worried that my best work might already be behind me, at least in my current fields of interest. Hence, my choices were to broaden my academic interests (which I did, into such areas as computer simulation); to shift into other areas of scholarly interest (which I also did, into writing textbooks); and to explore other careers, including entering the dreaded swamp of academic administration.

Actually, although I did have some interest in academic administration, it was largely closed off to me. My department was a small one, and we already benefited from a relatively young and effective department chairman. The alternative to department leadership was to become more actively involved in the myriad faculty service activities that characterize research universities. I already had been quite actively involved in department activities, chairing our committees on curriculum, nuclear reactor safety, and department review. By the mid-1970s, I had graduated to college-wide activities, first chairing the College of Engineering's curriculum committee and then serving on several department review committees.

My involvement with broader, university-wide issues began with my election to the executive board of the graduate school. I look back on this experience as one of the more intellectually stimulating and rewarding of my faculty service activities. Many of the university's most distinguished faculty members were elected to serve on the board, and the issues it considered were both fascinating and consequential. It stimulated me to think more broadly about the university and higher education, while developing both a better understanding of and relationships with academic programs across the university. Because of the executive nature of the board's activities, we frequently met with deans and department chairs from various academic units.

This service was followed by an even more intensive experience with academic administration, when I was asked to serve on and later chair the faculty advisory committee to the provost. The Academic Affairs Advisory Committee (AAAC) was a committee of the university's Senate Assembly (the faculty senate), charged with advising the provost and undertaking studies on various issues of concern to the Office of Academic Affairs. Since the provost at Michigan was not only the chief academic officer but also the chief budget officer of the university, the AAAC could get into almost anything having to do with the university.[5] I should note that I served on this body through two important transitions, first as Harold Shapiro succeeded Frank Rhodes as provost of the university and then as Shapiro succeeded Robben Fleming as president of the university. This committee gave me a ringside seat in observing the leadership skills of two individuals who would go on to become two of the most distinguished university presidents of the twentieth century (Rhodes at Cornell and Shapiro at both Michigan and Princeton).

During my tenure as chair of the AAAC, we launched a major study to evaluate the quality of the research environment on campus, including such controversial issues as indirect cost recovery and cost sharing, as well as administrative and technical support of research and faculty incentives for generating sponsored funding. This entire study was a bit sensitive, since it overlapped several vice presidential areas. Although we had strong support from the provost, we were somewhat threatening to both of the vice presidential areas of research and finance. Nevertheless, we plowed ahead, stirring up considerable interest and releasing a hard-hitting report warning the university that it needed to move quickly to address the deteriorating state of the research environment, before it lost both top faculty and research funding. This was an issue that I would continue to keep front and center both during my tenure as dean of engineering and eventually as provost and president. I believe that it was largely because of the persistence and effectiveness of this effort that we were able not only to improve the research environment on campus but also to propel Michigan, during the early 1990s, from eighth to first in the nation in sponsored research activities.

There is a saying in academic circles that no good deed goes unpunished, and hence my committee service continued for the next few years, first on the university's Budget Priorities Committee, a joint group of faculty, deans, and executive officers who made the key decisions on reviewing academic and administrative units for major budget reductions, including possible discontinuance. My final service assignment was my election to the university's faculty senate and then a nomination to its executive committee. At the time, I would probably have viewed my career as a faculty politician as just about complete had I been able to serve on this committee and eventually be elected as its chair—the chair of faculty governance at the university. However, fate was to intervene.

TRAPPED IN THE GRAVITATIONAL PULL OF ACADEMIC ADMINISTRATION

Late one evening in the spring of 1981, our home telephone rang. It was Billy Frye, provost of the university, with a request that I accept an appointment as dean of engineering. Both Anne and I were surprised (perhaps "shocked" is a more apt description), since I certainly was not one of the logical candidates in the yearlong search for an engineering dean. To be sure, both of us had been quite active in university affairs for a decade. But my administrative experience was essentially zero. I had never been a department chairman. I did not even have my own secretary, and I had never supervised anybody other than PhD students. Furthermore, I was only thirty-seven and relatively unknown inside the College of Engineering—although quite well known to the university's central administration because of my committee service.

Yet, perhaps because of the naïveté and brash confidence of youth, I quickly accepted Frye's offer, even though it brought with it the responsibilities for one of the university's largest schools, with over 300 faculty and staff, 6,000 students, and a budget of $30 million. After all, for the last several years, I had been one of a number of junior faculty members complaining loudly and bitterly about the deplorable state of the college. Now my bet had been called. I had been challenged with an opportunity to actually do something about it.

Like most of my subsequent assignments in academic administration at Michigan, my role as dean of engineering started almost immediately.[6] I was introduced to the faculty two days after accepting the position. One month later, I moved into the dean's office. During my period as dean-elect, I began meeting individually with each of the leaders of the college: its department chairs, associate deans, and key faculty. It was my good fortune to be sufficiently naive to simply assume that I would be able to select my own team, and I surprised each of my predecessor's associate deans by thanking them for their service and offering to help them return to the faculty. In my first meeting with the department chairs, two of the most powerful chairmen, who had also been candidates for the dean's position, attempted the usual power play by threatening that they would step down if they did not get their way. I simply called their bluff by thanking them for their service and asking them for help in searching for their successors, leaving both a bit stunned when I left their offices.

Another piece of good fortune was the willingness of several of the college's most outstanding young faculty to join me in the new administration, including Chuck Vest, who later succeeded me as dean and provost and eventually became president of MIT; Dan Atkins, who later became the founding dean of Michigan's new School of Information; and Scott Fogler, one of the nation's leaders in the pedagogy of engineering education. Bill Frye had taken a chance by turning the leadership of the college over to the young faculty. In a similar spirit, our team moved rapidly to restructure and rebuild the college. During our brief five-year tenure in the dean's office, our team was able to reenergize Michigan engineering. Through a combination of strong lobbying in Lansing and the support of the university's central administration, we were able to triple the base budget of the college. We completed the thirty-year-long effort to move the college to the university's North Campus. We also recruited over 120 new faculty, doubled PhD production, tripled sponsored research support, and boosted the reputation of the college from that of an also-ran to one of the top five engineering schools in the nation. We established strong ties with industry, including strong support for our effort to build one of the most advanced computer systems in the nation.

Although I was only dean of engineering for a brief five-year period, the lessons learned during this experience stayed with me throughout my career as an academic leader. First was the importance of people. Clearly, academic institutions and programs are intensely people-dependent enterprises. The secret to success is simple: attract the very best people; provide them with the support, encouragement, and opportunity to push to the limits of their talents and dreams; then get out of their way.

There is a corollary here: if you are going to place a big bet on the future, make certain that you place it on your best people and your best programs. It is wise to always invest in areas of strength, building on them to gain the momentum to move into new areas. For this reason, we placed our largest bets—and they were very large, indeed (amounting to tens of millions of dollars)—on such programs as the Center for Integrated Manufacturing, the Solid State Electronics Laboratory, the Center for Ultrafast Optics, and the Computer Aided Engineering Network. The converse to the preceding corollary is also true: it is very dangerous to make major investments in areas of weakness in an effort to build new areas of excellence. This almost never succeeds.

My next lesson learned as dean was the importance of consistency and persistence. It is essential to stay on message both to internal constituencies (e.g., the faculty) and to external patrons (e.g., the central administration, industry, and alumni). Any uncertainty or wavering will rapidly erode the effort to build support.

In a similar sense, speed and timing are very important. Looking back two decades later, it is difficult to understand just how rapidly we pushed ahead our blitzkrieg to rebuild the College of Engineering. But it is also my belief that this was, in part, the key to our success. We were able to accelerate rapidly, building momentum along a number of fronts. Success in one area propagated to others, almost like a chain reaction. Restructuring the salary program to reward achievement drove faculty effort and morale, which in turn established a credible case for greater university support. The completion of the move to a new campus was key in recruiting strong faculty members who rapidly established the college as a major player in key national research initiatives. The experience of rebuilding the university's College of Engineering taught me that to take advantage of the opportunities, one needs to have the capacity to move very rapidly. Timing is everything. Windows of opportunity open and close very rapidly, whether in the university, state government, or Washington.

Important, too, is developing, executing, and holding to a clear strategy. Too often, academic leaders tend to react to—or even resist—external pressures and opportunities rather than taking strong, decisive actions to determine and pursue their own goals. Since I was a scientist-engineer, it is not surprising that I tended to be a leader comfortable with strategic thinking. Yet it should also be acknowledged that my particular style of planning and decision making was rather unorthodox, sometimes baffling both our university planning staff and my colleagues alike.

Once, I overheard a colleague describe my style as "fire, ready, aim," as I launched salvo after salvo of agendas and initiatives. This was not a consequence of impatience or lack of discipline. Rather, it grew from my increasing sense that traditional planning approaches were simply ineffective during periods of great change. Far too many leaders, when confronted with uncertainty, tend to fall into a mode of "ready, aim . . . ready, aim . . . ready, aim . . ." and never make a decision. By the time they are finally forced to pull the trigger, the target has moved out of range. Hence, there was indeed logic to my "anticipatory, scattershot" approach to planning and decision making.[7] I also believed that incremental change based on traditional, well-understood paradigms might be the most dangerous course of all, because those paradigms may simply not be adequate to adapt to a time of very rapid change. If the status quo is no longer an option, if the existing paradigms are no longer valid, then more radical transformation becomes the wisest course.[8] Furthermore, during times of very rapid change and uncertainty, it is sometimes necessary to launch the actions associated with a preliminary strategy long before it is carefully thought through and completely developed.

However, pushing full speed ahead does not always lead to success. The decision process in a university can become overloaded and driven into a state of paralysis. If one asks for too much at once, the system can lock up into indecisiveness. It was important to learn how to manage the flow of requests and when subtle pressure was more effective than an all-out assault.

Beyond that, we also learned that sometimes, in order to break a logjam of indecision, it was necessary to think outside of the box. It took a great deal of creativity and ingenuity to keep the decision process moving ahead. In addition to creativity, there were also times when we needed to be prepared to push all of our chips into the center of the table. For example, when the university was frozen on its decision concerning the move of the College of Engineering to the North Campus, we offered to deplete our entire discretionary funding capacity and loan the provost $2 million to get the show on the road. When Harold Shapiro and Bill Frye were unwilling to challenge the vice president for research over our proposal for research incentives, we found a way to accomplish the same objective while avoiding executive politics. To reestablish merit rather than longevity as the primary determinant of compensation, we doubled the salaries of all assistant and associate professors in the college, an action that incurred the wrath of many of our less-active senior faculty. But we were prepared to take the heat in order to make the necessary investments in the college's future.

The importance of teamwork runs throughout my years as dean and, afterward, provost and president. The sense of teamwork among our dean's team, department chairs, executive committee, and faculty was truly extraordinary. It clearly cut through the usual hierarchy of authority that characterizes administrative organizations. This is not to say that we avoided responsibility. Sooner or later someone had to lead the troops into battle—and suffer the consequences if the battlefield strategy was a failure. I have long become convinced that academic leadership is never effective from far behind the front lines.

Working with such a young, energetic, and talented team to rebuild the College of Engineering was an exhilarating experience, but by the mid-1980s, I was beginning to wonder what I could do for an encore. The college had undergone such dramatic change that I and my colleagues worried that the solidification of its gains might require a different leadership style than the "go for it" approach we had encouraged during our tenure. We had stretched the college in all directions, strengthening the faculty, the student body, the quality of academic programs, the facilities, and the budget. It was time to let it cure a bit with a different type of leadership. Of course, during the years I served as dean, I had been probed about other opportunities. But Anne and I were not ready to leave Ann Arbor and the university just yet.

As fate would have it, we really did not have to leave, since the provost position at Michigan opened up when Bill Frye decided in the fall of 1985 to return the following spring to his native Georgia as provost at Emory University. Harold Shapiro launched a long and quite involved search for Frye's replacement. On the positive side for me, Michigan had never selected a provost from outside the university, in part because of the concern that the learning curve was simply too steep and unforgiving in a university of its size and complexity. However, in over 175 years of Michigan history, the university had never selected anybody from engineering for a senior university position.[9]

Yet sometimes the impossible happens, and in March, while I was in Washington at a National Science Board meeting, I received a call from President Harold Shapiro's assistant asking me to return to Ann Arbor to discuss the position of provost. As in my earlier negotiations with the university, I reasoned that since our relationship would depend on a very high level of trust and confidence, I would be comfortable with whatever arrangement Shapiro devised. My only request was that I continue my service on the National Science Board, since I believed this to be of major importance to the university—and the nation, of course.

While my transition into the provost's office was about as rapid as that as my transition into the dean's—roughly six weeks between my acceptance of Shapiro's offer and taking over—there were some important differences. In sharp contrast to moving into a situation where a decade of relatively weak leadership had left the College of Engineering in shambles, I would be following in the footsteps of Billy Frye, one of the university's most able provosts, and I would be joining a very talented team of executive officers, led by a particularly insightful and effective president in Harold Shapiro. Hence, I immediately realized the importance of a smooth transition, with few personnel changes, so that I could not only build on Frye's past accomplishments and momentum but also reinforce the strong confidence that the faculty (and particularly the deans) had in his wisdom, compassion, and academic intuition to do the right thing. Frye graciously set aside a very considerable amount of time, and we met for many days to discuss the university, its challenges, and the role of the provost. It was clear from the outset that I had a great deal to learn.

As in my earlier transition to dean, I began a crash course in university-wide leadership by meeting with scores of faculty and administrators. Of particular priority here were meetings with the deans of our schools and colleges. While I already had established good peer-to-peer relationships with many of them, a new level of confidence and respect needed to be developed to support my role as their chief academic officer. I intentionally scheduled each of these meetings "on their turf" (i.e., in their offices) and followed quickly with tours of their schools. I received similar briefings from other university units, including a several-day immersion in the Medical Center (where I finally concluded that the best way to understand the complexities of this very large part of the university was to be admitted for a medical procedure).

It was important to gain a broader perspective, both historically and beyond the boundaries of the campus. I spent a considerable amount of time with the university's former presidents Harlan Hatcher and Robben Fleming, as well as traveling about the country to meet with an array of experienced education leaders, including the presidents and provosts of Harvard, Yale, Stanford, Illinois, Wisconsin, and Minnesota, as well as the heads of such university organizations as the Association of American Universities and the American Council on Education.

But clearly my most important meetings were with my new boss, Harold Shapiro. A strong relationship between the president and provost, based on mutual confidence and respect, is absolutely essential in university leadership, and despite his hectic calendar, he was always willing (and anxious) to meet with me both in the weeks prior to my becoming provost and then later throughout my tenure. We had an understanding that any time a matter of urgency arose, we would immediately set aside other activities to meet. As I have noted earlier, Harold Shapiro was a leader of truly remarkable intellect, with an exceptionally deep understanding of the nature of higher education and the particular character of the University of Michigan. One measure of how much I learned from him is the number of my notebooks filled with notes from our conversations.

Since Harold Shapiro had also served both as provost and faculty member at Michigan for almost two decades, he had accumulated a very broad experience and interest in the academic and financial intricacies of the university. He clearly knew far more than I did about many of the core activities of the university, as well as some of its particularly complex components, such as the Medical Center. I, however, had served as dean of one of the larger professional schools (engineering) and was a scientist with extensive Washington experience (serving on the National Science Board). Furthermore, I was probably more comfortable with strategic visioning than with focusing on details. Hence, although this relationship only lasted 18 months before Shapiro left for the presidency of Princeton, it worked quite well, since we complemented one another in a partnership.

Through these early conversations with Shapiro, Frye, and others in the university, it became increasingly clear that while I would be filling some very big shoes in a particularly able central administration, the university was facing some serious issues that would require a bolder and more comprehensive strategy. This was one of the key reasons that Harold Shapiro selected me as his provost and also a key reason that I accepted the position. During the late 1970s and early 1980s, the university had experienced one of the most difficult periods in its history, with deep cuts in state appropriations, considerable campus unrest (particularly with respect to racial tensions), and the trauma of an extended period of budget cuts, program reviews, and retrenchment. Shapiro and Frye had done a masterful job of guiding the university through these rocky shoals, but the confidence of both faculty and staff was clearly shaken, and morale was low.

Hence, one of my major challenges was to shift the university from defense to offense, to restore a sense of optimism and excitement about the future. Key in this effort was to work with Shapiro to develop a new and compelling vision for the future of the university, a vision that would build on our traditions and strengths—our institutional saga—to earn the engagement and commitment of our campus community and to rebuild strong support from the public and private sector. In each meeting with faculty, deans, or executive officers, I tried to convey a sense of excitement and enthusiasm about the university's future. While I acknowledged that we still were not out of the woods yet and needed to continue to focus resources, the key was to give folks more of a sense of influence over their futures. Since most knew our success in rebuilding the College of Engineering, I tried to use some of the same themes: the importance of people; a philosophy of building from the grass roots up rather than from the top down; and strong encouragement of innovation, risk taking, and entrepreneurial behavior.

Harold Shapiro and I worked closely together to address some near-term challenges. The erosion in state support experienced during the early 1980s had essentially wiped out the university's discretionary capacity, particularly those resources available to fund new ventures. In my role as chief budget officer, I began to take steps to rebuild reserve funds, encouraging all of our academic and administrative units to control expenditures in an effort to build reserves at the local level, avoiding funding traps that might lead us into long-term funding commitments, and simply saying "no" more frequently (if ever so politely). Within a year, we had managed to restore all of the university's reserve accounts to the maximum levels they had achieved before the period of state budget cuts.

The second near-term objective was to raise the bar on faculty hiring and promotion decisions. As provost, Harold Shapiro had been quite rigorous in reviewing faculty promotion casebooks, a habit he carried with him into the presidency. Together, we moved to create an even higher level of expectation for our various schools and colleges, paying particular attention to those programs whose culture made such evaluations difficult (most particularly in large professional schools, such as the schools of law and medicine). As provost, I made it clear to the deans that my first role would be to challenge what I perceived to be weak cases and, rather than reject them outright, ask them to reconsider or provide additional justification. Usually this was sufficient, but in some cases, it was necessary to use back channels (a staff assistant) to warn deans about resubmission of particularly weak cases, since a provost has to take care not to overtly overrule deans in such a way that it undermines their credibility with their faculty.

Not surprisingly, while I was determined to build on the achievements of my predecessor and retained most of his administration, my style was quite different. Because of the complexity of the university, the dual role of the provost as both chief academic officer and chief budget officer, and the exceptionally large number of direct reporting lines (18 deans, six associate vice presidents or vice-provosts, and a flock of directors and staff for other administrative units), it was a real effort to avoid having all of one's waking hours consumed by standing committee meetings or responding to the in-box. Yet, with so many people dependent on decisions of the provost, the ability to quickly analyze situations and make decisions was essential. Nothing frustrates deans more than indecisiveness, since they are usually creative enough to respond to a negative decision but are frozen into inaction until a decision is made. Working closely with my staff, I was brutal in simplifying the calendar and delegating to others minor decisions, such as the control of small discretionary funds.

Yet another theme of the provost years that would continue into my presidency was the importance of building a greater sense of community within the institution. Whether due to the harsh climate or the years of agonizing budget cuts, people had retreated into their foxholes, cautious and conservative in their activities and protective of their turf, with a consequent erosion in both morale and loyalty to the institution. Since Anne had recently served as president of the university's Faculty Women's Club, she knew a great many members of the faculty family across the campus, and she began immediately to launch a wide array of events for students, faculty, and staff to draw together the campus community. Within a few weeks following my selection as provost, Anne had already established a new university tradition to honor newly promoted faculty each spring.

One of Anne's most important early efforts involved launching a series of monthly dinners held at the university's Inglis House estate to bring together 10 to 15 faculty couples from across the university. The intent was to provide faculty with new opportunities to reach beyond their disciplines, meet new people, and develop new friendships. The dinners also provided us with a marvelous opportunity to understand better what was on the faculty's mind. However, the logistics involved in carrying out the provost-faculty dinners (which were to become a university tradition that continues today) were considerable. This involved not only working with catering and clerical staff to design and conduct these events but also developing a faculty database capable of supporting the invitations to these monthly dinners. Anne also understood the importance of team building among the deans, since without some effort from the provost and president, the deans' naturally competitive natures could push the academic units apart. Each year, Anne would organize an array of events hosted by the provost (and later the president) for the deans and their spouses, from informal potluck suppers to events that showed off unusual aspects of the university.

Looking back over my notes in preparation for this book, I find the level of activity during my first year as provost quite incredible. I was involved in rebuilding the reserve funds of the university while achieving the strongest faculty salary program in a decade; creating the Michigan Mandate, which would become the cornerstone of our diversity effort during the 1990s; stimulating the construction of a series of important capital facilities for academic units (since the Replacement Hospital Project had been the primary focus of the preceding decade); launching an array of activities aimed at improving the undergraduate experience; negotiating new policies governing intercollegiate athletics; raising the standards for faculty promotion and tenure; leading a university-wide strategic planning effort; working with Anne to create a broad array of community events for students, faculty, and staff; and a host of other activities associated with the broad responsibilities of the provost. Perhaps because of the high level of energy and enthusiasm that accompanied such an active agenda, I was able to quickly earn the confidence, respect, and strong support of the deans.

In one sense, it is probably not surprising that I was able to hit the ground running, since both my university service experiences as a faculty member and my administrative experience as the dean of one of the university's largest schools prepared me well for leadership as provost. But it is also the case that my strong support of the directions in which Harold Shapiro and Billy Frye had led the university over the preceding decade allowed me to simply accelerate (rather than change course) and invest my time and energy in continuing this agenda. Many of the same approaches I had taken as dean of engineering seemed to be equally effective at the university level: shifting from reactive to strategic leadership, that is, gathering information by listening, analyzing, determining objectives, planning a course of action, building a team, and moving out rapidly; forming the deans into a leadership team; delegating responsibility, albeit with accountability for results; and conveying a sense of great energy and enthusiasm. Beyond my role as the chief budget officer for the academic programs of the university, I viewed my most important priority as working closely with the president and deans in developing a strategic vision for the university. Within a few months, we had not only initiated a major set of planning activities involving every school and college of the university, but I had also launched a series of initiatives that would later define my presidency: a major effort to increase the racial diversity of the campus community; a series of initiatives designed to improve the undergraduate experience; an initiative to expand the international activities of the university; an aggressive plan to improve the capital facilities of the university; a far-reaching effort to achieve leadership in the use of information technology; efforts to rebuild programs in the natural sciences; and the restructuring of several key professional schools (including the schools of dentistry, library science, and education).

As the activities of the Office of the Provost accelerated, Anne and I were asked to take on additional responsibilities. The provost position at Michigan was a particularly challenging one because of its broad range of responsibilities, since the provost serves not only as the chief academic officer of the university but also as the university's chief budget officer. The provost was also second in command and thereby empowered to serve as acting president in the event of the president's absence. Such a situation arose late in 1986, when Harold Shapiro took a brief sabbatical leave—spent partly in England and partly in New York, working at the Ford Foundation. During this period, I served as acting president in addition to my role as provost. This involved, among other activities, serving among the leaders of a Michigan expedition to the Rose Bowl in 1987. (We lost.)

ON THE BRINK

When Harold Shapiro asked me to accept the position of provost in April 1986, he conveyed his hope that I would commit to serving for at least five years. We both knew the Michigan provost position had frequently been a stepping-stone to a major university presidency (e.g., for Roger Heyns to the University of California, Berkeley; Frank Rhodes to Cornell; and Harold Shapiro at Michigan). However, Anne and I wanted to remain in Ann Arbor, so I signed on for the duration, assuming, naturally, that Harold Shapiro would remain as well.

Imagine our surprise when, almost exactly one year after I became provost, in May 1987, Harold pulled me aside the day before spring commencement to tell me he had accepted the presidency at Princeton. Actually, by that time I suspected something might be up, since rumor had it that Shapiro had been approached by Princeton during his sabbatical leave earlier that winter. Yet, although I had suspected that the ice might be getting thin under my current position at the university, I had remained solidly behind my commitment to remain as provost, turning aside several approaches concerning presidencies at other institutions.

When Shapiro's announcement became public, two things happened almost immediately that dramatically changed our lives. First, there was a very rapid transfer of power from Harold Shapiro to me. Although Shapiro was determined to serve until the end of the year (in part, to see through the completion of the current fund-raising campaign), it was clear that most faculty saw him not only as a lame duck but as one destined to fly off to another pond. Anyone either on or off the campus who needed a decision or a commitment that would last beyond Shapiro's final months came to me in my role as not only the second-ranking officer but also one who would be in place to honor the commitment after Harold's departure. (As an aside, it is interesting to note that Anne and I experienced a quite different situation following the announcement of our own decision to step down from the Michigan presidency and return to the faculty in 1996. Although I had expected that I would almost certainly experience some erosion of power during my last year as a lame-duck president, I continued to experience the full authority of the presidency until my last day in office. There was even an increase in the number of difficult issues or decisions flowing across my desk for resolution as the end of my tenure approached, as people wanted to tie up loose ends before I stepped down. In retrospect, I believe that this sharp contrast with Shapiro's loss of power was due to the simple fact that the university community knew that Anne and I were committed to staying at Michigan. Hence, the university continued to have full confidence in our leadership as long as we remained in the presidency.)

The second major change that occurred in our lives once Shapiro announced that he was stepping down was the recognition, both on our parts and on the part of the university community, that I was now viewed as a leading candidate to succeed him—whether I believed this would actually happen or not and whether I wished it to happen or not. Within a very short time, we were propelled into the search process beyond the point of no return. Looking back, both Anne and I realize that the provost assignment was probably our downfall. Even as dean, one still retains considerable credibility with the faculty: I was still able to do research and supervise graduate students—although I usually met with them during noontime jogging through the university's arboretum; Anne was able to maintain her network of friends while serving in such important roles as the president of the Faculty Women's Club. However, once we had been captured by the immense gravitational pull of the central administration, it was almost impossible to escape back to a normal faculty life. The Michigan provost position is a decidedly ephemeral role (even if the president remains for a longer period), since it is generally the first place other institutions look for a presidential candidate. Looking back now, Anne and I realize that the die was probably cast eventually to become a university president the minute I had accepted Shapiro's Faustian bargain to become provost.

To some degree, my path up the academic leadership ladder to the Michigan presidency was rather conventional, in the sense that it progressed naturally from professor to dean to provost and, finally, to president. Yet it stands in sharp contrast to the experiences of most of today's university presidents, since careers typically wander through several universities—or other roles in government or business—before landing in a presidency. During my years as president, there were only two other presidents among the 60 universities in the American Association of Universities who had spent their entire careers as faculty and academic leaders in a single institution (William Danforth at Washington University and Charles Young at the University of California, Los Angeles).

Of course, although my entire faculty and leadership experience had been at the University of Michigan, my own education had been forged in two other remarkable institutions: Yale University and Caltech. Yale has long viewed its educational experience as a preparation for leadership, and Caltech is characterized by a truly remarkable commitment to focus its efforts only in academic areas where it can be the very best. There was one further advantage in my own experience: the opportunity to learn the craft of university leadership from several of the most distinguished academic leaders of our times—Harlan Hatcher, Robben Fleming, Frank Rhodes, Harold Shapiro, and Billy Frye. In retrospect, a key to the role I played as Michigan's provost and president during my 10 years at the helm of the university was this combination of my experiences with three quite remarkable institutions—Michigan, Yale, and Caltech—and my relationships with some truly extraordinary academic leaders.

3

THE PRESIDENTIAL SEARCH

The search for and selection of a university president is a fascinating process. Considering the growing importance of the university in a knowledge-based society and the complexity of this leadership role, one would expect that a rigorous and informed process would be used to select a university president. This is certainly the case for most other academic leadership positions (e.g., department chairs, deans, or executive officers), whose occupants are typically selected by experienced academic leaders, assisted by faculty search committees, and driven by the recognition that the fate of academic programs—not to mention their own careers—rests on the quality of their selection. Yet, at the highest level of academic leadership, the selection of a university president is the responsibility of a governing board of lay citizens, few with extensive experience in either academic matters or the management of large, complex organizations. This board is aided by a faculty advisory committee with similarly limited knowledge concerning the role of the contemporary university president.

The contrast of a presidential search with the selection of leadership in other sectors of our society, such as business or government, could not be more severe. In the business world, the search for a corporate chief executive officer is conducted by a board of directors, composed primarily of experienced business leaders who understand the business and make their selection in full recognition of their legal and fiduciary responsibility and their liability for shareholder value. In government, leaders are chosen by popular election, with candidates put under extensive public scrutiny by the media and voters. Yet the selection of a university president is conducted in relative secrecy, by those quite detached from academic experience, fiduciary responsibility, or accountability to those most affected by the decision—namely, students, faculty, staff, patients, and others dependent on the welfare of the institution.

Actually, the selection of a university president is most similar to a political campaign. The search is surrounded by an unusual degree of public interest, both within the university community and beyond. Various constituencies attempt to influence the search with their particular political views and agendas. While some view the most important challenge of selecting a new president as sustaining or enhancing academic quality as top priority, others are more concerned with the implications of new leadership for peripheral activities (e.g., the university's athletic program), service activities, or perhaps even the university's stance on controversial political issues (e.g., affirmative action or gay rights). Local news media frequently treat the search as they would a political race, complete with leaks and speculation from unnamed sources. The search is generally long—frequently at least a year—and often distracted by legal issues and constraints, such as sunshine laws. But the selection of a university president has one important distinction from a political campaign: those most affected by the outcome have no vote.

THE SEARCH PROCESS

Most searches for university presidents begin rationally enough. After consultation with the faculty, the governing board appoints a group of distinguished faculty—perhaps augmented by representatives of other constituencies (students, staff, and alumni)—to serve as a screening committee, with the charge of sifting through the hundreds of nominations of candidates to determine a small group for consideration of the board. This task seems straightforward enough: the university can place advertisements of the position in various higher education magazines to attract attention to the search, and university leaders at other institutions can be contacted for suggested candidates. Yet there are many complications.

Few, if any, attractive candidates will formally apply for the position, since they are typically in senior leadership positions elsewhere—perhaps even as university presidents. Instead, the challenge to the screening committee is to identify qualified individuals and persuade them to become candidates in the search—typically in a very informal sense during the early stages of the search, to avoid compromising their current positions. During this process, the members of the screening committee may be lobbied hard by their colleagues, by special interest groups, and even occasionally by trustees, in an effort to place their preferred candidates on the short list that will be eventually submitted to the governing board.

In an effort both to expedite and protect the faculty search process, there is an increasing trend at most universities to use executive search firms to assist in the presidential search process. These search consultants are useful in helping the faculty search committees keep the search process on track, in gathering background information, in developing realistic timetables, and even in identifying key candidates. Furthermore, particularly for public institutions subject to sunshine laws, search consultants can provide a secure, confidential mechanism to communicate with potential candidates without public exposure, at least during the early stages of the search. Of course, there are sometimes downsides to the use of search consultants. Some consultants tend to take on too many assignments at one time and devote inadequate attention to thoroughly checking background references. Other consultants, while experienced in searches for corporate executives, have relatively little experience with the arcane world of higher education and simply do not know how to generate an adequate list of attractive candidates. Perhaps most serious are those rare instances in which search consultants attempt to influence the search process by pushing a preferred candidate. Yet most consultants act in a highly professional way and view their role as one of facilitating, rather than influencing, the search. If selected carefully and used properly by the screening committee and the governing board, executive search consultants can be invaluable to an effective search.

While the early stage of screening candidates usually proceeds in a methodical fashion (particularly if assisted by an experienced search consultant), the final selection process by the governing board more frequently than not involves a bizarre interplay of politics and personalities. The search process for public universities is frequently constrained by sunshine laws—notably those laws requiring public meetings of governing bodies and allowing press access to written materials via laws upholding the freedom of information. In many states, these laws require not only that the final slate of candidates be made public but, moreover, that these candidates be interviewed and even compared and selected in public by the governing board. These public beauty pageants can be extremely disruptive both to the integrity of the search process and to the reputation of the candidates. A great many attractive candidates simply will not participate in such a public circus, because of the high risk such public exposure presents to their current positions. Universities subject to such sunshine laws generally find their candidate pools restricted to those who really have nothing to lose by public exposure—those in lower positions (e.g., provosts or deans), leaders of smaller or less prominent institutions, or perhaps even politicians or corporate executives. For these candidates, public exposure poses little risk, and there is some potential for gain in their being identified as presidential candidates.

The interview process conducted by the governing board, whether public or private, is rarely a very effective way to assess the credentials of candidates. As former University of Texas president Peter Flawn has noted, many a governing board has been burned by "a charmer, an accomplished candidate for president who is charming and engaging, eloquent about 'the academy,' politically astute, yet who, once in the job, will turn the management over to vice-presidents, enjoy the emoluments, entertaining, and social interactions for a few years, and then move on, leaving the institution as good as the vice-presidents can make it."[1] Flawn observes that only in extraordinary situations does the charisma last for more than three years.

Governing board members are lobbied hard both by internal constituencies (faculty, students, and administrators) and by external constituencies (alumni, key donors, politicians, special interest groups, and the press). Since the actual group of trustees making the selection is usually rather small, strong personalities among governing board members can have a powerful influence over the outcome. Some university presidential searches are wired from the beginning, with powerful board members manipulating the search to favor preferred internal or external candidates. The politics of presidential selection becomes particularly intense for public universities, since the open nature of these searches allows the media to have unusual influence in not only evaluating candidates but actually putting political pressure on governing board members to support particular individuals. Sometimes political groups sabotage the candidacy of individuals by misrepresenting the background of a candidate or leaking false information to the media. Many who have participated in good faith in public university searches have been seriously compromised.

Most governing boards launch the search process for a successor within several weeks after a president announces the intention to step down. Presidents who resign to accept an appointment at another institution generally leave within a few months, much to the relief of governing boards and university faculties, since lame ducks generally make very ineffective leaders. When a president decides to return to the faculty or retire, typically announcing in the fall that she or he will leave at the end of the academic year the following spring, there is usually the flexibility to allow more time for a transition. Yet even in these situations, interim leadership is generally required, since the search for a new president inevitably takes longer than anticipated, typically a year or more.

During this interim period, it is customary for the governing board to ask a senior member of the faculty or the administration to serve as interim or acting president until the search is completed and the new president assumes the post. Sometimes this is one of the senior vice presidents or deans. On occasions, a past president will be asked to come out of retirement to serve in the interim role for several months.

This interim period can be awkward and stressful both for the institution and for the governing board. Rarely do interim presidents have sufficient authority to provide strong leadership. Even if the governing board grants them the power to be decisive, their limited term as an interim leader undermines their credibility both on campus and beyond. Most governing boards try to avoid appointing potential candidates, such as the provost, to these interim posts, both to keep from distorting the search process—that is, to maintain a level playing field for all candidates—and to maintain as much normalcy as possible within the administrative team. Woe to those provosts with interest in the presidency who are asked to assume such interim roles, since the complexities of both interim university leadership and the search process itself are likely to doom their candidacy.

Whether formally announced through a public vote or a press release, the final decision to select a university president is usually made in private. It generally involves a negotiation among governing board members. Consequently, the search all too frequently results in the selection of the least common denominator, that is, the candidate who least offends the most trustees.

A quick review of the history of the University of Michigan, including the more recent oral histories of its leaders, makes it clear that Michigan is no exception to this strongly political process of presidential selection. Each presidential search at Michigan has been unique. Some have been truly bizarre. In fact, most Michigan presidents have not even been the regents' first choice (including such distinguished leaders as Henry Tappan and James Angell, perhaps Michigan's greatest presidents).[2] In the end, the result of each search has been a consequence more of board politics and personalities than of any broader consideration of the university's needs of the moment, saga of the past, or potential for the future.

THE PRESIDENTIAL SEARCH: A VICTIM'S PERSPECTIVE

Perhaps the most vivid way to illustrate the complexities of a presidential search is to describe my own personal experience in being selected as Michigan's president, a process my wife, Anne, once compared to a 14-month pregnancy. Our situation was made all the more difficult because of the fact that as both provost and behind-the-scenes president, I was continually under the microscope as a potential presidential candidate. It rapidly became apparent that there would be only one internal candidate in the search: me. The search process itself essentially consisted of comparing one external candidate after another against me as a calibration. While this probably was good training for the stressful public role of the contemporary university presidency, it could also be a bit unnerving, particularly when the comparisons were kept confidential to the search committee. Nevertheless, within a very short period, I concluded that we had been dragged into the search process far too deeply to withdraw without harming the university. Anne and I felt we had no choice but to stick it out until the end.

As provost of the university at the time that Harold Shapiro announced in May of 1987 his decision to accept the presidency at Princeton, I was faced with the challenge of providing leadership for the academic programs of the university during the interim period between presidents and with the possibility of being an internal candidate for his successor. Although many viewed me as the most viable internal candidate to succeed Shapiro, I knew that presidential searches were very complex (particularly in public universities with an elected governing board) and that it was quite likely that an external candidate would be chosen by the regents. If that were to occur, it was possible that I would be out of a job, since the new president would likely select his or her own provost. Yet Anne and I felt a very strong loyalty to the university and particularly to the deans who had become our family during my service in the provost role. Hence, we decided together to commit ourselves to providing whatever leadership we could in the provost role and to guiding and stabilizing the university through the transition between presidents, although we had no idea at the time that this period would last for almost 14 months. Although I continued to be approached by other universities concerning presidencies during this period, I turned these aside to focus on my duties as provost (and occasional behind-the-scenes chief executive officer) of the university.

The first order of business was to meet with outgoing president Harold Shapiro to more clearly define our roles and then to meet with the deans to seek both their counsel and support. In my experience, there are two different approaches to leaving a presidency. Some departing presidents simply check out, leaving whatever mess remains for their successor to clean up. Others remain for a time, attempting to complete key agendas and to clean up any loose ends for their successor, although this may be difficult as one's authority and credibility rapidly erode during a lame-duck period. Harold Shapiro, always loyal and responsible to the university to the end of his tenure, chose the latter approach.

In my early discussions with Harold, I stressed the importance of his support during his remaining months. As provost, not only would I become, by default, the primary source of continuity during the leadership transition, but it was also likely that I would eventually be blamed for any mistakes made during the interregnum, since I would be the one left behind. In particular, I asked not only to be kept in the loop on all major decisions but for his assistance in building stronger relationships with the executive officers. No matter how hard an outgoing president tries, it is very difficult to shift the loyalty of the executive officers and staff to the interim leadership, since they know they are likely to soon be reporting to someone else. Hence, court politics can run rampant; petty turf battles, challenges to authority, and recalcitrance are commonplace. Equally important was the outgoing president's role in keeping the governing board on course, focused both on its ongoing responsibilities and on its efforts to conduct a search for the next president. At Michigan, this was difficult because of the deep political divisions on the board and its tendencies toward micromanagement, which were likely to break out in the power vacuum that would develop during the lame-duck period.

Next, I turned to a series of meetings with the deans, since they would play such a key role in ensuring a stable leadership transition. In our discussions, I stressed my belief that it would be a serious mistake simply to adopt a "steady as she goes" approach. This was a very critical period in the university's history, and we could not afford to waste it through inaction. We were already far along in the strategic leadership effort that Harold Shapiro and I had launched the year before, and we could not put on hold such important initiatives as the Michigan Mandate, improving undergraduate education, building needed capital facilities, and strengthening state and federal relations.

But we also understood that the transition period would not be a time for business as usual, so we had to select carefully our priorities.

Shapiro and I agreed that an important element of this strategy would be to enable greater involvement of the deans in campus-wide leadership. To this end, I created a number of high-level advisory groups involving the deans. While this created some degree of overload for the deans, adding considerable responsibilities beyond their schools and colleges, they appreciated the opportunity to become more actively involved in university-wide leadership during the transition. This deeper engagement of the deans was so effective that I continued it during my presidency.

In a similar spirit of building university momentum during the transition, I strongly supported the efforts of both Harold Shapiro (as a lame duck) and Robben Fleming (as interim president) to proceed with searches to fill several senior personnel positions (including vice president for finance, general counsel, chancellor of our Dearborn campus, and athletic director), even though filling these positions would limit the ability of the next president to build his or her own executive team. Because of the considerable uncertainly about the length of time that would be required to search for and install a new president, we all agreed that the university was best served by moving ahead with these searches.

The final issue facing the university leadership during the interim had to do with maintaining control of the agenda in the face of the usual distractions that characterize university campuses: for example, student activism (in our case, student disciplinary policies; campus security; and various "isms," such as racism, sexism, and extremism), faculty issues (compensation, health benefits, parking), government relations (state appropriations, political intrusion on university autonomy), and media exposés (enabled by sunshine laws, such as the Freedom of Information Act and the Open Meetings Act). The deans and I cautioned Shapiro and Fleming against taking any actions that might trigger campus disruptions and instability during the interim period, such as forcing through a new student disciplinary policy.

Despite the efforts of outgoing president Harold Shapiro and interim president Robben Fleming and despite the strong support of the university's deans, the wear and tear of leading the university from the provost position during this interim period (either directly or behind the scenes) was considerable for both Anne and me. During the holiday season, after the Shapiros left for Princeton and while the rest of the executive officers flew to Florida for the annual bowl trip of the Michigan football team, Anne and I remained behind in Ann Arbor to keep watch over the university (a typical provost role) and to take a deep breath in preparation for the final stage of the presidential search.

Part of the problem was the awkward nature of the search itself. The university's regents had begun the search process by fanning out across the country, talking with other university leaders, in an effort to educate themselves about the key issues facing higher education and to identify leading candidates. While this was a perfectly reasonable—indeed, laudable—objective, the personalities of some members of the board rapidly proceeded to turn off several of the most attractive candidates. This was complicated by disagreement among the board members as to just who would lead the formal search process and how it would be organized. Without the guidance of an executive search consultant, the search began to unravel. By fall, it was in a shambles. As the faculty members on the search committee became more and more frustrated with the slow pace of the search, they were finally able to persuade the regents to retain an executive search consultant to get things back on track. Even so, by early fall, it became apparent that the search process was simply not moving ahead rapidly enough to have a new president selected and ready to go by the time Harold Shapiro planned to leave for Princeton.

The role of provost of the university is complex enough without taking on the additional responsibilities of the presidency. My brief experience in handling both roles simultaneously when I had served as acting president during Harold Shapiro's brief sabbatical left me little appetite to continue as interim president. Fortunately, the board of regents had the wisdom to ask a former Michigan president, Robben Fleming, to return in the interim role between Harold Shapiro's departure and the installation of a new president, a period that would last roughly nine months. Yet, although Robben Fleming was widely respected by the faculty, particularly skillful in handling controversy, and supported by the regents, he had not been actively involved in university issues for almost a decade. Since he was identified as the interim choice in the fall, it gave him an opportunity to come up to speed on several of the various issues affecting the university. It also provided me with ample opportunity to work with him and develop a close relationship that would be essential to operating smoothly through the transition.

While it was a duty above and beyond the call, I had the sense that Robben Fleming was actually rather excited to be returning to the fray. Since he was wise enough to realize that there was no way that he could master in such a short period the many complex issues involving the university or the many details required for its management, he decided at an early stage to focus his personal efforts on a few issues that aligned with his strengths and then to rely on his executive officer team to handle the other details. Key among his priorities were resolving the racial tensions that had developed during the last years of the Shapiro administration, the issue of a student disciplinary policy, and two key searches—for an athletic director and a chief financial officer. While Fleming recognized that as provost—both chief academic officer and chief budget officer—I would be handling many of the details in running the university behind the scenes, our relationship was such that if he felt I was headed in the wrong direction, he would immediately tell me, so that we could reevaluate and, if necessary, make midcourse corrections. Working with Fleming also gave me an opportunity to learn from his extraordinary people skills, particularly in handling adversarial situations.

Even working as a team with Robben Fleming and the other executive officers, I found the task of maintaining the momentum of the university during the transition period difficult. The newspapers carried continual speculation about the presidential search, including frequent rumors about the list of candidates. During the search process, Anne and I were asked to participate in a series of interviews for the presidency. I first met with the joint committee of faculty, students, and alumni. Then we were both asked to dine at Inglis House with the regents comprising the search committee. Of course, we knew that several external candidates were undergoing a similar process.

As the search approached its final stages in late spring, the papers became more active with speculation about the search candidates. This was a rather depressing time for Anne and me. It was not that we had a burning lust for the Michigan presidency; we had been happy in both my roles as dean and then provost. It was, rather, the recognition of our vulnerability. We both had played a highly visible role in leading the university and sustaining its momentum during the interim period since Harold Shapiro's announcement of his resignation. If another candidate were selected, there would be strong pressure on me not only to step down from the provost position but to leave the university. We were well aware that one of the hazards of moving up the pyramid of academic administration was that there was less and less room as one moved toward the top. As the end of the interregnum approached, we realized that the best way to make certain we stayed at Michigan was to be selected as its next president, since returning to the faculty would be difficult at this late stage of the search process. Yet from the rumors reported in the newspapers and the total silence from the regents, we concluded that this was probably not in the cards. During this final phase, the regent's search committee had even pulled away from their search consultant, so even this channel of information about the search disappeared.

Finally, on the Sunday afternoon when we had just returned from our daughter's commencement at Yale, I received a mysterious phone call from the regent who was chair of the search committee, asking me to meet him the next day at the university's Inglis House retreat. Typical of my interactions with the board, there was absolutely no indication of the reason for the meeting. I called the search consultant that evening, and he, too, was totally in the dark. Both of us decided that the odds were about equal between two possibilities. I would either be offered the presidency or told to get ready to welcome another as the next Michigan president.

The next morning, I went to the meeting prepared for either possibility. Two regents met me. After about 15 seconds of chitchat, they said that they were authorized by the board to offer me the presidency. Not being one to beat about the bush, I said that I had made a personal commitment that if I were going to remain in the search until the end, it would be with the understanding that if offered the position, I would accept it—but with one caveat: there was another party that had to be a part of this decision—Anne—since I viewed the presidency as a two-person position. I felt it important that they make a similar request to her. They agreed, and so I called to invite her over to the meeting. Anne had also realized that the Inglis House meeting could go either way. When I asked her to come out to join us, she expressed some relief—but also some anxiety. Nevertheless, together, we agreed to accept the presidency. We really had no choice.

However, there was a technicality here. In an effort to comply with the state's Open Meetings Act, the regents had utilized a process of forming a subquorum subcommittee to conduct the actual search. They believed that to fully comply with state law, it was necessary to conduct a public meeting of the full board, at which I would be interviewed. There, the search subcommittee would submit its recommendation, and the formal vote would be taken. Two days later, just prior to the regents' meeting, I assembled the staff of the Office of the Provost and briefed them on the decision to "move downstairs" to the Office of the President. There were probably more sighs of relief than sad farewells, since they, too, understood the alternatives all too well. The regents' meeting itself was relatively noneventful. As one regent put it, the interview consisted largely of lobbing me a few softballs to hit out of the park, such as "What do you think the largest challenges facing the university are?" Each regent had the opportunity to ask one question, then the senior regent, as chair of the search committee, introduced a resolution to appoint me as the eleventh president of the university. The regents approved it unanimously.

Since the regents' meeting was public, there were enough people in attendance to require the use of the anteroom. Beyond our daughters, there were a number of our friends on the faculty. There were also a number of university personalities, such as football coach Bo Schembechler. Needless to say, Bo stole the headlines with his statement "He was my choice!" In general, there was a very positive reception to the selection, both on the campus and in the media. We were well known to the university community, and there seemed to be a sense of confidence in the direction that we would lead.

The rest of day was spent calling numerous VIPs: the governor, key legislators, other Michigan university presidents, the mayor, industry leaders, and student government leaders, most of whom I already knew personally from my days as dean and then provost. One particular conversation stands out: a senior editor of the *Detroit Free Press* and longtime friend of the university asked to drop by for a brief conversation. He pledged his strong support, but he also wanted to convey an early warning. He feared that the increasing fragmentation of the political parties in Michigan, controlled as they were by an ever-narrower block of special interests, would continue to have a very negative impact on Michigan's board of regents, causing increasing politicization of our governing board and putting both the university and its president at some risk. He suggested that this might be my most formidable challenge as president. As I was to find later, he was right on target.

The presidential search that led to my presidency had already been complicated not only by conflicts among board members (particularly the behavior of one maverick board member who attempted to sabotage the end phase of the search by discouraging one of the finalists)[3] but even more by the intrusion of the media, using the state's Open Meetings Act. Several papers brought suit against the regents for violating the act, which was finally upheld in 1994 by a local judge, who decided, in a fit of pique, to punish the university by demanding that every document concerning the search be opened to the public, including letters of personal reference and personal notes. Although my skin had grown thick enough to weather such exposure, many other candidates involved in the search were seriously embarrassed by the judge's action. It would not be until 2001 that a similar case brought against a presidential search conducted by Michigan State University would make it to the Michigan Supreme Court and receive a ruling that the university's constitutional autonomy and the responsibilities of governing boards overrode the application of the Open Meetings Act to presidential searches.

On a more positive note, since I had been in various faculty and leadership roles at the university for almost twenty years, I understood well the Michigan institutional saga. Furthermore, in my role as provost, I had worked closely with Harold Shapiro and the deans in designing the strategic leadership agenda intended as the vision for the university as it approached the twenty-first century. Hence, I was able to hit the ground running almost immediately as president-elect (and still provost); and long before I would formally assume the presidency in September, I had begun to define and put into place the key themes that would characterize my administration: diversity, globalization, and our evolution into a knowledge-driven society.[4] Hence, by the time of my formal inauguration in October of 1988, the university had emerged from its interregnum and was already accelerating rapidly.

A POSTMORTEM

The difficult task of leading the university through a transition between presidents had come to an end. Despite the long and somewhat confusing presidential search, my leadership team took pride in not only keeping the university on track during the transition but actually making some significant progress on an array of issues, ranging from race relations to resource allocation to intercollegiate athletics. There was a certain personal toll, since Anne and I entered the presidency a bit weary from this task. But our relief at being able to stay at Michigan and our excitement about the challenges and opportunities ahead kept us in high spirits. Perhaps as well, our blissful ignorance about just how challenging the months ahead would be also played an important role in helping us approach our new roles with a spirit of optimism.

In looking back at the experience, there appear to be several lessons to be learned. Of course, the first caveat concerns the awkward position of internal candidates in such searches, particularly when they are in senior positions, such as provosts or interim presidents. All too frequently, this is a no-win situation. As in my case, most such internal candidates are likely to be used as stalking horses in the search, serving as a calibration for one external candidate after another. Furthermore, being held up as a visible candidate during such an extended period invites anyone and everyone to register their views (and take their best shot at the incumbent). The public exposure is unrelenting, and the pressure is intense.

Although such internal candidates are sometimes selected, this is more frequently a result of being the last available candidate in the pool after external candidates have dropped out rather than the first choice of the board. It is also frequently the case that when the board decides to go outside, the inside candidates are left high and dry as damaged goods. Not only do they represent a potential threat to the arriving president-elect, but their credibility as a candidate elsewhere is sometimes damaged beyond repair.

Maintaining the momentum and stability of the university from my position as provost through the long transition period was challenging enough, without the additional complexities and burdens of being a candidate in the search. Try as I might always to act in what I perceived as the best interests of the university (even though there were times when this would get me crosswise with several of the regents, potentially damaging my status as a candidate for the presidency), there was always second-guessing from some on campus about whether I was "campaigning" or whether commitments made during the interim would be sustained by the next president. This situation would have been made even more difficult had I served as interim president. Looking back on my experience, I have concluded that, in general, universities should not select as interim presidents those who might be regarded as candidates. Furthermore, in my own experience, my health, sanity, and good humor might have been better served had I simply declined at the outset to be considered for the presidency.

Hence, from my perspective, at least, I would strongly recommend against accepting an appointment as an interim if one has aspirations for a permanent appointment. If you are already a provost when the presidency opens up, you are in an awkward position. Both your life and your leadership would be best served by issuing an immediate Sherman statement: "If nominated, I will not run; if elected, I will not serve." However, if you are determined to continue to lead even as a candidate, you had better develop a thick skin and be prepared for disappointment.

SOME ADVICE FOR PRESIDENTIAL SEARCH COMMITTEES AND UNIVERSITY GOVERNING BOARDS

Clearly, the selection of a university president is the most important responsibility of a governing board, since it not only must sustain the institution's momentum but also set its course for the future. Mistakes made in a presidential search that result in the selection of a candidate lacking the necessary experience or skills or whose personality conflicts with the character and culture of the institution can cause very serious damage that may take many years to heal. Faculty advisory committees and search consultants can assist in the process, but in the end, the board must accept full responsibility for the success of the presidential search. It is the governing board's judgment that is on the line. The board must take ownership of the search process from day one.

University presidential searches are considerably more difficult than leadership searches in the corporate or government sector. There are a very large number of constituencies who need to be consulted in the search (e.g., faculty, administrators, alumni, key donors, and students). For public universities, public exposure and the constraints imposed by sunshine laws, such as the Open Meetings Act, pose a considerable challenge. Beyond that, the rumor network on and among campuses is quite strong, so that there are invariably leaks to the press as the search plods along. But the most significant challenge is how to conduct a search when both those screening candidates (e.g., faculty) and those making the final selection (i.e., governing board members) are hindered by quite limited knowledge about the nature or role of the contemporary university president. Furthermore, all too often, board members with considerable experience in evaluating and selecting talent in their own careers in business, government, or learned professions tend to leave their wisdom and judgment behind when they enter a boardroom to select a university president and rely instead on highly subjective and personal reactions to the candidates.

Hence, in the spirit of the Chinese proverb "To know the road ahead, ask those who are coming back," let me offer a few words of advice to governing boards faced with a presidential search. What checklist should the governing board give the faculty search committee and the executive search consultant? Of course, the specific wish list will depend on the institution, its challenges and its opportunities. But there are some generic qualifications for a university president.

First, there are matters of character, hard to measure, but obviously of great importance. These include such attributes as integrity, courage, fair-mindedness, a respect for the truth, compassion, and a fundamental and profound understanding of academic culture. The leadership of an educational institution requires a certain degree of moral authority; hence, moral character and behavior become quite important.

Second, there are a number of characteristics, also obvious, but somewhat easier to measure from a candidate's track record. For most institutions, a president must have a credible academic record. This demands strong credentials as a teacher and a scholar. Otherwise, the faculty will not take the president very seriously as a peer, and neither will peer institutions. Strong, demonstrable management skills are also required. After all, the contemporary university is one of the most complex institutions in our society. In these days of increasing legal and financial accountability, universities appoint amateurs to campus leadership at their own risk. However, one must here resist the assumption of many outside of higher education (including many executive search consultants) that the contemporary president's role is similar in style and compensation to chief executive officers in the corporate world.

An array of other experiences are useful (although not mandatory) in candidates for university presidencies. These include familiarity with state and federal relations; experience with private fund-raising; and, perhaps unfortunately, some understanding of the complex world of intercollegiate athletics. A candidate's abilities in all these areas can be easily assessed by thoroughly examining a candidate's past experience and record of achievement.

Some governing boards, particularly those selected through political processes, place a candidate's political skills as an overriding factor in the selection of a president. To be sure, the leaders of both public and private universities require political skill to advance their institution's interests with federal, state, and local government and to handle the array of complex political issues and constituencies within the university. But a university president is called on to provide leadership of many types: executive, academic, moral, and strategic, in addition to political. All too frequently, while politically adept leaders may be effective in pleasing politically determined boards or politically elected state leaders, they may be totally lacking in the intellectual skills necessary to lead an academic institution or the executive skills necessary to manage the complexity of the contemporary university. While political skills alone may be sufficient for many government roles (indeed, they are sometimes the only visible skills of those elected to public office), far more is necessary for university leadership. Many presidents who are the most able politicians have become absolute disasters for the long-term welfare of their institution, since their actions and decisions tend to be based on the near-term imperatives of the political process rather than the long-term interests of the institution. While such leadership might be tolerated for the short term if paired with strong, experienced academic administrators in such roles as provosts and deans, selecting a university president who has only political skills and is isolated from academic traditions and values can lead to disaster.

Beyond these obvious criteria, there is another set of qualifications, again hard to measure, but of particular importance at this moment in the history of public higher education in America. My own experience would suggest the importance of a strong commitment to excellence, including the ability to recognize excellence when it is present and to admit when it is absent—a perspective drilled into me by such mentors as Harold Shapiro, Billy Frye, and Frank Rhodes. Today, presidents need both an understanding of the importance of and a driving passion to achieve diversity, along with a willingness to achieve and defend equality for all members of the university community. As the university's chief recruiter of talent, presidents require an impeccable "taste" in the choice of people. They need the ability to identify and attract the most outstanding talent into key leadership positions in the university, to shape them into teams, and to provide them with strong support and leadership.

As I stress throughout this book, to be successful, presidents must have the capacity to comprehend and the willingness to respect the institutional saga of the university they will lead. They also should have the confidence and wisdom to build on the contributions of their predecessors, even if it is natural that they will tend to chart their own course to the future. Governing boards should seek candidates with personalities and experiences well aligned with the particular character and needs of the institution. For example, selecting a prima donna president to lead the prima donna faculty characterizing some elite U.S. universities can lead to disaster. If the aim is to select a president capable of elevating the academic quality of an institution, the candidate should have experience—either as an administrator or faculty member (or perhaps even student)—with an institution higher up in the pecking order. Here, boards should resist the pressure to determine presidents by the issues of the moment and should instead seek candidates capable of positioning the institution for challenges and opportunities a decade or more in the future.

Finally, it is my belief that presidential searches should seek leaders—those who will seize the helm and guide the institution, rather than simply serve as a representative of the institution to its many constituencies. Although governing boards and faculty senates sometimes shy away from such candidates, times of challenge and change require strong leadership. Of course, leadership goes far beyond management skills and involves the capacity to develop a compelling vision for the institution and to build support for this vision within the university community and among its various stakeholders. It goes without saying that such leadership will require, in turn, immense physical stamina, undiminished energy, and a very thick skin.

Most of these important characteristics should be easily discernible from the track record of candidates and not left simply to the vagaries of superficial impressions from interviews. Candidates with the experience and achievement necessary to be considered as a university president will likely have a track record a mile wide and a mile deep to examine. The typical career path to a university presidency—traversing as it does a sequence of administrative assignments as department chair, dean, and provost—provides search committees and governing boards with ample opportunities to assess the full qualifications of presidential candidates long before they are invited to the campus.

With these formidable qualifications in mind, where should governing boards and search committees look for university presidents? Unfortunately, the pool of attractive candidates considered by most searches is rather small. In fact, the same names keep coming up time and time again, until they are finally selected for a position or ruled out permanently because of some discovered fatal flaw. Perhaps this should not be surprising, since most advisors (usually former university presidents) and executive search consultants have relatively short-range radars and tend to keep scanning the same highly visible leadership positions, such as provosts or deans in major institutions.

Another issue of concern is whether institutions should give preference to internal or external candidates. Most institutions seek a balance among internal and external candidates in filling key academic leadership positions, such as department chairs and deans. But these days, it is rare for a university president to be chosen from internal candidates. In fact, recent surveys indicate that 80 percent of the time, governing boards will select external candidates.[5]

While trapped in an airport one day, I conducted a back-of-the-envelope comparison of inside versus outside presidential appointments over the past several decades at major research universities and arrived at some interesting conclusions. During this period, roughly 85 percent of the presidential searches for Big Ten universities have ended with the selection of external candidates. The Ivy League is a bit more balanced, with a fifty-fifty split, although this is primarily due to the tendency of Harvard, Yale, and Princeton to go with internal candidates, while the rest usually go outside. California stands out as the other extreme, with 75 percent of the selections at the University of California and Stanford being insiders.

Let me suggest two unsubstantiated speculations about these results. First, the better the institution, the more willing it seems to be to consider internal candidates, that is, to grow its own. Here, Harvard, Yale, Princeton, Stanford, and the University of California stand out (although I suppose I could add Wisconsin and Michigan, at least during some periods of their history). It takes a strong sense of institutional self-confidence to assume that the best leader would be one of your own faculty members. Second, there is a particularly pronounced trend for the governing boards of public universities to select new presidents from outside. To some extent, this may simply result from the notion that "the grass is always greener on the other side of the fence"—or, perhaps more accurately, that "the devil you don't know is always more appealing than the devil you do"—at least when it comes to university presidents. But it could also be a sign that governing boards, particularly in public universities, have become ever more political and insecure in their selection of leadership, believing they can better control external candidates who arrive on campus with no local constituency of support. Ironically, the history of several institutions that today tend always to look outside suggests that their best presidents in years past have come from inside (with John Hannah at Michigan State and William Friday at North Carolina being prime examples).

Finally, this tendency could also be evidence of the rather low priority given to leadership development within our universities. Governing board members who have served as directors on publicly traded corporations realize the importance of succession planning that involves not only identifying a leadership depth chart but recruiting and developing junior executives with leadership potential. It is my belief that governing boards should demand that similar attention be given to succession planning and leadership development in higher education.

An unfortunate consequence of the tendency of governing boards to look outside for university leadership is accompanied by another characteristic of today's university presidents: the number of institutions where they have served as faculty or administrators as they climb the leadership ladder during their careers. To some extent, institution hopping among academic administrators is perfectly logical. As I noted earlier, the leadership pyramid narrows markedly as one climbs up the ladder, and since the rungs back to faculty positions in one's field tend to evaporate, there is little choice but to move to another institution for further advancement. So, too, some presidents have used an institution-hopping strategy to move up the ladder of institutional quality, establishing a reputation as a leader at one institution, then jumping to a similar post at an institution of higher reputation—or, in some cases, just leaving town before the lynch mob catches up with them. Yet the phenomenon of the vagabond president has recently become even more pronounced, with many administrators serving not only as academic leaders (chairs, deans, provosts, presidents) in several institutions but even as presidents in several different universities. While it takes a rare talent to be able to adapt to new institutions and provide effective leadership, it is also the case that it takes a newcomer time to understand the institutional saga of a university and much longer to have a substantial and enduring impact on the institution—at least five years and more likely a decade for most universities. From this perspective, it is not surprising that many perceive a leadership vacuum within the higher education community these days, since the tendency of governing boards to recruit presidents from outside has led to a generation of short-timers who tend to bounce off institutions without making a dent. It is also understandable why many faculties seem weary and frustrated from the effort to adjust to one externally appointed president after another, each lasting for only a few years before moving on to another assignment, without the time to achieve the leadership continuity necessary to build institutional momentum.

Finally, a word about just how boards should approach the recruitment of their top candidates. Executive search consultants and compensation consultants tend to stress the importance of competitive compensation. Yet I believe that these evaluations tend to be biased, since consultant fees are frequently indexed to executive compensation levels. Furthermore, the recent inflation in presidential compensation, with salaries no longer simply at the top of the faculty but now beginning to approach those of even football coaches in both the magnitude and the complexity of the compensation scheme,[6] is driving a wedge not only between the faculty and the administration but between the public and higher education.

Although this view may not be shared by governing boards or even many faculty members, I would raise a flag of concern that the university presidency may be evolving away from an academic leadership assignment to a separate profession, with its own unique professional characteristics—including compensation packages—quite apart from those of the faculty. In years past, at most universities, the salaries of academic administrators (e.g., the president, executive officers, and deans) have been generally comparable to those of the top faculty. It was felt important that these academic leaders be seen as senior members of the faculty rather than corporate officers. Rewarding a university president like a corporate CEO threatens to open up a psychological gap between the faculty and the administration (where the faculty no longer views the president—and other senior administrators—as "one of us"), thereby decoupling the president from the academic core of the university and undercutting his or her effectiveness at leading the institution. Derek Bok notes: "A huge presidential salary tends to exacerbate tensions that too often exist between faculty and administration. At critical moments, however, when academic leaders need to rally the faculty to make special efforts for the good of the institution, the distance between highly paid presidents and their professors can be costly indeed."[7]

From many years of experience in assisting in the selection and recruitment of academic leaders, it continues to be my belief that top talent is rarely lured by dollars alone. To be sure, a competitive salary is viewed by some candidates as a measure of how much you want them. But it is rarely the deciding factor. Far more important is the challenge, opportunity, and prestige of building a high-quality institution or academic program. Many candidates are seeking new opportunities because they have been blocked by the narrowing pyramid of the academic hierarchy in their own institution. Some are after wealth and fame, though usually not from their university salary but, rather, from outside their academic appointment, through corporate boards, national commissions, or other opportunities. Some actually view academic leadership as a higher calling, with emotional rewards and satisfaction that simply cannot be quantified in terms of compensation. And some, believe it or not, have acquired a sense of loyalty to a particular university and view such assignments as a duty of service. Skeptics of this perspective might just consider the list of institutions with the highest executive salaries. For the most part, these are the places you have to pay talented people to go, not those institutions capable of attracting them with their quality and reputation. Put slightly differently, the higher the risk of the position, the higher the compensation necessary to attract strong candidates. If a president cannot depend on the board to support him or her when the going gets tough, it is natural to seek to protect oneself in the event that the tough have to get going.

I offer a final comment here about the dangers posed by the professionalization of the university presidency—whether by a widening gap between the faculty and the president because of celebrity compensation levels or because the itinerant careers of many professional university presidents rarely allow the opportunity to build the strong bonds with the faculty necessary to understand the distinctive institutional sagas of the universities they are leading. There is ample experience from both government and the corporate sector to suggest that leaders without the experience or appreciation for the "business" of an organization can get their organization into serious trouble, threatening its very survival. Of most concern here is the lack of institutional understanding and loyalty evident when a president strives more for personal achievement as an academic administrator than for the higher calling of loyally serving an institution while keeping its institutional welfare the primary concern. The professional university president may be yet another sign that the nature of the contemporary university has outstripped the capacity of the traditional approach to its governance—for example, such traditions as lay governing boards and shared governance among boards, faculty, and administrators. To the degree that this creates a cadre of professional university leaders with limited experience and attachment to the faculty and the core teaching and scholarly efforts of the university, it will almost certainly threaten the fundamental academic values and traditions of the university.

SOME ADVICE FOR CANDIDATES FOR UNIVERSITY PRESIDENCIES

While there are many attractive and rewarding aspects of a university presidency, those tempted to consider such appointments should be aware that such roles are accompanied by significant risks. Reporting to a governing board of lay citizens is considerably different than the reporting lines characterizing most academic leadership positions in a university (e.g., chair, dean, or provost) where one reports to academic peers. The president's relationship with the lay board is a complex one, particularly when it has the political nature characterizing most public universities. Unlike the reporting relationship of a CEO to a board of directors, populated in most cases by peers in the business profession, the university governing board has little direct experience in understanding either the academic nature of the institution or a means of evaluating the president. Usually, the relationship with the board is sustained through a personal relationship with the board chair or a small executive committee, hence it will change when the board composition changes—a particular challenge for the small, politically determined boards characterizing public universities. This creates a certain instability to the appointment, since the board relationship will change with its composition.

In the past, many presidents served "at the pleasure of the board," which was akin to being a wife of Henry VIII as long as he was willing. My own appointment was of this character, and one of my regents always took great delight in announcing publicly that the first item on the agenda of each meeting should be a vote on whether or not to fire the president. If the board chose not to, it should proceed with the business of the meeting. In fact, the tenures of many presidents of public universities do, in effect, continue from meeting to meeting, always threatened by a volatile issue or a change in board composition that will create a majority of votes opposed to their leadership. In sharp contrast to an elected public official, such as a governor with a fixed term of office, the electorate for a public university president (the board) can ask for a recall at any time.

For this reason, many presidents today (indeed, most in public universities) insist on a firm contract stipulating the nature of the appointment for a fixed period (e.g., five years). But in contrast to golden parachutes characterizing the employment agreements for most corporate executives, most university presidents have rather weak postemployment agreements, such as a year's salary while they find another job. In most cases, it is far easier to fire a president than a football coach (which suggests that more university presidents should learn from their athletics colleagues to hire a top-notch attorney or agent to negotiate their contract). This intrinsic vulnerability of the position is not particularly conducive to courageous, visionary leadership. Nor is it capable of attracting many of the most talented potential leaders into these positions.

At the same time, let me caution candidates against being too demanding as they approach the negotiation for a university presidency, since excessive greed could well plant land mines that return to haunt them later. For example, while it is natural to seek generous compensation (particularly if one is concerned about the risk posed by a political governing board), keep in mind that a president with compensation too far above the faculty is asking for trouble. Similarly, some judgment must be present in negotiating perquisites, such as modifications to the presidential mansion, transportation, office, or football box. Remember, you are not being hired as king or queen but, rather, as a servant of the institution and the public to which it is accountable.

SO WHAT ARE WE SUPPOSED TO DO NOW?

Once a university governing board has selected and recruited a new president and enjoyed the euphoria of relief and congratulations for a job well done, it can relax. Right? Wrong! The next task is to make certain that the board provides the president with the support necessary to be successful and advance the interests of the institution. In fact, developing a strong relationship of mutual trust, confidence, and respect between the president and governing board is one of the most important factors in determining the success of a presidency.

First, it is essential that during the selection and recruiting process, there has been an agreement up front on the relative priority of presidential duties, since this will form the basis for further evaluation of the president's performance. If the board believes that the academic quality of the institution should be taken to the next level or that a major institutional transformation should occur, it had better be prepared to fully support strong presidential action and to take the inevitable heat when sacred cows are sacrificed. If the board has been foolish enough to put fund-raising or state politics as its highest priorities, it should be aware that it is unlikely to get strong academic leadership.

Next, it is very important for the governing board to make certain that the newly appointed president gets off on the right foot. Too many times, new presidents feel abandoned by their boards during those critical early days of their tenure. The governing board must find opportunities to demonstrate their strong support for the agenda of the new president. For presidents new to the campus, the board should also take steps to link the president to the university community, including influential faculty and former university presidents.

The next task is to determine whether they made the right decision. Put another way, how does a board know when it has made a mistake in appointing a new president, and what can they do about it? During the past several years, we have seen an unusually high attrition rate among university presidents at leading institutions. Some of these departures have been triggered by cosmic events (e.g., a faculty vote of no confidence or a political onslaught by the media or politicians), but in most cases, the governing board deserves more blame than the president. In some cases, the board simply selected a president whose style was incompatible with the institution they were expected to lead—a situation that should have clearly been recognized, anticipated, and avoided before the appointment was made. In other cases, there was not a clear understanding between the board and the president about objectives. There are also examples of a failure of nerves, when a president marching into battle looked back only to find the board had turned about and was beating a hasty retreat. Again, a thorough presidential search, a wise selection, and a careful and candid up-front negotiation could have avoided these disasters.

Over time, both institutional needs and presidential abilities can change. It is the governing board's responsibility to continually monitor the quality and effectiveness of the leadership of its institution. This requires a rigorous approach to the evaluation of presidential performance. Just as many board members seem to leave behind their experience and common sense from their own professions when they hire university presidents, they frequently do the same when they evaluate a president's performance. In the corporate world, boards of directors have well-defined measures of executive performance based on shareholder value, such as achieving goals in such measures as earnings per share, revenue growth, and profit margins. Indeed, bonus compensation is directly determined by such quantitative measures. The key principle is clear. University presidents should be evaluated on what their institutions accomplish, not simply on issues of personal style or appearance. Yet, just as lay boards bring little experience to selection of the leaders of academic institutions, they are similarly limited in their capacity to evaluate a university president, since it is hard for them to understand measures of university progress without an academic background. Even when quantitative measures are used, these tend to be simplistic, such as gift income (which is usually determined by cultivation of potential donors many years earlier); university rankings in, for example, *U.S. News and World Report* (which are of questionable validity and also are determined by investments years earlier); or the win-loss record of the football team.

Hence, most boards evaluate their presidents on a highly subjective basis, by how people (particularly board members) "feel" about them, which all too often depends on whether the president has been responsive to a particular personal request or perk. Sometimes, boards tap into the gossip networks or seek out the opinion of faculty or staff members they know. But few boards seek an objective evaluation of just how the institution is doing, which would be the best measure of presidential performance.

There are several key indicators of whether a university presidency is going to be successful, even at a very early stage. Here, one must look beyond the superficial and symbolic activities of the president to gain an assessment of substance. After all, most presidents will enjoy a honeymoon of popular support from students, faculty, alumni, and perhaps even the local media during their first few months.

First, one should focus on the ability of the president to build a strong leadership team. The quality of executive officers, deans, and senior faculty determines the quality of the institution. While some changes among executive officers, deans, and senior staff are to be expected with a new administration, warning flags should go up immediately if the new president launches a series of purges of long-standing, successful and loyal academic and administrative leaders—particularly if the new leader is from outside the university. Inexperienced or insecure presidents sometimes try to wipe the slate of existing leadership clean, replacing long-serving officers and staff by their own appointments, with the primary criteria being loyalty to the new regime. Beware, as well, of presidents who insist on selecting external candidates for most open positions, since this approach is likely aimed at solidifying personal power rather than improving the quality of the institution. It is important to recall here that universities tend to evolve according to long-standing institutional sagas—traditions, practices, and values. To begin a presidency by eliminating those academic leaders (executive officers and deans) and senior administrative staff members who understand and can help sustain these traditions is not only damaging to the institution; it is almost certain to lead to a failure in presidential leadership.

The second warning sign also has to do with recruiting and team building. The university president is the institution's leading recruiter. Successful presidents have the ability both to identify topflight talent and to recruit it into key university leadership positions. Incompetent presidents eventually surround themselves with weak appointments, creating a cascade of incompetence that flows down through the institution, paralyzing even successful activities and resulting in a downward-glide path.

Third, university presidents are looked to for their vision for the future of the institution. Successful presidents should be able to work with the university community to generate a shared sense of participation in both creating and striving toward a vision. To be sure, this is always difficult for those unfamiliar with the people, traditions, and culture of an institution. This is all the more reason why successful presidents seek a mixture of old and new on their leadership teams.

Finally—and this is most important—the success of a presidency should always be assessed by asking a simple question: is the university better when the president leaves than when he or she arrived? Of course, this assessment cannot occur until long after a president's tenure ends. From this perspective, only history itself will validate the wisdom of a governing board in conducting a presidential search.

Clearly, I am not a big fan of the current process for selecting university presidents. It has always struck me as bizarre that we leave the selection of leaders of such important institutions to a group of lay citizens who have limited experience and understanding of the complex nature of a university and the intricacies of academic life and who are often heavily influenced by politics (particularly in the case of public universities) and influential observers (e.g., wealthy alumni or powerful football coaches). Even board members with extensive experience from other sectors, such as corporate governance, all too frequently leave behind their judgment (not to mention their values and integrity) when it comes to selecting a university president. Presidential selection tends to be based on the most subjective intuition—

sometimes the flimsiest of whims—rather than on the thorough due diligence that would be demanded for a corporate CEO.

Some suggest that the selection of a university president is more akin to that of a major political election of a governor or even a U.S. president, where the votes of lay citizens also determine the outcome. But political candidates are required to parade in front of the body politic for many months, thoroughly examined by the press and challenged by their opponents, to give voters a better sense of whom they should support. Contrast this with the backroom process used in most university searches, particularly in the endgame, when the governing board must decide among the finalists. No matter how well intentioned or determined, few search consultants are able to penetrate and comprehend the complexities of faculty or peer evaluations of presidential candidates. Laws concerning privacy and freedom of information make the process even more difficult, forcing many consultants to rely on a well-worn (and frequently stale) pool of potential candidates. It is little wonder that few internal candidates are selected for these posts, since they are usually not yet on the search consultants' radarscopes, which tend to be dominated by professional institution hoppers.

It is ironic, indeed, that universities that put great effort into the very thorough evaluations of faculty candidates for hiring, promotion, tenure, and academic leadership roles tolerate such a cavalier approach to the selection of their leadership at the top. In over two decades of tracking presidential searches through the nation, I must confess that I have yet to see a search conducted with the thoroughness and rigor of a faculty tenure evaluation. Whether due to the questionable competence of governing boards, the limited ability or self-interest of search consultants, the detached view of faculty search committees who feel that their recommendations will not be heard in any event, or a belief that most university presidents simply are not very relevant to the activities of teaching and research in the trenches, it is a fact of university life today that the presidential selection process in American higher education is sadly lacking in rigor, insight, and, at times, even integrity.

PART II

Presidential Leadership

4

PRESIDENTIAL LEADERSHIP

There are many contrasting perceptions of a university president. In many countries, the post is traditionally an honorific position elected by the faculty. In nations with strong central ministries of education, it is not uncommon for the university president to be considered an administrative bureaucrat. Even in the United States many trustees and some faculty members tend to think of the president as a hired hand of the governing board. However, the charters of most American colleges and universities define the president as a chief executive officer, with ultimate executive authority and responsibility for all decisions made within the institution.

This leadership role is complicated by the scale and diversity of the contemporary university, comparable to that of major global corporations or government agencies. Today's university conducts many activities, some nonprofit, some publicly regulated, and some operating in intensely competitive marketplaces. Universities teach students, conduct research for various clients, provide health care, engage in economic development, stimulate social change, and provide mass entertainment (e.g., college sports). Of course, the university also has higher purposes, such as preserving our cultural heritage, challenging the norms and beliefs of our society, and preparing the educated citizens necessary to sustain our democracy. Yet, despite the fact that university presidents have executive responsibilities for all of these activities and purposes, the position has surprisingly little authority. The president reports to a governing board of lay citizens with limited understanding of academic matters and must lead, persuade, or consult with numerous constituencies (e.g., faculty and students) that tend to resist authority. Hence, the university presidency requires an extremely delicate and subtle form of leadership, sometimes based more on style than substance and usually more inclined to build consensus rather than take decisive action. The very phrases used to characterize academic leadership, such as "herding cats" or "moving cemeteries," suggest the complexity of the university presidency. Universities are led, not managed.

There are numerous approaches to university leadership. Some presidents focus on sustaining momentum and stability during difficult times; others attempt to take their institution up a notch, improving the reputations of academic programs (or, God forbid, building a winning football team). Many presidents view the complex, tradition-bound nature of a university as quite resistant to major change and soon conclude that it is perhaps best, or at least safest, to focus their attention on a small set of issues where their leadership can have an impact. Others view their presidency as simply another step along a career path, either from one university to another or, perhaps, between public and private life. Hence, they are disinclined to stir things up, letting the institution drift along until they jump to their next ship. Fortunately, most university presidents, even if passing briefly through a particular leadership assignment, set institutional welfare as a high priority. On rare occasions, one encounters presidents who view themselves as change agents, setting bold visions for their institution and launching strategic efforts to move toward these visions. Like generals who lead their troops into battle rather than sending orders from far behind the front lines, these leaders recognize that winning the war sometimes requires personal sacrifice. The risks associated with proposing bold visions and leading change are high, and the tenure of such leaders is usually short. But their impact on both their institution and higher education more broadly can be considerable.

Regardless of personal proclivities, successful presidential leadership styles must be responsive to both the nature of the institution and the demands of the times. The character of each institution—its size, mission, and culture—and, most important, its institutional saga will tolerate certain styles and reject others. Authoritarian leadership might be effective or even demanded at some institutions, but the culture of creative anarchies, such as Michigan, Berkeley, or Harvard, will demand a more subtle approach to building grassroots support for any initiative. Similarly, the turbulent 1960s and financially stressed 1980s required different leadership styles than the market-driven challenges and opportunities of the early twenty-first century. It is important that university presidents be capable of adapting their own leadership styles to fit the needs of their institution. Rigidity is not a particularly valuable trait for either the effectiveness or even the survival of university leaders.

In earlier chapters, I have described my own path to the presidency of the University of Michigan (from faculty member to campus politician to academic administrator), throughout which I learned the trade of university leadership from several of the most distinguished academic leaders of our generation. Yet presidential leadership cannot be learned only as an understudy. It requires on-the-job training—rather, baptism by fire—in facing the challenge of day-to-day decisions of major import, defending the university against hostile forces both from without and within, and enduring the slings and arrows of those who view the university president as a convenient target to promote their particular issue or concern. In a sense then, the chapters in part 2 of this book, on the arcane topic of presidential leadership, are taken from my own "course notes," compiled from personal experiences, occasional successes, and predictable failures.

THE ELEMENTS OF PRESIDENTIAL LEADERSHIP

Rather than beginning this discussion with such issues as presidential style and philosophy, it seems more constructive to consider the various facets of leadership that are required by the important position of university president. Each of these elements of presidential leadership will be considered in more detail in subsequent chapters, but it is useful to summarize them here at the outset.

Clearly, as the chief executive officer of the university, the president has a range of executive leadership responsibilities, such as supervising the university administration; ensuring the quality and integrity of academic programs; managing human, financial, and capital assets; and being accountable to the governing board (and the public) for the welfare of the university. In a sense, the responsibility for everything involving the university usually ends up on the president's desk—where the buck stops—whether the president is directly involved or even informed about the matter or not. The corporate side of the university—the professional staff responsible for its financial operations, plant maintenance, public relations, and so forth—generally functions according to the business hierarchy of command, communications, and control. After all, major universities are in reality very complex multibillion-dollar enterprises, with all of the accountability and demands of a modern business. Yet the academic organization of the university is best characterized as a creative anarchy. Faculty members possess two perquisites that are extraordinary in contemporary society: academic freedom, which means that faculty members can study, teach, or say essentially anything they wish; and tenure, which implies lifetime employment and security. Faculty members do what they want to do, and there is precious little that administrators can do to steer them in directions where they do not wish to go.

As chief executive officer, the president is responsible for recruiting the key leadership of the university, not simply the executive officers, but also the deans and even, on occasion, key faculty members. This headhunting function is absolutely essential, since universities are only as good as the leaders of their academic programs, whether in administrative roles (e.g., department chairs and deans) or in intellectual roles (e.g., chaired professors). Equally important is the president's capacity to manage the relationship between the governing board and the university. Since most governing board members have little knowledge and even less experience with the core teaching and research activities of the university, a university president must devote considerable time and effort to educating the board, helping to shape its agenda, and providing the necessary background on key issues. Woe be to the president—and the university—whose governing board members believe they know more about the institution than the president.

In terms of executive leadership, the Office of the President is usually ground zero in any university crisis. Whether the university faces a student protest, an athletics scandal, a financial misstep, or a political attack, the president is usually the point person in crisis management. This has serious implications for scheduling the president's calendar, since in such a complex institution as the contemporary university, a considerable amount of the time of the leadership will invariably be consumed by unanticipated crises. Crisis management and all the other elements of executive leadership—building a leadership team, financial management, building campuses, and leading governing boards—are covered in some detail in chapter 5.

Another role of university presidents is academic leadership. Although the faculty usually expects the university president to focus on government relations, fund-raising, and keeping the governing board out of its hair, the most successful university presidents are capable of not only understanding academic issues but also shaping the evolution of academic programs and enhancing the academic reputation of the university. To be sure, academic leadership must be exercised with great care (even sleight of hand)—through the appointment of key academic leaders (e.g., deans or department chairs) or by obtaining the funds to stimulate the faculty to launch new academic programs. However, since it is my belief that the most successful university presidents, regardless of institutional type, are deeply involved in academic matters, I devote considerable attention to this subject in chapter 6.

The same ambiguity characterizes another role of university presidents, political leadership. The management of the university's political relationships with various constituencies—state government, federal government, and various special interest groups—rests eventually with the president. Just as faculties may resist presidential involvement in academic matters that they regard as their domain, governing boards (particularly those for public universities) can pummel a president for overinvolvement in public or political issues—at least those not aligned with their particular political persuasion. Yet both constituencies will demand some expertise in academics and politics during the presidential search process. Moreover, most successful presidents find that their credibility as proven academics and their skills as politicians, both on and off campus, are essential to their ability to lead their university. Chapter 7 is devoted to a discussion of political leadership, replete with some lessons learned from my personal school of hard knocks.

Although institutional needs and opportunities are different today than, say, a century ago, universities—just as our broader society—still require moral leadership. Universities, their communities, and their constituencies do seek guidance on such key moral issues as social diversity, civic responsibility, and social justice. Skillful presidents can transform crises—such as a racial incident, student misbehavior, or an athletics scandal—into teachable moments for moral leadership. Moreover, while the moral voice of the university president is sometimes drowned out by the din of political chatter, most presidents have ample opportunity to use their bully pulpit to speak out with courage and conviction on moral issues faced by our society, thereby providing role models for their students and perhaps even illuminating the discussion of moral issues with the perspective of the learned academy. Furthermore, through personal behavior, a leader can frequently influence the values and practices of an organization. If presidents value integrity, openness, truth, and compassion in their personal activities, these characteristics are more likely to be embraced and valued by those within their universities. By the same token, if a president is arrogant or insensitive, deals harshly with subordinates, or is truth- and candor-impaired, these traits, too, will rapidly propagate throughout the institution.

The presidential family also plays a pastoral role. In a very real sense, the president and spouse are the dad and mom of the extended university family. Students look to them for parental support, even as they routinely reject official actions in loco parentis. Faculty and staff also seek nurturing care and sympathetic understanding during difficult times for the university. To both those inside and those outside the system, presidents are expected to be cheerleaders for their university, always upbeat and optimistic, even though they frequently share the concerns and are subject to the same stresses as the rest of the campus community. The topic of pastoral care and that of moral leadership more generally are considered in chapter 8.

Finally, there is the "vision thing"—providing strategic leadership of the university toward significant goals. All too often, the tenure of presidents is sufficiently brief and their loyalty to a given institution is sufficiently shallow that acting in the long-term interests and evolution of the university is not a major priority. So, too, it is not uncommon to find presidents who tend to prefer backing into the future, by lauding the past with a nostalgic glow that confuses myth with reality. Strategic leadership requires a sense of institutional saga, a keen understanding of current challenges and opportunities, and the ability to see future possibilities. It also requires the skills necessary to engage a university community and build support for a vision of the future, as well as the energy, determination, and courage to lead toward these objectives. Strategic leadership is not an easy task, to be sure, and deserves the attention provided to it in chapter 9.

SEVERAL UNIQUE ASPECTS OF UNIVERSITY LEADERSHIP

Today's university president is expected to be part chief executive officer, intellectual leader of the faculty, educational leader, occasional parent to the students, political lobbyist with both state and federal government, cheerleader for the university, spokesman to the media, fund-raiser, entertainer, and servant to the governing board. Large institutions require strong executive leadership; public institutions need political acumen; and smaller institutions seek a greater degree of hands-on engagement with faculty and students in academic issues. And the performance in any particular one of these roles is usually considered as the singular basis for evaluating the president's performance by the correspondingly affected constituency.

Of course, this multiplicity of leadership roles is not unique to the university presidency. Corporate and government leaders must also contend with multidimensional roles. Yet there are several aspects of university leadership that set the university presidency apart from other leadership roles in our society. Perhaps the most significant difference is in the authority of the position, since universities are led more by building consensus than issuing orders. University presidents rarely enjoy the authority commensurate with the responsibilities of their positions. Although the responsibility for everything involving the university usually floats up to the president's desk, direct authority for university activities almost invariably rests elsewhere. This mismatch between responsibility and authority is unparalleled in other social institutions. As one colleague put it, universities may have shared governance, but nobody wants to share power with the president.[1]

Faculty members resist—indeed, deplore—the command-and-control style of leadership characterizing the traditional pyramid organizations of business and government. Most among the faculty are offended by any suggestion that the university can be compared to other institutional forms, such as corporations and governments. The academy takes great pride in functioning as a creative anarchy. Yet the faculty also recognizes the need for leadership, not in details of teaching and scholarship, but in the abstract—in providing a vision for their university and in stimulating a sense of optimism and excitement. They also seek protection from the forces that rage outside the university's ivy-covered walls: politics, greed, anti-intellectualism, and mediocrity that would threaten the most important academic values of the university.

The corporate side of the university—the professional staff responsible for its financial operations, plant maintenance, public relations, and so forth—might be expected to behave more according to the business hierarchy of command, communication, and control. After all, as I noted earlier in this chapter, major universities are very complex multibillion-dollar enterprises, with all of the accountability and demands of a modern business. Yet here, too, one finds an erosion of the normal lines of authority, almost as if the culture of the faculty ("I'll do it only if I choose to") has infected the professional staff. Indeed, this blurring of academic and corporate cultures has been one of the great challenges in putting into place the effective total quality management programs so successful in the business world.

So, too, the student body generally tends to resist leadership. After all, many young students are at the age when challenging authority is an important part of growing up. Whether a situation involves a residence hall supervisor, a classroom instructor, or even the president of the university, student refusal to accept the authority necessary for effective leadership can be problematic. Yet students are generally the first to demand that the president speak out on important issues about which they feel strongly.

One might expect that governing boards would seek and support strong leadership for their universities. Yet such characteristics as energy, vision, and even experience are sometimes viewed not only as of low importance but perhaps even as a threat to the authority of the board. This is particularly the case for public universities, where the politics surrounding board selection and action can become dominant. Although most members on the boards of public universities approach their responsibilities as a high calling to public service, there are always a few who impose on their roles a wide array of extraneous political agendas, and to these latter individuals, a strong president may be viewed as an inconvenience.

It is little wonder, then, that many people, including some university presidents, are quite convinced that the contemporary university has become immune to leadership. Presidential leadership does occur and, in many cases, is extremely effective. But it usually is accomplished through subtle influence rather than pushing ahead—by first seeding awareness and discussion of issues and building support to prepare the way for decisions, preferably reflecting grassroots participation (even if the seeds have been quietly planted by the administration). Although organizational theorists view such an approach as a small-win strategy,[2] it seems appropriate to quote the advice given by a more ancient authority, Lao Tzu, who says:

> Undertake difficult tasks
>   by approaching what is easy in them;
> Do great deeds
>   by focusing on their minute aspects.
> All difficulties under heaven arise from what is easy.
> All great things under heaven arise from what is minute.
> For this reason,
>   the sage never strives to do what is great.
> Therefore
>   he can achieve greatness.[3]

Of course, there are those times of urgency when a "just do it" approach is necessary, such as when confronting a financial or political crisis. Furthermore, blockbuster goals are sometimes the key to igniting necessary levels of institutional excitement and energy. But universities move like ocean liners, ponderously but with considerable momentum.

The rapid and profound nature of the changes occurring in our world today poses formidable challenges to tradition-bound institutions, such as the university. The pace of a university is quite different from that of a corporation responding to quarterly earnings statements or a government reacting to election cycles. In business, management approaches change in a highly strategic fashion, launching a comprehensive process of planning and transformation. In political circles, sometimes a strong leader with a big idea can captivate the electorate, building momentum for change. The creative anarchy arising from a faculty culture that prizes individual freedom and consensual decision making poses quite a different challenge to the university. Most big ideas from top administrators are treated with either disdain (under that assumption "This, too, shall pass") or ridicule. The same usually occurs for formal strategic planning efforts, unless, of course, they are attached to clearly perceived budget consequences or faculty rewards. The academic tradition of extensive consultation, debate, and consensus building before any substantive decision is made or action taken poses a particular challenge in this regard, since this process is frequently incapable of keeping pace with the profound changes swirling about higher education.

One of the biggest challenges for academic leaders is to avoid becoming a slave to the in-box, spending most of their time on the hundreds of microissues that arise in a university. The myriad issues and an overloaded calendar can distract a president from the broader issues that can only be addressed by the chief executive officer of the institution. Too many presidents, perhaps frustrated with the slow pace of the academic decision process or the anarchy of the faculty, become preoccupied with more routine activities, such as fund-raising, campus construction, or even intercollegiate athletics.

Because of the unforgiving political environment of the president, even the seemingly most inconsequential decision can explode in one's face. A decision not to accept a speaking request from a key constituency, denial of a personal request by a board member to admit a relative to a selective academic program, or a slip of the tongue with a politically incorrect phrase at a public appearance—all can bring disaster. Hence, the challenge to the president is how to keep the focus at the strategic level when the routine flow of activities through the Office of the President contains occasionally explosive elements. Part of the answer is to make certain that the office has at least one politically sensitive staff member who can act as the canary in the mine shaft, always on the alert for possible danger. But sooner or later, no matter how experienced, all presidents get blindsided by a seemingly innocuous decision or action that creates a political firestorm. Hence, damage control can become as important as the presidential decision process.

There is a growing epidemic of presidential turnover that is both a consequence of these problems and a factor that contributes to them. The average tenure for the presidents of major public universities is about five years, too brief to provide the stability in leadership necessary for achieving effective change.[4] While some of these changes in university leadership are the result of natural processes, such as retirement, others reflect the serious challenges and stresses faced by universities, which all too frequently destabilize their leadership. The politics of college campuses (from students to faculty to governing boards), coupled with external pressures (exerted by state and federal governments, alumni, sports fans, the media, and the public at large), make the presidency of a public university a very hazardous profession these days. At a time when universities require courageous and visionary leadership, the presidency position's eroding tenure and deteriorating attractiveness pose a significant threat to the future of these institutions.

Finally, it is important to stress once again just how critical the relationship between the governing board and the president is in determining the success of a university presidency. Of course, the authority necessary to lead the institution is delegated directly from the board. Furthermore, the board has the primary responsibility for evaluating the performance of the president. Faculties can take votes of no confidence, students can protest, and politicians and the media can complain, but if the governing board supports the president, then the position is secure. In fact, when a university presidency crashes and burns, it is usually the consequence of a poor search by the governing board or the eroding support it has provided an incumbent president that has caused most of the damage. Successful presidents and capable governing boards usually go hand in hand.

THE MANY STYLES AND PHILOSOPHIES OF PRESIDENTIAL LEADERSHIP

Over the years, I have had the privilege of studying under and working with scores of university presidents who were, for the most part, talented leaders with distinguished academic credentials striving to do the best for their institutions. The leadership styles and philosophies of these academic leaders were just as varied as those among leaders in any other walk of life. In fact, they were more so, perhaps because of the random paths that led to a presidency and the awkward process of being selected by a board of lay citizens.

Perhaps long ago some university presidents could be characterized as gentlemen scholars—for example, Tappan of Michigan, Eliot of Harvard, and Gilman of Johns Hopkins. However, there is probably as much myth as reality to this legend of the giants of the past. A more careful reading of the historical papers of university presidents (including those of the University of Michigan) reveals that as many rogues and scalawags populated these high leadership positions as did scholars and visionaries.

Today, we find many styles of leadership. Of course, most university presidents have at least a modicum of political skill. Otherwise, they would have never been selected for these positions, nor would they long survive. But some take this political approach to an extreme, as did several of my colleagues who heavily populated their personal staff with press relations experts (always sending an advance team to scout out any public appearance) and would likely get lost en route between the airport and a meeting in Washington without a personal escort. Some university presidents become so skillful at the political arena that they easily move into public life, Woodrow Wilson of Princeton being the most noted example. While this is both understandable and commendable, today's counterflow of politicians moving into university presidencies raises some flags of concern, since the caldron of political life is not necessarily the best training ground for those who are to lead academic institutions. While those universities led by politicians sometimes prosper for the near term due to enhanced appropriations or federal largesse through legislative earmarks (pork barrel), they rarely improve in academic quality.

As this chapter has stressed, the executive responsibilities of university presidents require some degree of management skills. Fortunately, most presidents have developed these through a sequence of earlier leadership experiences (e.g., department chair, dean, and provost). But this can also be taken to the extreme, where the president becomes more of a technocrat or corporate CEO than an academic leader. Still others adopt more of a military approach, commanding their executive staff much as a general would command the troops. Of course, while the administrative staff of a university can adapt to such authoritarian styles, the creative anarchy characterizing the faculty will rebel or simply ignore general-presidents and continue with their own agendas.

Other presidents adopt more of an imperial style, viewing their anointment by the governing board as conferring a divine right to behave as an emperor-king. Occasionally, these are benign rulers, more in the Louis XIV mode, who enjoy the perquisites of presidential life—the president's mansion, chauffeur-driven limousines, trips to exotic destinations, and mixing with the rich and famous—and focus their leadership activities on personal whims. Far more sinister are those who become carried away with their own sense of privilege and importance, evolving into imperial rulers more along the lines of Henry VIII, taking perverse pleasure in power as well as perks and propagating a sense of fear and dread throughout the institution ("Off with their heads!"). While this description may sound like an extreme, power-obsessed presidents installed and tolerated by inattentive governing boards occur more frequently than one might expect and have caused great damage in higher education. Universities have a relatively weak form of the check-and-balance mechanisms characterizing other social institutions (e.g., governments with voters and corporations with shareholders), since their governing boards tend to be isolated from campus happenings and unaware of abusive leadership.

At the other extreme of presidential style is the stylish charmer,[5] those presidents who mesmerize the naive with their articulation of such academic phrases as "the life of the mind," are capable of balancing a teacup on their knee while discussing estate planning with aging dowagers, and keep the board happy with perks and flattery. These talents are not necessarily bad, of course. But all too frequently, the charmer president is also hopelessly hapless, either uninterested in or incapable of dealing with the myriad of complex academic and administrative issues that determine whether the university flourishes or flounders.

Just as there are many leadership styles, there are also many different philosophies of presidential leadership. Some presidents adopt a fatalistic approach, taking to heart the idea that the university is basically unmanageable. They focus their attention on a small set of issues, usually tactical in nature, and let the institution essentially drift undirected in other areas. They view their role as representing the university rather than leading it. This laissez-faire approach assumes that the university will do fine on its own. Indeed, most institutions can drift along for a time without strategic direction, although they will eventually find themselves mired in a swamp of commitments that are largely reactive rather than strategic.

Typically, such minimalist presidents will focus on a few external activities, such as schmoozing state politicians to build political support or achieving elite frequent-flier status flying about the country prospecting for donors in fund-raising efforts. Some presidents become consumed by institutional character flaws: for example, rogue governing boards that require excessive time, attention, and pampering; or building winning football programs that dominate the attention of the institution, its alumni, and the public. Others fall into the "Yes, Minister!" trap, essentially allowing their calendar to be determined by personal staff and allowing themselves to be enslaved to the in-box and to all of the flotsam and jetsam, minutia and trivia, that flow through the Office of the President. Although certainly frustrating—and certainly not strategic for the institution—minimalist presidents are probably better than those presidents who float at the periphery of institutional concerns, pursuing their own personal agenda while the rest of the university burns, out of sight, out of mind. Furthermore, some presidents can be quite effective focusing their attention primarily on tactical issues when they are convinced that the institution is already headed in the right direction.

Of course, there are obvious deficiencies in all of these stereotypes. Major university campuses require, at least somewhere in the upper echelon of the university administration, the full suite of leadership skills—academic intuition, financial skills, political acumen, public relations, strategic vision, people skills, and a deep understanding of the fundamental values and nature of an academic community. This is particularly the case at very large institutions, such as the University of Michigan, which has an unusually challenging combination of breadth, quality, tradition, and capacity—the largest campus, the largest budget, the largest university hospital, the largest sponsored research activity, and of course, the nation's largest football stadium. In fact, the great challenge of the Michigan presidency is to protect the fragile character of the university's academic programs from being overwhelmed or pulled asunder by the ever-present distraction and threat of the Athletic Department on one end of the campus and the Medical Center on the other. Needless to say, presidents detached from the academic enterprise, surrounded by inexperienced executive officers, and overly influenced by the whims of ambitious athletic directors or hospital administrators can soon drive the university into the ditch.

Far more constructive are those presidents who are determined to uplift the academic quality of the institution, by raising standards, challenging weak promotion cases, and recruiting top-notch faculty. Perhaps the best Michigan example of this approach was Harold Shapiro, who, from his early days as provost and then through his presidency, was absolutely insistent on the highest academic standards for the university. Although his determination to raise the bar on faculty hiring, promotion, and tenure sometimes rankled complacent faculty and occasionally undermined deans, it clearly elevated the quality of the university to a degree that few others were able to achieve. It also demonstrated quite convincingly that academic leaders can have a major impact on institutional quality—if they are determined enough, have the academic background to recognize quality, and have the courage to point out where it is weak.

Some presidents are particularly skillful at grasping opportunities, or rescuing victory from the jaws of defeat. Robben Fleming exhibited this skill at a particularly important moment, when campus disruptions could have seriously and permanently damaged the University of Michigan. His long experience as a labor mediator had taught him that sometimes conflict is necessary to create the most effective path to compromise.

Perhaps the rarest of university leaders are those capable of strategic vision, who view themselves as change agents, setting bold visions for their institution and launching efforts to move toward these visions. These leaders recognize that winning the war sometimes requires personal sacrifice. The risks associated with proposing bold visions and leading change are high, and the tenure of such leaders is short—at least in public universities. Michigan's own experience suggests that visionary leaders, such as Henry Tappan, are rarely appreciated in their time by their faculties and particularly their governing boards, but they can have great eventual impact on their universities. In the case of a leading institution like Michigan, they can have a broader impact on the evolution of higher education, as demonstrated by the long-standing influence of Tappan on American higher education.

ADAPTING LEADERSHIP STYLES TO THE TIMES AND THE INSTITUTION

Presidential styles are rarely powerful enough to change the culture of an institution, much less its institutional saga. Presidents can lead universities in new directions or boost its quality. But prospects for a long tenure—or even survival—are slim indeed for those presidents whose styles are incompatible with the institutional saga of a university.

For example, the postwar years of the 1940s and 1950s were a time of prosperous economy, growing populations, and an expanding demand for higher education, first as a consequence of returning veterans under the GI Bill and later through the efforts of the Truman Commission to extend the opportunity for a college education to all

Americans. Hence, it was a time for university presidents who could grasp the opportunity to grow their institutions, for example, Harlan Hatcher at Michigan and John Hannah at Michigan State.

In contrast, the 1960s and early 1970s were a time of protest, triggered first by the Free Speech Movement and civil rights and later by the Vietnam War (and the draft). Universities sought leaders with the skills to handle dissent and confrontation. Many came from backgrounds in labor mediation, such as Robben Fleming at Michigan and Clark Kerr at the University of California. There were also many casualties among those presidents from an earlier time who simply could not adapt to the confrontational climate of the 1960s.

The late 1970s and 1980s required still different leadership styles as the economy weakened, driven first by rising energy prices (the OPEC oil embargo) and later by industrial competition from Japan. While the nation fell into recession, many industrial states, such as Michigan, faced depression-level hardships, with serious shortfalls in tax revenue and, consequently, deep cuts in appropriations to higher education. This was a time of retrenchment, focusing resources on highest priority, and generating new revenue streams through private fund-raising and student fees. Leaders with strong financial skill (and intuition)—such as Harold Shapiro at Michigan, Jack Peltason at the University of California, and Arnold Weber at Northwestern—were key to the abilities of their institutions to restructure themselves financially to thrive in an era of constrained resources.

Although financial pressures relaxed—at least temporarily—in the late 1980s and 1990s, universities required strong entrepreneurial leadership capable of grasping the opportunities presented by the end of the cold war, the increasing diversity of the American population, the forces of globalization, and the extraordinary transformation of the U.S. economy from making things (manufacturing) to creating and applying new knowledge, driven in part by such rapidly evolving technologies as the computer, telecommunications, and transportation. Perhaps indicative of the needs of higher education during this period was the appearance of university presidents with science and engineering backgrounds. While these university leaders were comfortable with the technology reshaping our society, even more important was a leadership style stressing teamwork, risk taking, and entrepreneurial energy and capable of providing new visions for the university of the twenty-first century.

Equally important is a presidential leadership style compatible with (or adaptable to) the unique character of the institution. Let me again illustrate this with the University of Michigan. Because of Michigan's exceptionally large size, intellectual breadth, and complexity, power is very widely distributed among academic and administrative units. Michigan is clearly a deans' university, in which the authority and responsibility of deans as academic leaders are very strong. At least over the long term, good things happen in academic programs because of good deans and good department chairs (and conversely, good programs attract good deans and department chairs). Yet, despite this dispersal of power, Michigan is also an institution where team building is greatly valued. Deans come together quite easily as teams—particularly if encouraged by the provost and president—and willingly work on university-wide priorities. Similarly, effective presidents can mold the executive officers of the university into teams rather than playing one off against another: for example, it is more effective to say, "I would like you folks to work together to give me your considered opinion on this matter," rather than to say, "Each of you tell me what you would recommend, and then I will make a decision."

The trailblazer character of the Michigan saga demands a risk-tolerant environment in which initiatives are encouraged at all levels—students, faculty, and staff. For example, the university intentionally distributes available resources among a number of independent funds, so that entrepreneurial faculty with good ideas rarely have to accept no as an answer but instead can simply turn to another potential source of support. The most important play in the Michigan playbook for entrepreneurs is the end run, since Michigan administrators not only tolerate but encourage faculty, students, and staff to bypass bureaucratic barriers. For example, it is quite common for faculty to bypass deans and appeal directly to the provost or president, just as many, including the deans—and occasionally even a coach or athletic director—will occasionally find opportunities to execute an end run to the regents, a relatively easy thing to do since half of them live in Ann Arbor. Once faculty, chairs, and deans learn the Michigan culture, they quickly learn that the university also tolerates end runs to state or federal government (e.g., the governor, the legislature, Congress, or federal agencies). To be sure, sometimes a senior administrator might growl at them—particularly a vice president for government relations who is worried about coordinating university relations with the state or a president who is worried about inappropriate influence on a regent. Most Michigan presidents soon learn that since these end runs are so ingrained in the culture of the university, they will happen quite naturally. Presidents come to understand that attempts to stifle end runs are not only likely to be ineffective but could discourage many of the most creative, loyal, and well-intentioned people in the university. Hence, it is far better to accept the end run as a Michigan tradition. Some of us even quietly encouraged this practice, since we had used it quite effectively ourselves during our own roles as faculty and deans.

A final characteristic of university leadership as it is evidenced at Michigan is worth mention here: perhaps because of Michigan's long tradition of decentralization (even anarchy), university-wide faculty governance through a faculty senate has been relatively ineffective at Michigan. Just as with the administration, the real power among the faculty and the ability to have great impact on the institution resides at the school, college, or department level, where powerful senior faculty, executive committees, chairs, and deans have the authority to address the key challenges and opportunities facing their academic programs. Should this power structure become distorted with poor appointments or weak faculty, the end-run culture acts as a check and balance by rapidly communicating such problems up or around the chain of command to the provost, the president, or even the regents.

From this discussion, it should be apparent that a top-down leadership style is quite incompatible with the Michigan culture. Those presidents who have chosen to ignore this reality or who have attempted to reign in this distributed power (i.e., to tame the Michigan anarchy) have inevitably failed, suffering a short tenure with inconsequential impact. This does not mean that Michigan will tolerate a weak president. Presidents unable to adapt to the Michigan trailblazing saga—that is, presidents who are hesitant to push all the chips into the center of the table on a major initiative or incapable of keeping pace with the high energy level of the campus—will soon be rejected or at least ignored by the faculty. Michigan embraces bold visions, and without these, effective leadership of the university is simply impossible.

Of course, Michigan probably represents one of the extremes of a highly decentralized academic anarchy, although many other institutions with exceptionally strong faculty lie in a similar regime of the governance spectrum. There are other institutions that not only tolerate strong, centralized leadership but actually require it. Some are at an early stage of evolution and require strong, top-down leadership to set the priorities and make the tough lifeboat decisions to move the institution to the next rung in quality.

So, too, different institutional types will require a different balance and priority among the various leadership roles of the president. While competent financial management and energetic fund-raising are essential to all institutions, the roles of academic, moral, and pastoral leadership are perhaps more critical to the presidents of smaller institutions, particularly those with the missions of liberal arts colleges. Here, the size of the faculty and student body demand a more hands-on engagement in campus life by the president. In sharp contrast, the executive leadership demands on the president of a multicampus system become far more important, since recruiting campus leadership, managing the financial operations, and working closely with the governing board become the key priorities. In fact, many system presidents are quite detached from the campuses of the system and are similar to corporate CEOs, much to the frustration of system presidents who miss the excitement of an academic campus. Yet there are also frustrations for campus chancellors unfortunate enough to have the university system's office close by, since there is an inevitable tendency for the system president to become overly involved on the campus. Not surprisingly, the chancellorship of campuses with system offices tends to turn over quite rapidly.

A MATTER OF PERSONAL STYLE

As I mentioned earlier, I always viewed myself first and foremost as a member of the faculty of the university, regarding academic administration not as a professional career in itself but, rather, as public service to my institution. Perhaps this explains my tendency to bring a value system formed in the groves of academe to my various leadership assignments. This is best illustrated with several examples.

It was my good fortune to have as mentors some quite distinguished university leaders, along with some exceptionally capable administrative colleagues. Although I always sought and listened carefully to their advice, it is also clear that my style was considerably different. For example, most of my colleagues tended to stress the importance of approaching issues in a very measured, low-key way: encouraging staff to analyze issues and bring forward recommendations, always trying to stimulate ideas at the grassroots level, letting them simmer a bit before revealing support, and never moving rapidly with an initiative associated with the Office of the President (or with the Office of the Provost or any dean's office). I was warned about leaping ahead of people during conversations (a personal character flaw of mine), since this can be misinterpreted as not listening rather than quickly grasping their points and moving ahead to consider their implementation. I was cautioned to be always very sensitive to the political implications of any issue. This extended to tolerating even the most offensive behavior of individuals if they had sufficient political clout (e.g., legislators, congressmen, or governing board members). A president (or provost or dean) was never supposed to be seen as critical of such behavior, even if it was damaging to the university or its people. Instead, I was advised to find someone else to beard the tiger, to carry the bad news, to take the flack. Academic leaders were praised for their Teflon coats, not their courageous defense of the institution.

Unfortunately, try as I might to adopt such a laid-back style, I could no more do this than a pig could fly. While such a passive style might make everybody feel better, the challenges and opportunities of the times (not to mention my particular leadership skills) demanded a more activist style, based on decisiveness and action rather than conversation and contemplation. I preferred an open management style, playing all my cards face up so that folks always knew where I was coming from. I also tended toward a more kamikaze style, perhaps dating from my football days, since I preferred to confront challenges rather directly, usually by leading the troops into battle rather than giving orders from far behind enemy lines.

More fundamentally, I had a very deep-seated belief that universities were profoundly human endeavors, that good things happened because good people made them happen with their talent and dedication, especially when they were provided with the support, encouragement, and freedom to push to the limits of their abilities. In this spirit, I always sought to build and work with teams of talented people, much as I had during my engineering days. I sought to surround myself with people smarter and more talented than I was, recognizing that this was the key not only to my own success as a leader but, more important, to the future of the institution.

Years of laboring in the trenches had taught me that the best ideas and creativity flowed upward through the university from its faculty, students, and staff. Hence, I viewed my leadership challenge as that of a farmer, planting questions and issues, cultivating discussion and debate, and then harvesting and implementing the best ideas. The key was always tapping into the energy, interest, and creativity that exists in great abundance at the grassroots level of the institution.

In each of my leadership roles, I also felt a sense of deep responsibility to act always in the best interests of the institution and its people, with little concern about my own future. After all, my administrative assignments (dean, provost, president) were brief excursions from my fundamental role as a faculty member (scientist and engineer), not an all-consuming career in and of themselves. Hence, my approach to important issues tended toward "Damn the torpedoes, full speed ahead!" rather than "What do you think we should do?" If the decision was obvious and the need (or opportunity) was great, I preferred just to go ahead and get it done. It mattered little to me and my leadership teams who had the great idea or who would get credit (although I was likely to take the blame); the only concern was that the institution would benefit. To be sure, some toes were trampled: the political reaction could be intense (particularly on such controversial issues as tuition, diversity, and gay rights), and the risk could be considerable. But whether the job was to rebuild the College of Engineering or to transform Michigan into a university for the twenty-first century, I was appointed to get it done, I was determined to get on with it, and I did. Key in this approach was a determination to never believe that my position was more important than my objectives. Job security was never first priority. As dean, provost, and then president, I was quite comfortable putting my job on the line, not as a threat or ultimatum, but, rather, as a quiet recognition on my part that I was prepared to face consequences of failure in high-risk activities if they were important to the institution.

Yet another personal leadership characteristic of mine—perhaps arising out of my background as a scientist and engineer—was that I tended to be somewhat more concerned about the future than the present. One of our regents suggested that I differed from many other Michigan presidents because I envisioned the university as it should be in 10 or 20 years rather than just 5. He added, "Considering how slowly the ship turns, it takes a lot of time to make those course adjustments." I did indeed view my strength as strategic leadership, providing the vision, energy, and excitement to move toward blockbuster goals rather than delving into the details of tactical decisions.

Many organizations are characterized by a bimodal distribution of leadership, consisting of young leaders who know what to do but have little experience on how to get it done (and, as a result, get very frustrated) and more senior leadership who know how to get things done but have either forgotten what to do or lost their will (becoming recalcitrant). I sought to build a bridge between bold visions and pragmatic experience. We spent a great deal of time working with next-generation leadership, identifying potential leaders, placing them in key positions, and trying to pair them with wise, experienced old salts. Those who were both smart and able took advantage of this, learning and developing into capable leaders. Those who were headstrong and stubborn usually flamed out at a low level of administration.

Not surprisingly, I had my share of critics. Many believed I pushed too hard, not respecting or using the traditional university process of consultation and collegiality—or, perhaps more appropriately, delay and procrastination. Some regents complained about the pace I set, their complaints fed in part by faculty set in their ways. Some of my executive officers and deans would have preferred that I spent more time fund-raising out of town (and out of their hair). Special interest groups appreciated my concern and support, but they worried about a "white European male" getting too involved in influencing their agenda, even if I managed to achieve many of their objectives at a rapid pace. Folks absorbed in process tended to favor building bottom-up consensus over decisive action. The list of examples could go on and on. I was even criticized for being too visionary, perhaps too far ahead of the faculty.

But as Theodore Roosevelt stated, "Far better it is to dare mighty things, to win glorious triumphs, even though checkered by failure, than to take rank with those poor spirits who neither enjoy much nor suffer much, because they live in the grey twilight that knows not victory nor defeat."[6] My presidential leadership style proved capable of achieving rapid, permanent change and very significant enhancement of quality, momentum, and excitement in extremely short time periods. Hence, I finally concluded, or at least rationalized, that my "go for it" style was just what was needed to bring the sleeping Michigan giant to life. I decided not to worry too much about the carping and, instead, to just nod politely, grow an extra layer of skin, and push ahead. I explained once to some critics of the Michigan Mandate, our diversity agenda: "I guess the real point is that people have to look at what actually happens rather than conjecturing about whether I meant what I said. If these things do not happen, then I deserve to be harshly criticized if not ignored. But if we succeed, then folks should acknowledge success, respect that action for what it delivered, and get on with things."

MOVERS AND SHAKERS, PUSHERS AND COASTERS: THE IMPACT OF THE PRESIDENCY

It has always amused me how universities, much like other social organizations, tend to cycle back and forth between periods of acceleration, coasting, and perhaps slowing to a halt or even sliding back down the hill. As president, I always used to view my role of leadership as pushing as much as pulling. I likened it to pushing a stalled car until it achieved sufficient momentum to start again. Yet it was always possible that my successor would back off and enjoy coasting, though hopefully not rolling to a halt.

This ebb and flow in leadership should not be so surprising, since it characterizes most of the history of a university. In Michigan's early years, Tappan, Angell, Burton, and Hatcher were clearly pushers, determined to build the university, taking it to higher levels of achievement and capacity. Each was followed by successors who tended to accept the resulting quality or capacity of the university as they inherited it, consolidating gains and perhaps addressing other issues, sometimes dictated by challenges beyond the campus, such as the Great Depression, the world wars, and the social disruption of 1960s activism.

Both Harold Shapiro and I pushed hard to build the quality, financial strength, and leadership of the university. We restored reserves, built new revenue streams, and increased endowment by a factor of 10. We rebuilt the campuses; established new standards for faculty hiring, promotion, and tenure; and raised expectations for the performance of academic and administrative units. We decentralized authority and accountability with strong incentives and launched a number of important community and world leadership projects (the Replacement Hospital Project, the Michigan Mandate, and building the Internet). Fortunately, at least in the history of the University of Michigan, the pushers seem to have achieved sufficient momentum for the institution to ride through the next coasting period with quality intact.

LEADERSHIP FOR A TIME OF CHANGE

Because of the imbalance between responsibility and authority, the presidency of a university is certainly one of the more challenging roles in our society. Yet it is nevertheless a position of great significance. While a particular style of leadership may be appropriate for a particular institution at a particular time, the general leadership attributes outlined in this chapter seem to be of universal importance.[7]

Governing boards, faculty, students, alumni, and the press tend to judge a university president on the issues of the day. However, the true impact of presidents on their institutions is usually not apparent for many years after their tenure. I believe that the most effective university presidents are those capable of always setting institutional welfare above personal objectives—or, at times, even professional survival. While political skill is a valuable trait in avoiding confrontation, appeasement is rarely the route to institutional greatness. Successful university presidents must occasionally take risks and demonstrate courage. Decisions and actions must always be taken within the perspective of the long-standing history and traditions of the university, and they must be taken not only for the benefit of those currently served by the institution but on behalf of future generations.

All too frequently, particularly in universities, the environment is simply not tolerant of strong leadership. It is not surprising that many university presidents and other academic leaders take the easy way out, deferring to the whims of outspoken faculty members or the political agendas of governing boards and accepting that their role is to act more as representatives of their institutions than as strong leaders. Why should they rock the boat when their tenure is only a few brief years? It is little wonder that weak leadership characterizes much of higher education. In many institutions, the other partners in the academic tradition of shared governance—the faculty and the governing board—would not have it any other way.

There is a growing epidemic of presidential turnover that is both a consequence of these problems and a factor that contributes to them. The average tenure for the university president is too brief to provide the stability necessary for institutional advancement, much less achieving effective change. Hardly a week passes without another report of a university president swept aside by a faculty vote of no confidence, abandoned by a rogue governing board, or leaving an institution behind in search of greener pastures. At a time when universities require courageous and visionary leadership, the eroding tenure and deteriorating attractiveness of the university presidency pose a significant threat to higher education in America.

We live in a time of great change, an increasingly global society, knitted together by pervasive communications and transportation technologies and driven by the exponential growth of new knowledge. It is a time of challenge and contradiction, as an ever-increasing human population threatens global sustainability; a global, knowledge-driven economy places a new premium on workforce skills and hence education; governments place increasing confidence in market forces to reflect public priorities; and shifting geopolitical tensions driven by the great disparity in wealth and power about the globe trigger new concerns about national security. More than in any previous time, the strength, prosperity, and leadership of the United States require a highly educated citizenry and, hence, a world-class system of higher education capable of meeting the changing educational, research, and service needs of a knowledge-driven society. Yet at the same time, changing population demographics, social priorities, and economic constraints require both university leadership and policy makers to reconsider the most fundamental public purposes of higher education.

We will need strong leadership in the years ahead, as academia faces even more fundamental questioning. Politicians, pundits, and the public increasingly challenge us at the same time that social, economic, and technological forces increasingly drive us. No question is out of bounds: What is our purpose? What are we to teach and how are we to teach it? Who teaches under what terms? Who measures quality, and who decides what measures to apply? Who pays for education and research? Who benefits? Who governs and how? What and how much public service is part of our mission? What are appropriate alliances, partnerships, and sponsorships?

To face these challenges and respond effectively to the rapidly changing needs of society, the university requires strong, visionary, and courageous leadership. This, in turn, requires governing boards, faculties, and a public understanding that will not only tolerate but demand strong presidential leadership. Clearly, those universities capable of attracting and supporting strong, decisive, and visionary leadership will not only survive with quality intact but will likely flourish during this era of great change in higher education.

5

EXECUTIVE LEADERSHIP

In the United States, the charters of most colleges and universities provide the president with the executive authority for all aspects and activities of the institution. The responsibilities of this role as chief executive officer are both immense and complex. Although most people tend to think of the university in very traditional ways (e.g., with images of students in classrooms, scholars in libraries, and scientists in laboratories), the reality is far more complex. In a sense, the modern research university has many of the characteristics of an international conglomerate of highly diverse businesses.

To illustrate, consider the various business lines of the University of Michigan from a corporate perspective. In 2006, the "U of M, Inc.," operated a $1.6 billion educational business enrolling more than 58,000 students on its three campuses. The annual budget of its research and development activities was $800 million. Its $1.8 billion health care system had 1.2 million patient visits in its various hospitals and provided managed care to a population of 300,000. The university's activities are truly international in scope, providing educational, research, and service activities throughout the world both through an array of campuses abroad and through Internet services, a business line amounting to $200 million. Even its sports entertainment line, the Michigan Wolverines, has scale more comparable to professional franchises—even larger because Michigan Stadium's capacity of 112,000 is the largest in the nation. The activities of the university have become so vast that it even has its own captive insurance company, Veritas. The university's other characteristics of note include 34,000 employees, an annual budget of $4.5 billion, an endowment of $7 billion (and almost $10 billion under active management), and over 25 million square feet of facilities—which would rank it 350th as a corporation on the Fortune 500 list.

Many of the major universities in America are characterized by very similar organizational structures, indicative of their multiple missions and diverse array of constituencies. In some ways, the university is even more complex than corporations or governments, because of the diversity of its many activities, some nonprofit, some publicly regulated, and some operating in intensely competitive marketplaces. It teaches students, conducts research for various clients, provides health care, engages in economic development, stimulates social change, and provides mass entertainment (athletics). Many of these activities are conducted on a global scale.

Clearly, as the chief executive officer of this complex organization, the university president has leadership responsibilities comparable to those of the CEO of a major corporation or the governor of a state. Although many of the constituencies of the university—its faculty, its students, and perhaps even some of its trustees—would decry such a corporate view, the burden of the welfare of the institution as a multinational conglomerate, rests with the president. With billion-dollar budgets, populations of students, faculty, and staff numbering in the tens of thousands, and activities spanning the range from instruction to research to health care to economic development, financial issues are highly complex and consequential, particularly in the harsh light of public scrutiny and accountability. Presidents must worry about where to obtain the funds necessary to support academic programs and how these funds are spent (resource acquisition and allocation, budget development). They are responsible for building and maintaining the campus environment necessary for quality teaching and research (capital facilities). They are held accountable for the integrity of the institution (financial audits, compliance with state and federal regulations). And they must manage the university's relationships with its multiple stakeholders (public relations, government relations, and marketing).

In addition to the ongoing academic and administrative decisions necessary to keep the university moving ahead, there are always unforeseen events that require immediate attention and rapid decision making. For example, when student activism explodes on the campus, an athletic violation is uncovered, or the university is attacked by politicians or the media, crisis management becomes critical. While the handling of such matters requires the time and attention of many senior university administrators (from deans to executive officers and governing boards), crisis management frequently becomes the responsibility of the university president. At any meeting of university presidents, the frequent disruption of pagers and cell phones provides evidence of just how tightly contemporary university leaders are coupled to the issues of the day.

Although many university presidents focus most of their effort on external activities (e.g., political lobbying or private fund-raising) and tend to delegate many of their management responsibilities, they will eventually be held accountable by the faculty, the governing board, and the public for the efficient operation and integrity of their institution. Hence, although delegation of executive authority and responsibility to competent professional staff and other academic leaders is clearly necessary, so, too, are sufficient administrative experience and management skills to know where a president's attention is required, as well as the people skills to identify, recruit, and lead talented administrators.

Like other complex organizations in business or government, the university requires a high quality of professional management and administration in such areas as finance, legal affairs, physical plant maintenance, and information technology. Universities of long ago were treated by our society—and its various government bodies—as largely well-intentioned and benign stewards of truth, justice, and the American way. Today, we find that the university faces the same pressures, standards, and demands for accountability characterizing any billion-dollar public corporation.

THE EXECUTIVE OFFICER TEAM

One of the great myths concerning higher education in America—and one that is particularly appealing to faculty members, trustees, and legislators alike—is that university administrations are bloated and excessive. In reality, most universities have quite lean management structures, inherited from earlier times when academic life was much simpler and institutions were far smaller. Typically, the number of administrative positions (and executive officers) in a university is only a small fraction of the number of senior administrators found in corporations or government agencies of comparable size. Furthermore, in contrast to corporations or government agencies, universities have quite shallow organizational structures. For example, there are typically only five organizational levels in the academic ranks (president, provost, dean, department chair, and faculty member), leading to an exceptionally broad, horizontal organizational structure at the senior level.

The direct line reports of the university president are comprised of the executive officers of the university, with such titles as vice president or vice-chancellor in various functional areas—for example, academic affairs, research, student affairs, business and finance, fundraising, and government relations. The success or failure of the university president depends on the quality of the people appointed to these positions. Hence, one of the most important responsibilities of the president is recruiting, building, and leading a quality team of executive officers.

Surprisingly, for one of the nation's largest and most complex universities in the world, the University of Michigan has a very small central administration. During my tenure we operated with a very lean team of executive officers, with only six vice presidents, plus two chancellors for the Dearborn and Flint campuses. Although this has increased modestly in recent years, it remains only one-half to one-third the number of executive officers at most other universities. Such a lean administration could only succeed with outstanding people, hence a premium is placed on developing or recruiting the very best people into these key positions. Their success requires, in turn, recruiting outstanding senior staff in each of their organizations, a stress on quality that tends to propagate throughout the institution.

At Michigan, the two key executive positions are the provost (and vice president for academic affairs) and the chief financial officer (and vice president for business and finance). Much as in corporate organization, the president, provost, and vice president for business and finance represent the executive leadership core of chief executive officer (CEO), chief operating officer (COO), and chief financial officer (CFO). In 1992, I added the modifier *executive* to the titles of both the provost and the vice president and CFO, to distinguish their line-reporting responsibilities for all academic and administrative units of the university, including the regional campuses in Dearborn and Flint. Other vice presidents—such as those for research, student affairs, development, and government relations—generally had staff roles, although some had large administrative units reporting to them (e.g., student housing and research administration).

Next to the president, the provost (or chief academic officer) is the most important leader in the university. In effect, the provost is the chief operating officer of the university, with the line-reporting responsibility for all of the academic units of the university: schools and colleges through their deans; centers and institutes through their directors; and a host of academic service units, such as admissions and financial aid. The provost also serves as second in command and backup to the president and is usually tapped as acting president when the president is on leave or absent for an extended period.

Clearly, the position of the provost at a major university is daunting, as suggested by the formal definition used for the role at Michigan: "The provost is the intellectual and scholarly leader of the university, with ultimate responsibility for all academic programs, operations, initiatives, and budgets." To clearly establish the priority of the academic mission of the institution, the Michigan provost also functions as the chief budget officer, preparing the budget that determines the detailed allocation of resources throughout the university and thereby integrating the academic and budget functions and priorities. Furthermore, the provost is given veto power over all other executive officers (with the exception of the president, of course) on issues that have implications for the academic activities of the university. This includes, for example, capital facilities, research priorities, student affairs, the priorities in university fund-raising, those aspects of the Medical Center that have impact on academic programs, and even intercollegiate athletics, particularly in such areas as student admission and eligibility. Not surprisingly, the Office of the Provost is characterized by a very flat organization, with reporting lines for 18 deans; four associate vice presidents; numerous directors of academic service units, such as admissions and financial aid; and sundry interdisciplinary research centers and institutes.

Perhaps because of its vast size and complexity, Michigan has usually selected insiders as provosts. Hence, it is logical that the relationship between provost and president is frequently an inside/outside division of roles. Most often, the provost serves as chief operating officer, managing the internal affairs of the institution, while the president serves as CEO and "chairman of the board," managing the university's external relationships (actions involving state and federal government, fund-raising, public relations, intercollegiate athletics) and its sensitive relationships with the governing board (which could be extraordinarily time-consuming with a politically elected body).

The unusual responsibility and authority of Michigan's provost position and the quality of the academic leaders who have served in this role give it high visibility and influence on the national scene. However, it also identifies the position as an important source of university leadership, as evidenced by the number of Michigan provosts who have gone on to university presidencies. Yet the turnover in the position can be a considerable challenge to the president.[1]

The relationship between the provost and the president is a very critical one. Early in my faculty days at Michigan, I had the privilege of chairing the faculty advisory committee to two provosts, Frank Rhodes and Harold Shapiro, who later went on to become distinguished university presidents. As a dean, I reported to yet another exceptionally able provost, Billy Frye, who would later become chancellor at Emory University. During my own brief stint as provost, I worked closely with Harold Shapiro as president. Hence, I had the opportunity to experience or observe a variety of different relationships between presidents and provosts.

My relationship with Chuck Vest, the first provost to serve Michigan after I was appointed president, worked very well. Although we had common academic experiences, we had quite different styles, which were well adapted to the approach of "good cop, bad cop" (i.e., Chuck and me). We had worked closely together in the College of Engineering and continued this relationship into the central administration. Chuck knew well my strengths and weaknesses, as did I his. Hence, we both knew when to leave one another well enough alone and when backup was advisable.

Unfortunately, Chuck remained in the provost role for only 18 months before he was approached by MIT about their presidency. Although he was very concerned about leaving after such a brief stint as provost, we both viewed the MIT offer as a call to national service that left him little choice but to accept. I reconvened the provost search committee and asked its members whether we should start a new search from scratch or just reevaluate their earlier candidate list. They rapidly converged on a recommendation for Gil Whitaker, dean of Michigan's School of Business and a very skillful administrator, who was instrumental in completing Michigan's journey to becoming a privately financed public university. My relationship with Gil was more complex than my relationship with Chuck. Gil and I could be characterized as more of a peer-to-peer team, since we had once served together as deans of major schools, spending most of our earlier careers at Michigan in a more competitive relationship.

Just prior to my last year as president, Gil Whitaker stepped down as provost, and a new search was launched. However, since my decision to return to the faculty happened during this search, I decided to name one of our deans as an interim provost during my lame-duck year, so that my successor could have the opportunity to select his or her own provost. In discussions with the deans, there was unanimous support expressed for Bernie Machen, then dean of the dental school, for this interim role. He continued in this interim role for another year, serving under interim president Homer Neal and then briefly with Lee Bollinger before accepting the presidency of the University of Utah (and later the University of Florida).

The third member of the executive leadership core at Michigan and many other institutions is the chief financial officer, with responsibility for the financial, capital, and human resource assets of the university as well as its financial integrity. Needless to say, in an institution with billions of dollars of assets, hundreds of major facilities, tens of thousands of employees, and mission-critical obligations (e.g., health care), the position of vice president and chief financial officer (VPCFO) requires quite exceptional skills and experience. Michigan has been fortunate in attracting several extraordinarily talented individuals into this position: Wilbur Pierpont, James Brinkerhoff, and Farris Womack, viewed by many as among the finest VPCFOs in the nation during the last half of the twentieth century. I was particularly fortunate to have as my VPCFO Farris Womack, who brought great experience gained through similar service at the University of Arkansas and the University of North Carolina. He also brought great integrity and a thorough understanding not only of financial and business operations but also of the politics surrounding public universities.

There are many models of presidential leadership of an executive officer team. Some presidents prefer to act essentially as a judge, asking each executive officer to bring a recommendation on a particular issue and then selecting one of these options. Other presidents prefer to deal with the executive officers as a team, posing an issue to the group and asking them to thrash out the options until they reach agreement on a preferred direction. Still other presidents prefer a more authoritarian approach (much like a football coach), giving specific assignments to each member of the team within their narrowly defined range of responsibilities.

Some university presidents tend to stress loyalty or subservience in their appointments. Others prefer to surround themselves with the best people they can find, recognizing that their own success—indeed, their survival—will depend on the talents of their executive officer team. This latter approach was certainly my belief and practice, since I realized that in an institution as complex as Michigan, only the very best people could provide the leadership necessary. Fortunately, my executive officers rarely hesitated to say what they thought, even if they knew it was not what I wanted to hear. Furthermore, if I was wrong, they were encouraged to tell me so in no uncertain terms. Fortunately, my ego could tolerate criticism, and I was quite willing to change directions when a better idea was put forward.[2]

A strong team of executive officers fills the important role of placing checks and balances on the president. The unforgiving environment of the president as chief executive officer, particularly in a public institution, demands great rigor in assessing the appropriateness of all decisions, including their compliance with various university and public policies. Presidential decisions must be vetted with such important bodies as the governing board, with disclosure and transparency issues, and with an array of political considerations as seen by various constituencies both on and off the campus. Since no president can (or should) rely strictly on his or her own judgment across such a broad array of issues, the executive officers—particularly the team of provost, VPCFO, and general counsel—play an absolutely critical role in checking and challenging possible presidential decisions. In large part because of the demanding sense of rigor and integrity of Farris Womack as my VPCFO, all aspects of my presidential decisions and activities were given particular scrutiny, including thorough audits of all compensation issues, travel activities, and presidential expenses.

It was sometimes quite a challenge to hold together such a group of strong personalities. Teamwork was essential, but it was also sometimes a challenge when strongly held and differing views existed. While presidents are well advised to appoint strong and capable executive officers and work to mold them into a team, it is also essential to establish firm ground rules that while disagreements and debates on complex university issues and policies are both encouraged and tolerated, these should be kept "within the family." Once the executive officer team (or, in some cases, the president) has reached a decision, it is essential to present a united front beyond the executive conference room. Efforts by an executive officer to carry disagreement to members of the university community or perhaps even the governing board should be discouraged in the strongest possible terms, since this amounts, in effect, to mutiny. Executive officers who feel so strongly about an issue that they would betray the trust and confidence of their colleagues should seriously consider resignation—rather than revolution—as the principled course.

At Michigan, there has been a long-standing practice of balancing internal versus external appointments to senior administrative positions, typically at a fifty-fifty percentage level, in an effort to preserve institutional memory and momentum while bringing new ideas and energy. Yet, perhaps because of the complexity of the university, it is frequently the case that outsiders have difficulty in understanding the institution (or its institutional saga) well enough to be effective leaders. While these external candidates may be capable, their institution-hopping careers can undermine both their ability to understand the culture and traditions of the university and the perception of their loyalty to their new institution.

One of the most difficult tasks of a university president is to evaluate the performance of the administrative team (both executive officers and deans) and make changes when necessary. Here, particular caution must be taken at the outset of a new presidency. All too often, governing boards and new presidents adopt the philosophy of a changing political administration, sweeping through the layers of leadership of the institution and replacing many long-serving and experienced administrators. While such administrative housecleaning is understandable in the political environment of state or federal governments, which are sustained by an experienced and immovable civil service, it can lead to absolute disaster in universities heavily dependent on loyal and experienced staff to balance the administrative inexperience and naïveté of academic administrators. Yet it is also the case that the longer a president is in office, the more difficult personnel changes can become. In part, this arises because of the personal relationships that executive officers and deans develop with important constituencies within or beyond the university—for example, key faculty, governing board members, and alumni.

As with any chief executive officer, the staffing of the personal activities of a university president is important. Beyond a skilled executive secretary capable of handling the myriad calendar events and personal contacts, university presidents require talented staff to handle relations with multiple constituencies, including faculty, trustees, donors, politicians, and numerous VIP visitors to the campus. So, too, the personal appearances required of the presidency require speech writing and advance preparations. Since the office of the president is ground zero for inquiries and official communications of the university, it must be managed with an exceptionally high degree of accuracy and integrity. Mistakes (e.g., in written correspondence or notes) that might be tolerated elsewhere in the university can lead to disaster for a president. Hence, both the quality of secretarial staff and the rigorous oversight of office activities become essential.

Of course, there is considerable variation in how university presidents handle their personal staffing. In some elite private universities, presidents are able to function with a very small personal staff consisting of an executive secretary—usually of superb quality—supported by a receptionist and perhaps several correspondence and appointment secretaries. However, in larger public universities, the multiple constituencies of the university generally require a larger staff, more typical of a senior public official, such as a governor or senator. For most presidents, the level of support they require is more akin to a political figure than a corporate CEO, since their most sensitive relationships tend to be with peer constituencies—such as faculty, donors, government officials, or trustees—rather than with internal subordinates.

Some presidents staff this public role to the extreme, with specialized teams to handle calendar management, speech writing, advance logistics, travel arrangements, and intercollegiate athletics (a world unto itself). One of my colleagues had a large staff that knew in advance every person that would be in a meeting with the president; staff members would quietly whisper the names of each person approaching the president and would make certain that the speaking podium was located so that the president's best side would always face the cameras. Other presidents demand sophisticated travel arrangements, requiring that they always be met at a destination by a staff member with transportation to whisk them away to a scheduled appointment.

Part of the challenge of staffing the presidency involves the constituencies with whom they interact. For example, staff trained in handling donors or politicians are usually ill suited to managing relationships with faculty. So, too, it is difficult to find executive secretaries with the skills and tact to field phone calls from irate faculty one minute and inquisitive reporters the next, then perhaps a governor or senator, followed by a particularly insistent trustee. Hence, hiring intelligent, talented, and sensitive staff of the highest quality is key in providing adequate support to the president.

This raises another challenge, since the more talented the staff member is, the more he or she tends to acquire—and deserve—his or her own independent agenda and responsibilities beyond those of simply supporting the day-to-day needs of the president. All too often, a president soon finds that personal staffing erodes, leaving the president with a growing load of personal speech writing, meeting planning, and donor and public relations activities. This is particularly true if the president tends to rely on more senior administrators (e.g., the director of development or government relations) to handle the president's personal support. Many was the time I would arrive at a gathering and be left to fend for myself while staff huddled in the corner chatting among themselves. The reality is that despite the best of intentions, the more senior the staff member is, the less likely he or she is to set the personal support of the president as the highest priority.

GO DOWNTOWN AND GET THE MONEY

Like other enterprises in our society, the operation of a university requires the acquisition of adequate resources to support its activities. This is a complex task for academic institutions, because of both the wide array of their activities and the great diversity of the constituencies they serve. The not-for-profit culture of the university, whether public or private, requires a different approach to the development of a business plan than one would find in business or commerce.

The university president, as CEO, has the lead responsibility in attracting the funds required by the institution, from state and federal government, donors, student fees, hospital revenues—whatever it takes. Harold Shapiro captured this well by noting a quote from an early issue of *Harpers Weekly:* "A university president is supposed to go downtown and get the money. He is not supposed to have ideas on public affairs; that is what trustees are for. He is not supposed to have ideas on education; that is what the faculty is for. He is supposed to go downtown and get the money."[3]

Of course, much of a president's time is spent as a salesperson, persuading state government to provide adequate appropriations or encouraging donors to make gifts to the university. The president is also the leader of an entrepreneurial organization of faculty seeking research grants and contracts from federal and industrial sponsors or marketing the clinical services of the university medical center or the entertainment value of athletic programs. Although the provost generally determines the required level of student tuition and fees, it is the president's responsibility to sell this recommendation to the governing board.

In times of budget constraints, presidents may play a key role in demanding cost-containment efforts or resource reallocation. Many of the executive decisions made by presidents and their executive officer team involve difficult financial issues, such as where to take budget cuts to meet revenue shortfalls, including the possible discontinuance of academic or administrative units. This is a particular challenge since the budget culture on most campuses begins with the assumption that all current activities are both worthwhile and necessary and that it is the responsibility of the administration to generate the revenue not only to sustain but to grow these activities. Beyond that, since there are always an array of worthwhile proposals for expanding ongoing activities or launching new activities, the university always seeks additional resources. The possibility of reallocating resources away from ongoing activities to fund new endeavors, "innovation by substitution," is an alien concept on many campuses. Strategies from the business world aimed at cutting costs and increasing productivity also tend to bounce off academic institutions.

Finally, the president has the same fiduciary responsibilities as the governing board. In the end, the president is responsible for the financial integrity of the institution, not simply for assuring that revenues balance expenditures, but for justifying each expenditure as appropriate, necessary, and cost effective. Increasingly, university presidents are finding, just as have corporate CEOs, that a rigorous audit process (e.g., internal and external auditors and a competent audit committee from the governing board) is essential in these times of stringent public and private accountability. For public universities, the issues of accountability and transparency become extremely important, particularly in such areas as compensation.[4]

While not as devastating as during the years of my predecessor, the financial challenges faced by the University of Michigan during my presidency were considerable. The state support of the university continued to erode during the late 1980s and early 1990s, dropping to less than 10 percent of the university's total operating budget and less than 20 percent of its academic budget by 1996. As I was fond of saying (and being quoted), during the last half of the twentieth century, the University of Michigan was forced to evolve from "state-supported" to "state-assisted" to "state-related" to what might only be characterized as "state-located." One of my colleagues went even further by suggesting that the University of Michigan became only a "state-molested" university, referring to the abuse it sometimes received from opportunistic state politicians.

My leadership team continued a three-tiered strategy developed during the Shapiro years: (1) effective cost containment, (2) decentralized management of resources, and (3) aggressive development of alternative revenue sources. Following the recommendations of a major task force on costs chaired by then dean of business administration Gil Whitaker, Michigan implemented an institution-wide total quality management program that empowered staff and faculty at all levels to seek ways to enhance the quality of their activities while constraining costs. The university moved toward more realistic pricing of both internal and external services (e.g., facilities maintenance, tuition and fees, research overhead). In the early 1990s, it completed the decentralization of both resource and cost management to the unit level, through a budgeting system similar to that used in many private universities.

As evidence of the effectiveness of these efforts, by the mid-1990s, peer comparisons ranked the University of Michigan's administrative costs (as a percentage of total expenditures) third lowest among major research universities. Yet another sign of Michigan's efficient use of resources was that while essentially all of the university's programs were ranked among the top 10 nationally in academic quality, Michigan ranked roughly fortieth in terms of expenditures per student or faculty member. Put another way, it was able to provide an education comparable to the quality of the most distinguished private institutions at typically one-third the cost.

An important element of the Michigan strategy involved far more aggressive management of the assets of the university—its financial assets; its capital facilities; and, of course, its most valuable assets, its people. Michigan's chief financial officer Farris Womack moved rapidly in the late 1980s to put into place a sophisticated program to manage the investments of the university. He built a strong internal investment management team augmented by knowledgeable external advisors, including several university alumni. Particular attention was focused on the university endowment, which amounted to only $250 million in 1988, small by peer standards and quite conservatively managed. Through Womack's aggressive investment management, coupled with a highly successful fund-raising effort, the university increased its endowment to over $2.5 billion by 1996—a truly remarkable growth of tenfold. As the university continued to harvest from Womack's investments, the endowment rose to over $7 billion in 2006. During the 1990s, Michigan consistently ranked among the national leaders in endowment earnings. Similar attention was focused on the management of the university's financial reserves, such as operating capital and short-term funds. By establishing the concept of a centralized bank, Womack was able to bring under sophisticated investment management more than $2 billion of additional funds associated with the various operating units of the university.

The university also took steps to price its services more realistically. Although the university had long charged tuition at the level of private universities to out-of-state students (acknowledging a state policy that dictated that state tax dollars could be used only for the support of Michigan residents), in-state tuition had been kept at only token levels throughout the 1960s and 1970s. However, as state support declined, it became clear that the eroding state subsidy of the cost of education for Michigan residents no longer justified these low tuitions. Throughout the 1980s, the university began to raise in-state tuitions to more realistic levels, although this frequently triggered political attacks from both state government and the media. By the mid-1990s, student tuition revenue had been increased to over $500 million (rising to over $700 million by 2006), far exceeding the university's annual state appropriation of $300 million. Throughout this period of tuition restructuring, Michigan was able to increase the financial aid awarded to students, so that it could sustain its policy that no in-state student would be denied a Michigan education for lack of economic means.

The financial strength of the university also benefited from the remarkable success of its faculty in attracting research grants and contracts from both the federal government and industry. These grants and contracts were rewarded with strong incentives and were supported by effective Washington relations efforts. As I noted earlier, Michigan rose to a position of national leadership by measure of its research activity, and by 1996, its sponsored research support was over $500 million per year—substantially larger than its state support.

Michigan was one of the first public universities to recognize the importance of private fund-raising, with the $55 million campaign of the 1960s and the $180 million campaign of the 1980s. However, as the prospects for state support became dimmer, it became clear that private support would extend beyond providing simply the margin of excellence for the university's academic programs, to include increasingly providing their base operating funds as well. Early in my administration, we set a very aggressive goal to build private support (as measured by the combination of gifts received and income distributed from endowment) to a level comparable to state support by the year 2000.[5] To this end, Michigan launched the largest fund-raising campaign in the history of public higher education, by setting as a goal the raising of $1 billion by mid-1997. The fund-raising effort was extraordinarily successful and ended up raising more than $1.4 billion, boosting total annual private support, including endowment distribution, to over $350 million per year by the end of the decade.

Yet here I would offer a word of caution about the role of the president in fund-raising activities. In an era of what seem like ever-increasing costs and ever-declining public support, private giving is clearly important. Furthermore, the president must play a key role both in the symbolic leadership of fund-raising campaigns and in making "the ask" and closing the deal for major gifts. Yet this effort has to be kept in perspective, since private giving typically represents less than 10 percent of the revenue base of a major university, such as Michigan. Put another way, I viewed my financial challenge as president to help raise the roughly $3 billion each year it cost to run the university. Hence, while soliciting gifts was important, so was making the case for adequate state support, lobbying Washington for federal research grants, making the case to our regents for adequate tuition levels, investing our assets wisely, and developing business plans for various auxiliary activities (e.g., the University Hospital and intercollegiate athletics). Hence, while fund-raising is certainly important, presidents should carefully budget their personal efforts to reflect realistically the balance of revenue sources.

Of course, one way to enhance the security of a presidency is to launch a multiyear fund-raising campaign, since it is hard to dislodge a sitting president while a campaign is under way. Furthermore, a campaign can be used to shift attention from more controversial issues that threaten a presidency to an activity that benefits the institution while building a constituency of wealthy fund-raising volunteers to support the president. Perhaps this is not an adequate justification in and of itself for launching a megacampaign, but threatened presidents certainly occasionally use this practice.

Yet another comment on fund-raising strategies seems appropriate here. There is a disturbing tendency, particularly in institutions rather new to the fund-raising game, to sell the naming rights for almost anything in the university. At Michigan, we found that our policy of requiring at least a 50 percent contribution for donor naming of a facility was frequently circumvented by ambitious fund-raisers (or demanding donors). Even more unfortunate was the tendency of aggressive deans to sell naming rights within their schools—perhaps even the name of the school itself—for gifts that were far too modest. Here, it is important for presidents to recognize that naming university assets—and particularly academic programs—can lead one down a slippery slope to selling the heritage and perhaps even the reputation of their institution.

A combined strategy of effective cost containment, sophisticated asset management, and alternative resource development provided the University of Michigan with extraordinary financial strength, despite continued deterioration in state support. As one measure of this financial integrity, in 1997, Michigan became the first public university in history (along with the University of Texas) to have Wall Street raise its credit rating to the highest level (Aaa), making it comparable to the wealthiest private universities. Perhaps a better way to describe the University of Michigan's financial status was to characterize it as a privately financed public university, supported by a broad array of constituencies at the national—indeed, international—level, albeit with a strong mission focused on state needs. Just as a private university, Michigan was now earning the majority of its support in the competitive marketplace (i.e., via tuition, research grants, and gifts). It was allocating and managing its resources much as private universities.

In retrospect, I would identify several key philosophical elements in our financial strategy. First was an extremely conservative approach to budgeting and financial management, drawing much of its impetus from Harold Shapiro's leadership during the difficult days of the early 1980s. The school of hard knocks taught us to be extremely conservative in estimating revenues, whether from state appropriations, student tuition, federal research support, or private giving. This conservatism was also evident in our determination to rebuild the reserve funds of the university. To be sure, we were not afraid to place very big bets when the right opportunity arose. For example, in 1980, during a particularly difficult financial time for the university, Harold Shapiro bet the ranch on launching the $300 million Replacement Hospital Project, then one of the largest public construction projects in the history of the state of Michigan. Aided by the university's exceptionally high credit rating, we placed similar bets in launching a massive renovation of key academic facilities at a time when interest rates were at an all-time low. We tempered these financial risks by always insisting that they be in areas of the university's established strength, betting on our best people in our strongest programs.

Second, we were determined to focus resources (and cuts) rather than spread them across the board. Shapiro's "smaller but better" philosophy was continued during my administration, with a determination to sacrifice breadth and capacity, when necessary, in an effort to sustain and enhance quality. This was accompanied by an "innovation through substitution" philosophy that funded the new through reallocation from the old.

Third, we made a conscious decision to involve the entire university community in key financial decisions. These included resource allocation, where to take budget cuts, and priorities in new revenue strategies, such as our $1.4 billion fund-raising campaign. We believed that only through broad participation would we achieve support for the difficult decisions that would be required to focus resources on key university priorities.

Finally, we understood that leadership was most effective when it could demonstrate directly a commitment to cost containment and financial priorities at the level of the central administration. The most significant financial impact arose from our conservative budgeting approach and our unusually lean administration. But we also believed it important to demonstrate restraint and frugality in more visible areas, such as university events (fund-raising events, commencements, regents' activities) and facilities (particularly the President's House).

The lessons from the Michigan experience seem clear: the financial challenges to higher education will likely compel most universities to restructure their financial activities, from resource acquisition and allocation to financial and asset management to cost containment. More specifically, our experience from the 1980s and 1990s suggests that universities need to explore financial models that strive to build far more diversified funding portfolios. In particular, public universities need to become less dependent on state appropriations (and more independent from state regulation). Through endowment, they need to build the reserve capacity to provide resilience against the inevitable ebb and flow of public support. The allocation and management of resources, the containment of costs, and the adoption of efficiency measures from business (e.g., systems reengineering and Total Quality Management) can be important strategies, provided they are suitably aligned with the values and culture of academic communities. Most important, all universities, public and private, must become more entrepreneurial and strategic, achieving a more flexible resource base and adopting management methods that will allow them to thrive despite the vicissitudes of the economic cycle. Clearly, the president's leadership in such financial restructuring is absolutely essential.

BRICKS AND MORTAR

While outstanding faculty, students, and staff are the key assets of a great university, the quality of facilities clearly influences the ability both to recruit outstanding people and to support their efforts to achieve excellence. Winston Churchill once stated: "We shape our buildings. Thereafter, they shape us."[6] Maintaining and enhancing the quality of the campus, buildings, grounds, and other infrastructure is a major priority of the university and must be a responsibility of the president. In most cases, the need for facilities and other campus improvements bubble up from the various programs of the university, then the president takes the lead in acquiring the resources necessary to support these projects. Although the needs of academic units should take precedence in capital improvements, any visit to a university campus will soon reveal that much of the activity exists in auxiliary units, such as the medical center, student housing, and intercollegiate athletics.

The majority of capital expansion at most universities these days occurs in their medical centers, driven by the need for renovation or growth in clinical facilities, the desire for additional research space in the life sciences, and the availability of substantial income from clinical activities. This is not surprising, considering that medical center budgets have typically increased at twice the rate of academic budgets throughout the past two decades (e.g., 10 percent per year for the medical center versus 5 percent per year for the rest of the university). The desire to increase clinical income drives the continual expansion of facilities, particularly in such lucrative areas as surgery and internal medicine, but also in satellite clinics designed to expand primary care activities that feed patients into university hospitals. Similarly, the extraordinary growth in federal support of biomedical research, now representing over 60 percent of all federal research and development on university campuses, has stimulated staggering investments in expensive new research facilities in the life sciences, such as molecular biology, genomics, proteomics, and biotechnology. There is a certain irony here: in contrast to pharmaceutical companies that tend to invest in "throwaway" research buildings because of the rapid obsolescence of research technology, universities prefer to hire expensive architects to design monumental facilities to last generations, even though these facilities will require several times their original capital costs for the renovations necessary to track technological changes.

In recent years, there has been a comparable level of capital expansion in athletic facilities. The wacko culture characterizing intercollegiate athletics presumes that the team that spends the most—or builds the most—wins the most. Hence, there has been a costly race to invest hundreds of millions of dollars in expanding football stadiums and basketball pavilions, specialized training facilities, academic counseling centers, plush offices for the ever-expanding athletic staff, and even museums designed to impress recruits and fans alike with past athletic accomplishments. While much of this investment (e.g., in bigger and better training facilities or the most expensive artificial turf fields) is driven by competitive forces, some of the largest investments (e.g., skyboxes for wealthy fans and corporate clients, sophisticated television systems, or on-campus stores for marketing sports paraphernalia) have been made as a marketing device. Most athletic departments tend to borrow the funds to build such facilities, depending on future revenue from ticket sales, television contracts, or licensing to cover the debt, although most of these loans are actually secured with a university pledge of income from student fees. The debt load on several of the major athletic programs is considerable, ranging into the hundreds of millions of dollars for many institutions and requiring that new revenue be generated through clever and occasionally even coercive mechanisms, such as seat taxes and skyboxes (ironically given a highly favorable, if somewhat perverse, tax treatment by the Internal Revenue Service).

Although the core activities of the university involve teaching and scholarship, capital investments in facilities for academic programs has lagged far behind investments in auxiliary activities, such as medical care and intercollegiate athletics. In part, this has to do with constraints on the funding sources available for academic facilities (e.g., state appropriations, private gifts, or debt financing based on student fees). But it is also due to the relative autonomy of most auxiliary units, portraying (at least in myth, if not in reality) their financial independence from the rest of the university. Most universities tend to be far more parsimonious when spending funds on new classroom or library space than when investing in major expansion of the football stadium or university hospital. As a result, the quality of academic space on many campuses, particularly in public universities, has deteriorated quite significantly during the hard economic times of the early 1980s, the early 1990s, and the early twenty-first century.

From this perspective, the rebuilding of the University of Michigan's academic campuses in the 1990s ranks as a remarkable accomplishment. During the decade from 1986 to 1996, the university completed over $2 billion of major construction projects that provided essentially every academic program of the university with a physical environment of unprecedented quality. Several factors converged simultaneously to provide the university with a remarkable window of opportunity for rebuilding its campuses. First, falling interest rates, coupled with Michigan's high credit rating, made it quite inexpensive to borrow money. Second, because of a weak economy, there were few competing construction projects under way in the private sector, hence construction costs were quite low. Third, the university's success in auxiliary activities (including private support, clinical revenue, and fees for continuing education) was beginning to generate substantial revenue. Fourth, Michigan was able to convince a new governor to launch major state programs for capital facilities, with the understanding that the university would match the state effort through the use of its own funds.

There was also a substantial effort to improve the landscaping and appearance of the campus. Pride in place—on the part of students, faculty, and staff—is important in maintaining the quality of a campus. Once the quality of facilities begins to deteriorate, not only do people dread going to their working or learning environments, but they lose any sense of personal responsibility for maintaining the appearance of a campus. Students begin to trash the campus by tacking flyers everywhere and chalking sidewalks and buildings. Faculty and staff simply ignore the accumulating debris and graffiti. Each Sunday morning, my wife, Anne, and I would take a walk about the campus, pulling down posters, picking up trash, and noting where graffiti needed to be removed. But such efforts were simply fingers plugging the holes in the dike until the general quality of the campus was improved through the massive capital investments of the mid-1990s. A sense of pride in the campus was restored, and the campus community accepted a spirit of personal responsibility in keeping it in tip-top shape. The lessons learned from three decades of neglect should not be forgotten.

The role of the president in such projects was considerable, not so much in determining priorities or architectural design, but in acquiring the resources and smoothing the approval process. However, some caution is also warranted here. Perhaps because of the "edifice complex" (the desire to see one's impact on a campus or to leave monuments behind), many university presidents become obsessed with bricks-and-mortar projects. They retain "signature" architects as campus planners and commission them to make architectural statements on the campus. Unfortunately, this leads to disaster in many cases, since prominent architects frequently have little understanding of the culture of a campus or the facility needs of academic programs. Many ambitious projects come in at costs far higher than original estimates or result in buildings that are dysfunctional for their original intent. Furthermore, since the lifetime costs to operate buildings generally exceeds their original construction cost, far too many signature architectural projects become white elephants, placing a heavy burden on academic budgets, while meeting the original objectives in only a marginal fashion.

Although I had always had a strong personal interest in architecture (not only taking Vincent Scully's famous course on modern architecture at Yale, but actually working for an architecture-engineering firm in the 1960s), I stayed far away from any direct involvement in architectural issues as president. Instead, I relied heavily on the chief financial officer and his experienced staff in our plant extension department, who worked closely with the provost, deans, and faculty in academic units to develop realistic program statements and then utilized competitive bidding processes and strong project management to make certain that capital projects moved ahead smoothly, remained within cost estimates, and met program objectives. As the CEO of an organization spending hundreds of millions of dollars per year on capital facilities, I was not about to inject amateur architectural interests or whims into major expenditures addressing critical needs of the campus.

CRISIS MANAGEMENT

One reason that university presidencies are so stressful is the role presidents play in responding to crisis. Each president has a particular suite of skills and talents, but regardless of their particular strengths, all presidents are expected to play key leadership roles during times of emergency. I found that because of the size and complexity of the University of Michigan, such incidents were both frequent and almost always unpredictable, bubbling up out of the complexity of the institution and its multiple constituencies. I considered it essential to develop a strategy for handling such crises. Otherwise, my leadership team would have found ourselves continually in a reactive mode, responding to one crisis after another. Our strategic framework not only enabled us to respond to unanticipated challenges but also sometimes allowed us to transform a crisis into an opportunity that helped the university move toward an important objective. For example, the student activism over racial incidents on campus created both an awareness of racial inequity and a willingness to consider institutional change, which allowed us to launch the Michigan Mandate, our strategy for achieving campus diversity. The violations in the university's baseball program allowed the administration to put into place a far more effective audit mechanism and to strengthen the university's compliance with conference and NCAA rules. The political attacks launched by a new president at Michigan State University gave the University of Michigan the ammunition it needed to activate a powerful network of alumni and friends across the state.

Sometimes we were able to anticipate incidents. For example, we knew that as the NCAA Final Four approached, the local newspapers would try to spring on us a trumped-up attack concerning a presumed scandal in our athletic programs, only to follow several weeks later with a back-page retraction that there was little substance to the rumor. In a year when the labor contract was up for renegotiation with the union representing graduate teaching assistants, we could anticipate an unusual amount of student disruption of regents' meetings. Major confrontations with the government—such as a congressional witch hunt on perceived abuses of federal research contracts or tuition increases—would inevitably involve Michigan, as one of the most visible universities in the nation.

Many of the major initiatives of the university would attract unusual attention. For example, our diversity efforts (and the associated student activism) drew political activists, ranging from state legislators to presidential candidates (e.g., Jesse Jackson) to conservative groups (e.g., the Center for Individual Rights). Our effort to negotiate steep discounts on computer purchases for our students riled local retailers, who sought to limit the practice by lobbying state government.

At the start of each academic year, several of us would meet to identify possible sources of crisis in the months ahead, develop possible strategies to head them off, and assign responsibility to a member of the executive officer team. Of course, many issues were one-day wonders that go with the territory (e.g., student protests or legislative thrashing) and did not merit any special action. Students would always pursue activities designed to upset their elders. There would always be politicians out to score points against the academy. Human character flaws, such as greed and dishonesty, were just as prevalent in a university community as they were in broader society. But some issues, such as racial unrest, could have lasting impact that could not only harm the university but distract the leadership from other important priorities. For these issues, some degree of anticipation and planning was desirable.

Fortunately, I had learned well from my predecessors two cardinal rules about dealing with such disruptions. First, from Robben Fleming I learned that while we should tolerate peaceful protest, including even an occasional takeover of an office, we had to draw the line when university functions (teaching, research, administrative operations) were seriously disrupted or when staff, faculty, or students were threatened. From Harold Shapiro I learned the importance both of never taking action in the face of a threat and of setting definite time limits (24 to 48 hours) after which we would proceed with arrest. While we always took great care to avoid harming protestors, we would also not shy away from arrest if we determined that the function or personnel of the university were threatened.

Yet it was still common to be taken completely by surprise on issues. One of the great thrills of leading the University of Michigan involved opening up the local newspaper and reading a sensationalized account of a university activity revealed only through the release of materials under the Freedom of Information Act (FOIA). There were two systemic problems here. First, the university was an extraordinarily complex enterprise, and it was about as unrealistic to expect that the central administration would know about every detail of university activity as it would be to expect that the White House would know everything about the operations of the federal government. But even more difficult was the intrusive and insidious nature of the state of Michigan's FOIA, which both the media and others with an ax to grind used to go fishing into all aspects of university operations, looking for possible embarrassments. Clearly, any complex organization requires some degree of confidentiality in its operations, particularly when it comes to matters involving sensitive personnel or financial matters. Yet the blunt nature of the Michigan FOIA and its extension by the courts exposed all aspects of university operations to the prying eyes of the press.

Always being at ready condition—or DEFCON 3[7]—for potential crises can be both stressful and wearing. Further, to sustain both the loyalty and morale of staff, the president and other senior officers frequently had to take the heat for situations they knew all too well were the responsibility of others. This went with the territory, although to the great detriment of the university and the health and humor of the president.

THE CHALLENGES OF EXECUTIVE LEADERSHIP

Although the American university has become one of the most complex institutions in modern society—far more complex, for example, than most corporations or governments—its management and governance could best be described as "amateur." Although competent professionals have usually been sought to manage key administrative areas (e.g., investments, finances, and facilities), the general leadership, management, and governance of the university has been the responsibility of either academics or lay board members. Many universities take great pride in the fact that they not only are led and managed by "true academics" with little professional experience but also are governed by lay boards with little business or educational experience.

Yet leadership and executive responsibilities frequently overlap. In these days of increasing legal, financial, and political accountability, universities appoint amateurs to campus leadership roles at their own risk. Like other major institutions in our society, we must demand new levels of accountability of the university for the integrity of its financial operations, the quality of its services, and the stewardship of its resources. To keep their institutions moving ahead, presidents require some capacity for planning and priority setting, organizing and institution building, decision making and delegation. Perhaps most important of all, they need the ability to recruit and lead teams of talented administrators.

It is also important to seek individuals with some experience in managing large organizations with line responsibilities (e.g., hiring and firing people). Here, again, I believe it is foolhardy to ask someone with only modest leadership experience to move to the helm of a vast university with thousands of employees and with budgets in the hundreds of millions (or even billions) of dollars. Too much is at stake, including the welfare of thousands of faculty, staff, and students.

Finally, it is important for a university president to have had some direct experience—as an academic leader, a faculty member, or even as a student—with the quality to which the institution aspires. Setting the bar for program quality and recruiting talent are critical executive responsibilities of the president. It is difficult to lead—indeed, even to comprehend—an institution of a quality considerably above that of one's personal experience.

Occasionally, inexperienced or insecure governing boards will intentionally select weak leadership—that is, individuals who clearly do not have the experience or level of previous achievement that would qualify them for a major university presidency. Such individuals are sometimes viewed as far more controllable and nonthreatening to board members. But these presidents quickly become overwhelmed by the complexity of their roles and all too frequently follow the same pattern of insecurity, by selecting subordinates even less qualified than they are. As a result, some universities have had to contend with a cascade of incompetence, a kind of sequential Peter Principle in which inexperienced amateurs, in far over their heads, populate most of the administrative positions in an institution.

Even with adequate training and experience, the administration of the contemporary university faces many challenges. Most institutions lack serious financial planning—which is not surprising given that the faculty usually resists any suggestion that academic units should develop a business plan. Universities are plagued by a serious incompatibility in the responsibility and authority assigned to those in administration. All too often, those charged with the responsibility for various activities simply are not provided with the authority to carry out these tasks. By the same token, many with relatively little responsibility have great ability to prevent decisive action. It is little wonder that the university administration is frequently unable and unwilling to tackle such major issues as the downsizing or elimination of obsolete programs to free up resources for new initiatives.

Patience is yet another important trait for executive leaders of universities. Campuses have their own leisurely timescales, driven by the time-honored processes of considered reflection and consensus that have long characterized the academy. Change in the university proceeds in slow, linear, incremental steps—improving, expanding, contracting, and reforming without altering its fundamental institutional mission, approach, or structure.

Another executive skill that applies almost exclusively to the president in contrast to other academic leaders and executive officers is the ability to relate to and guide a university governing board. All university presidents serve at the pleasure of governing boards. They are both hired and possibly fired by such boards, and they take key policy direction from this body. The ability to communicate with the board and to understand and to some degree shape its dynamics is important for a university president, just as it would be for a corporate CEO and a board of directors. Yet the lay character of the university governing board presents a particular challenge, since without guidance, governing boards can drift into areas where they are not only unable to fulfill their responsibilities but may actually damage their institution. Unless the president guides them on such issues, they will almost certainly founder.

The complexity of the university and the day-to-day pace of events (many of them unexpected) that require the attention of the president can become highly distracting. The ability of a president to see the forest for the trees, to look beyond the battles of the moment to the objectives that should be pursued for the long term, is a particularly important leadership trait. One of the great challenges of leading very complex organizations is preventing the concerns of today from obscuring the opportunities for tomorrow. Although leaders must deal with moments of crisis, they must not allow these challenges of the moment to distract them from pursuing a longer-range vision for the future of their institution, whether it be a corporation, a public body, or a university.

As a scientist and engineer, I was rarely daunted by the complexities of executive leadership. Actually, management is just a form of problem solving, an activity for which engineers are well trained. All of the elements used to solve engineering problems fit the executive role quite well, including the ability to identify and define problems; to synthesize, verify, and evaluate solutions; and to present results. Perhaps even more significant was the fact that my training as a theoretical physicist gave me the ability to rapidly assess and extract the key elements of complex issues, focusing on the forest rather than the trees. I preferred to focus my attention on the big picture and to delegate the myriad details associated with university operations to others, unless they were tasks that only the president could address (e.g., negotiations with the governor or making the pitch to a key donor). To be sure, this tendency to focus on the fundamentals led to my frustration with the endless committee meetings and appointments that characterize the calendar of senior academic administrators. But in the end, this ability of the president to stay above the fray is essential to keep the university on course even as it is buffeted by strong economic, social, and political forces both on and off the campus.

Even so, I was not immune from the ever-present threat of being pecked to death by turkeys, as both time and attention were consumed by a host of issues that were of relatively minor importance to the long-term welfare of the university but that seemed of cosmic significance to one constituency or another. I used to classify these as the "p" issues, since they included such topics as parking, pay, the Plant Department, political correctness, and so on. I used to implore our faculty senate to focus on such strategic issues as the appropriate balance between undergraduate and professional education or the challenge of tenure to a faculty with increasingly diverse activities and situations (e.g., child or elder care, clinical care responsibilities). Yet, time after time, elected faculty governance would come back to the "p" issues, once even assigning faculty members to roam around the university's parking decks to see who was taking up faculty parking spaces.

So, too, university presidents grow weary of the court politics that usually surround positions of power (real or perceived). Leading a team of strong administrative officers inevitably involves smoothing out conflicts and occasionally even picking winners and losers. It is also the case that the best executive officers and deans are usually quite ambitious and seek further advancement, including perhaps even a university presidency (particularly at such an institution as Michigan). Knitting these leaders into a cohesive team where institutional priorities dominate personal agendas can sometimes be a challenge, requiring extensive face time in one-on-one meetings. This becomes even more difficult when a particular administrator either falls short of satisfactory performance or decides to go his or her own way, even to the point of disloyalty to the institution or the president. In such cases, the necessary personnel changes are sometimes made difficult because of the political or personal sensitivities of key faculty groups or even the governing board.[8]

Most university presidents have very limited powers to deal with such issues and responsibilities, from the most strategic to the most trivial. Too many governing board members become immersed in management details or focused on personal or special interest agendas. Faculties have become highly fragmented, comfortable in their narrow scholarly world, and demanding of excessive consultation before any decisions can be made. Both trustees and faculty alike are threatened by anyone who would challenge the status quo, leaving scattered throughout our institutions a large herd of sacred cows—obsolete programs, outdated practices, archaic policies—grazing on the seed corn of the future and defended by those determined to hang onto power and perquisites, even at the expense of the institution's future. Public opinion is largely reactionary and, when manipulated by the media, can block even the most urgently needed change. It is little wonder that many university presidents sometimes conclude that the only way to get anything accomplished within the political environment of the university is by heeding the old adage "It is simpler to ask forgiveness than to seek permission."

6

ACADEMIC LEADERSHIP

Early college presidents were expected to provide academic leadership. In some nineteenth-century institutions, the president was not only the most distinguished scholar but the only scholar. The intellectual influence of presidents on the faculty, the governing board, and the students was profound, as suggested by a Michigan student's admiration of President Tappan: "He was an immense personality. It was a liberal education even for the stupid to be slightly acquainted with him."[1]

Today, the president's role in academic affairs remains important but must be exercised in a more delicate fashion. Technically, the shared governance policies of most universities delegate academic decisions (e.g., criteria for student admissions, faculty hiring and promotion, curriculum development, and awarding degrees) to the faculty. Hence, the faculty usually expects the university president to focus on political relations, fund-raising, and protecting their academic programs (e.g., from threats of dominance posed by intercollegiate athletics and the medical center) and to keep hands off academic matters.

Yet the most successful university presidents are capable not only of understanding academic issues but also of shaping the evolution of academic programs and enhancing the academic reputation of their university. After all, if the success or failure of a presidency will be based on the goal of leaving the university better than one inherited it, it is hard to imagine how one could achieve this without some involvement in the core activities of the institution: teaching and scholarship. But this requires both skill and diplomacy, since faculty reaction to a president's heavy-handed intrusion into academic affairs can be fierce. Presidential influence is more generally exercised through the appointment of key academic leaders (e.g., deans or department chairs), by obtaining the funds to stimulate the faculty to launch new academic programs, or by influencing the balance among academic priorities.

There are some presidents—though they are unfortunately a rarity these days—who have had both the scholarly credentials and interests to play a significant role in shaping the intellectual direction of a university. Michigan has benefited from several such leaders. For example, James Angell attracted extraordinary scholars, such as John Dewey; Harlan Hatcher, himself a distinguished scholar and professor of English literature, raised the quality of the university even as it doubled in size; and Harold Shapiro brought his own deep understanding of the history of the university and the changing nature of a liberal education to his efforts, as provost and then as president, to enhance the quality of the university's students, faculty, and programs.

However, buried among academic programs are numerous land mines that pose serious risks to those presidents inclined to meddle in academic affairs. Again, the history of the University of Michigan provides important lessons. The university's first president, Henry Tappan, stirred the wrath of several faculty members and the local newspapers when he tried to build a true university in Ann Arbor that emphasized scholarship on a par with instruction. In the 1920s, Michigan president C. C. Little failed when his attempt to impose the Harvard model of a university college for undergraduate education was strongly resisted by the university's faculty.

As I noted earlier in this book, my own academic perspectives were shaped first by Yale, perhaps the most faithful replication of the college system of Oxford and Cambridge in America; then by Caltech, embracing a culture driven by absolute scientific brilliance in research for both faculty and students; and finally in Michigan's nuclear science and engineering program, a truly interdisciplinary program spanning the range from the microscopic phenomena of nuclear and atomic physics to the design of such mammoth projects as billion-dollar nuclear power plants and thermonuclear fusion systems. I had learned early to distinguish the collegiate focus on the intellectual growth and socialization of young students from the broader roles of the university in creating, propagating, and applying new knowledge, so I had come to agree with Eliot's observation "A college is a place to which a young man is sent; a university is a place to which he goes!"[2] Hence, while I understood the University of Michigan's important role in undergraduate education, I also believed its impact went far beyond this, to encompass graduate education, professional education, scholarship and research, and an exceptionally broad array of activities in applying advanced knowledge such as medical care, international development, and promoting cultural vitality. Combining the concepts of John Henry Cardinal Newman and Henry Tappan provided my working definition of the university: a community of masters and scholars (*universitas magistorium et scholarium*), a school of universal learning (Newman), embracing every branch of knowledge and all possible means for making new investigations and thus advancing knowledge (Tappan).[3]

THE ACADEMIC CLOCKWORK

It has been said that the organization of the contemporary university—its array of departments, schools, and colleges—more resembles the organization of nineteenth-century knowledge than the contemporary scholarly landscape. However, I prefer the astronomical analogy of a solar system. This Copernican view of the university places at the center its liberal arts college, including the academic disciplines of the humanities, natural sciences, and social sciences. About this academic sun orbit four very large and powerful professional schools: engineering, law, business, and medicine. Many university presidents consider the medical school to actually be a massive black hole rather than a planet, since it tends to suck resources away from both the liberal arts and other academic planets of the university solar system, never to be seen again. Moving still farther away from the liberal arts core, one finds an array of smaller planetary bodies corresponding to various professional schools (architecture, education, social work, dentistry, public health, public policy) and schools of fine arts (art, music, dance). Here again, the massive gravitational pull of the medical school attempts to pull the smaller health sciences schools (nursing, dentistry, public health, pharmacy) into orbits about it as moons, although this is vigorously resisted by their deans. Continuing with the astronomical analogy, extracurricular activities, such as intercollegiate athletics and student activism, might be similar to comets in the Oort cloud, out of sight and out of mind—at least until they tumble into the orbits of academic planets, where they can cause great havoc, if not cosmic extinction of important academic values.

Private universities, particularly those evolving from the colonial colleges, are generally built around undergraduate colleges based on the liberal arts disciplines (e.g., Harvard College and Yale College). In contrast, public universities are built more on a foundation provided by the key professional schools, the big four being engineering, business, law, and medicine (plus agriculture in land-grant universities), with the liberal arts college primarily serving the general education needs of undergraduates. Yet, just as with private universities, the quality of the liberal arts college is generally the key factor determining the quality of the institution, since it has a profound impact on the quality of professional schools.

Of course, there is always an ebb and flow in the fortunes of particular academic programs, as university priorities shift in response to societal needs. During my years at Michigan, the university lurched from embracing the priorities of the Great Society in the 1960s by placing emphasis on the social sciences and related professional schools such as education and social work to an emphasis on the health sciences in the 1970s, with major investments in medicine, dentistry, nursing, public health, and pharmacy—culminating in the $260 million commitment to the major new University Hospital in 1978. As both the state and the nation became concerned with such issues as economic competitiveness and industrial productivity in the early 1980s, the university once again shifted priorities, to focus on engineering and business administration. Most recently, an aging baby boomer population concerned about its health has demanded massive federal programs in the biomedical sciences, and the university has reacted with major billion-dollar investments in an expansion of the Medical Center and the building of the Life Sciences Institute.

The academic and professional disciplines—departments, schools, colleges—tend to dominate the modern university, developing curriculum, marshaling resources, administering programs, and doling out rewards (e.g., tenure). However, the traditional disciplines can pose a major impediment to change, since in their faculty recruiting efforts, they frequently tend to clone their existing professors rather than seeking to move in new directions stimulated by bright, young minds. Despite the importance and strength of traditional departments, schools, and colleges, most campuses still have many examples of worn-out academic programs that manage to limp along, draining resources from more vital areas and constraining the university's capacity to change.

ACADEMIC LEADERSHIP

To be sure, the broad responsibilities of the president as chief executive officer of the university limit the time and opportunity to provide academic leadership. Furthermore, the academic programs of the institution report through the deans to the provost as the chief academic officer. Although other executive officers (e.g., the vice president for research or the vice president for student affairs) can influence academic activities (e.g., sponsored research and the student living-learning environment), the provost generally is regarded as the point person for academic leadership. Yet university presidents, even at large research universities or university systems, can have considerable impact on the academic programs of the university.

Perhaps the most difficult and certainly controversial administrative actions are those that establish priorities among various academic programs. A skillful president can bias the university system for resource allocation such that new proposals tend to win out over those that aim to sustain or strengthen established programs. While this requires some intellectual good taste on the part of both president and provost, it is an extremely important device for navigating the university toward the future rather than drifting along on currents from the past. During good times with growing budgets, this amounts to picking winners and losers. During hard times, when resources are declining, this amounts to lifeboat decisions about which units will survive and which may be discontinued. Although most universities find it important to put into place well-defined policies for academic program reduction and discontinuance, with ample mechanisms for consultation, in the end the president usually shoulders the eventual blame for these decisions, whether it is deserved or not.

The triad of criteria for such decisions typically involves consideration of program quality, centrality, and cost-effectiveness. Some institutions use this in a highly quantitative way: a provost of a leading research university once told me that his institution simply plotted the national ranking of each of their academic programs versus their cost per student, then targeted those units in the lower right quadrant (e.g., low reputation and high cost) for potential elimination. For most institutions, the considerations that determine university academic priorities are far more subjective and subtle. I learned this the hard way as provost, when I had my proposal for refining the university's policies on academic program discontinuation soundly trounced by a negative vote of 80 to 2 by the faculty senate. (Harold Shapiro went ahead and implemented the proposal anyway, providing another lesson in presidential leadership.)

Presidents sometimes have the opportunity to influence broad university priorities, such as the balance between teaching and research. At large public universities, there is usually a concern about the appropriate balance between well-funded professional schools, such as business, law, and medicine, and the liberal arts disciplines, particularly in the arts and the humanities. Although many people think of such a university as Michigan as dominated by its liberal arts college and undergraduate education, these programs represent less than 30 percent of the faculty and 15 percent of the budget. In contrast, the Medical School and the associated University Hospital represent over 50 percent of the budget of the university and roughly two-thirds of its staff. One lesson that Michigan presidents soon learn is the importance of protecting the fragile academic core of the university from the potential distortion posed by health sciences due to their unusual access to resources, such as clinical income and federal research grants. These resources fuel a constant growth (over 10 percent a year at Michigan), which can soon take over a campus and begin to intrude on the space and funds available for other academic programs.

For example, during the 1970s and early 1980s, the massive investment in the new University Hospital diverted state funding away from academic priorities into clinical facilities for almost a decade, not only at the University of Michigan but throughout the state. My administration was able to achieve some rebalancing, with a particularly intensive effort to rebuild the core academic facilities of our College of Literature, Science, and Arts (LS&A). During the early years, this was done through the provision of additional operating funds as well as through special initiatives that benefited LS&A: for example, priority given to rebuilding the natural sciences,[4] additional funding designed to improve the quality of first-year undergraduate education, and special salary programs for outstanding faculty. However, in later years, we went beyond this to launch an ambitious program to renovate or rebuild all of the buildings housing LS&A programs, which had deteriorated during the 1970s and 1980s as the university had addressed other capital priorities, such as the University Hospital. In the decade from 1986 to 1996, the university invested more than $350 million in capital facilities for LS&A, essentially rebuilding the entire Central Campus area.

Within a university, there is a definite hierarchy of academic prestige—or, perhaps better stated, an intellectual pecking order. In a sense, the more abstract and detached a discipline is from the real world, the higher its prestige. In this ranking, perhaps mathematics or philosophy would be at the pinnacle, with the natural sciences and humanities next, followed by the social sciences and the arts. The professional schools fall much lower down the hierarchy, with law, medicine, and engineering followed by the health professions, social work, and education.

Yet there is another pecking order in higher education, a ranking among, rather than within, institutions. Some of these are determined by popular rankings, such as those produced annually by *U.S. News and World Report.* Although academics decry these commercial beauty pageants, which are based on such nonsensical parameters as endowment per student (which, of course, rules out all large public universities) and the fraction of students rejected (which emphasizes elitism over access), the rankings nevertheless influence the enrollment decisions of students and parents, strike terror into the hearts of admissions officers, and (most significant for *U.S. News and World Report*) sell lots of magazines.[5]

While universities tend to trumpet it when their programs are ranked highly in such comparisons and to either hide or deride the rankings when they fall, most deans, provosts, and presidents look elsewhere to measure the quality of their academic programs and institutions. Once every decade, the National Research Council (of the National Academies) conducts a very comprehensive survey of graduate programs across the disciplines, using an array of more empirical measures, such as faculty awards, frequency of citations of scholarly publications, success in winning federal research grants, and graduate-level performance on standardized tests. These rankings are taken far more seriously, so much so that within several years of their publication, many universities have changed both the leadership and the investment in those programs ranked low by the NRC survey, and the faculty of their higher-ranked programs have become recruiting targets by wealthier universities. But since the NRC rankings occur only once a decade, university leaders must also look elsewhere to assess the quality of their programs.

The most common—and, to my mind, effective—evaluation tool involves peer assessment, subjective ratings of program quality by deans, department chairs, and distinguished faculty members. Since these academic leaders are continually involved in recruiting new faculty or evaluating the promotion or tenure cases of their own faculty members, they usually have a pretty good sense of which departments are at the top (or on the way up) and which are weak (or on the way down). Presidents, provosts, and deans keep their ears to the ground to pick up on these conversations. It is not only their business to develop an accurate assessment of the quality of their own programs but also their responsibility to take action to enhance the reputation of their institution. In some cases, this amounts to putting together a package to recruit a new superstar in a particular area. In other cases, it involves additional funds or new facilities to improve the unit.

There are also occasions—rare as they may be—when a university decides to simply throw in the towel and shut a program down for a damning trilogy of faults: it is not good enough, too expensive, and/or not central enough to the rest of the university. Since outright academic program discontinuance is difficult because of faculty tenure, the elimination of weak programs is usually accomplished by finesse. For example, a smaller unit may be merged into a larger academic unit, where it will disappear gradually; or an academic program may undergo reorganization, which is portrayed as merely renaming the program but, in effect, eliminates the box on the organization chart for the target unit.

As president, I would conduct an annual analysis of the ebb and flow of senior faculty across all of our academic units, to track our efforts to attract and retain top-notch talent. My leadership team kept a scorecard on the ability to attract (or raid) faculty talent on a department-by-department basis, along with our capacity to retain our best faculty members in the face of offers from competing institutions. This was not only a good way to evaluate the strength of our academic leadership at the level of department chairs and deans, but it was also an excellent way for the president and provost to monitor the ongoing health of the university. It also kept the pressure on me as president, since achieving competitive faculty compensation and quality environments for education and research were ultimately my responsibility.

On a more general level, we developed a comprehensive annual report, "The Michigan Metrics," which served as a "dashboard" (in modern business parlance) on which to track a broad set of data concerning academic quality, financial integrity, and institutional leadership. While this annual snapshot of university vital signs was probably not useful in the way that a corporate balance sheet or income statement would be, the use of such longitudinal data gave a good sense of whether the university was climbing in altitude or on a downward-glide path—or, more seriously, headed for a crash. Again, with academic leadership, as in other aspects of the university presidency, one should never forget that results are what count.

One of my colleagues, Charles Eisendrath, director of the university's Journalist-in-Residence Program, once proposed to me a "fish foodball theory" of faculty behavior. He noted that faculty activities are usually randomly distributed, much like fish swimming in an aquarium, and that just as fish will quickly align to go after a ball of food suspended in their tank, faculty will soon align their activities to go after new funds. All one needs to do is create financial incentives. A couple of examples illustrate.

During the 1980s, when I was dean of engineering and then provost of the university, we were concerned that the university was underrecovering the true costs of federally sponsored research through excessive institutional cost sharing and inadequate overhead (so-called indirect costs) on federal grants. The faculty did not have much sympathy with this concern, since such overhead charges usually came off the top of their research grants, at the expense of such worthy priorities as laboratory equipment, technical staff, and graduate student support. Yet indirect costs were very real costs that had to be paid by someone—if not by the federal sponsor, then by the university, from such sources as tuition revenue or state appropriation. To change the faculty perception, we used a very simple device. Each year, we would distribute back to faculty members in discretionary accounts a certain fraction of the overhead recovered on their federal grants. Although this was generally a small amount (typically 5 percent or less of the recovered funds), the accounts were totally discretionary and under the direct control of the faculty member who was the principal investigator on the grant. They could be used for supporting a graduate student, traveling to a technical meeting, purchasing a computer, or carpeting one's office—any expenditure appropriate for university funds. This very modest incentive program drove a sea change in faculty attitudes toward indirect cost recovery—as well as toward more general grant and contract support. Over the next decade, Michigan rose from eighth to first in the nation in federal research support, due to the strong entrepreneurial efforts of our faculty stimulated by strong research incentives to reward faculty grantsmanship.

Presidents can sometimes influence priorities by adjusting the balance between the sustained support for ongoing initiatives and the funding aimed at stimulating new initiatives. As the university's provost, each year Harold Shapiro reallocated 1 percent of the base budget of all university units, both academic and administrative, into a University Priority Fund, to stimulate and support new activities in such areas as undergraduate education, diversity, and interdisciplinary scholarship. This was later augmented by a $5 million grant from the Kellogg Foundation and a match from the university, to create a Presidential Initiative Fund aimed at providing the president with resources to stimulate new academic initiatives. As these mechanisms, which allowed small onetime allocations, were continued year after year, they resulted in rather significant reallocations from ongoing activities (which saw their budgets declining to 99 percent, 98 percent, 97 percent, etc. each year) into key university priorities—that is, from the old to the new. As provost, I continued this process, selecting as early priorities the areas of undergraduate education and diversity. For example, we created a competition for proposals to attract more senior faculty into teaching undergraduate classes. We used incentive funds to support Target of Opportunity programs for minority faculty and PhD students. Later, we added interdisciplinary scholarship, international programs, the arts, and several other priorities that benefited greatly from the grassroots interest, involvement, and creativity of faculty attracted by the potential of additional resources.

Here, a word is appropriate about a sharply contrasting approach, perhaps best captured by the phrase "presidential whim" rather than "presidential initiative." Rather than establishing incentives of significant resources, allocated on a peer-reviewed, merit basis, some presidents instead attempt to stimulate faculty engagement by indicating their personal interest in a particular topic. While this may create a few headlines in the university press releases, the best faculty members will usually ignore such presidential whims unless they align with their own interests. The lesson to be learned here is that academic leadership is most effective and powerful if it taps into the energy, interests, and creativity of the faculty at the grassroots level. Providing an Eisendrath fish foodball of resources to fund faculty initiatives aimed at a broad university priority, such as undergraduate education or diversity, tends to align best with the highly entrepreneurial nature of the faculty culture.

FACULTY QUALITY

The principal academic resource of a university is its faculty. The quality and commitment of the faculty determine the excellence of the academic programs of a university, the quality of its student body, the excellence of its teaching and scholarship, its capacity to serve broader society through public service, and the resources it is able to attract from public and private sources. The quality of the faculty is determined by many factors, such as resource commitments and capital facilities, but none more critical than the standards applied in recruitment, promotion, and tenure decisions.

Each appointment to the faculty and each promotion within its ranks must be seen as both a significant decision and an important opportunity. In theory, at least, these decisions should always be made with the quality of the university always foremost in mind. Policies, procedures, and practices characterizing the appointment, role, reward, and responsibilities of the faculty should be consistent with the overall goals of the institution and the changing environment in which it finds itself. In practice, however, these decisions tend to be made at the level of individual disciplinary departments, with relatively little consideration given to broader institutional concerns or long-range implications.

Certainly the most controversial, complex, and misunderstood issue related to the faculty in higher education, at least in the minds of the public, is tenure. In theory, tenure is the key mechanism for protecting academic freedom and for defending faculty members against political attack both within and outside the university. In practice, it has become something quite different: job security, protecting both outstanding and incompetent faculty alike, not only from political intrusion, but also from a host of performance issues that could lead to dismissal in many other walks of life. Of course, it is this presumed guarantee of job security that so infuriates many members of the public, some of whom have felt the sting of corporate downsizing or job competition.

Because tenure represents such a major commitment by a university, it should only be awarded to a faculty member after a rigorous process of evaluation. Most university faculty members believe that tenure is a valuable and important practice in the core academic disciplines of the university, where independent teaching and scholarship require some protection from criticism and controversy. This privilege should also enable tenured faculty members to accept greater responsibility for the interests of the university, rather than focusing solely on personal objectives. But even within the academy, many are beginning to question the appropriateness of current tenure practices. The abolition of mandatory retirement policies is leading to an aging faculty cohort insulated from rigorous performance accountability by tenure, a situation depriving young scholars of faculty opportunities. Increasingly, the academy itself is acknowledging that both the concept and the practice of tenure—particularly when interpreted as guaranteed lifetime employment—need to be reevaluated.

Yet only the most foolhardy would attempt to reevaluate tenure within a single institution, since the marketplace for the best faculty is highly competitive. Any challenge to the status quo of tenure must be mounted by a coalition of institutions. When I was chair of the Big Ten Conference (which is actually as much an academic organization of 12 institutions—including the University of Chicago—as it is an athletic conference), we invited the provosts and chairs of the faculty senates of our universities to a daylong conference in the mid-1990s to discuss tenure and the faculty contract. Needless to say, one workshop does not a sustained movement make, but the discussion did suggest that the faculties of at least this set of research universities are more open to considering change than one might expect.

Through active participation in tenure decisions, university presidents and provosts can have considerable impact on the quality of the faculty of their university. Harold Shapiro demonstrated this to me, first in his role as provost and then as president (see chapter 2). I continued his practice of direct and strong involvement in hiring, promotion, and tenure decisions. Once, I actually challenged over 50 percent of the recommendations from the Medical School, observing that they all looked like they had been prepared from the same word processor template.[6] My philosophy was summarized in a communication to the school's dean and executive committee: "Put yourself in my shoes for a moment. In the course of a year I am asked to evaluate and rule on hundreds of appointments for all conceivable academic and professional appointments. Indeed, I will be shortly receiving 70 recommendations from your school. The issue here is tenure. In my view the decision to offer tenure is the most important decision we make in this university. It is also my most important responsibility, since these decisions affect the institution for decades to come. The burden must be on the unit to demonstrate that the candidate has the degree of excellence, of achievement, necessary to merit tenure. You have not done so on many of these recommendations, and until that case has been made I am unable to support tenure for these individuals."[7]

The faculty members of research universities are well aware that their careers—their compensation, promotion, and tenure—are determined primarily by their research productivity as measured by publications and grantsmanship, since these activities contribute most directly to scholarly reputation and hence market value. This reward climate helps to tip the scales away from undergraduate teaching, public service, and institutional loyalty, especially when quantitative measures of research productivity or grantsmanship replace more balanced judgments of the quality of research and professional work. The growing pressures on faculty to generate the resources necessary to support their activities are immense.[8] At a university like Michigan, with roughly 2,500 faculty members generating over $800 million of research grants per year, this can amount to an expectation that each faculty member will generate hundreds of thousands of research dollars per year, a heavy burden for those who also carry significant instructional, administrative, and service responsibilities. For example, consider the plight of the young faculty member in medicine, responsible for teaching medical students and residents; providing sufficient clinical revenue to support not only his or her salary but also the overhead of the medical center; securing sufficient research grants to support laboratories, graduate students, and postdoctoral fellows; exploiting opportunities for technology transfer and business start-ups; and building the scholarly momentum and reputation to achieve tenure. Consider as well the conflict that inevitably arises among responsibilities to students, patients, scholarship, and professional colleagues. Not an easy life!

As a consequence, the American research university has developed a freewheeling entrepreneurial spirit, perhaps best captured by the words of one university president who boasted, "Faculty at our university can do anything they wish—provided they can attract the money to support what they want to do." We might view the university of today as a loose federation of faculty entrepreneurs, who drive the evolution of the university to fulfill their individual goals.[9] In a sense, the research university has become a highly adaptable knowledge conglomerate because of the interests and efforts of our faculty. An increasing share of externally provided resources flow directly to faculty entrepreneurs as research grants and contracts from the federal government, corporations, and private foundations. These research programs act as quasi-independent revenue centers with very considerable influence, frequently at odds with more formal faculty governance structures, such as faculty senates. The result is a transactional culture in which everything is up for negotiation. It is *Let's Make a Deal* writ large.

Since the academic promotion ladder is relatively short (consisting essentially of the three levels of assistant professor, associate professor, and professor), the faculty reward culture can become one-dimensional, based primarily on salary. Although faculty honors and awards (including endowed professorial chairs) are common in higher education, faculty members tend to measure their relative worth in terms of salary. Laws upholding the freedom of information require many public universities to publish faculty salaries. Even in private universities, one's salary can usually be compared to the salaries of others either through the informal grapevine or through testing the marketplace by exploring offers from other institutions. Hence, the faculty reward structure creates a highly competitive environment that extends beyond a single institution into a national or even global marketplace for the very best faculty talent.

University presidents can have a significant impact on faculty compensation policies, which are key to recruiting, rewarding, and retaining top talent. While attracting the necessary resources and making the case for adequate faculty salaries to legislatures and trustees is an important responsibility of the president, perhaps even more so is the articulation of an effective faculty compensation policy that achieves an optimum balance among such criteria as merit, market, and equity. At Michigan, I put into place the following general policy for faculty compensation:

1. The average compensation for full professors at Michigan was set at the top of public universities.
2. However, the best faculty members at Michigan would be compensated at levels comparable to those of the best public and private universities.
3. The average compensation for assistant professors and associate professors was set to be the highest in the nation among public and private universities, since Michigan's tradition was to develop faculty from within rather than recruit at senior ranks through raids, and hence we needed to recruit the very best junior faculty.
4. Deans and directors were compensated at levels comparable to the best public and private universities.
5. Annual salary increases were based entirely on merit (i.e., no cost-of-living increase), occasionally adjusted by market or equity considerations.

It was then my responsibility as president to attract the resources necessary to support such a policy and to make an effective case to the regents, the legislature, and the public as to why such compensation was vital to the university's quality. The success of this aggressive strategy was demonstrated by comparative data. By the early 1990s, Michigan's faculty salaries had passed those at the University of California, Berkeley, to become first among all public universities. At the level of assistant and associate professor, they were first in the nation, ahead of all public and private peers.

Faculty members learn quickly that the best way to increase compensation and rise through the ranks is to periodically test their market value by exploring positions in other institutions. Although many professors would prefer to remain at a single institution through their career, the strong market-determined character of faculty compensation may force them to jump from institution to institution at various stages in their career. Here, once again, the influence of the president can become important.

University presidents are usually not involved in routine faculty recruiting, since in the typical university, hundreds of searches are under way at any particular time. However, on occasion, the president is brought into the search process to lure a major faculty superstar to the campus. The president will also occasionally play a similar role in attempting to persuade a distinguished faculty member to remain in the face of an attractive offer from another institution. Since so many such efforts to retain a faculty member at Michigan were in competition with West Coast universities, I used to carefully place picture books on the San Francisco earthquakes or other West Coast calamities (e.g., freeway traffic) on the coffee table in my office prior to my meeting with the faculty member. As president, I would also occasionally become involved in recruiting senior minority faculty, in part because of my hands-on involvement in the Michigan Mandate, a strategic effort to increase the university's commitment to diversity.

However, perhaps my most significant impact on faculty recruiting was through particular policy initiatives. My own academic experiences at Yale and Caltech had convinced me that much of the momentum of academic institutions is driven by a few truly exceptional, visionary, and exciting appointments—what I called "essential singularities" (drawing on my mathematical background)—that set the pace for our academic programs. Hence, we created a Target of Opportunity program intended to strongly encourage academic units to recruit such candidates. Usually, faculty searches are heavily constrained by programmatic requirements, such as to search for a historian in Southeast Asian studies or a physicist in superstring theory. However, first as dean and then as provost and president, I would set aside special funds intended to fund appointments for truly exceptional candidates, regardless of area of expertise. We challenged the academic units to identify exceptional hiring opportunities and then bring us proposals for funding the necessary positions. If these proposals looked promising, we would commit from central resources the base and start-up funding necessary to recruit the candidates. We later extended this program to the recruiting of outstanding minority faculty, with great success.

Of course, such singular scholars are not always the easiest people to accommodate. Some are demanding prima donnas, requiring high maintenance by deans, provosts, and even presidents. It was my role to stroke these folks, sometimes assisting deans in meeting their needs and demands, sometimes simply reassuring them that the university was honored to have them on our faculty and strongly supported their work. Their passion for their work, their unrelenting commitment to achievement, and the exceptionally high standards that accompanied their great talent set the pace for their students, their colleagues, and the university.

Academic leaders spend much of their time either attempting to recruit outstanding faculty members to their institution or fending off raids on their faculty by other institutions. Although there have been attempts in the past to impose certain rules of behavior on faculty recruiting (e.g., through informal agreements that institutions will refrain from recruiting faculty just prior to the start of a new academic year or avoid using the promise of reduced teaching load to lure a research star), it remains a no-holds-barred and quite ruthless competition. The wealthier and more prestigious an institution is, the more aggressively it plays the game.

There is an insidious nature to this intensely competitive market for faculty talent. First, such recruiting efforts are a major factor in driving up the costs of a college education. The competition for faculty superstars can be intense and very expensive. The size of an offer put together to lure a star faculty member away or of the counteroffer the home university puts on the table to retain the individual can seriously distort broader faculty compensation patterns. Furthermore, such offers usually go far beyond simply salary and can involve a considerable dowry including laboratory space, research support, graduate and research assistants, and, yes, sometimes even a reduced teaching load.

Not only does such an effort tax the available resources of a university, but the recruitment package may seriously distort the existing faculty reward structure and lead to the loss of key faculty who feel jilted by the offer to their new colleague. Even more serious are those instances in which an up-and-aspiring university recruits a big-name faculty member past his or her prime—an "extinct volcano." While the reputations of these individuals may add luster to the institution, their excessive compensation and declining productivity can discourage more junior faculty and actually harm program quality over the long term.

Beyond this, several of the wealthiest private universities play a particularly damaging role within higher education by preferring to build their faculties through raiding other institutions rather than developing them through ranks from within. Their vast endowments allow them to make offers to faculty members that simply cannot be matched by public universities. When challenged about their predatory faculty raids on public universities, the elite private institutions generally respond by suggesting a trickle-down theory. Such free-market competition, they argue, enhances the quality of all faculties and institutions. Yet this philosophy promotes the fundamental premise that the very best faculty members should be at the wealthiest institutions. Such predatory behavior can decimate the quality of programs in other universities by raiding their best faculty, who have been nurtured and developed at considerable expense. Even unsuccessful attempts to raid faculty can result in a serious distortion of resource allocation in the target institution, as it desperately attempts to retain its best faculty stars.

SELECTION AND RECRUITMENT OF ACADEMIC LEADERSHIP

University presidents can have the most direct impact on academic quality through the selection and/or recruiting of key academic leaders. After all, universities are intensely people-dependent organizations, with the faculty as the key to both the quality and the reputation of the institution. Clearly, the provost is the most important appointment by the president, since this individual serves as the chief academic officer as well as the reporting line for the deans. Beyond the provost's responsibility as chief operating officer and second in command, the selection of a provost must take into account the president's own role and focus. For example, for presidents who are required to devote much of their time to external matters (e.g., fund-raising, alumni relations, and politics) or who are consumed by internal responsibilities (e.g., athletics, medical affairs, or keeping the governing board happy), the provost may assume a much more significant role in managing the affairs of the campus. At a very complex institution, such as the University of Michigan, it is difficult for outsiders to come up to speed fast enough to survive in the position. Hence, many large universities tend to appoint provosts from within, drawing from among the deans of the larger schools and colleges (particularly the liberal arts college).

The president is also responsible for the selection and evaluation of the executive officers of the university. Unlike government administrators or corporate executives, senior officers at most universities do not serve merely at the pleasure (or whim) of the president. Rather, they are regarded as members of a leadership team that provides continuity from presidency to presidency.

Most university presidents also work closely with their provosts in the selection and recruitment of deans, since these are the key line officers in determining the quality of academic programs. This is particularly critical at a deans' university—such as Michigan—where the dean's role is characterized by an unusual degree of authority (and responsibility) for the leadership of their schools and colleges. In the end, the quality of academic programs is determined more by the ability of deans than by any other factor. At Michigan, some deans lead academic units as large as most universities (e.g., the liberal arts college has over 20,000 students, and the Medical School has over 1,000 faculty). Hence, it is absolutely essential for the president to play an active role in selecting, recruiting, and evaluating deans, since mistakes can sometimes take years to correct, with rather considerable implications for academic programs.

Since deanships are such critical appointments, Michigan developed a practice in which the president, provost, and other senior officers kept their eye out for junior colleagues with leadership potential, providing them with opportunities for leadership development. Just as with deans, changes in executive officers can become complex, particularly when the motivation was a poor performance evaluation or a necessary change in institutional direction. Increasingly, institutions are choosing to negotiate contracts with senior officers that not only spell out conditions of the appointment (e.g., authority and compensation) but also specify exit strategies, along with golden parachutes (taking a lesson from football coaches).

TINKERING WITH TIME BOMBS

Presidents with strong academic backgrounds can become so fascinated with the myriad academic programs of the university that they are tempted to tinker with its academic mechanisms. Such was my own case, since after roughly two decades of experience at Michigan, I had accumulated a large inventory of ideas about the academic organization of the university. Although my many years as a faculty member, dean, and provost had provided ample warning of the hazards that await those academic leaders venturing down the path of academic transformation, the temptation to tinker was simply too great.

Like most new presidents, I inherited a broad array of here-and-now academic issues that simply could not be ignored or delayed. For example, the university was only beginning to emerge from a decade-long trauma of budget cuts and reallocation—the "smaller but better" days of the early 1980s—and there were still difficult decisions about which units would win (i.e., survive) and which would lose (and perhaps disappear). So, too, there was a clear imbalance between supporting administrative and auxiliary activities (notably the massive growth of the Medical Center) and meeting the needs of core academic units, particularly in Michigan's large liberal arts college. There were deans to appoint—and deans to replace. There was a new executive officer team to build. And of course, there were the inevitable battles, on behalf of the quality and integrity of the university, that only the president could fight—battles against external threats from legislators, governors, Congress, and the media and even against internal threats, such as the Athletic Department.

Yet my real interests concerned more fundamental and strategic academic issues, although prying loose the time from the in-box and the travel calendar to consider academic issues was always a challenge. Among the first issues to draw my attention was undergraduate education. My own experiences in graduate and professional education provided a very broad view of Michigan as predominantly a university rather than a college dominated by undergraduate education. To some degree, I agreed with such predecessors as Henry Tappan and James Angell that the considerable intellectual assets of a great university can sometimes be wasted on the socialization of young students. Yet I also realized that the University of Michigan had an important responsibility to provide high-quality undergraduate education—indeed, we enrolled over 22,000 students in our undergraduate programs. Furthermore, recent studies had suggested that the institution was too reliant on large lecture courses and teaching assistants and was failing to take advantage of the student residential environment as a potential learning opportunity.

Hence, improving the quality of the undergraduate experience became one of my earliest priorities as both provost and president. Following the Eisendrath fish foodball theory, my leadership team created the Undergraduate Initiative Fund to provide over $1 million each year of grants to faculty projects at the grassroots level aimed at improving undergraduate education. We created a group of distinguished university professorships to honor outstanding undergraduate teaching. Major investments were made in restructuring introductory courses, particularly in the sciences. We built into the base budget $500,000 per year to methodically upgrade and maintain the quality of all classrooms for our undergraduate programs. We launched a massive effort to rebuild the physical environment for undergraduate education. Efforts were made to create more learning experiences outside of the classroom through student research projects, community service, and special learning environments in the resident halls. Perhaps most important, the deans began to include rigorous evaluations of teaching in faculty recruiting, promotion, and tenure.

Similar efforts were launched to improve the quality of graduate and professional education. The Medical School completely restructured the medical curriculum to provide students with early clinical experience. The School of Business redesigned its MBA program to stress teamwork and community service. The College of Engineering introduced new professional degrees at the master's and doctorate level to respond to the needs of industry for practice-oriented professionals. The School of Dentistry underwent a particularly profound restructuring of its educational, research, and service programs. The Institute for Public Policy Studies was restructured into a new School of Public Policy (later named after Michigan alumnus Gerald R. Ford). And under the leadership of Dan Atkins, a colleague from my days as dean of the College of Engineering, the School of Library Science was transformed into a new School of Information—the first of its kind in the nation—developing entirely new academic programs in the management of knowledge resources.

International education was also given high priority. Following planning efforts led in the 1980s while I was provost, a series of steps were taken to broaden and coordinate the university's international activities. The university created a new International Institute to coordinate international programs. It continued to expand its relationship with academic institutions abroad, with particular emphasis on Asia and Europe. Of particular note were the distance-learning efforts of the School of Business, which used computer and telecommunications technology, along with corporate partnerships, to establish overseas campuses in Hong Kong, Seoul, Sao Paulo, Paris, and London.

Yet even as our leadership team successfully implemented this broad agenda, it was becoming increasingly clear to many of us that we needed to ask some more fundamental questions about the nature of learning and scholarship at such a major research university. For example, most of our efforts to improve the quality of undergraduate education were working within the traditional paradigm of four-year degree programs in disciplinary majors designed for high school graduates and approached through solitary (and, all too frequently, passive) pedagogical methods. Yet society was demanding far more radical changes. Hence, as president, I began to challenge our faculty to consider bolder initiatives.

For example, it was clear that in a world in which our graduates would be required to change careers many times during their lives, a highly specialized undergraduate education became less and less appropriate. Instead, more emphasis needed to be placed on breadth of knowledge, on critical thinking, and on the acquisition of learning skills—that is, on a truly liberal education. In a sense, an undergraduate education should prepare a student for a lifetime of further learning. Yet how could we create a truly coherent undergraduate learning experience as long as we allowed the disciplines to dominate the academic undergraduate curriculum? How could we address the fact that most of our graduates are quantitatively illiterate, with a totally inadequate preparation in intellectual disciplines that will shape their lives, such as science, mathematics, and technology?

The challenge was to develop a rigorous undergraduate degree program that would prepare students for the full range of further educational opportunities, from professions including medicine, law, business, engineering, and teaching to further graduate studies across a broad range of disciplines from English to mathematics. Far from being a renaissance degree, such a "bachelors of liberal learning" would be more akin to the type of education universities once tried to provide a century ago, before the deification of academic disciplines took over our institutions and our curriculum.

To this end, I suggested that the university broaden the responsibility for undergraduate education beyond our liberal arts departments, to include the faculties of our professional schools. While well received by the faculties of the schools of medicine, business, and engineering, these efforts were strongly resisted, perhaps understandably, by the faculty of our liberal arts disciplines. Of course, this should not be surprising to those familiar with Michigan's institutional saga and with C. C. Little's failed efforts to develop a "university college" (see chapter 1). To counter these concerns, my leadership team came up with a major project, the Gateway Campus, which was intended to become the focal point of undergraduate education at Michigan, if we had been able to get it funded.

The plan was to build a major cluster of facilities on the university's Central Campus that would provide a physical space that would be clearly identified by students, faculty, and alumni as the university's focal point for undergraduate education. It would include major facilities for undergraduate instruction, including lecture halls, classroom clusters, and multimedia spaces. It would also house several of our most important museum collections. We referred to the complex as the Gateway Campus both because of its role in providing students with the gateway to their undergraduate education and because of its function as a gateway to the campus for various external communities attracted by Michigan's museum collections and performing arts.

A financing plan was developed for the Gateway Campus, using a combination of private gifts, state support, and internal university funds. However, we were unable to raise the nucleus private support (estimated at $75 million) to launch the project. Today, instead of being a space marked by commitment to undergraduate education, the proposed site for the Gateway Center has become the location of the massive Life Sciences Institute, a complex primarily devoted to research and postgraduate education (and representing, to many, a beachhead for the Medical School on the university's liberal arts campus).

Far more successful was a similar effort to build a multidisciplinary center on the university's North Campus. The Media Union was developed with a somewhat different theme: creativity and innovation. The university's North Campus is characterized by a very unusual collection of academic programs: art, architecture, engineering, music, the theatrical performing arts (drama, dance, musical theater), the new School of Information, and computer science. In contrast to many professional and academic disciplines that stress the analysis of what is or has been, these programs attempt to create or synthesize what has only been imagined. Hence, the deans of the schools containing these North Campus programs came up with a theme captured by the term "the Renaissance Campus"[10] and sought a major center to integrate and support the multidisciplinary activities supporting these creative activities.

Working closely with the governor I was able to obtain a commitment of $70 million of state funds for the project, along with unusual flexibility in its planning. This enabled me to pull together a highly creative team of faculty and deans and challenge them: "Here is $70 million. Design us a facility for a twenty-first century university!" Together, they came up with a fascinating new concept, best captured by the name of the new Media Union, which was a play on the name of the Michigan Union of the Central Campus (the nation's first student union) but also suggested the merging of various media (art, music, architecture, engineering) and senses (sight, hearing, touch, etc.) into a space designed to stimulate creativity and innovation. I found written in one of my notebooks from the time: "This could well be the most important project the university will undertake in the decade ahead, since it could well define what the twenty-first–century university will become. But we need to keep it low key to avoid scaring people. Let's keep it on track by just using an occasional nudge, a 'just trust me,' or 'humor your president.'"

Our $2 billion effort to rebuild the campus gave us many other opportunities to stimulate new intellectual activities, even though the Gateway Center on the Central Campus remained only a dream. An array of new research laboratories in the health sciences integrated clinical research with molecular genetics and proteomics. New facilities were created for interdisciplinary centers, such as the Institute for the Humanities, the International Institute, the Tauber Manufacturing Institute, and the Davison Institute for Developing Economies. And we continued to sprinkle the campus with new facilities aimed specifically to support undergraduate education.

We also sought to make more use of novel organizational structures. Michigan has long been a leader in establishing interdisciplinary centers and institutes that reach across disciplinary boundaries. However, we believed we needed to go further than this. We tried to create alternative virtual structures that drew together students, faculty, and staff in new ways. The Global Change Program and the Center for Molecular Medicine were such efforts. Some of these ideas worked. Others stayed on the drawing board, such as the concept of reorganizing disciplines to better link together academic and professional disciplines in key areas (e.g., linking the humanities with the visual and performing arts; the social sciences with professional schools, such as business, law, and education; or the physical sciences with engineering). The only linkage that eventually succeeded was that between the biological sciences and clinical disciplines, in part because the university's massive investment in the Life Sciences Institute enabled the integration of the basic sciences in the Medical School with the biological sciences in our liberal arts college.

Many lessons spill out of this array of triumphs and failures in academic leadership. First, it is difficult for the university leadership, at least at the level of the president, to have sufficient understanding of intellectual issues to determine the optimum organization of an academic institution. Top-down reorganization, while perhaps the quickest way to respond to present challenges, might just create new empires that would eventually dominate the institution and constrain change, just as our present discipline-based units sometimes do. Furthermore, it was clear that technology itself was challenging the basic organization of the University of Michigan. Such information and communications technologies as e-mail, instant messaging, and more sophisticated collaborative tools (known collectively as cyberinfrastructure) are allowing the formation and evolution of new types of knowledge communities engaged in learning and scholarly pursuits that are increasingly detached from both traditional academic units and the campuses themselves.

Hence, I became convinced that the most effective route to change for the long term was to encourage experimentation driven by our best faculty. Universities need to break the stranglehold of existing organizational structures dictated by traditional disciplines, and this can be accomplished by creating new grassroots incentives and opportunities to allow the institution to evolve more rapidly along changing intellectual lines. The Eisendrath fish foodball approach is always a good place to start.

THE CHALLENGES TO ACADEMIC LEADERSHIP BY THE PRESIDENT

The most serious challenges to the efforts of university presidents to provide academic leadership involve time and perception. All too many people—including faculty, trustees, and the public—view the president's primary job as "going downtown to get the money." Academic matters are presumed best left to the faculty. Some of the responsibility for this perception must rest with those presidents who have intentionally distanced themselves from the academic enterprise to focus more of their efforts on off-campus activities, such as private fund-raising, government relations, and corporate boards. Yet many university presidents remain quite active in academic affairs, at least on educational issues of major national import, such as diversity, student access, and undergraduate education. Others have taken on broader issues in their areas of expertise, such as international development, bioethics, and technological change. While it is true that some presidents simply do not have the time, the inclination, the experience, or the credibility to speak out on national issues, others have taken courageous stances on key issues of importance to higher education. Here, it is important to stress again the importance of the governing board, both in selecting presidents with a deep understanding of the academic nature of the university and in clearly charging them with the academic leadership of the institution as among their most important duties. Furthermore, the governing board plays a key role in both empowering and enabling the university president to provide broader leadership on behalf of higher education, defending the important values and traditions of higher education and articulating the importance of the university to contemporary society.

Those presidents associated with prominent universities have opportunities to represent the interests of higher education at the national level through such organizations as the Association of American Universities, the National Association of State Universities and Land-Grant Colleges, and the American Council on Education. Because of my background in science and engineering, I also had the opportunity to provide leadership through the National Academies and through such federal bodies as the National Science Board. However, like many presidents, I occasionally encountered regents uncomfortable with these broader roles—including one regent who actually tried to block my acceptance of the chairmanship of the National Science Board.

Many university presidents have served with great distinction as teachers and scholars and developed a strong understanding of academic values and culture. Yet the broader responsibilities of the university presidency—its executive role and its responsibility for managing the myriad external relationships of the universities with governments, donors, the media, and the public—lead many, particularly among the faculty, to assume that their president has set aside academic values in favor of corporate behavior as a chief executive officer. From time to time, most university presidents are criticized for accepting the "corporate" nature of the university administration or of their actions as chief executive officer of the institution. Woe be to the president who mistakenly uses terms from the business world, such as *employee* or *customer* or even *productivity.* Once, while I was in a foul mood after being beaten up at a meeting of my faculty senate for presumably using such business language, I went back to my office and used computer technology to run a word search on every one of my speeches, essays, and letters over my years as president (over 2,200 files), searching for the words *corporation* and *corporate.* To my surprise, I found that I had never referred to the university as a corporation. The computer search found only two instances of the use of the word *corporate.* In one, I suggested that the "corporate style of top-down management was totally inappropriate for a university." In the other, I suggested that the "corporate culture" of the university needed to be reexamined, actually referring to the "collective culture."

Quite in contrast to negative perceptions, I made a special effort to restructure the university administration so that it was more attentive to academic values, by seeking to appoint executive officers with academic experience. In most university administrations (including those before and after mine at Michigan), only the provost, the vice president for research, and (occasionally) the president have academic experience and credibility. However, by the end of my tenure, every one of my vice presidents—including those in such areas as finance, development, state relations, and secretary of the university—were experienced academics with doctorates and faculty appointments. Furthermore, most of our deans also had long records of distinction in scholarship and teaching. In this sense the Michigan administration provided a good example of true faculty governance, since we were all faculty members ourselves.

Although many people both within and external to the institution tend to evaluate university presidents on dollars raised through fund-raising or state appropriation, buildings built, football championships won, and perhaps trustee desires fulfilled, the true impact of a president on the academic quality of an institution is generally not apparent for years afterward, usually long after most presidents are gone and forgotten. The real key to an effective university presidency is the ability to attract and support talented people—students, staff, faculty, and particularly academic leaders. This people-focused character of academic leadership requires considerable experience with the core activities of the university: teaching and scholarship. It also requires good taste in identifying talent, strong recruiting skills in attracting it, the insight to develop it, and the persuasive ability to retain it. And it is almost never understood or acknowledged as the most critical role of the university president.

7

POLITICAL LEADERSHIP

Throughout the history of American higher education, the university presidency has had a strongly political character. Presidents are expected to be skillful in working with local, state, and federal governments, both to represent the interests of their universities and to protect them from unnecessary government intrusion and control. The success of their leadership is frequently measured in terms of political objectives, such as level of state appropriations or volume of federal research grants. Although such political skills are undeniably important for public universities, they are also essential for private colleges and universities, since these are clearly affected by government regulation and tend to benefit from public policies, such as those concerning taxes and student financial aid.

University presidents also need considerable skill in dealing with the multiple constituencies and myriad interests of the university community. University campuses are, by design, "free and ordered spaces" where important social issues can be debated.[1] Furthermore, as large, complex, and basically anarchical organizations, universities are frequently dominated by politics among their various constituencies—students, faculty, and staff. The faculty, by its very nature, tends both to be skeptical and to challenge leadership. Students are frequently at that age where challenging authority becomes almost a rite of passage. Governing boards, particularly at public institutions, tend to be highly political, bringing to the table many issues (e.g., tuition policy and affirmative action) that reflect fundamental political convictions. The size and impact of the contemporary university on its community, its region, and the nation itself can place the president at ground zero on major political controversies.

The political role of the president is particularly important in public universities. These institutions are not only dependent on public tax dollars for support but are subject to a complex array of government regulations and relationships at the local, state, and federal level, most of which tend to be highly reactive and resistant to change. By their very nature, public universities can become caldrons of boiling political controversy. From their governing boards (usually determined by either gubernatorial appointment or popular election) to the contentious nature of academic politics, student unrest, or strident attacks by the press, public university presidencies are subject to political stresses more intense than those in other arenas of higher education.

GROWING UP IN A ROUGH NEIGHBORHOOD

The University of Michigan, highlighted for its free and liberal spirit during its early years, has a long tradition of political activism on the part of its students, faculty, and alumni. Student concerns on and extending beyond the university's campus have frequently not only addressed but influenced major national issues, such as the Vietnam War, the environmental movement, and civil rights.

While Ann Arbor may be a small midwestern community, the university itself has always had more of the hard edge characterizing the urban centers of the Northeast. Sports fans might suggest that this flows naturally from Michigan's reputation in violent sports, such as football. Actually, it has evolved as a defensive mechanism to protect the university against the reality of its harsh political environment. In a sense, the University of Michigan grew up in a rough neighborhood and had to become lean and mean and capable of looking out for itself. Michigan is a state characterized by confrontational politics. It was long dominated by the automobile industry, which meant big companies, big labor unions, and big state government. During the last half of the twentieth century, as the state's economy and population faced the challenges and hardships driven by global competition and poverty in its industrial cities, this political atmosphere has become more strident, with organized labor fighting to retain its control of the Democratic Party, while the conservative communities of western Michigan, dominated by the religious Right, now control the Republican Party.

In many ways, Ann Arbor was an oasis, a liberal eastern community planted in the center of a tough midwestern state. It did not help the university that the politics of the city of Ann Arbor suffered a hangover from the protest days of the 1960s. The community continues to this day to mark its history of civil disobedience by celebrating each April 1 with the annual Hash Bash, where thousands come to promote and experience the evil weed, uninhibited by Ann Arbor's liberal laws governing the possession of marijuana.

Despite the changing nature of its economic and politics, the state of Michigan still has very much a blue-collar mentality today. This is perhaps best illustrated by a comment made to me by a senior executive of General Motors during my years as dean of the College of Engineering: "As long as we can put a car on the showroom floor for fewer dollars per pound than anybody else, we will dominate the global marketplace!" Of course, the Japanese demonstrated convincingly that people no longer buy cars by the pound—they choose quality instead. Similarly, in the global, knowledge-driven economy of the twenty-first century, it is the quality of a workforce that counts, as evidenced by the increasing tendency of American companies to outsource—rather, "offshore," in contemporary language—not only unskilled labor but high-skill activities, such as software engineering. Yet, higher education in Michigan tends to be treated at best with benign neglect and at worst as a convenient political whipping boy.

Much of the University of Michigan's political challenge was stimulated by its very success as one of the nation's leading research universities. Its aspirations for excellence were frequently met by state government and the public at large with the questions "Excellence for whom?" and "Excellence for what purpose?"—the assumption being that excellence really meant an elitism that would exclude their constituents. Furthermore, as one of the largest and most prominent universities in the nation, Michigan was frequently targeted by those in the federal government hoping to use it as a lynchpin for driving broader change in higher education. Since the university operates one of the nation's largest and financially most successful university medical centers, it was understandable that Michigan would be the target for federal efforts to reduce health care reimbursement and funding for medical training. The university's national leadership in sponsored research also made it an attractive target for the same congressional investigations that trampled Stanford in the early 1990s, ironically led by Michigan's own congressman John Dingle. However, unlike Stanford, Michigan was prepared and immediately responded to the congressional attack, not only with a strong public defense led by alumnus Mike Wallace, but also through back-channel conversations with the congressman, which successfully deflected the attack.[2]

There were other factors that frequently placed the university in the political bull's-eye. The success and visibility of the university's athletic programs—particularly its football team—made the university a primary target for the enforcement of gender equity through Title IX of the Education Amendments Act in the 1970s. As the largest employer in Ann Arbor, with vast assets in the billions of dollars, it was also natural that Michigan would become a popular target of litigation on almost every issue imaginable from those plaintiffs and lawyers who were hoping that the institution's deep pockets would lead to a quick settlement, regardless of the merits of the case.

Giving the university even more prominence were its institutional saga—to quote James Angell, "an uncommon education for the common man"—and its success in leading the struggle for campus diversity through such efforts as the Michigan Mandate, which doubled minority student and faculty representation on campus during the early 1990s. Hence, it was not surprising that the institution would become a target for conservative groups seeking to challenge and roll back affirmative action policies in college admissions, an effort that would lead to the important Supreme Court decision of 2003 and later in 2006 to a referendum amending the state constitution to ban affirmative action in Michigan.

As the point person on controversial issues in higher education, the president of a university is frequently placed under a political microscope by politicians, the press, and the university community itself. Of course, all presidents have certain political preferences on most issues, but it is extremely important to keep these carefully veiled. However, in contrast to many skillful public leaders who, like a chameleon, are able to change their political colors depending on the situation, I took a more honest, if occasionally perplexing, approach. During my early tenure, the Michigan governor (James Blanchard) was a Democrat, and the U.S. presidents (Ronald Reagan and George Bush) were Republicans. During my later years as president, this situation was completely reversed, with a Republican governor (John Engler) and a Democratic president (Bill Clinton). As UM president and as chair of the National Science Board, I participated in both state and national arenas, so I had to be very careful not to get caught in a political crossfire.

On occasion, I suffered the usual problems of public leaders by getting mislabeled as in one political camp or the other. The Democrats believed that since I was a friend of Governor Engler and a White House appointee of Presidents Reagan and Bush, I must surely be a Republican. The Republicans viewed my stances in support of diversity and gay rights as telltale signs of a Democrat. My true political background and beliefs were far more complex. I had been raised as a dyed-in-the-wool Missouri Democrat in the tradition of Harry Truman. My mother was a long-standing chairperson of the Democratic Party of Carroll County, Missouri, and my sister was the producer of the conservative viewpoint used on WGBH's program *The Advocates.* I grew up a fan of Kennedy and McCarthy. Yet I developed an independent streak in the 1960s and 1970s. I generally stayed in the middle of the road, almost always voting a split ticket. In fact, a Progressive at heart, I would probably be most comfortable as a member of Teddy Roosevelt's Bull Moose Party. In reality, I was simply not a political partisan. Nor was I politically impaired, as was suggested by some of my more political colleagues. Rather, I held a more complex set of values than the terms *liberal* or *conservative* would tolerate, values that would manifest themselves on a case-by-case basis during my presidency. With this confession now on the record, let me move on to consider the political leadership of the university president.

DEFENDING THE UNIVERSITY

One of the most important roles of the president is to protect the university from hostile political forces, both internal and external, that could cause it great harm. At the beginning of each academic year, my Michigan leadership team of executive officers would meet together for a risk-assessment session, to predict the most significant political threats to the university and develop strategies for its defense. We actually developed a threat chart identifying the greatest concerns for the year ahead. At the top of the chart would usually be the governor, since whether by opportunistic intent or just neglect, this state leader was frequently the source of many of the woes facing higher education in the state. Close behind was the state legislature, dominated during my tenure by graduates of Michigan State University, who took great delight in thrashing that arrogant institution in Ann Arbor. Washington also posed an ongoing threat, usually through the meddling of federal agencies or congressional action. There were times when even members of our own Michigan congressional delegation would make the list—for example, when manipulated by their staff into taking positions hostile to the university in order to win political influence or visibility at the national level.

Next on the chart would be the media, particularly the hometown newspapers—which in Michigan's case included not only the *Ann Arbor News* but also the Detroit papers. While most hometown newspaper editors soon realize that university controversies stimulate public interest and advertising sales, the Ann Arbor paper occasionally was led by people who actually carried a chip on their shoulders about the university—perhaps because Michigan was perceived as elitist and arrogant, because of rocky town-gown relations, or even because we refused to invest heavily in building degree programs in journalism (flames occasionally fanned by several of our own faculty members). We usually did not bother listing the student newspaper, the *Michigan Daily,* as a major threat, since it tended to be more preoccupied with college sports or student causes, such as disciplinary policies.

We never included any students, faculty, or staff on our threat chart. We realized that student activism, while occasionally annoying to administrators, was nevertheless an important and positive element of the Michigan saga. To be sure, Michigan had its share of outspoken students and faculty members, some enjoying the spotlight of campus politics, some content as squeaky wheels pushing one personal agenda or another, and some speaking out on issues of considerable importance to the institution or broader society. But generally we regarded this as a normal—indeed, desirable—characteristic of a campus with an activist tradition. We preferred to not only tolerate but actually encourage such behavior, even when, in one case, it led to the Supreme Court case on affirmative action. Although we occasionally had outspoken staff members as well, particularly on union issues, most staff were intensely loyal university citizens whom we viewed as strong allies rather than threats.

We did include on our threat chart an occasional member of our board of regents. We viewed most members of the board as conscientious public servants, basically supportive of the university, although some had their particular hang-ups, such as football, campus architecture, or student rights. However, we always had one or two regents who were renegades, frequently seizing on opportunities to embarrass or even disrupt the university to promote their personal visibility and political agenda.

Finally, there was the usual array of special interest groups (some on campus, some off) inclined to use the university as a convenient and highly visible target to further their particular cause. Here, the list was very long and ever changing. It spanned the political spectrum from the Marxist Left to the Genghis Khan Right.

State Relations

Public university presidents play important political roles in managing their universities' relationships with state government. The relationship between public universities and state government is complex and varies significantly from state to state. Some universities are structurally organized as components of state government, subject to the same hiring and business practices characterizing other state agencies. Others possess a certain autonomy from state government through constitutional provision or statute. All are influenced by the power of the public purse—by the nature and degree of state support.

Although the University of Michigan faced many of the challenges experienced by other state universities (inadequate state appropriations, intrusive sunshine laws, overregulation, politically motivated competition among state institutions, and a politically determined governing board), two characteristics of our relationship with the state were quite unique. First, as I noted in chapter 1, the university was given unusual autonomy in the state constitution, autonomy comparable to that of the legislature, government, and judiciary. While it was certainly subject to state funding decisions and regulations, the university's board of regents possessed exceptionally strong constitutionally derived powers over all academic activities of the institution. Second, because of the university's autonomy and its long history (first as a territorial institution and then later, in effect, as a national—and today, one might argue, world—university), it was determined to do whatever was necessary to protect both the quality of and access to its academic programs and its service to these broader constituencies.

In particular, the university refused to allow the quality of its academic programs to be determined by state appropriations, which were usually insufficient to support a world-class institution. Instead, it developed an array of alternative resources to supplement state support, including student tuition, federal research support, private giving, and auxiliary activities (e.g., clinical care). Furthermore, it used its constitutional autonomy to defend its commitment to serving a diverse population, reaching out not only to underserved minority communities but also to students from across the nation and around the world. While this philosophy of independence was key to the quality of the university and its ability to serve not simply the people of the state but those of the nation and the world, it did not always endear the university to state government, which tended to equate the university's independence with arrogance.

Political winds tend to shift over time, and this was certainly the case for the political fortunes of the University of Michigan. For its first century, the university enjoyed a privileged position. Many of its alumni were in the state legislature and in key positions in government and communities across the state. Political parties were disciplined, and special interests had not yet splintered party solidarity. In that environment, the university had little need to cultivate public understanding or grassroots support. A few leaders from the university met each year with the governor and leaders of the legislature to negotiate our appropriation. That was it. The university was valued and appreciated. A historic and intense public commitment to the support of public higher education characterized the founders of the University of Michigan and the generations of immigrants who followed, sacrificing to provide quality public education as the key to their children's future.

This situation changed dramatically in the 1950s and 1960s, because of the aggressive ambition of the other state colleges and universities and the laid-back and occasionally arrogant attitude of the University of Michigan. In the early 1950s, Michigan State's legendary president John Hannah transformed that institution from an agricultural college into a major university, relying on both his own political skill and UM's missteps. Hannah began, ironically enough, with football, by maneuvering Michigan State into the opening left by the University of Chicago's departure from big-time football and the Big Ten Conference. With this visibility, he then persuaded the state legislature to change the name from Michigan Agricultural College and later Michigan State College to Michigan State University, later adding professional schools such as medicine. The University of Michigan adamantly and unsuccessfully opposed each of these steps, finally attempting to save face by capitalizing the word *The* in its own name.[3] These unsuccessful battles firmly established UM's reputation in Lansing for arrogance (as in, "those arrogant asses from Ann Arbor").

A story contrasting the styles of the presidents of the two universities at the time illustrates the challenge. UM's president, Harlan Hatcher, a tall and distinguished English scholar, used to travel to Lansing to meet with legislators in his chauffeur-driven Lincoln. John Hannah, in shirtsleeves, would drive himself over in his Ford pickup to make the case to legislators more typically from farm country than big-city Detroit. A second story about Hannah is of interest here. During the 1950s and 1960s, the Michigan State campus was pockmarked with construction projects. The legend was that Hannah would get funds from the legislature for a single building, use the funds to dig the foundations of several more buildings, and then turn to the legislature for the funds to fill all those holes in the ground with new buildings.

A longtime leader of the state legislature portrayed the University of Michigan during this period of its history as a university led by a distinguished but conservative president and by moneyed Republican regents determined to hang onto the past. These leaders were surprised when the state legislature not only labeled Michigan as arrogant but actually took great delight in disadvantaging it relative to other public universities. The student protests on campus during the 1960s provided even more ammunition to those who wanted to attack Michigan for political reasons. The university entered the 1970s with both a bruised ego and a damaged reputation—at least in Lansing.

Slowly the university began to realize that the world had changed and that it no longer had monopoly on state support. The state was in the midst of a profound economic transformation that was driving change in the political environment. Political parties declined in influence. Special interest constituencies proliferated and organized to make their needs known and their influence felt. Even as the university became more central in responding to the needs of the state, it was also held more accountable to its many publics. Compounding the complexity of this situation was a growing socioeconomic shift in priorities at both the state and federal level. In Michigan, as in many other states, priorities shifted from investment in the future through strong support of education to a shorter-term focus, as represented by the growing expenditures for prisons, social services, and federal mandates (e.g., Medicaid), even as a conservative administration cut taxes in the 1990s. This was compounded by legislation that earmarked a portion of the state budget for K–12 education, leaving higher education to compete with corrections and social services for limited discretionary tax dollars. As a result, the state's support for higher education declined rapidly in real terms during the early 1980s and continued to drop, relative to inflation, throughout the remainder of the decade.

As an interim strategy, Michigan lowered its sights from hogging the entire trough to simply trying to stay even with Michigan State. But even this proved to be a formidable challenge, with Michigan

State alumni as governors (James Blanchard and John Engler) in the 1980s and 1990s. Although the University of Michigan at least managed to avoid being low man on the totem pole during the latter part of the 1970s, the university's Replacement Hospital Project exhausted the state's discretionary capacity to fund higher education capital facilities. The cupboard was bare.

The 1980s began with a deep national recession—read "depression" in Michigan, since when the nation gets a cold, Michigan catches pneumonia because of the sensitivity of the automobile industry to the national economy. Although the University of Michigan was not singled out for abuse, it suffered greatly along with the rest of higher education. It also faced an unusual alignment of the political planets when legislative champions for Michigan State University and Wayne State University assumed the chairs of the key higher education appropriation committees, along with a two-decade long succession of Michigan State alumni as governors.

There were many theories about what was actually happening. Despite the fact that the state's governors paid lip service to the unique role of the University of Michigan as the state's flagship university, none lifted a finger to help the university if political capital were at stake. As William Hubbard, former UM dean of medicine and Upjohn CEO, put it, the state was cursed with an extreme intolerance of extraordinary excellence. It was certainly true that an angry strain of populism ran throughout the state. One key legislator summarized the situation to me: "It is no longer possible for a kid like me to go to the University of Michigan. The university's prospects in Lansing are at a low point. The Senate is controlled by MSU Republicans more interested in agriculture and boosting their alma mater. The Democrats are simply not very effective, dominated by the Detroit Black Caucus. The key legislators are simply no longer swayed by public pressure. They cannot be intimidated, since they cannot be beaten in their districts."[4]

With fewer and fewer Michigan graduates in influential positions in state government, it was questionable whether a traditional approach to lobbying legislators would be effective. There were those who believed that UM bashing had become a popular sport in Lansing because the university no longer had allies with sufficient power or commitment to threaten retaliation. The university was drifting politically without a plan of attack or even an effective defense. Another Lansing observer put it this way: "Michigan is big, vulnerable, and doesn't dance very well!"

Actually, the 1980s started off a bit more positively for the university, when the new Blanchard administration made a special effort to recognize the impact of the research universities on the state's economy through the Research Excellence Fund, a special $30 million annual appropriation for campus-based research. As dean of the College of Engineering, I was able to help shape this legislation so that roughly $11 million of this annual appropriation flowed to the university. But this effort to differentiate among institutions and mission soon ran afoul of Lansing politics, and eventually the special funding for research disappeared. Blanchard's second term became a disaster for higher education when he realized, through polling, that he could get more votes by attacking the rising tuition levels of public universities—a consequence of inadequate state support—than investing in their capacity. State funding for higher education dropped from 12 percent to less than 8 percent of the state's budget during the decade. Even more dramatically, the state of Michigan fell into the bottom quartile in its support of higher education, dropping as low as forty-fifth in the nation at one point.

In summary, during the last half of the twentieth century, the University of Michigan's political influence in Lansing plummeted. Although changing external factors—such as the rise of populism, changing demographics, and the rise of the religious Right in western Michigan—were key factors, the university's presidents had been largely ineffective in reversing the situation since the 1940s. Ruthven's declining health prevented his active role in Lansing. Hatcher was effective with moneyed Republicans, but he was a poor match for John Hannah's shirtsleeve approach. Fleming relied heavily on others, keeping his powder dry for the periodic crises erupting on the campus during the volatile protest years of the 1960s and 1970s. Shapiro was dedicated and tireless, but the sharp mismatch of his thoughtful style with the crude populism and paranoia of the legislature was simply too great.

The key factor allowing the university to sustain its quality during this difficult period was its constitutional autonomy. Relying heavily on this autonomy to control its own destiny, the university began to increase both its tuition and its nonresident enrollments, to compensate for the loss of state support. Yet even the constitutional autonomy of the university faced formidable challenges from legislative efforts to control admissions, gubernatorial efforts to freeze tuition, and even media efforts (carried out under the guise of the state's sunshine laws) to control everything from presidential searches to regental elections.

This was the challenging political environment I faced when I became provost and then president in the late 1980s. Fortunately, I also inherited a top-notch state-relations team with experience on both sides of the aisle.[5] Although we soon reaffirmed the pragmatic conclusion of our predecessors that it was unlikely that the university would ever again benefit from its flagship status in Lansing, we also realized that we were destined to continue to lose in state politics as long as we stayed on the defensive, simply reacting to whatever trumped-up charge—concerning out-of-state enrollments, high tuition, racism on campus, and so on—that our enemies used to disadvantage us with respect to other state universities.

To test our assumptions, we decided to conduct a reality check with a number of the state's political and corporate leaders. Each was asked to challenge two assumptions about the future of state and university relations. The first was that because of the state's limited will and capacity to support higher education and due to a weakened economy and other social needs, the state would, at best, be able to support higher education at the level of a regional four-year college—not at the level of a world-class research university. The second assumption was that political pressures would make it increasingly difficult for state leaders to give priority to state support for flagship institutions and that, instead, strong political forces would drive a leveling process in which state appropriations per student would equalize across all state universities.

In the end, few of the leaders disagreed with our premises. Furthermore, all believed that the university's only prudent course was to assume that state support would continue to deteriorate throughout the 1990s. Consistent with the university's long-standing philosophy of refusing to let the state control our quality, first Harold Shapiro and then I embarked on a new strategy: (1) to build alternative revenue streams (tuition, federal grants and contracts, auxiliary enterprises, and private giving) to levels sufficient to compensate for the loss in state support; (2) to deploy our resources far more effectively than the university had done in the past, by focusing on quality at the possible expense of breadth and capacity, while striving to improve efficiency and productivity; and (3) to enhance the university's ability to control its own destiny, by defending our constitutional autonomy, building strong political support for our independence, and strengthening the quality of the university's board of regents.

We were well aware that the University of Michigan was a creature of the state constitution and was unlikely ever to separate itself from this constraint. Yet the political realities of the past several decades had shifted the university's Lansing strategy from offense (e.g., maximizing state support) to defense (i.e., minimizing the damage to the university from state government). We chose a different and more aggressive strategy: to move toward operating more like a private institution, while becoming less dependent on the state.

Associated with this increasingly pragmatic view of the future of the university as a public institution was a recognition that we should abandon strategies to advantage ourselves over other Michigan universities and instead direct our efforts to increasing the general state support for all of higher education, adopting the philosophy that a rising tide raises all boats. In the process, we also began to realize that we simply did not have a sophisticated capability for marketing and outreach. Hence, I began to spend much of my time as president during the early 1990s leading the presidents of Michigan's public universities in a series of political and public relations efforts throughout the state to make the case for enhanced support of higher education. Key in this effort at civic education was knitting together the interests of the state's universities through the Presidents' Council of State Universities of Michigan (PCSUM), which I chaired during the early 1990s.

Yet this remarkably effective spirit of cooperation was broken when new leadership at Michigan State University persuaded a new governor, who just happened to be an MSU alumnus, to disrupt the long-standing balance in appropriations among UM, MSU, and

Wayne State University to advantage his alma mater. Fortunately, the Wayne State president, David Adamany, and I were able to counter this with a treetops strategy and activate the influence of alumni and media throughout the state. In the end, we managed to block the MSU effort, but the strong spirit of cooperation among Michigan's public universities had been replaced by a conflict and discord that would last a decade in the state's higher education system.

These events provide an important case study of the impact—both positive and negative—that a state governor can have on public higher education. The deterioration in state support of the University of Michigan ironically began under a moderate Republican governor, William Milliken. Although in principle quite supportive of the University of Michigan as the state's flagship university (and a Yale graduate himself), Milliken refused to support the tax increases necessary to plug a hole in the state budget resulting from the deep recession of the late 1970s, thereby necessitating deep cuts in state appropriations for higher education. His Democratic successor, James Blanchard, was also quite supportive of higher education at first, but he soon became convinced by staff that he could win more votes by attacking the tuition charged by universities than by providing adequate state appropriations. Although Blanchard, an MSU alumnus, did not play favorites among state institutions, the adversarial approach taken by his staff toward higher education soon turned the universities against him.

Blanchard was succeeded by a moderate Republican governor, John Engler, who, while supportive of higher education, adopted a conservative financial policy based on tax cuts that allowed only inflationary growth in appropriations, rather than restoring earlier cuts to higher education during a boom period in the state's economy. His policy led to a structural imbalance in the state budget that triggered catastrophic cuts during the recession in the next decade. More serious, however, was Engler's willingness to join in a blatant effort to advantage his alma mater over the state's other universities. In the long run, this probably had more damaging impact on higher education than the actions of any other Michigan governor in modern times, because it destroyed a long-standing spirit of cooperation among the state's universities.

University presidents are responsible for building and sustaining favorable relationships with state governments. But in the end, they must play the hand they are dealt. They face few opportunities and many challenges when forced to deal with inattentive governors and term-limited legislatures.

Federal Government

Although the United States leaves most of the responsibility for higher education to the states and the private sector, the federal government does have a considerable influence on higher education, both through federal policies in such areas as student financial aid and through the direct support of such campus activities as research and health care. In fact, some people maintain that the most transformative changes in American higher education have usually been triggered by federal actions, such as the Land-Grant Acts of the nineteenth century, the GI Bill and government-university research partnership (resulting from Vannevar Bush's famous report "Science: The Endless Frontier") following World War II, and the Higher Education Acts of the 1960s.

As Washington became convinced that higher education was important to the future of the nation in the decades after World War II, the federal government began to provide funding to colleges and universities in support of research, housing, student financial aid, and key professional programs, such as medicine and engineering. Yet, with significant federal support came massive federal bureaucracy. Universities were forced to build large administrative organizations just to interact with the large administrative bureaucracies in Washington. Federal rules and regulations snared universities in a web of red tape that not only constrained their activities but became important cost drivers. Universities were frequently whipsawed about by unpredictable changes in Washington's stance toward higher education as the political winds shifted direction each election year.

With increasing involvement of the federal government in the affairs of higher education came additional responsibilities for the university president. Just as the presidents of state universities were expected to take the lead in relationships with governors and state legislatures, the presidents of major research universities became familiar figures in Washington. The University of Michigan joined many other universities in establishing well-staffed offices near Capitol Hill. Others retained professional lobbyists to advance (and protect) the interests of their institutions in such areas as student financial aid, federal research priorities, and health care financing. The national associations of universities—such as the American Council on Education, the Association of American Universities, and the National Association of State Universities and Land-Grant Colleges (known collectively as the "One Dupont Circle group" because of their location in Washington)—became, in effect, lobbying organizations on behalf of the interests of their universities.

As leader of one of the nation's leading research universities, Michigan's president should—indeed, must—be highly visible on the national stage, promoting higher education. So, too, with one of the nation's largest academic health centers, UM presidents have been heavily involved in federal health care policy. In my own case, service for over a decade as a member and then chair of the National Science Board and then as a member of the National Academies provided an important platform for advancing the interests of the nation's research universities.

With over eight thousand graduates living and working in the Washington area during the 1990s, Michigan's alumni network was a particularly powerful one, reaching into Congress, the administration, and even the White House itself—including, of course, former U.S. president Gerald R. Ford. Furthermore, the state of Michigan had very considerable influence in Congress, including four powerful "cardinals" as chairs of key congressional committees during the 1980s and early 1990s: John Dingell, William Ford, John Conyers, and Robert Carr. Yet the university also faced some unusual challenges in Washington. Although the Michigan congressional delegation was powerful, it rarely used its influence to attract resources to the state, leading to the ironic situation in which Michigan usually ranked last among the states in the return of federal tax dollars. Instead, their power was used to protect the interests of Michigan's principal industry, Big Auto (and, of course, Big Labor), from federal intrusion into such matters as automobile emissions, safety standards, and labor legislation. The one important exception was Michigan congressman William Ford, chair of the House Education and Labor Committee, who was an important force in the periodic reauthorization of the Higher Education Act. The university worked closely with Ford on such important national issues as the establishment of a direct student lending program designed to reduce the costs of federal loans to college students.

During my years as president, my leadership team substantially increased the university's presence in Washington by establishing a permanent office on Capital Hill, significantly expanding our federal relations staff, and mobilizing our extensive army of alumni in the Washington area. We strongly encouraged university faculty members to become actively involved in federal policy activities, and we provided politically active faculty with support through our Washington office and federal relations team. Perhaps most important, however, was our acceptance of a major role in acting on behalf of all of higher education on important issues ranging from research policy to student financial aid to health care to diversity. We encouraged our federal relations team to work closely with the various national higher education associations. This spirit of building alliances was very similar to that we had employed in our state-relations efforts, since we realized that the interests of the University of Michigan were best served when we helped advance the interests of all of higher education.

Yet while we looked for opportunities to benefit higher education, our basic federal strategy was more defensive than offensive. Unlike many other universities, we refused to use political influence to go after legislative earmarks that bypassed and undermined the peer review process. Instead, we closely monitored potential federal legislation and actions that might harm our efforts, a continuing challenge with the never-ending expansion of complex federal regulations in such areas as research policy, occupation safety, environmental impact, tax policy, and equal opportunity, as well as the confusing and frequently intrusive federal regulations aimed at higher education.

Community Relations

The relationship between a university and its surrounding community is usually a complex one, particularly in cities dominated by major universities—such as Madison, Berkeley, Austin, Chapel Hill, and Ann Arbor. Although town and gown are linked together with intertwined destinies, there is nevertheless always a tension between the two. On the plus side is the fact that the university provides the community with an extraordinary quality of life. It stimulates strong primary and secondary schools, provides rich cultural opportunities, and generates an exciting and cosmopolitan community. The income generated by the university insulates these communities from the economic roller coaster faced by most other cities. Without such universities, these cities would be like any other small towns in America; with them, they become exciting, cosmopolitan, richly diverse, and wonderful places to live and work. But there are also drawbacks. The impact of these universities—whether through parking, crowds, or student behavior—can create inevitable tensions between town and gown. Members of the city community who are not directly associated with the university are sometimes viewed as outsiders in the life of both the university and the city.

Since my wife, Anne, and I had been members of the Ann Arbor community for two decades before assuming the role as president, we saw this town-gown relationship from two sides. While we understood well the university's interests, we also had experienced frustration with the occasional negative impact of the university—rising property taxes as the university took more property off the tax rolls, traffic and parking congestion, student disruptions, and a frequent university attitude of insensitivity and even arrogance concerning city issues. Unfortunately, the contentious nature of Ann Arbor city politics, aggravated by an Open Meetings Act that required the televising of all meetings of government bodies (e.g., the city council or the school board), made interactions with city officials very difficult. Hence, we instead formed an informal group of community leaders, drawn primarily from the private sector, with whom the executive officers could meet monthly on a private basis. We also developed quite good relations with the mayors of the city, who not infrequently had strong university ties.[6]

Although this informal process did little to satisfy the appetite of the local media and City Council, it did provide a very productive mechanism for discussing important strategic issues facing the city and the university. It led to a genuine effort to strengthen relationships between the leadership of the university, the city government, and the local business community. It also established important informal channels of communication, so that neither town nor gown was taken off guard in important decisions. However, we were not successful in many of these efforts, since the barrier of local politics was sometimes too difficult to overcome.

Public Relations

The public's perception of higher education is ever changing. Public opinion surveys reveal that at the most general level, the public strongly supports high-quality education in our colleges and universities.[7] Surveys of leaders in the public and private sector believe that the United States continues to have the strongest higher education system in the world, a fact they believe to be of vital importance to our nation's future.[8] They believe it essential that higher education remain accessible to every qualified and motivated student, but they also remain convinced that the vast majority of these students can still get a college education if they want it. However, when one probes public attitudes more deeply, many concerns about cost, student behavior (alcohol, drugs, political activism), and intercollegiate athletics appear. There is a growing concern that too many students entering our universities are not sufficiently prepared academically to benefit from a college education.

Public universities have an obligation to communicate with the people who support us—to be open and accessible. People want to know what we are doing, where we are going. We have an obligation to be forthcoming. But here we face several major challenges. First, we have to be honest in admitting that communication with the public, especially via the press, does not always come easily to academics. We are not always comfortable when we try to reach a broader audience. We speak a highly specialized and more exacting language among ourselves, and it can be difficult to explain ourselves to others. But we need to communicate to the public to explain our mission, to convey the findings of our research, to share our learning.

Second, as I noted earlier, the public's perception of the nature and role of the modern university is inconsistent with reality. To be sure, we remain a place where one sends the kids off to college. Such concerns as cost, student behavior, athletics, and political correctness are real and of concern to us just as they are to the public. But the missions and the issues characterizing the contemporary university are far more complex than the media tends to portray them.

One of the curses of the American public is our willingness to embrace the simplest possible solutions to the most complex of problems. Higher education is certainly an example. People seem eager to believe that our system of higher education—still the envy of the world—is wasteful, inefficient, and ineffective and that its leaders are intent only on protecting their perquisites and privileges. Public university presidents recognize there is a very simple formula for popularity with the public:

1. Freeze tuition and faculty salaries
2. Support populist agendas, such as sunshine laws
3. Limit the enrollment of out-of-state students
4. Sustain the status quo at all costs
5. Win at football

But most university leaders also recognize this as a Faustian bargain, since it would also put their institutions at great risk with respect to academic program quality, diversity, and their capacity to serve society.

The Media

One of the facts of the modern university president's life is the public nature of position and the role of the press. This poses a particular challenge in a public university, subject to intrusive sunshine laws that can be used by determined reporters to pry into every aspect of the institution's operation and the private lives of its leaders. It is also a greater challenge when the university is located in a small city, where there is little other news.

In earlier times, the relationship between the university and the press was one of mutual trust and respect. Given the many values common to both the profession of journalism and the academy, journalists, faculty, and academic leaders related well to one another. The press understood the importance of the university, accepted its need for some degree of autonomy similar to its own First Amendment freedoms, and frequently worked to build public understanding and support for higher education.

In today's world, where all societal institutions have come under greater scrutiny by the media, universities prove to be no exception. Part of this is no doubt due to an increasingly adversarial approach taken by journalists toward all of society, embracing a certain distrust of everything and everyone as a necessary component of investigative journalism. Partly to blame is the arrogance of many members of the academy, university leaders among them, in assuming that the university is somehow less accountable to society than are other social institutions. But the shift in the media's approach is also due in part to the increasingly market-driven nature of contemporary journalism, as it merges with or is acquired by the entertainment industry and trades off journalistic values and integrity for market share and quarterly earnings statements.

Rare indeed is the newspaper that assigns high priority to covering higher education. Even in college towns, the local papers assign far more resources to covering athletics than to reporting on academics. While it is certainly true that the academy does not understand how the press operates, it is equally true that the press is remarkably ignorant of the major issues facing higher education.

Whether the local press is supportive or hostile depends most sensitively on the persuasion of the editor, who determines not only the editorial position of the paper but also which reporters are assigned to cover the higher education beat. For the first few years of my administration, we experienced relatively positive or at least benign treatment in the local papers. Looking back over press clippings, I was quite amazed to find a number of very positive editorials commending the university's actions or positions on most issues. However, eventually the local editor reached the conclusion of his predecessors: university controversy in a community dominated by a large university stirs up interest, sells papers, and, most significant, sells advertising. Hence a junkyard-dog reporter was assigned to cover the university and stir things up, and life became considerably more difficult.

THE LOYAL (AND SOMETIMES NOT SO LOYAL) OPPOSITION

Of course, the political role of the president is not confined to external constituencies, such as state and federal government, the public, or the media. With various internal constituencies (students, faculty, staff, trustees) and special interest groups always jockeying for position, university campuses can become political tempests. Although university presidents generally have relatively little influence over the university's political culture or political issues, they frequently receive demands to take one side or another, to make a statement, or to take action. At the very least, they are expected to manage the political battles, to prevent the intrusion of outside forces (e.g., government), and to create—as best they can—a level playing field for the debate over contentious issues. Throughout this effort, presidents are also expected to protect the interests, the values, and the reputation of the university.

For the most part, campus-based political activities are not only highly constructive but also can become important elements of the educational process. They represent one of the most important roles of the university in America, to challenge the status quo in a setting that allows free and thoughtful debate. Furthermore, most participants in these activities are well intentioned, if frequently quite passionate about their concerns. Faculty members voicing concerns about university policies or broader social issues are usually not only well informed but thoughtful and creative, willing to listen to and consider other points of view, even as they make persuasive arguments for their own views. Although students are frequently ill informed about particular issues (e.g., student disciplinary policies or campus safety), they are largely sincere in their beliefs—even though, in many cases, they have not learned yet the importance of allowing all sides of an issue to be heard.

Several examples of constructive campus-based debate during my tenure come to mind. The Supreme Court case that challenged the university's use of race as a factor in student admissions was stimulated by a long-standing Michigan faculty member, Carl Cohen, who passionately believed that in a truly diverse and egalitarian society, race simply should not be used as a factor in any decision. Cohen was also deeply loyal to the university, and although his opposition to university affirmative action policies triggered a national debate and expensive litigation, it was an important issue that deserved this attention. Although I disagreed strongly with Cohen's stance, we respected one another, and I actually encouraged this debate.

So, too, students who were passionate about particular issues were usually well intentioned and believed they were fighting on behalf of just causes. Students were the primary driving force and energy behind the Michigan Mandate, the university's massive effort to diversify its campus and extend educational opportunity to underserved populations. If students had not taken to the battlements on issues involving racial justice and tolerance on the campus, it is quite unlikely that the university would have moved as vigorously or successfully to equate social diversity with academic excellence. To be sure, there were times when the most contentious students would take on causes that would have been highly questionable to outsiders, such as the long-standing effort to eliminate the university's student disciplinary policy ("the Code"). Sometimes even their student colleagues would dismiss such efforts as nonsense.

Yet, on any campus, there are always those with agendas who utilize political mechanisms to seek personal objectives. Sometimes this is healthy, such as on those occasions when students simply view campus politics as a personal stepping-stone toward a political career after graduation. What better place to learn how to be an effective politician than in the safe, secure, no-fault environment of a university campus. However, more sinister were those who sought to use politics for personal vendettas or political gain at the expense of the institution. The real danger comes from those who take advantage of the free, open, and tolerant culture of a university in order to advance their personal agendas, in full recognition that they are trampling over the values of the university and exploiting the good intentions of others in order to pursue their own perverse ends. In a sense, these mavericks become infectious diseases, poisoning the academic culture, which frequently is unable to identify their real motives, much less defend against them.

Particularly vulnerable to manipulation by malevolent purposes is elected faculty governance. While faculty governance at the level of academic departments and colleges continues to be both effective and essential for such academic matters as curriculum development, faculty hiring, and tenure evaluation, it is increasingly difficult to achieve true faculty participation in broader university matters through elected bodies, such as faculty senates, which are particularly vulnerable to takeover by single interest faculty groups. At Michigan, these faculty coups typically erupted from the Medical School, since its size (over 1,000 faculty), faculty stress level (due to heavy clinical loads), and top-down administrative culture frequently left disgruntled faculty members with little recourse but to look beyond the school itself to express their frustrations.

A second university component that is particularly vulnerable to political manipulation is the university's board of regents. Of course, every university governing board has its mavericks, members who are particularly outspoken with bizarre views, unusually self-serving, or occasionally even hostile to the university. This is particularly the case with public universities, since their governing board members are selected through a political process and usually come with particular political views. Most governing board members are able to set aside these political interests when the interests of the institution are at stake. However, there are always those who use their position on the board to push personal or political agendas despite the damage it could do to the university.

The Michigan governing board has always had its share of these mavericks—going back to the time of the first elected board, in which a particularly aggressive regent managed to take over the board as its chairman and then orchestrate a successful effort to fire the university's first president, Henry Tappan, despite the fact that Tappan was viewed as one of the most effective and visionary university leaders in the history of American higher education. What has made this fact of life particularly difficult to handle has been the small size of Michigan's board, since with only eight members, one curmudgeon can have very considerable influence. This brings me to the last and most sensitive political responsibility of the presidency: reporting to, working with, advising, educating, and shaping the agenda of the governing board of the university.

THE PRESIDENT AND THE GOVERNING BOARD

In a formal sense, at least, the relationship of a university president to the institution's governing board has some similarities with that between a CEO and a corporate board of directors. The board has the legal authority and fiduciary responsibility for the institution. It can make policy and hire and fire the president just like a corporate board. However, there is one major difference. In contrast to corporate board members selected for their experience and knowledge of business practices (as is now required by law, e.g., the Sarbanes-Oxley Act), many university board members have little understanding about what really goes on in a university, since they have never been in faculty roles. Moreover, Harold Shapiro has noted, "Despite much rhetoric to the contrary, members of the board generally show little sustained interest in the needs and aspirations of the members of the academic community, and vice versa." Hence, the role of a president, beyond that of leading the university's management team to implement the boards policies and directives, is to educate the board sufficiently that it becomes a positive force for the university. Furthermore, the president both represents the faculty to the governing board and similarly represents the board to the faculty. Again I quote Shapiro: "A key leadership challenge for the university president is to ensure that the governing board, in both public and private universities, comes to view the education and research programs of the university and the internal intellectual culture necessary to support these as providing a very valuable social product—one well worth considerable investment despite many risks."[9]

Here, it is important to state once again that most university governing board members—whether elected, appointed, or self-selected—are conscientious volunteers, strongly committed to the welfare of their university. Yet they are frequently caught in a system of governance that is increasingly incompatible with the growing complexity and importance of the contemporary university. The lay character of boards, their vulnerability to disruption by renegade members, and their lack of accountability can put the university at some risk.

Put in somewhat more colorful language, many public university presidents believe that their first responsibility is to protect the university from its governing board, to keep it focused on those areas of policies where it has both responsibility and educable expertise and away from dabbling in management, campus politics, labor contracts, and the football program. This challenge is made all the more difficult by the deeply ingrained practice of end-running that characterizes the creative anarchy of a university. Physicians treating governing board members will lobby about Medical Center issues. Most trustees enjoy the celebrity treatment provided by the Athletic Department and present a ready ear to the concerns of the coaches and the athletic director. Even the most political of trustees exhibits a thin skin when it comes to treatment in the local newspapers, either on campus or in the community. Of course, some are not above leaking confidential information in an effort to ingratiate themselves with the press. Some will use their position to feather their own nest, by exerting pressure to admit the children of friends or procure the best football tickets for business or political associates. Perhaps of most concern are those trustees who develop a messianic character, believing they are the chosen ones with the duty to keep the university on the straight and narrow path. Sometimes this tendency can characterize an entire governing board, which comes to believe it is more important than the institution it "serves"—a somewhat different concept than "governs," I admit.

Board discipline is a very important, yet delicate, process. Just as a chain is only as strong as its weakest link, a university governing board is only as good as its worst member—particularly in the case of the small, political boards characterizing public universities. The public antics of one regent are frequently viewed by the university community and beyond as reflecting the quality of the entire board. All too often, governing board members, like politicians everywhere, rush to defend their colleagues regardless of how reprehensible their behavior has been. It has always struck me as odd that boards will circle the wagons to defend even the most outrageous behavior of their board colleagues, apparently not realizing that by failing to discipline inappropriate behavior by their colleagues, they are perceived on the campus and beyond as accomplices in the transgression. The president and other officers of the university are put in an awkward position when a board ignores inappropriate behavior by one of its members, usually with the rationalization "Well, a trustee has to have some latitude."

The task of carrying bad tidings to the board should fall to the university secretary, who is responsible for maintaining both the activities and the relationships of the board. As is true of the secretary of a corporate board of directors, the role of a university secretary is absolutely critical and increasingly requires considerable expertise as well as skillful rapport (not to mention a thick skin). Presidents should beware of board secretaries who back away from the difficult relationships that sometimes arise between board members and faculty or administrators—or, far worse, who become more loyal to the board than the president, a situation that will likely lead to either the secretary's termination or the president's resignation.

Universities are very complex, and it takes even the most sophisticated governing board members years to begin to understand them, if ever. Hopefully the timescales for leadership within a governing board are sufficiently long that just as cream rises to the top, the more senior, respected, and knowledgeable board members will gradually move into roles where they can lead, influence, and educate their colleagues. Woe be to a president and university if senior board members disappear prematurely, leaving behind only inexperienced colleagues. Although this rarely happens with private governing boards (because of their process of self-selection), it is an all-too-frequent occurrence with public boards, due to political shifts triggered by a change in governor or electorate.

Many people believe that the deterioration in the quality of governing boards, the confusion concerning their roles, and the increasingly political nature of their activities pose a serious threat to the quality and reputation of higher education.[10] Beyond the dangers posed to their institutions, the burdens malcontent governing board members place on their presidents can be significant, including the amount of time required to accommodate the special interests of board members, the abuse presidents receive from board members with strong personal or political agendas, and the increasing tentativeness presidents exhibit because they never know whether their boards will support or attack them. While perhaps superficially reassuring government leaders, the media, and the public that greater oversight and accountability is being exercised, the long-term damage such rogue board members can cause to an institution are considerable and represent a very major challenge to effective presidential leadership and to their more conscientious colleagues on the governing board.

THE BROADER POLITICAL AGENDA OF THE UNIVERSITY AND THE UNIVERSITY PRESIDENCY

The university president is both responsible for and responsive to the myriad and diverse political relationships both external and internal to the university. For example, much of the attention of my administration at Michigan was directed at building far stronger relationships with the multitude of external and internal constituencies served by and supporting the university. Efforts were made to strengthen bonds with both state and federal government, ranging from systemic initiatives (e.g., opening and staffing new offices in Lansing and Washington) to developing personal relationships with key public leaders (e.g., the governor, the White House, Michigan's congressional delegation). A parallel effort was made to develop more effective relationships with the media at the local, state, and national level.

The challenges faced in establishing our relevance and credibility to this array of interests and at the same time sustaining our fundamental values and purposes were formidable. This balancing act faced serious problems: the diversity—indeed, incompatibility—of the values, needs, and expectations of these various constituencies who all view higher education through quite different lenses; the tension between such responsiveness and the university's role as a center of learning where all ideas can be freely questioned in light of reason; the increasing narrowness of the public's support for higher education—a "What have you done for me lately?" attitude—and an increasing sense of competitiveness with other interests and sectors and other urgent social needs for a decreasing pool of public and private dollars. Needless to say, balancing the university's relationships with these many different constituencies proves to be quite an acrobatic feat—a high-wire act, performed without a safety net. No matter how a university structures its external relations activities, the primary responsibilities eventually come to rest on the desk of the president. The management of this complex web of relationships requires clear goals, a carefully developed strategy, and an effective organizational structure.

Beyond the responsibility for managing the relationships of the university with a multitude of external and internal constituencies, university presidents also should play an important role as public figures who articulate and exemplify the values of higher education. This is particularly important during a period when higher education has become increasingly important to our society. In an increasingly knowledge-driven society, more and more people seek education as their hope for a better future—the key to good jobs and careers, to meaningful and fulfilling lives. The knowledge created on our campuses addresses many of the most urgent needs of society—for example, health care, national security, economic competitiveness, and environmental protection. The complexity of our world, the impact of technology, the insecurity of employment, and the uncertainty of our times have led all sectors of our society to identify education in general and higher education in particular as key to the future.

Yet in the midst of this growing importance—indeed, perhaps because of it—higher education has also become the focus of increasing concerns and criticism. Many see the contemporary university as big, self-centered, and even greedy, as it gouges parents with high tuition and inappropriately charges government for research. Some characterize our students as spoiled and badly behaved and our faculties as irresponsibly lazy. Our campuses are portrayed as citadels of intolerance, plagued by a long list of "isms"—racism, sexism, elitism, and extremism. Some have even charged us with an erosion of our most fundamental academic values, using as examples the faculty's lack of concern for undergraduate education, numerous well-publicized cases of scientific fraud or misconduct, and incidents of political correctness.

While there is certainly much that is refutable in many of these criticisms, it would be a mistake simply to dismiss them. They do represent the genuine concerns of the American public—albeit characterized by a great misunderstanding of what we are and what we do. They also contain a good deal of truth about us. Hence, the role of the university president is to listen carefully to these broader concerns and attempt to address them, both by participating in a broader effort of civic education and by leading internal efforts to better align the academy with public purpose and accountability.

Much of my tenure at Michigan was spent in such activities, working closely with other university presidents at the local, state, or national level to strengthen the relationship between higher education and the body politic. For example, the treetops effort to build a leadership network across the state of Michigan on behalf of higher education was largely driven by the University of Michigan's leadership. Working closely with various national organizations, such as the Association of American Universities and the American Council on Education, several of us worked to build the Science Coalition, comprised of leaders of American industry, to defend the nation's research efforts against the budget-slashing mentality triggered by the Gramm-Rudman Act of the 1980s. One of our most interesting efforts was to convince the presidents of the Big Ten universities that they should commit the free commercial time they received in broadcasting their NCAA football and basketball games to promoting the benefits of higher education rather than simply their own institutions. Here, the prominent Chicago advertising company Leo Burnett contributed a pro bono effort to help produce several quite stunning 60-second commercials highlighting the importance of higher education to the nation, an effort that pushed this important message into hundreds of millions of households.

Yet this last example also illustrates the challenges of persuading university presidents to commit time and effort beyond the interests of their own institutions, since as several of the Big Ten presidencies turned over, the new presidents soon reclaimed these valuable broadcasting minutes for promoting their own universities. More generally, while many university presidents provide important leadership for all of higher education, committing great time and effort, others look only for ways to advantage their own institutions, remaining aloof from such cooperative ventures. This insular tendency of some university presidents can be particularly damaging when it involves leading universities that have long been depended on to advance the cause of higher education.

THE HAZARDS OF POLITICAL LEADERSHIP

Today, many universities find that the most formidable forces controlling their destiny are political in nature. When you get right down to it, universities are victims of their own success. Our world has entered an era in which educated people and the ideas they produce have truly become the wealth of nations, and universities are clearly identified as the prime producers of that wealth. This central role means that more people today have a stake in higher education. More people want to harness it to their own ends. We have become more visible and more vulnerable as institutions. We attract more constituents and support, but we also attract more opponents.

There are many lessons to be learned from the experiences of my leadership team at Michigan. First among these is the importance of flexibility and agility in navigating through the ever-shifting winds of the political environment. The years of my presidency saw state government swing from a liberal Democratic governor and Democratically controlled legislature to a moderate Republican governor and a divided statehouse. This occurred at the same time that the opposite transition was occurring in Washington, from the Reagan White House and a Democratic Congress to the Clinton years, followed by the Newt-onian revolution (à la Gingrich) in Congress that led to Republican control. Each shift not only required rebuilding new relationships with new leaders and their staffs but accommodating the new philosophies that accompanied shifts in political stripes. Such transitions became even more frequent and complex with the introduction of term limits in many states (including Michigan).

Political earthquakes at the federal or state level also propagate strong tremors into public universities. New governors appoint or influence the nomination and election of new governing board members. Woe be to the president who has been too closely associated with the outgoing political powers, particularly in those states where the tradition has been to regard public universities as just another component of state government, subservient to the political party in power.

To some degree, the changing political environment of the university reflects a more fundamental shift from issue-oriented to image-dominated politics at all levels—federal, state, and local. Public opinion drives political contributions, and vice versa, and these determine successful candidates and eventually legislation. Policy is largely an aftermath exercise, since the agenda is really set by polling and political contributions. Issues, strategy, and the "vision thing" are largely left on the sidelines. Since higher education has never been particularly influential either in determining public opinion or in making campaign contributions, the university is left with only the option of reacting as best it can to the agenda set by others.

Political leadership is both challenging and hazardous to the university president. For some presidents, the concern about stepping on a political land mine becomes almost an obsession, always on their mind and always dominating their actions. Each time the president stands in harm's way, there is always a chance of a fatal blow. The political environment of the academic presidency is unusually unforgiving. Most politicians can make mistake after mistake without fear of consequence, since recalls are almost impossible (except in California) and since the next election is usually far enough in the future that missteps will be forgotten or forgiven. In contrast, university presidents usually serve at the pleasure of lay governing boards that are subjected to the continual assessment of the president by faculty, alumni, and the media. In a sense, the president must be engaged in a continuous political campaign to build support and avoid a vote of no confidence, since one step on a political land mine can bring disaster.

In the end, it is important for the president to recognize that politics is a contact sport. While truth, justice, and rational persuasion were the cornerstone of our efforts at Michigan, there were times when we had to take off the gloves to defend the institution—to stand up to governors who wanted to weaken the university's autonomy, legislators attacking our affirmative action programs, or congressmen launching yet another investigation into trumped-up charges for their political gain. This was never easy, since the natural tendency of most university staff is to immediately go on the defensive, to avoid making waves. One of my executive officers with extensive experience at other public universities lamented, "We just don't have enough folks around here willing to pick up a sword and fight on behalf of the university!" He certainly was willing, and so was I. But we were also well aware that the army of faculty and staff, friends and allies, that was marching behind us was inevitably modest and might quickly dissipate in the face of intense political pressure.

There were times when I thought of my political role as roughly akin to that of a tired, old sheriff in a frontier town in the American West. Every day I would have to drag my bruised, scarred carcass out of bed, strap on my guns, and go out into the main street to face whatever gunslingers had ridden in to shoot up the town that day. Sometimes these were politicians; other times the media; still other times special interest groups on campus; even occasionally other university leaders, such as deans or regents. Each time I went into battle to defend the university, I knew that one day I would run into someone faster on the draw than I was. In retrospect, it is amazing that I managed to perform this particular duty of the presidency for almost a decade with only a few scars to show for the effort.

Yet tentativeness in the face of such political threats can itself be a danger, since failing to take prompt action can make many situations even worse. Procrastination and, worse yet, avoidance can lead to disaster in the unforgiving political environment of the university. Hence, effective presidents must approach their task with a certain sense of adventure, since once a university leader begins to be concerned about mere survival as a priority, he or she rapidly becomes ineffective. It is only by taking chances, by doing things, that you accomplish anything. After all, if all one wants to do is to be king, czar, emperor, or CEO, there are lots of more enjoyable, rewarding, and secure opportunities than a university presidency.

8

MORAL LEADERSHIP

As both an educator and the leader of a large and diverse learning community, a university president is occasionally called on to provide a certain degree of moral leadership. Of course, today's presidents no longer are expected to teach the capstone course in moral philosophy, but they do have both the opportunity and the obligation to provide leadership on an array of value-related issues on the campus, ranging from the protection of academic values to institutional integrity to the pastoral care of students, faculty, staff, and other members of the university family.

Certainly, this is a natural and appropriate role of presidents in areas related to student behavior, from substance abuse to vandalism of the campus to sexual or racial harassment. Although incidents are less frequent, the conduct of faculty and staff also sometimes merits both decisive action and perhaps even public comment to protect the integrity of the institution. In today's post–Sarbanes-Oxley corporate environment, institutional integrity in such areas as finance and business practices has become all-important. While some presidents choose to delegate value-related activities to others, such as student affairs staff, the provost and deans, or financial officers and internal auditors (depending on the issue), others use these incidents as teachable moments to stress the important values of educational institutions.

However, there are many university activities in which the opportunity for moral leadership by the president is complicated because of ambiguity or risk. One clear example would be causes concerned with human rights and dignity, particularly in such sensitive areas as racial diversity or gay rights. Most university presidents embrace the fundamental values underlying such causes, those of equal opportunity and social justice. Yet how many presidents are willing to use the bully pulpit of their office or take decisive actions to address these issues, when progress may be difficult and when considerable risks are posed by an increasingly conservative society—not to mention the strongly held views of many political leaders in national, state, and university governance? It is little wonder that many presidents decide to keep their powder dry and let others carry on the battle.

Another obvious opportunity for moral leadership involves intercollegiate athletics, where rampant commercialism has not only exploited young student-athletes but also imposes a show-business culture that is corrosive to academic values. How many university presidents are willing to challenge the intractable training and traveling schedules that interfere with the academic progress of student-athletes or their exposure to the risk of serious injury that accompanies competition at a professional level, just to satisfy the demands of the viewing public, the greed of celebrity coaches, and the insatiable appetites of ambitious athletic directors for more revenue and grander facilities?

Many deplore the relative silence of university presidents on broader social issues, such as corporate integrity, poverty, and international conflict. The usual rationalization for this silence is that the demands placed on the presidency by the complexity of the contemporary university simply do not allow issue-related activities, suggesting that management responsibilities, fund-raising, and political duties swamp the time available for moral and ethical leadership.[1] Some even suspect the influence of other considerations, such as the fear of alienating donors or triggering political retaliation. Today, most university presidents are acutely sensitive to the need to distinguish when they are speaking and acting ex cathedra (i.e., on behalf of their institution) and when they are merely stating their own personal views on a subject. Concerning his presidency at Brown University,

Vartan Gregorian noted: "It is not natural for me, but I must speak with tact and diplomacy. I have come to agree with Lord Chesterfield that wisdom is like carrying a watch. Unless asked, you don't have to tell everybody what time it is."[2] Beyond this, however, is the simple fact that many people—perhaps most in our society—no longer believe that university presidents have any particular expertise or wisdom concerning issues beyond their campus. Some even question whether many presidents—hired more as fund-raisers, politicians, and managers, have the academic training—intellectual vision, and moral authority to address such issues even on their campuses.

However, in defense of my colleagues, it has been my experience that a great many college and university leaders do provide moral leadership, but through deeds rather than words. Here, we must remember that early college presidents led very small institutions, typically with fewer than several hundred students and a dozen faculty members, in an age in which rhetoric was the primary means of addressing moral issues. Today, the contemporary university president assumes a role as a chief executive officer, addressing issues both on campus and off through example, decision, and action. Instead of measuring moral leadership by the statements of university presidents on controversial issues, it may be more appropriate to study instead their decisions and actions. This latter perspective most clearly reflects my own view of the university president's role in moral leadership, as I believe strongly in the admonition "Don't listen to what I say, but instead watch what I do!"

THE CHALLENGES TO MORAL LEADERSHIP

An ancient Chinese proverb states, "The way to do is to be." Clearly, moral leadership at the university begins at the top, with the integrity, both real and perceived, of the president. University leaders who have problems with personal integrity and morality are unlikely to command the high ground and possess the credibility necessary for moral leadership. Although some are able to disguise these shortcomings in the near term, one cannot fool all of the people all of the time.

I am not talking here so much about university presidents who are outright scoundrels, although the university presidency has probably attracted its fair share of such miscreants throughout history. Rather, I am more concerned with those who fail to see any correlation between their personal behavior and their expectations for the integrity of their institution. To be sure, many of the trappings of the presidency have a royal character: a large, stately home; chauffeur-driven cars; first-class travel and lodging; a large and humble staff; VIP treatment; a lifestyle of the rich and famous. But when presidents begin to demand such royal treatment as an entitlement of rank, creating and enjoying court life much like a seventeenth-century French monarch, setting themselves above the norms constraining other members of the campus community in such areas as financial accountability and personal austerity, they quickly lose their ethical compass, not to mention their moral authority.

The examples are all too numerous. In some cases, they amount simply to bad judgment, such as excessive expenditures on the president's housing. Other cases involve more serious ethical lapses, such as tolerating the exploitation of students or sacrificing institutional welfare for personal career advancement. While this can be self-correcting—as history provides many examples when losing one's head over excessive personal expenditures leads to losing one's head by the ax—the damage to the integrity of the institution can be considerable.

Truth is another area where many presidents can have difficulty. New presidents are sometimes unaccustomed to the public attention given their every word, and when blindsided at a public presentation, they may sometimes cut corners with the truth. Other presidents come from backgrounds in law or politics, where distorting the truth is not only accepted but admired. Needless to say, a cavalier disregard for the truth can soon trample academic values.

Somewhat more abstract, yet of comparable importance to moral leadership, is an understanding and acceptance of those key values and traditions that undergird an institution. Some of these are fundamental academic values, such as academic freedom, scholarly integrity, and openness. Others trace back to the institutional saga—the history and culture—of the particular institution. Effective presidents accept, build on, reinforce, and vigorously defend such values. Institution-hopping short-timers ignore them.

As in other leadership areas, one can find ample examples of most of the dos and don'ts in the history of Michigan's presidency. Although a forceful advocate for scholarly values, Michigan's first president, Henry Tappan, preferred a lifestyle a bit too flamboyant for the frontier village that was then Ann Arbor (including a taste for fine wines), an important factor in undermining his leadership. C. C. Little met his demise in part by choosing the wrong areas for moral leadership, criticizing temperance and promoting birth control in a conservative state. On the positive end of the scale are such presidents as James Angell and Robben Fleming. When Angell became president of the University of Michigan, it was already one of the largest public universities in the nation. A man of strong Christian faith, Angell thought it natural to suggest that state and public universities should have the same deeply rooted concern for religious values as their older counterparts among the denominational colleges.[3] Perhaps of most significance for the future of the university, however, was his articulation of a more fundamental purpose of public higher education, aimed at serving the working class, the common man. Among Michigan's more recent presidents, Robben Fleming was known as a person of high integrity, with small-town Midwestern roots and a modest lifestyle. His modesty and tolerant manner, formed from years of mediating contentious labor contracts, were factors that contributed to the strong public support he received when he spoke out courageously on such controversial matters as the Vietnam War and racial justice.

The entrepreneurial nature of the contemporary university, in which individual faculty and staff are increasingly responsible for generating the resources to support their activities from myriad sources, can undermine not only the sense of loyalty to the institution but any common agreement and acceptance of fundamental values. The many communities of the multiversity respond to different values and different moral perspectives. The social disruptions of the student movements of the 1960s and 1970s, leading to the rejection of not only in loco parentis but also the traditional values of the university (perceived as part of the oppressive establishment), were also contributors to this loss of moral cohesiveness. As universities accepted less moral responsibility for the lives of students and lowered expectations for faculty loyalty, they severed the linkages to their tradition, heritage, and values.

While certainly challenging, the vast, complex, and frequently political responsibilities of the contemporary president should not be used as an excuse to avoid moral leadership. Effective leadership usually entails a certain degree of risk. Moreover, to change an institution in a fundamental way, the president has to lead from the front lines, not from a command bunker far from the action.

To illustrate the opportunity for moral leadership by the president of today's university, I have chosen several examples from my own experience at the University of Michigan: the university's leadership in demonstrating the importance of diversity to excellence in higher education, its effort to change the student culture to stress personal responsibility, and the importance of integrity in the university's business practices. Each example illustrates somewhat different aspects of both the opportunity for and the challenge to the moral leadership of the contemporary university president. Finally, although somewhat tangential to moral and ethical leadership, I have included in this chapter a discussion of the president's responsibility for providing pastoral care and concern for the diverse elements of the campus community.

SOCIAL DIVERSITY AND ACADEMIC EXCELLENCE

The effort of the University of Michigan to bring diverse racial and ethnic groups more fully into the life of the university in the 1980s provides an excellent example of the moral leadership that can be exerted by a university president. This process of institutional transformation was guided by a strategic plan known as the Michigan Mandate, which achieved very significant progress toward the objective of social diversity and led eventually to a landmark decision by the U.S. Supreme Court in 2003.

As with most of higher education, the history of diversity at Michigan is complex and often contradictory. There have been many times when the institution seemed to take a step forward, only to be followed by two steps backward. As I noted in the discussion of its institutional saga in chapter 1, Michigan was one of the earliest universities to admit African Americans and women in the late nineteenth century. It took pride in its large enrollments of international students at a time when the state itself was decidedly insular. Yet it faltered as minority enrollments languished and racial tensions flared in the 1960s and 1970s, only to be jolted occasionally into ineffective action by student activism—the Black Action Movement in the 1970s and the United Coalition against Racism in the 1980s. Nonetheless, access and equality have always been central goals of the institution. Michigan has consistently been at the forefront of the struggle for inclusiveness in higher education.

When I became provost and then president in the late 1980s, it had become apparent that the university had made inadequate progress in its goal to reflect the rich diversity of our nation and our world among its faculty, students, and staff. In assessing this situation, we concluded that although the university had approached the challenge of serving an increasingly diverse population with the best of intentions, it simply had not developed and executed a plan capable of achieving sustainable results. More significant, we believed that achieving our goals for a diverse campus would require a very major change in the institution itself.

The long-term strategic focus of our planning proved to be critical, because universities do not change quickly and easily any more than do the societies of which they are a part. Michigan would have to leave behind many reactive and uncoordinated efforts that had characterized its past and move toward a more strategic approach designed to achieve long-term systemic change. Sacrifices would be necessary as traditional roles and privileges were challenged. In particular, we understood the limitations of focusing only on affirmative action—that is, on access, retention, and representation. The key, rather, would be to focus on the success of underrepresented minorities on our campus, as students, as faculty, and as leaders. We believed that without deeper, more fundamental institutional change, these efforts by themselves would inevitably fail—as they had throughout the 1970s and 1980s.

The challenge was to persuade the university community that there was a real stake for everyone in seizing the moment to chart a more diverse future. People needed to believe that the gains to be achieved through diversity would more than compensate for the necessary sacrifices. The first and most important step was to link diversity and excellence as the two most compelling goals before the institution, recognizing that these goals were not only complementary but would be tightly linked in the multicultural society characterizing our nation and the world in the future. As we moved ahead, we began to refer to the plan as The Michigan Mandate: A Strategic Linking of Academic Excellence and Social Diversity.[4]

The mission and goals of the Michigan Mandate were stated quite simply: (1) to recognize that diversity and excellence are complementary and compelling goals for the university and to make a firm commitment to their achievement; (2) to commit to the recruitment, support, and success of members of historically underrepresented groups among our students, faculty, staff, and leadership; and (3) to build on our campus an environment that sought, nourished, and sustained diversity and pluralism and that valued and respected the dignity and worth of every individual. A series of carefully focused strategic actions was developed to move the university toward these objectives. These actions were framed by the values and traditions of the university and by an understanding of our unique culture, characterized by a high degree of faculty and unit freedom and autonomy and animated by a highly competitive and entrepreneurial spirit. The strategy was both complex and pervasive, involving not only a considerable commitment of resources (e.g., fully funding all financial aid for minority graduate students) but also some highly innovative programs, such as our Target of Opportunity program for recruiting minority faculty.[5] It also was one of those efforts that we believed required personal leadership by the president, since only by demonstrating commitment from the top could we demand and achieve comparable commitments throughout the institution.

By the mid-1990s, Michigan could point to significant progress in achieving diversity. The presence of underrepresented minority students, faculty, and staff on our campus more than doubled over the decade of the effort. Perhaps more significant, the success of underrepresented minorities at the university improved even more remarkably, with graduation rates rising to the highest among public universities, promotion and tenure success of minority faculty members becoming comparable to that of their majority colleagues, and growth in the number of appointments of minorities to leadership positions in the university. Not only did the campus climate became more accepting and supportive of diversity, but students and faculty began to be attracted to Michigan because of its growing reputation for a diverse campus. Perhaps most significant, as the campus became more racially and ethnically diverse, the quality of the students, faculty, and academic programs of the university increased to their highest level in history. This latter fact reinforced our contention that the aspirations of diversity and excellence were not only compatible but, in fact, highly correlated. By every measure, the Michigan Mandate was a remarkable success, moving the university beyond our original goals of a more diverse campus.

But, of course, this story does not end with the successful achievements of the Michigan Mandate in 1996, when I stepped down as president. Beginning with litigation in Texas (the Hopwood decision) and then successful referendum efforts in California and Washington, conservative groups, such as the Center for Individual Rights, began to attack such policies as the use of race in college admissions. Perhaps because of the University of Michigan's success in the Michigan Mandate, the university soon became a target for those groups seeking to reverse affirmative action, with two cases filed against the university in 1997—one challenging the admissions policies of undergraduates and a second challenging those in our Law School. Although I had been succeeded by Lee Bollinger by that time, I was still named personally as a defendant in one of the cases (as the "et al." in the *Gratz vs. Bollinger et al.* case). I had little influence on the strategies to defend both cases to the level of the Supreme Court, aside from giving day after day of depositions and having all of the records of my presidency digitized, archived, and posted publicly by our university history library.[6]

At Michigan, we felt it was important that we carry the water for the rest of higher education toward reestablishing this important principle. Throughout our history, our university has been committed to extending more broadly educational opportunities to the working class, to women, to racial and ethnic minorities, and to students from every state and nation. It was natural for us to lead yet another battle for equity and social justice.

Although the 2003 Supreme Court decisions were split, supporting the use of race in the admissions policies of our Law School and opposing the formula-based approach used for undergraduate admissions, the most important ruling in both cases stated, in the words of the Court: "Student body diversity is a compelling state interest that can justify the use of race in university admission. When race-based action is necessary to further a compelling governmental interest, such action does not violate the constitutional guarantee of equal protection so long as the narrow-tailoring requirement is also satisfied."[7] Hence, the Supreme Court decisions on the Michigan cases reaffirmed the policies and practices long used by the selective colleges and universities throughout the United States. More significant, it reaffirmed the importance of diversity in higher education and established the principle that, with appropriate design, race could be used as a factor in programs aimed at achieving diverse campuses. Hence, the battle was won, as the principle was firmly established by the highest court of the land. Or so we thought.

While an important battle had been won with the Supreme Court ruling, we soon learned that the war for diversity in higher education was far from over. As university lawyers across the nation began to ponder over the Court ruling, they persuaded their institutions to accept a very narrow interpretation of the Supreme Court decisions as the safest course. Actually, this pattern began to appear at the University of Michigan during the early stages of the litigation process. Even as the university launched the expensive legal battle (following my presidency) to defend the use of race in college admissions, it throttled back many of the effective policies and programs created by the Michigan Mandate, in part out of concern that these might complicate the litigation battle. As a consequence, the enrollment of underrepresented minorities began almost immediately to drop at Michigan, eventually declining from 1996 to 2002 by almost 25 percent overall and by as much as 50 percent in some of our professional schools. Although there was an effort to rationalize this decline by suggesting that the publicity given the litigation over admissions policies was discouraging minority applicants, there is little doubt in my mind that it was the dismantling of the Michigan Mandate that really set the university back.

Since the Supreme Court decision, many universities have begun to back away from programs aimed at recruitment, financial aid, and academic enrichment for minority undergraduate students, either eliminating entirely such programs or opening them up to nonminority students from low-income households. Threats of further litigation by conservative groups have intensified this retrenchment. As a consequence, the enrollments of underrepresented minorities are dropping again in many universities across the nation (including Michigan).[8] After the years of effort in building successful programs, such as the Michigan Mandate, and defending the importance of diversity in higher education all the way to the Supreme Court, it would be tragic indeed if the decisions in the Michigan case caused more harm than good by unleashing the lawyers on the nation's campuses to block successful efforts to broaden educational opportunity and advance the cause of social justice.

Ironically, the uses of affirmative action (and programs that involved racial preference) were not high on the agenda of the Michigan Mandate. Rather, our success involved commitment, engagement, and accountability for results. Yet there is ample evidence today, from such states as California and Texas, that a restriction to race-neutral policies will drastically limit the ability of elite programs and institutions to reflect diversity in any meaningful way. Former University of California president Richard Atkinson noted in a recent address in Ann Arbor: "Proposition 209 asked the University of California to attract a student body that reflects the state's diversity while ignoring two of the major constituents of this diversity—race and ethnicity. A decade later, the legacy of this contradictory mandate is clear. Despite enormous efforts, we have failed badly to achieve the goal of a student body that encompasses California's diverse population. The evidence suggests that without attention to race and ethnicity this goal will ultimately recede into impossibility."[9]

In 2006, Michigan voters approved a constitutional referendum to ban the use of affirmative action in public institutions similar to that of California's Proposition 209. This referendum will prevent Michigan colleges and universities from using the narrowly tailored prescriptions of the 2003 Supreme Court decision. It is likely that the University of Michigan will see a rapid decline in campus diversity similar to that which has occurred in California. Yet it also seems clear that many people today believe that, despite the importance of diversity, racial preferences are contrary to American values of individual rights and the policy of color blindness that animated the Civil Rights Act of 1964. Atkinson suggests that we need a new strategy that recognizes the continuing corrosive force of racial inequality but does not stop there. We need a strategy grounded in the broad American tradition of opportunity, because opportunity is a value that Americans understand and support. We need a strategy that makes it clear that our society has a stake in ensuring every American an opportunity to succeed and that every American, in turn, has a stake in equality of opportunities and social justice in our nation.

Even while pursuing the racial diversity goals of the Michigan Mandate, we realized we could not ignore another glaring inequity in campus life. If we meant to embrace diversity in its full meaning, we had to attend to the long-standing concerns of women faculty, students, and staff. Here, once again, it took time—and considerable effort by many women colleagues (including my wife and daughters)—to educate me and the rest of my administration to the point where we began to understand that the university simply had not succeeded in including and empowering women as full and equal partners in all aspects of its life and leadership.

Despite the increasing pools of women in many fields, the number of new faculty hires and promotion of women had changed only slowly during the late twentieth century in most research universities. In some disciplines, such as the physical sciences and engineering, the shortages were particularly acute. We continued to suffer from the "glass ceiling" phenomenon: that is, because of hidden prejudice, women were unable to break through to the ranks of senior faculty and administrators, though no formal constraints prohibited their advancement. The proportion of women decreased steadily as one moved up the academic ladder. Additionally, there appeared to be an increasing tendency to hire women off the tenure track as postdoctoral scholars, lecturers, clinicians, or research scientists. The rigid division among various faculty appointments offered little or no opportunity for these women to move into tenured faculty positions.

Many of our concerns derived from the extreme concentration of women in positions of lower status and power—as students, lower-paid staff, and junior faculty. The most effective lever for change might well be a rapid increase in the number of women holding positions of high status, visibility, and power. This would change not only the balance of power in decision making but also the perception of who and what matters in the university. Finally, we realized that we needed to bring university policies and practices into better alignment with the needs and concerns of women students in a number of areas, including campus safety, student housing, student life, financial aid, and child care.

To address these challenges, the university developed and executed a second strategic effort, known as the Michigan Agenda for Women. While the actions proposed were intended to address the concerns of women students, faculty, and staff, many of them benefited men as well. In developing the Michigan Agenda, we knew that different strategies were necessary for different parts of the university. Academic units varied enormously in the degree to which women participated as faculty, staff, and students. What might work in one area could fail miserably in another. Some fields, such as the physical sciences, had few women represented among their students and faculty. For them, it was necessary to design and implement a strategy that spanned the entire pipeline, from K–12 outreach to undergraduate and graduate education to faculty recruiting and development. For other fields, such as the social sciences or law, there already was a strong pool of women students, and the challenge became one of attracting women from this pool into graduate and professional studies and eventually into academe. Still other units, such as education and many departments in humanities and sciences, had strong participation of women among students and junior faculty but suffered from low participation in the senior ranks and in leadership roles.

As with the Michigan Mandate, the vision was again both simple yet compelling: that by the year 2000 the university would become the leader among American universities in promoting and achieving the success of women as faculty, students, and staff. Again, as president, I took a highly personal role in this effort, meeting with hundreds of groups on and off campus, to listen to their concerns and invite their participation in the initiative. There was significant rapid progress on many fronts for women students, faculty, and staff, including the appointment of a number of senior women faculty and administrators as deans and executive officers, improvement in campus safety, and improvement of family care policies and child care resources. In 1997, Michigan appointed its first woman provost, Nancy Cantor (now president at Syracuse University). Finally, in 2002, the University of Michigan named its first woman president, Mary Sue Coleman.

The university also took steps to eliminate those factors that prevented other groups from participating fully in its activities. For example, we extended our antidiscrimination policies to encompass sexual orientation and extended staff benefits and housing opportunities to same-sex couples. This was a particularly controversial action, because it was strongly opposed not only by the religious Right but also by several of the university's regents. Yet this was an issue of equity long frustrating to many faculty, staff, and students and required attention. Harold Shapiro had tried on several occasions, without success, to persuade the regents to extend its antidiscrimination policies to include the gay community. Finally, with a supportive, albeit short-lived, Democratic majority among the regents, I decided to move ahead rapidly to put in the policy while there was still political support, no matter how slim. The anticipated negative reaction was rapid and angry, including an attempt by the Michigan state legislature to deduct from our appropriation the estimated cost of the same-sex couple benefits (effectively blocked by our constitutional autonomy), a personal phone call from our Republican governor (although it was a call he did not want to make, and he did not insist on any particular action), and a concerted and successful effort to place two conservative Republican candidates on our board of regents in the next election (resulting in the horror of a 4–4 divided board during my last two years as president). We were determined to defend this action, however, as part of a broader strategy. We had become convinced that the university had both a compelling interest in and responsibility to create a welcoming community, encouraging respect for diversity in all of the characteristics that can be used to describe humankind: age, race, ethnicity, nationality, gender, religious belief, sexual orientation, political beliefs, economic background, geographical background.

STUDENT AFFAIRS

The social disruptions of the student protest movements of the 1960s and 1970s led to the rejection of not only in loco parentis but many of the traditional values of the university, which were also perceived as the agenda of the oppressive establishment. As students pushed the faculty and the administration out of their lives, the universities themselves accepted less moral responsibility for the lives of students, in part out of fear of liability and litigation that might result from a deeper engagement and in part because of the shift in faculty interests and loyalty in the entrepreneurial university. As a consequence, the students in most large universities lost the linkages to many of those institutional values and traditions that had shaped the learning and lives of earlier generations.

My own educational experience had been in the early 1960s when such value-laden issues as the civil rights movement energized the campuses, in contrast to the later nihilistic protests against the establishment. Hence, I believed strongly in the role of the university president to provide moral leadership for the student body. In my early speeches, I challenged students to understand that freedom must be earned through responsible behavior. More specifically, I called for "a new respect for limits that carries with it concern for the moral values and restraints that unify communities and keep human conduct within acceptable bounds." I maintained: "Universities cannot avoid the task. Like it or not, they will affect the moral development of their students by the ways in which they administer their rules of conduct, by the standard they achieve in dealing with ethical issues confronting the institution, by the many who counsel their students and coach their athletic teams." I went on to urge that "universities should be among the first to reaffirm the importance of basic values, such as honesty, promise keeping, free expression, and nonviolence, for these are not only principles essential to civilized society; they are values on which all learning and discovery ultimately depend."[10]

Two particular actions illustrate this approach: the effort to put into place a student disciplinary policy and my efforts to change the destructive culture of our fraternities. One of the university's hangovers from the volatile days of the 1970s had been the absence of a code of student conduct. The elimination of this policy in 1974 had been intended only as a temporary lapse pending the development and adoption of a new and more contemporary code. But student government was given veto power over the process, and it had consistently exercised this veto to prevent the development or adoption of a new disciplinary policy. As a result, the university had gone for almost 15 years without any of the student disciplinary policies characterizing essentially every other university in the nation. The only option available for student disciplinary action was to utilize an obscure regents' bylaw that gave the president the authority to intervene personally to handle each incident. Although the university knew it was at some risk in the absence of such a student code—and was indeed out of compliance with federal laws that required such policies to govern such areas as substance abuse—each time an effort was made to develop a code, it was blocked by activist students (occasionally aided and abetted by a maverick regent, who appeared in this case to be a libertarian at heart).[11]

Yet another issue of great concern to many of our students, campus safety, also provided opportunities for protest to students who resented any authority. For most of the university's history, Ann Arbor was a rather simple and safe residential community. But as southeastern Michigan evolved in the postwar era into a metroplex with intricate freeway networks linking communities together, Ann Arbor acquired more of an urban character, with all of the safety concerns plaguing any large city. While many aspects of campus safety could be addressed through straightforward and noncontroversial actions, such as improving lighting or putting security locks on residence hall entrances, there was one issue unique to the university proved to be more volatile: the absence of a campus police force. Unlike most other large universities in America, the university had never developed its own campus police and instead relied on community police and sheriff's deputies. Throughout the 1980s, it became more and more evident that local law enforcement authorities simply would never regard the university as their top priority. Their responsiveness to campus crime and other safety concerns was increasingly intermittent and unreliable. Furthermore, most other universities had found that the training and sensitivity required by police dealing with students was far more likely to be present in a campus-based police organization than in any community police force.

The issues of both the code of student conduct and a campus police force came into focus in 1992, when a university task force on campus safety strongly recommended that both be established. Although surveys indicated that most students supported both steps, a number of student groups (including student government and the *Michigan Daily*) rapidly assembled a coalition to protest under the slogan "No cops, no codes, no guns." Like most protests resisting efforts to bring the university in line with the rest of higher education, this one rapidly faded. The campus police force was established and demonstrated not only that they could reduce crime on campus but, further, that they were far more sensitive to student needs and concerns than the local Ann Arbor police. Several years later, students again protested, this time to urge more deployment of campus police in preference to the use of city police.

There was also major change in Greek life during my years at the helm. Since the 1960s, the university had generally kept at arm's-length distance from fraternities and sororities, even though over 6,000 undergraduates each year chose these as their residential environment. This reluctance to become involved grew, in part, from the university's concern about liability for the institution should it become too closely linked with fraternity behavior. This attitude of benign neglect changed in the late 1980s, when the university—and the Ann Arbor community—became increasingly concerned about a series of fraternity incidents involving drinking and sexual harassment. The university concluded that it had a major responsibility, both to its students and to the Ann Arbor community, to become more involved with the Greeks.

As president, I finally decided it was time to step in and called a special meeting with the presidents of all of the university's fraternities, to address the growing concerns about their destructive behavior. I reminded them of Michigan's heritage of leadership, and I challenged them to strengthen their own capacity to discipline renegade members through such organizations as the Interfraternity Council. Although I issued a strong challenge for self-discipline, I also indicated quite clearly that the university would act with whatever force was necessary to protect the student body and the surrounding community. (More precisely, I suggested that if their disruptive behavior continued, I would come down on fraternities "like a ton of bricks.")

This challenge was picked up by fraternity leaders, and a new spirit of responsible behavior and discipline began to appear. Policies were adopted forbidding drinking during rush, along with strong sanctions against entertaining minors from the Ann Arbor community in the houses. With the arrival of Maureen Hartford as vice president for student affairs, the university took further steps by hiring a staff member to serve as liaison with the Greeks. This is not to suggest that misbehavior in Greek life vanished from the campus. Indeed, several fraternities suffered from such a pattern of poor behavior that their national organizations agreed to withdraw their charter, hence they were removed from campus. But in general, the nature of Greek life became one of far greater responsibility and self-discipline.

INSTITUTIONAL INTEGRITY

Closely related to a president's responsibility for moral leadership are those values and ethical principles undergirding institutional integrity. Mark Yudolf, chancellor of the University of Texas, has observed: "This is the era of Enron; this is the era of disclosure. This wave has already swept over the public schools, and now it is approaching higher education. Either you help to shape this accountability revolution so that it is done in an intelligent way, or you're going to get swept over by it."[12] Of course, part of the problem is the very complexity of the issues and ethical incidents. To be sure, there are obvious cases that amount essentially to criminal activity: for example, the cases with Enron, Tyco, and WorldCom. But how should one deal with more subtle business practices, such as the predatory behavior of Microsoft to prevent competitors from accessing their operating system, the American automobile industry's efforts to block enhanced fuel economy, or the decisions of pharmaceutical companies to ignore the needs of children for vaccinations and instead focus drug development to the far more lucrative market of aging baby boomers?

Higher education has its own list of high-profile ethical lapses: the loss of life in clinical trials conducted by faculty with interests in associated spin-off companies; the blatant conflict of interest of trustees cutting business deals with one another at their institutions' expense; college sports scandals involving sexual assault and substance abuse; and a host of extreme cases of faculty misbehavior in such areas as scientific integrity, sexual harassment of students, and so forth. But here, too, there are more subtle issues that raise serious ethical questions: the "management," rather than the "avoidance," of conflict of interest in the commercialization of intellectual property, which is clearly distorting the scientific enterprise, limiting publication and even cooperation among investigators; the tolerance of the abysmal graduation rates of college football and basketball players (now well under 50 percent), which clearly represent exploitation of these young students at a time when their coaches' compensation has soared to truly obscene levels; and the exposure of our students to credit-card scams and other predatory commercial practices on our campuses. Just as with the business community, lapses in ethical behavior can cause very great damage to the reputation and integrity of the university and of higher education more generally, undermining its privileged place in our society.

When one institution stumbles, we all get tarnished, as public opinion surveys clearly indicate. It all comes down to the need to make judgments and decisions on increasingly complex cases. This requires a solid foundation of institutional values that frequently goes beyond what the law would require. It also requires an extensive program of education about fundamental institutional and social values for students, faculty, and staff—not just a focus on the laws. Put another way, just as with the business community, universities are at increasing risk if they lack a clearly understood and accepted code of ethics and a process for educating the university community and continually reviewing and revising, when necessary, both the code of ethics and the policies and guidelines for its implementation.

So where are the key areas of concern? Clearly, we must include those areas that relate directly to the fundamental education and scholarly mission of the university, such as academic integrity and research accountability. But universities are also places charged with developing human potential and serving society. Hence, there are such concerns as faculty-student relationships, exploitation of students, and the protection of human subjects. Since universities are places where the young are not only educated but socialized, they also confront such issues as student disciplinary policies, substance abuse concerns, sexual harassment and assault, and a host of "isms" (e.g., racism, sexism, elitism, and extremism). Finally, since many of our institutions are multibillion-dollar global conglomerates, higher education also faces most of the same challenges with business practices characterizing any publicly traded corporation.

Today, many factors are intensifying both the importance and the complexity of ethical behavior in higher education. For example, the soaring commercialism of intellectual property, increasing university dependence on business activities (e.g., endowment management), faculty dependence on external compensation (consulting, publishing, equity interests), and increasing pressures on auxiliary activities (e.g., hospitals and intercollegiate athletics) raise serious issues of conflict of interest and business practice, comparable to those addressed by the Sarbanes-Oxley Act in the corporate setting. As mission creep continues to expand the complexity and scope of universities with new enterprises, it also entails new risks, such as the equity interests associated with technology transfer, real estate ventures, expansion of health care systems, international activities, and technology (software piracy). Driving it all is the increasingly Darwinian nature of the competitive environment in higher education—for the best faculty and students, for research grants and private gifts, for winning athletic programs, and for reputation.

More fundamentally, in an era in which the marketplace is replacing public policy in determining the nature of higher education in America, one must question the degree to which financial gain is replacing public purpose in determining the actions of universities and their faculty, staff, students, and governing boards. I believe we have reached a tipping point that requires more rigorous attention to institutional values and ethical practices in higher education. Clearly, the privileged place of universities demands higher standards than those simply required by law or public perception. After all, values are far more important than laws. There is a very significant difference between legal behavior and ethical behavior. The law provides very little guidance as to what is or is not ethical behavior, particularly in an academic institution where such values as academic freedom, rigorous scholarly inquiry, and openness require higher standards than those merely tolerated by the law.

The lesson of the past several years of corporate misbehavior—from Enron, WorldCom, and so on—involves the importance of both process and transparency. The corrective medicine of the Sarbanes-Oxley Act demands that corporations and their boards of directors not only have to be fiscally accountable but also have to be able to prove it. Some universities, such as the University of Texas, have already adopted such reforms as best practices. There are increasing calls to strengthen financial controls at colleges, not simply by government, but also by credit-rating agencies, accounting and law firms, and private foundations. But while these may pose challenges—albeit necessary—the call for greater accountability and transparency may also present important opportunities.

Here, governing boards must be particularly attentive, since they will increasingly be held to the same standards as the boards of directors of publicly traded corporations, both in their own competency and in the processes they utilize for assuring institutional integrity. Furthermore, governing boards must be more scrupulous in their oversight of both the compensation and the expenditures of senior university administrators, with particular attention paid to the university president. In public universities, this extends to transparency, since the failure to disclose key aspects of presidential compensation or expenditures can be just as damaging politically as the inappropriate nature of these decisions.

Finally, achieving public trust and confidence in higher education may require some reform of the academy itself. The academy claims to be a profession, much like law, medicine, and engineering. Members of such learned professions agree to maintain high standards of performance, to restrain self-interest, and to promote ideals of public service in areas of responsibility. In return, society grants them substantial autonomy to regulate themselves.

Many of the recent scandals in business practices resulted from professionals—such as accountants, lawyers, bankers, security analysts, and corporate officers—allowing self-interest and greed to trump integrity. Rather than acting as a constraint against excess, they facilitated unrestrained self-interest. As a result, their professions are increasingly losing their autonomy, as government steps in to provide strict regulations for professional practice (e.g., through the Sarbanes-Oxley Act), largely because the professions have lost the public trust.

There is an important lesson here for higher education. Like other professions, the professoriat is granted the autonomy of academic freedom as long as it is able to demonstrate that it has the capacity to set and enforce standards for ethical behavior. Yet, in all candor, it has failed to do so. Such ethical codes as those adopted by the American Association of University Professors and various disciplinary societies are largely vague and toothless. The evidence suggests that many faculty members fail to set high standards for the behavior of their colleagues, frequently tolerating the most blatant misbehavior of colleagues. The academy's credibility to students is undermined by inattention to teaching, exploitation of student relationships, and numerous examples of conflict of interest (e.g., scholarly ethics).

As a result of its benign neglect of professional ethics, the professoriat could find itself facing the same intrusion of regulation and constraint now characterizing the legal, accounting, and business professions, should the public lose confidence that it is upholding its end of the social contract that provides academic freedom and autonomy. Trustees need to act to hold the professoriat more accountable for maintaining its end of the social compact. They should require orientation programs for new faculty and include substantial material on ethics and values in graduate education, as these are key to producing the next generation of professors.

More specifically, the increasing demand for institutional accountability and integrity may provide an important opportunity to reinsert the subject of values and ethics into the curriculum. Key to institutional integrity is an understanding and acceptance of those values and traditions that undergird an institution. Some of these are fundamental academic values, such as academic freedom, scholarly integrity, and openness. Others trace back to the institutional saga—the history and culture—of the particular institution. But unfortunately, all discussion of such values seems to be missing from campus these days. Presidential and trustee leadership can fill some of the gap created by faculty reluctance to discuss moral values with students. Today's climate of increasing public scrutiny and accountability may present an opportunity. It is now easier to make the case that it is time for universities to take strong action to stimulate a dialogue concerning and a commitment to embracing fundamental values and ethics in their activities—certainly in their practices, but perhaps even more so in their fundamental activities of teaching and scholarship.

THE BULLY PULPIT

It was my experience that opportunities for moral leadership by the president were not only abundant but also highly influential. The examples described in this chapter were important and, to be sure, required a certain amount of intestinal fortitude and tolerance for danger. But they concerned only the mainstream interests of the university.

Like other presidents of major universities, including my predecessors at Michigan, I also used the bully pulpit to address moral issues of broader social import, such as the deteriorating social foundations of our families and communities, the growing divisions in our society (by race, class, age, religion, political persuasion), the increasing distrust of social institutions, the eroding appreciation of quality, and the growing imbalance created by consumption to satisfy present desires at the expense of investment for the future. After such fire-and-brimstone addresses, I would always try to end on an upbeat note, albeit one of challenge.

> America—and Michigan—have called upon some generations more than others for exceptional service and sacrifice, to defend and preserve our way of life for future generations, from taming Frontier America and the Revolutionary War to the Civil War, securing through suffrage the voting rights of all of our citizens, World Wars I and II, and the Civil Rights Movement. Americans have always answered the call. Now, no less than in those earlier struggles, our generation must rise to the challenge to serve. This time there are no foreign enemies. Our battlefield is at home and with ourselves. I've no doubt that in

the end we will prevail through our collective wisdom and resolve.

Of course, with each sacred cow challenged, with each ox gored, I would use up a bit more political capital. But I believed these were messages that folks needed to hear, and as president of the University of Michigan, it was my responsibility to be the messenger, even if it shortened my tenure in the process. Sometimes people even agreed with me. Or at least they respected my right to be heard.[13]

PASTORAL CARE

The contemporary university is much like a city, comprised of a bewildering array of neighborhoods and communities. To the faculty, it has almost a feudal structure, divided up into highly specialized academic units, frequently with little interaction even with disciplinary neighbors, much less with the rest of the campus. To the student body, the university is an exciting, confusing, and sometimes frustrating complexity of challenges and opportunities, rules and regulations, drawing students together only in major events, such as fall football games or campus protests. To the staff, the university has a more subtle character, with the parts woven together by policies, procedures, and practices evolving over decades, all too frequently invisible or ignored by the students and faculty. In some ways, the modern university is so complex, so multifaceted, that it seems that the closer one is to it and the more intimately one is involved with its activities, the harder it is to understand its entirety and the more likely one is to miss the forest for the trees.

But a university is also a diverse community of many families: faculty, staff, and students; deans and executive officers; office staff and former presidents. As university president, one not only becomes a member of each of these families but also assumes responsibilities to understand, support, encourage, and protect them, to understand their concerns and their aspirations, and to advance their causes. This pastoral role is among the most important and challenging, yet also most rewarding, aspects of university leadership.

In the early days of American higher education, many college presidents played a direct role in student life, knowing each student by name and following their progress, much as would the headmaster of a preparatory academy. Yet from its earliest days, Michigan's presidents followed a different path. They sought to build not simply a college but instead a great university where faculty scholarship and professional education would be placed on an equal footing with the training and socialization of young adults. Both Henry Tappan and James Angell were strongly opposed to such college traditions as dormitories and rigid discipline. They believed that students should be treated as adults, living independently in the community, rather than subjected to a common and carefully prescribed living experience. Later attempts to impose the collegiate model at Michigan, such as those by C. C. Little, met fierce resistance from both faculty and students alike—and continue to do so today.

Beyond this striking difference in educational philosophy, the size and diversity of such large universities as Michigan, with tens of thousands of students spread across hundreds of different disciplines and professional majors, dictates much of the presidential role with respect to students. Certainly, the president may have significant impact on the student body through involvement in key policy areas, such as admissions, student conduct, and student extracurricular activities (including, of course, intercollegiate athletics). But much of the president's direct interaction with students involves symbolic activities—for example, presiding over such student events as convocations, honors ceremonies, and, of course, commencement.

Some university presidents still attempt to teach a regularly scheduled course and hold office hours for students. Others maintain research programs—even laboratories—and advise graduate students. Yet first as provost and then as president, I soon became convinced that the complexity, unpredictability, and importance of presidential duties and responsibilities outweighed any substantive or symbolic value to taking on the additional burden of regularly scheduled courses (although I did spend much of my time educating legislators, trustees, alumni, and even the faculty on the intricacies of the contemporary university). Instead, I used other methods to keep in touch with students and student issues, including regular visits as a guest lecturer (sometimes unannounced) in a wide array of undergraduate and graduate classes; frequent meals with students in residence halls; regular meetings with leaders of various student groups, such as student government and the student newspaper; and a series of events that my wife, Anne, would arrange at the President's House for various student groups throughout the university year—on a schedule compatible with other obligations and responsibilities.

Campuses with an activist student body pose a particularly exhilarating challenge for the president. Michigan's tradition of activism, while being a source of great energy and excitement, had its drawbacks, particularly when the issues and agendas were more annoying than compelling—for example, opposing all rules governing student behavior or legalizing marijuana. Student protests can distract the attention of the institution and the president from other, more compelling priorities, such as achieving academic excellence. They can dominate the local headlines and occasionally trigger strong political responses, sometimes favoring student issues, sometimes opposing them. Student protests can also catch the attention of the university's governing board. Hence, like it or not, a university president frequently becomes the point person in dealing with student protests.

To be sure, on many occasions, student activism has had a very positive effect in raising issues of great importance—for example, the protest against the Vietnam War in the 1960s, the environmental movement in the 1970s, and the campaign to raise awareness of social injustice and the plight of underrepresented minority communities through the latter half of the twentieth century. Yet there is an ebb and flow to student activism, just as there is to broader political life. This flow is determined not only by social issues of the times (e.g., an unpopular war, the draft, an economic downturn, the lack of jobs for graduating students) but also by the quality of student leadership, since pulling together such movements requires some talent. There were occasional flare-ups of student activism during my years as a campus administrator, sometimes over such important issues as racial tolerance or gay rights, sometimes over cosmic concerns that have long since lost any relevance, such as establishing Ann Arbor as a nuclear-free zone. I found the students involved to be quite sincere and committed to their cause, and I must confess that there have been many moments of peace and quiet on the campus when I have longed for a more activist student body.

In my inauguration address, I began my comments to the faculty by observing: "It is sometimes said that great universities are run by their faculties, for their faculties. Clearly the quality of our institutions is determined by the quality of our faculty—by their talents, their commitments, and their actions."[14] This faculty-centric statement reflected well my own perspective, shaped by two decades of toiling in the faculty vineyards at Michigan—teaching, conducting research, advising students, hustling research grants, and serving on faculty committee after committee after committee. Similarly, my wife, Anne, had served in numerous leadership roles with university faculty and community groups.

Anne and I had developed empathy for faculty life through personal experience, understanding well the stresses of promotion and tenure decisions, the relative poverty of junior faculty, and the frustrations of faculty politics. From this background, we understood clearly our obligation to serve the faculty of the university in various leadership roles—first as dean, then as provost, and finally as president. Yet even in these leadership roles, we continued to view ourselves as first and foremost members of the university's faculty community, on temporary assignment to administrative positions. Of course, despite our best efforts, many of our friends and colleagues among the faculty began to pull away from us, whether because of the faculty's natural suspicion of all administrators, because of their perception that we no longer had time for our old activities and friends, or because we were being held prisoner in the fortress of the administration building, out of sight, out of touch, and out of mind.

The deans themselves form yet another family of the university, occasionally in competition with one another, more frequently working together, but always requiring the attention and the pastoral care of the president and the provost. Being a faculty member is the best job in a university (with the most prestige, the most freedom, and the most opportunity), but if one has to be an academic administrator, the next best role—at least at Michigan—is that of a dean. Although some of Michigan's academic units (e.g., the College of Literature, Science, and the Arts and the School of Medicine) rival major universities in their size, financial resources, and organizational complexity, both the size and the intellectual span of most UM schools and colleges is just about right to allow true leadership. To be sure, deans have to answer in both directions, to the provost from above and to their faculty from below. But their capacity to control both their own destiny and that of their school is far beyond that of most administrators.

Since the University of Michigan is so heavily dependent on the quality of its deans, most presidents and provosts make a great effort to attract the very best people into these important positions. It is my belief that great universities have great deans. Hence, it is important for the president and provost to work closely together not only in the appointment and support of these key academic leaders but also to build a sense of community among them, establishing friendships and bonds, since these, in turn, glue together the university. Perhaps because of our own experience as members of the "deans' family," Anne and I were always on the lookout for new ways to involve the deans more intimately in the leadership of the university.

We took similar pride in the quality of the executive leadership team of the university, which I believed to be one of the strongest in the nation, both during my administration and throughout the university's earlier history. The executive officers were also a family, although, quite unlike the deans, they were characterized by great diversity in roles and backgrounds: some were line officers; others were in staff roles. Although many of the executive officers at most universities come from outside the academy (e.g., business and law), Michigan had a very unusual situation during my years as president: all of our senior officers had academic roots, some even with ongoing teaching and research responsibilities. This not only provided the leadership team with a deep understanding of academic issues but gave us important flexibility in breaking down the usual bureaucracy to form multiofficer teams to address key issues, such as federal research policy, fund-raising, resource allocation, and even academic policy—issues that would be constrained to administrative silos in other universities.

The UM board of regents comprised yet another family requiring pastoral care by the president. Although most of our governing board members were dedicated public servants with a strong interest and loyalty to the university, there were among some members, as with any family, occasional disagreements—indeed, long-standing feuds—that might last months or even years. But this was not surprising for a governing board that owed both its election and its support to highly partisan political constituencies.

Although Anne and I tried to be attentive to the concerns of both current and past board members, our position was complicated by the fact that we were occasionally viewed by some regents as hired hands, totally subservient and submissive to their particular requests and occasional whims. Although every effort was made to treat the regents with respect, concern, and attentiveness, the great diversity among the attitudes of individual regents toward the role of the president and the first lady made the task extremely complex, as it had been for our predecessors over the years. Most presidents of public universities know these challenges well.

Students and faculty members tend to take the staff of a university pretty much for granted. While they understand these are the people who "keep the trains running on time" and who provide them with the environment they need for teaching and research, most view staff as only the supporting cast for the real stars, the faculty. When staff come to mind at all, it is usually as a source of complaints. To many faculty members, such service units as the Plant Department, the Purchasing Department, and the Office of University Audits are sometimes viewed as the enemy.

Yet with each step up the ladder of academic administration, my wife and I came to appreciate more just how critical the staff was to both the functioning and the continuity of the university. It became clear to us that throughout the university, whether at the level of secretaries, custodians, or groundskeepers or the rarified heights of senior administrators for finance, hospital operations, or facilities construction and management, the quality of the university's staff, coupled with their commitment and dedication, was actually just as important as the faculty in making Michigan the remarkable institution it has become. In some ways, it was even more so, since unlike many faculty members, who view their first responsibilities as to their discipline or perhaps their careers, most staff members are true professionals, deeply committed to the welfare of the university as their highest priority, many dedicating their entire careers to the institution. Most staff members serve the university far longer than the faculty, who tend to be lured away by the marketplace. This was impressed on me twice each year, when the president would host a banquet to honor staff with long-term service—20, 30, even 40 years. In a very real sense, it is frequently the staff that provide, through years of service, the continuity of both the culture of the university and its commitment to excellence. Put another way, the staff perpetuate the institutional saga of the university as much as do the students, faculty, or alumni.

Beyond their skill, competence, and dedication to the university, there was also a remarkable spirit of teamwork among staff members. We found ourselves working with them not so much as supervisors but, rather, as colleagues. In time, we began to view our presidential roles as more akin to those of staff than faculty, in the sense that our first obligation was always to the welfare of the university rather than to our academic discipline or professional career.

While intensely loyal to the university, staff also require pastoral care from the president, particularly during difficult times, such as budget cuts—sometimes involving layoffs—or campus unrest. Anne and I always gave the highest priority to events that demonstrated the importance of staff to the university and our strong support for their efforts. Whenever launching a major strategic effort, such as the Michigan Mandate or the Michigan Agenda for Women, I would meet with numerous staff groups throughout the university to explain the effort and seek their advice and counsel. We made it a point to attend or host staff receptions, for example, to honor a retiring staff member or celebrate an important achievement. While we understood the central role of faculty in determining the quality of academic programs, we felt it was important that the president always be seen, in word and in deed, as committed to the welfare of the entire university community—students, faculty, and staff—in a balanced sense.

In our presidential roles, Anne and I were always very conscious of being part of another very important Michigan family comprised of former presidents and first ladies of the university. We believed ourselves particularly fortunate in having several of these former presidential teams—the Hatchers, the Flemings, and the Smiths—living in Ann Arbor, with the Shapiros only a phone call away at Princeton. This gave us access to almost half a century of experience and wisdom.

We made it a point not only to seek the advice and counsel of earlier presidents and spouses whenever we could but also to involve them as completely in the life of the university as they wished to be. We made certain that they were invited to all major campus activities, such as dinners, receptions, commencements, and VIP visits. This conscious effort to involve the former presidents in the life of the university was intended not only to take advantage of their experience and wisdom but to better establish a sense of continuity. We realized that each presidency built on the accomplishments of its predecessors, and we wanted to make certain this was recognized throughout the university.

We also immensely enjoyed the friendship of the Hatchers, Flemings, Smiths, and Shapiros. There was a bond that only those who serve in the presidential role can understand. Even after one of our interim presidents, Allen Smith, passed away, we felt it very important to keep his wife, Alene, involved in university activities. When we had the opportunity to honor the Shapiros by naming the newly renovated undergraduate library after them, Anne went all out to design events for the Shapiros and their families, to convey a sense of the university's appreciation for their efforts.

Both Anne and I believed it important always to keep in mind the historical context for leadership. Such institutions as the University of Michigan have existed for centuries and will continue to do so, served by generation after generation of leaders. To serve the university, any Michigan president must understand and acknowledge the accomplishments of his or her predecessors and build on their achievements. Each president must strive to pass along to his or her successor an institution that is better, stronger, and more vital than the one he or she inherited. Indeed, this strong tradition of improvement from one presidency to the next has long been the guiding spirit of the university's leaders.

While Michigan enjoys an intense loyalty among its students, faculty, and staff, it can also be a tough environment for many. It is a very large and complex institution, frequently immersed in controversial social and political issues. The Michigan campus culture has evolved to accommodate a tough political neighborhood. The president's challenge is to provide pastoral care and leadership for a highly diverse campus community that, left to its own devices, could become highly fragmented—that is, to create community in a cold climate.

During my presidency, Anne and I sought to temper somewhat the university's hardened character by stressing certain "c" words: *community, communication, comity, cooperation, civility, caring, concern,* and *commitment*—in contrast to the harsher "c" words *competition, complaining, conniving,* and *conflict.* (Anne suggested adding some other "c" words just for students, such as *cleanliness* and *chastity,* but she soon realized this was a hopeless cause.) Particularly during a period of change, we believed that we needed to better link together the various cultures, values, and experiences that characterized our campus community. We also sought to build a greater sense of pride in and loyalty to the institution, pulling people together with a common vision and commitment to the achievement of excellence.

Some of the most important changes occurring at the university during the decade of my leadership affected the various family cultures of the university. The student culture evolved beyond the distrust and confrontation born in the 1960s to a spirit of mutual respect and trust with the administration. The university's commitment to diversity through such major strategic efforts as the Michigan Mandate and the Michigan Agenda for Women would never have been possible without such a major change in the campus climate. So too, the staff culture became more tolerant of change, in part because of our efforts to recognize the staff's loyalty and immense contributions to the university.

Changes occurred far more slowly in the faculty culture, because of its complexity and diversity. Fundamental academic values—academic freedom, intellectual integrity, striving for excellence—still dominated this culture, as they must in any great university. However, there seemed to be a growing sense of adventure and excitement throughout the university, as both faculty and staff were more willing to take risks, to try new things, and to tolerate failure as part of the learning process. While the university was still not yet where it needed to be in encouraging the level of experimentation and adventure necessary to define its future, it seemed clear that this spirit was beginning to take hold.

PERSONAL TRAITS AND TRAPS

Each president approaches the challenge of moral leadership in a unique way, shaped by his or her own experiences, personality, and deeply held values. As a skilled labor negotiator, Robben Fleming looked for teachable moments even during the most stressful moments of confrontation, always able to control his own demeanor while those about him lost theirs. His calm, reassuring approach to difficult issues, tempered at times with a Midwestern sense of humor, served him well in providing moral leadership.

In contrast, Harold Shapiro always gave careful and deep thought to the values underlying major issues, such as racism on campus or faculty governance. One could always be certain that Shapiro not only listened carefully but read thoroughly the arguments and concerns of others and that he had given matters great thought. Although he found it more difficult than did Fleming to remain emotionally detached from many issues, his careful, thoughtful approach was understood and accepted by all (or at least most).

Clearly, I was neither a skilled negotiator nor always a sufficiently thoughtful (or even rational) leader. But my small-town Midwestern roots gave me a "what you see is what you get" reputation. One of the leaders of the Michigan Mandate, Charles Moody, stated, "If President Duderstadt tells you he is going to do something, you can take it to the bank."

Along with these personality characteristics (possibly flaws to some), I also enjoyed taking on apparently insurmountable challenges, in part because sometimes I actually managed to accomplish something. Even if I occasionally failed, I rationalized that someone had to do it, and it might as well be me. After all, that goes with the territory of the presidency.

Taking on issues of values and morality can be hazardous to one's health, not to mention one's career. Not only are they usually controversial, but they also frequently demand leadership on the front lines.

I firmly believe that only a leader who is willing to carry the flag into battle can move such complex agendas ahead, albeit at considerable personal risk. This is perhaps the reason why so few institutions make progress in such complex areas as social diversity. Several examples illustrate this philosophy.

Many viewed as a significant risk my decision to deliver a sermon on the importance of social diversity at Detroit's largest African American church, the Hartford Memorial Baptist Church. But it was key to building the broad support we needed for the Michigan Mandate. In a similar sense, going over alone to meet with all of the deans and department chairs of the Medical School to read them the riot act about their failures to provide more opportunities for minorities and women students and faculty probably left some bruises (and grudges). But it certainly got the message across.

So, too, did my decision to address the Michigan Quarterback Club, a large body of the football team's most rabid fans, which excluded women from their meetings. It would have been easier to take the politician's approach of simply blasting their behavior in the press, although I suspect that this would have simply bounced off their stag policies. Instead, by using a personal appearance as a teachable moment, I was able to convince them that there was simply no place in the university for gender discrimination and that it was my intent to remove their university recognition if women were not promptly and fully integrated into their activities. Needless to say, the change was immediate and permanent, even if the grumbling continued for a few months.

My support of such issues as diversity and gay rights posed certain dangers from the political environment. On any given issue, presidents may decide that this is not the ditch they choose to die in. But sometimes, risking one's tenure is necessary to sustain one's personal integrity. Diversity was clearly one such issue for me. Although the university's efforts to achieve diversity received the strong support of most members of the university community and alumni, these efforts were not accomplished without considerable resistance. In the mid-1990s, the mood of the nation began to shift toward the Right, and the university was attacked more frequently for its stances on such issues as affirmative action and gay rights. Indeed, during the last year of my tenure, even as other institutions, such as the University of California, were backing away from affirmative action programs, I publicly reaffirmed Michigan's strong commitment to the Michigan Mandate, with the strong support of the campus community, and established even further the university's leadership in higher education.

Yet these political forces began to affect the university's board of regents, resulting in the election of new conservative members who joined others on the board who had opposed the university's diversity efforts. There was little doubt that my deep commitment to diversity and outspoken efforts to lead the university in this direction were not well received by many beyond the campus, who preferred a far more conservative—and socially homogeneous—campus. In retrospect, I have little doubt that these efforts consumed a great deal of my political capital—with the regents, with political leaders in the state, and perhaps with the media. It can be argued that they were instrumental in eroding regental support to the point where, months later, I would conclude that I no longer had sufficient support to continue my ambitious agenda for university transformation. Yet I also believe that I would probably choose to fight in this ditch again, even knowing the outcome. There are few causes that are clearly worthy of such sacrifices. Social justice and equity are certainly among them.

9

STRATEGIC LEADERSHIP

One of first questions usually posed to candidates for university presidencies concerns their vision for the future of the institution. However, beyond such platitudes as "enhancing the life of the mind" or winning a national championship in a revenue sport, the development of a vision for the future of a university is an extremely difficult task. Universities are notoriously complex institutions whose evolution is strongly influenced by their unique cultures, histories, and traditions. Even those internal candidates possessing intimate familiarity with the institution can find the development of a vision an uphill struggle. Imagine the plight of external candidates, unfamiliar with the institutional saga of the university and given only a brief honeymoon period to propose their vision and plan for the future of the institution.

Yet there have been numerous examples in which visionary university leaders were able to craft both a compelling vision for the future of their institutions and a successful strategy for achieving it. Some notable twentieth-century examples include Clark Kerr, who designed and built the greatest university system in the world in the University of California; Frederick Terman, who transformed Stanford into the scientific and technological powerhouse that created Silicon Valley; Richard Cyert, who led Carnegie Mellon University to a position of leadership in key areas, such as computer science; Charles Young, who transformed the University of California, Los Angeles, from a city college into a great research university; and Richard Atkinson, who led the young University of California campus in San Diego to become one of the leading research universities in the world in less than two decades. Although many Wolverines would hate to admit it, this list would also include John Hannah, who transformed Michigan Agriculture College into a world-class research university, Michigan State University.

The University of Michigan has been fortunate to have been led by visionary presidents during various periods of its long history. Henry Tappan transformed Michigan into one of the nation's first true universities. James Angell and, much later, Harlan Hatcher presided over periods of extraordinary growth in the university. Harold Shapiro understood the need for Michigan to transform itself into a predominantly privately supported university characterized by high standards if it was to sustain its quality during an extended period of weakened public support.

While there are many examples of visionary leadership in higher education, it is also fair to suggest that it is certainly not the norm. Beyond the challenge of developing a bold vision for a university's future, leading the institution toward such visions can be a hazardous task. It is little wonder that most university presidents tend to polish the status quo rather than proposing new paradigms, content to allow their institution to drift along without rocking the boat, until they disembark for their next leadership assignment.

Yet while the status quo may be the safest course for survival of university presidents, it can pose substantial risks to the institution. Universities that drift along, without a vision or strong leadership, can founder on rocky shoals. Although a university may seem to be doing just fine with benign neglect from the administration building, over a longer period of time a series of short-term tactical decisions will dictate a de facto strategy that may not be in the long-range interests of the university. Leading a university during a time of great social change without some formal planning process is a bit like navigating the Titanic through an iceberg floe in the dead of night. Simply reacting to challenges and opportunities as they arise can eventually sink the ship.

At Michigan, we had encountered a particularly large iceberg during the early 1980s with the loss of much of our state support. Harold Shapiro and his administrative team had done an admirable job at addressing the near-term crisis through a "smaller but better" strategy. But Shapiro realized the need to develop a longer-term planning process capable of not only navigating the treacherous waters ahead but seizing the opportunities presented by an increasingly knowledge-intensive society. This was to be my primary assignment when he lured me from my position as dean of the College of Engineering to become the university's provost in 1985. The two of us were to work closely together, as president and provost, to design and launch just such a planning process, although he would remind me, "Man plans while God laughs!"

Here, we accepted several key assumptions. First, we recognized that the University of Michigan was a very complex system, responding to the cumulative effects of its history as well as to its interactions with the changing external world. Despite this complexity, we believed it critical that the university take responsibility for its own future, rather than having its future determined for it by external forces and pressures. In particular, we sought a far more strategic and opportunistic approach to leadership, rather than simply reacting to the changing world about us. Second, we believed that the University of Michigan would face a period of unusual opportunity, responsibility, and challenge in the 1990s. During this pivotal decade, it could—indeed, must—seize control of its own destiny by charting a course to take it into the next century. Finally, we were convinced that the challenges facing higher education in the late twentieth century required a new paradigm for the university in America and that the University of Michigan was in an excellent position to develop this model for the nation, just as it had in earlier times through its trailblazing saga.

THE APPROACH

As dean, as provost, and then as president, I sought progressive, flexible, and adaptive planning processes, capable of responding to a dynamic environment and an uncertain—indeed, unknowable—future. My goal was to develop flexible strategies that avoided rigid paths or deep ruts and positioned the university to take advantage of windows of opportunity to pursue well-defined objectives as they arose. In a sense, I utilized an informed dead-reckoning approach, in which one first selected strategic objectives—where we wanted to go—and then followed whichever path seemed appropriate at the time, possibly shifting paths as strategic plans were updated and as additional information and experience dictated. I never assumed that the planning framework was rigid, since what might appear first as constraints could, with skill and cleverness, frequently be transformed into opportunities. When state appropriations were cut, my team used this as an opportunity to convince donors that since they no longer provided as much funding to the university when they paid their taxes on April 15, they should shift to funding us through private giving, much like a private university. When publishers dramatically increased the cost of serials to our libraries, we were able to convince the Big Ten universities that it was time to set aside competition and share library resources, creating, in effect, a gigantic resource with over 78 million volumes.

Another aspect of our planning was the belief that the real creativity, innovation, and wisdom in a university existed at the grassroots level, among faculty, students, and staff. Hence, every planning effort involved numerous planning groups—some formal, some ad hoc—that played a very essential role in guiding our efforts. Many brainstorming sessions at the President's House went late into the evening, challenging assumptions, proposing alternatives, and wondering "what if." I viewed my role as stimulating, harvesting, shaping, and refining the ideas bubbling up from the university community.

As I have stressed throughout this book, long-enduring institutions, such as universities, need to begin with an understanding of their history, tradition, and values—their institutional saga. These form the initial conditions for any planning process. Beyond this, it is important to gain an understanding of possible constraints that might restrict planning options, since these might be challenged and relaxed. In our case, a faltering Michigan economy that was no longer able to support a world-class public research university was clearly a serious concern. But so, too, were an array of demographic issues, such as the need to serve underrepresented minority communities and to embrace diversity as key to our capacity to serve an increasingly diverse state, nation, and world. Michigan's long history of international activities had sensitized us to the growing trends of globalization, just as the university's leadership in developing and implementing new technologies, such as the Internet, had given us a good perspective of technological change.

Key in the planning effort was the task of developing a vision statement for the university, a task made particularly difficult by the very broad range of activities and roles of the institution. I began by challenging our planning groups to come up with a single word to characterize our future, such as *excellence* or *public* or *diversity.* Next, I asked the groups to combine several of these words into a descriptive phrase, such as "a leading, public, research university." Finally, I asked them to use this exercise to develop, in a phrase (or, rather, a bumper-sticker slogan), a vision for the university's future. Here, there were lots of suggestions (accompanied by lots of discussion): "the nation's leading public university" (but why not simply "the world's leading university"?), "the university of the common man" (or even "the university of the poor"?), "America's university" (but was this not rather impolitic for a "state" university?), and so on.

Soon our planning efforts began to converge on a vision stressing two important themes: leadership and excellence. Looking back over the history of the university, we realized that quality by itself was never quite enough for Michigan. Here, the aspiration of going beyond excellence to achieve true leadership clearly reflected our understanding of the university's history as a trailblazer. This process eventually led to the following planning vision for the 1990s:

> Vision 2000: To position the University of Michigan to become a leading university of the twentieth century, through the quality and leadership of its programs, and through the achievements of its students, faculty, and staff.

Such a leadership vision required a comprehensive strategy based on improving and optimizing the key characteristics of the university: quality, capacity (size), and breadth (comprehensiveness). Yet even at this early stage of visioning, the campus community became both engaged and energized in exercises to determine the university's future.

THE ACTION PLAN

Of course, vision statements are empty without follow-through, actions, and results. To shift the institution into action mode, my administrative team set out several general challenges—which I termed "the challenges of excellence"—for the next phase of the planning exercise. First, we asked for a rededication to the achievement of excellence. It was time for Michigan to pick up the pace, by building a level of intensity and expectation that compelled us to settle for nothing less than the best in the performance of faculty, students, and programs. We encouraged the university to strive for even higher quality, since it would be the achievement of excellence that would set us apart and provide us with the visibility to attract the elements so essential to the enterprise—human and financial resources, outstanding students and faculty, and support from the public and private sectors.

Second, if we were to achieve excellence, we needed to commit ourselves to focusing resources. In decades past, regular increases in public support had allowed the university to attempt to do a great many things with a great many people and to attempt to do them all very well. However, in the future of constrained resources that we faced, we could no longer afford to be all things to all people. Quality had to take priority over the breadth and capacity of our programs and become our primary objective.

Third, as we focused our resources to achieve excellence, we needed to keep in mind that our highest priority was academic excellence—outstanding teaching, research, and scholarship. The University of Michigan's reputation would not be built on the football field. It would be based on the quality of its activities in scholarship and learning.

Fourth, the university needed to be responsive to changing intellectual currents. Academic leadership demanded pursuing the paths of discovery that influence the evolution of intellectual disciplines. We were increasingly finding that the most exciting work was occurring not within traditional disciplines but, rather, at the interfaces between traditional disciplines, where there was a collision of ideas that could lead to new knowledge. At Michigan, we wanted to stimulate a transition to a change-oriented culture in which creativity, initiative, and innovation were valued. We needed to do more than simply respond grudgingly to change; we needed to relish and stimulate it.

Fifth, the university faced the challenge of diversity and pluralism. Our ability to achieve excellence in teaching, scholarship, and service would be determined over time by the diversity of our campus community. We accepted our responsibility to reach out to and increase the participation of those racial, ethnic, and cultural groups not adequately represented among our students, faculty, and staff. Beyond this, we faced the challenge of building an environment of mutual understanding and respect that not only tolerated diversity but sought out and embraced it as an essential objective of the university. Here, we were clearly sowing the seeds that would later grow into the Michigan Mandate and the Michigan Agenda for Women.

Finally, to achieve the objective of leadership, we proposed to focus wherever possible on exciting, bold initiatives, consistent with the Michigan saga as a trailblazer. We aimed to stimulate, encourage, and support more high-risk activities. As steps in this direction, we began to reallocate each year a portion of the university's academic base budget into a Strategic Initiative Fund designed to support a competitive grants program addressing key university priorities, such as undergraduate education, diversity, and interdisciplinary scholarship. This fund was augmented by private support. Once again, the fish foodball theory of university behavior (see chapter 6) came into play, as highly creative proposals and initiatives began to bubble up from faculty, students, and staff to address each of our priorities.

Some of our initiatives were obvious, if challenging. We set a goal of building private support for the university to levels comparable to our annual state appropriation, which not only led to the first $1 billion fund-raising campaign for a public university but also stimulated a far more aggressive strategy for investing the university's assets, including its growing endowment. We developed new strategies for rebuilding the university's campuses with internal funding and private support, rather than waiting for the next round of state support for capital facilities. We provided deans and directors with strong authority, along with accountability, in the control of their own revenues and expenditures, essentially completing the decentralization of the university's financial management begun under Harold Shapiro.

We were prepared to make major investments in high-risk intellectual activities, but only in those areas where we had established strength. Some of these investments achieved spectacular success. For example, our investment in the management of NSFnet resulted in the creation of the Internet. Other investments failed, such as the major (but premature) effort to build the nation's first clinical programs in human gene therapy. But even in failure we learned valuable lessons. To create even more of a spirit of innovation, we sprinkled several "skunk works" activities about the campus (analogous to the famous Lockheed Skunk Works), some in existing academic units, such as the transformation of our School of Library Science into a School of Information, and some in new multidisciplinary facilities, such as the Media Union (see chapter 6).

Finally, we set a series of stretch goals, including becoming the national leader in such areas as campus diversity, sponsored research activity, faculty salaries, clinical operations, and the global outreach of our academic programs. As we began to make progress on our strategic goals, we fell into a pattern of raising the bar, compressing the timetable, and upping the ante. By the early 1990s, we began to realize something very surprising: we were not only achieving our objectives, but in most cases, we were going far beyond the goals we had originally set. The strategic goals associated with Vision 2000 were essentially achieved by 1993, seven years ahead of schedule. Hence, we soon began to wonder what to do for an encore.

LESSONS LEARNED AND THE GROWING CONCERN

There are many lessons, both good and bad, to be learned from Michigan's comprehensive planning effort during the 1980s and early 1990s, particularly when it turns out to be remarkably successful. Beyond the obvious challenges (to build on the institutional saga; to keep your eyes on the goals; to be candid, demanding, and evidence-based in your appraisal of progress and generous in your praise of achievement), other challenges arose from both the nature and the particular history of the university. I had recognized early in my provost role how important it was to shift the university away from a reactive, crisis mode to a more strategic focus after the trauma of state budget cuts and difficult reallocation decisions during the 1980s. Yet this was very difficult for some of our academic units. Not surprisingly, long-range planning was difficult for such a large and diverse academic unit as our College of Literature, Sciences, and the Arts, with almost 1,000 faculty, 20,000 students, and 45 departments. But, to our surprise, it was equally difficult for some of our professional schools, such as our School of Business, which had difficulty understanding the planning process or accepting any vision other than "We want to be better than Harvard!"

After the hard financial times of the 1980s, it was similarly difficult to re-create the risk-taking culture that had been such an important part of the Michigan institutional saga as a trailblazer. Institutions all too frequently choose a timid course of incremental, reactive change because they view a more strategically driven transformation process as too risky. They are worried about making a mistake, about heading in the wrong direction or failing. While they are aware that this incremental approach can occasionally miss an opportunity, many mature organizations would prefer the risk of missed opportunity to the danger of heading into the unknown.[1]

Yet in the end, through considerable effort by the administration in engaging the university community (and perhaps a certain tolerance for the planning inclinations of an engineer as president—actually, of two engineers for a time, as the provost position was filled first by Chuck Vest and then by Gil Whitaker, a former dean of the School of Business), the planning process was successful in achieving essentially all of our original goals. The Vision 2000 strategy, designed to move the university toward both the leadership vision and the strategic intent of transformation, succeeded beyond our wildest expectations. But this very success turned out to be one of our most formidable challenges.

With each step we took, with every project we launched, with each objective we achieved, I became increasingly uneasy. The closer the university approached its vision for the future, the more distant and uncertain it appeared to me, and the less confident I became that we were headed in the right direction. It became increasingly clear that the forces driving change in our society were far stronger and more profound that we had first thought. Furthermore, many of the social, economic, and technological forces driving change in higher education were disruptive in nature, leading to quite unpredictable futures. The future was becoming less certain as the range of possibilities expanded to include more radical alternatives.

Put another way, I became convinced that the Vision 2000 effort, while bold and challenging, was in reality only a positioning strategy, designed to achieve excellence and leadership, but within the current paradigm of the university in twentieth-century America. To be sure, this effort accomplished many of the tasks necessary to prepare the university for the new century, such as financial restructuring, diversifying our campuses, and rebuilding our physical environment for teaching and research. But the real challenge lay ahead: to transform the university so that it could better serve a rapidly changing society. We had now positioned the university for leadership. The next task was to determine where it would lead. By the early 1990s, it had become apparent that we needed to shift from our Vision 2000 plan, based on a series of small wins with an occasional opportunistic surge, to a bolder agenda based on blockbuster goals. Put another way, we needed to shift from positioning the university as a leading twentieth-century institution to transforming it into a twenty-first-century university designed to serve a profoundly different world.

INSTITUTIONAL TRANSFORMATION

So how does an institution as large, complex, and bound by tradition as the University of Michigan go about the process of transformation? Sometimes, one can stimulate change simply by buying it with additional resources. More frequently, transformational change involves first laboriously building a consensus necessary for grassroots support. But there are also times when change requires a more Machiavellian approach, using finesse—perhaps even by stealth of night—to disguise as small wins actions that were in reality aimed at blockbuster goals. And I must confess that there were times when, weary of the endless meetings with group after group (including, at times, our own governing board) to build consensus, we decided instead to take the Nike approach and "just do it," that is, to move ahead with top-down decisions and rapid execution—although in these cases, the president usually bears the burden of blame and hence the responsibility for the necessary apologies.

Michigan's own history provides many examples of both the payoffs and the risks of institutional transformation. Tappan's effort in the 1850s to transform a small frontier college into a true university was certainly important in the history of American higher education, although it cost him his job in the end. Little's effort in the 1920s to restore the collegiate model was also a transformative effort, but it failed to align with Michigan's history and tradition. During a period of relative prosperity, Hatcher had the capacity to launch numerous transformative initiatives important for the university—for example, the Residential College, the Pilot Program, and the Center for Research on Learning and Teaching. But during the 1960s, this transformation effort went unstable, as the university was overtaken by political activism that sought not to transform but, rather, to destroy the establishment. This illustrates the danger that arises when a change process becomes entangled with ideology and special interest agendas that divert it from the original goals. In the best scenario, the values and traditions of the institution will provide important limits on the process of change, so that the transformation process does not lead to a destructive outcome.

Of course, I was no stranger to transformation efforts, some highly successful—for example, the rebuilding of the University's College of Engineering, the Michigan Mandate and Michigan Agenda for Women, and the transformation of the university's research environment. But there had also been failures—for instance, the effort to better align auxiliary activities, such as the Athletic Department and the Medical Center, with the core academic values of the university; the attempt to shift the regents' perception of their roles from that of political governors to loyal trustees of the institution; and the effort to build stronger coalitions of universities, such as the Big Ten Conference, to work together on common goals. Through these efforts (both the successful and the unsuccessful) and from the experience of other organizations in both the private and public sector, it was clear that the more ambitious goal of institution-wide transformation—the reinvention of the university itself—would depend heavily on several key factors.

First, I recognized the importance of properly defining the real challenges of the transformation process. The challenge, as is so often the case, was neither financial nor organizational. Rather, it was the degree of cultural change required. We had to transform a set of rigid habits of thought and arrangements that were currently incapable of responding to change either rapidly or radically enough.[2]

Second, it was important to achieve true faculty participation in the design and implementation of the transformation process. This was true in part because the transformation of faculty culture is generally the biggest challenge of all. I believe that faculty participation should involve its true intellectual leadership rather than the political leadership more common to elected faculty governance.

Third, experience in other sectors suggested that externalities—both groups and events—were not only very helpful but probably necessary to lend credibility to the process and to assist in putting controversial issues (e.g., tenure reform) on the table. Unfortunately, universities—like most organizations in the corporate sector—rarely have been able to achieve major change through the motivation of opportunity and excitement alone. Rather, it takes a crisis to get people to take the transformation effort seriously, and sometimes even this is not sufficient.

Finally, it was clear that the task of leading transformation could not be delegated. Rather, as president, I would need to play a critical role both as a leader and as an educator in designing, implementing, and selling the transformation process, particularly with the faculty. Furthermore, my presidential leadership had to be visible out in front of the troops rather than far behind the front lines.

Hence, in 1993, the university turned toward a bolder vision aimed at providing leadership through institutional transformation. This objective, termed "Vision 2017" in reference to the date of the two-hundredth anniversary of the university's founding, was designed to provide Michigan with the capacity to reinvent its very nature, to transform itself into an institution better capable of serving a new world in a new century. This transformation strategy contrasted sharply with the earlier, positioning strategy that had guided the university during the 1980s. It sought to build the capacity, the energy, the excitement, and the risk-taking culture necessary for the university to explore entirely new paradigms of teaching, research, and service. It sought to remove the constraints that would prevent the university from responding to the needs of a rapidly changing society—to remove unnecessary processes and administrative structures; to question existing premises and arrangements; and to challenge, excite, and embolden the members of the university community.

Of course, much of the preparation for this transformation had already occurred earlier in my presidency, when several of the major strategic thrusts were launched. A series of planning groups, both formal and ad hoc, had been meeting to consider the future of the university. This effort included the strategic planning teams of the late 1980s, ad hoc meetings of faculty across the university, and numerous joint retreats of executive officers, deans, and faculty leaders. A presidential advisory committee of external advisors had been formed and had been meeting regularly on strategic issues for several years. Extended strategic discussions with the board of regents had been initiated and would continue through the transformation effort.

However, we needed something beyond this, to break our thinking out of the box, expanding our sense of the possible to encompass even highly unlikely alternatives. To this end, we first took advantage of the presence on our business school faculty of C. K. Prahalad, one of the world's most influential corporate strategists, asking him to lead a group of senior administration and faculty leaders through the same strategic process that he had conducted for the executive leadership of many of the major corporations in the world. We followed this by inviting Robert Zemsky, both an important thought leader in higher education and an experienced facilitator of strategic discussions, to lead several sessions of a roundtable group, including junior faculty members as well as senior leadership.

The Vision 2000 strategy required a careful optimization of the interrelated characteristics of institutional quality, size, and breadth. Transformation would require more: tapping the trailblazing spirit of the Michigan saga. It would emphasize risk taking and innovation. It would demand the bold agenda of reinventing the university for a new era and a new world.

To capture a bolder vision of the university's future, we turned to C. K. Prahalad for his concept of *strategic intent*.[3] The traditional approach to strategic planning focuses on the fit between existing resources and current opportunities. Strategic intent is a stretch vision that intentionally creates an extreme misfit between current resources and future objectives and thus requires institutional transformation to build new capabilities. Michigan developed the following strategic intent:

> The Strategic Intent (Vision 2017): To provide the university with the capacity to reinvent itself as an institution more capable of serving a changing state, nation, and world.

Vision 2017 depended for its success on sustaining our most cherished values and our hopes for the future: excellence, leadership, critical and rational inquiry, liberal learning, diversity, caring and concern, community, and excitement. In addition, we paid particular attention to those elements of the university's institutional saga that were important to preserve, as well as those values and characteristics that were our fundamental aspirations. The figure that follows summarizes this aspect of our transformation process. Around the core of values and characteristics are arranged a number of possible paradigms of the university. While none of these alone would appropriately describe the university as it entered its third century, each was a possible component of our institution, as seen by various constituents. Put another way, each of these paradigms was a possible pathway toward the university of the twenty-first century. Each was also a pathway we believed should be explored in our effort to better understand our future.

We proposed four simply stated goals to help move the university beyond the leadership positioning of Vision 2000 and toward the paradigm shifting of Vision 2017:

Goal 1: To attract, retain, support, and empower exceptional students, faculty, and staff

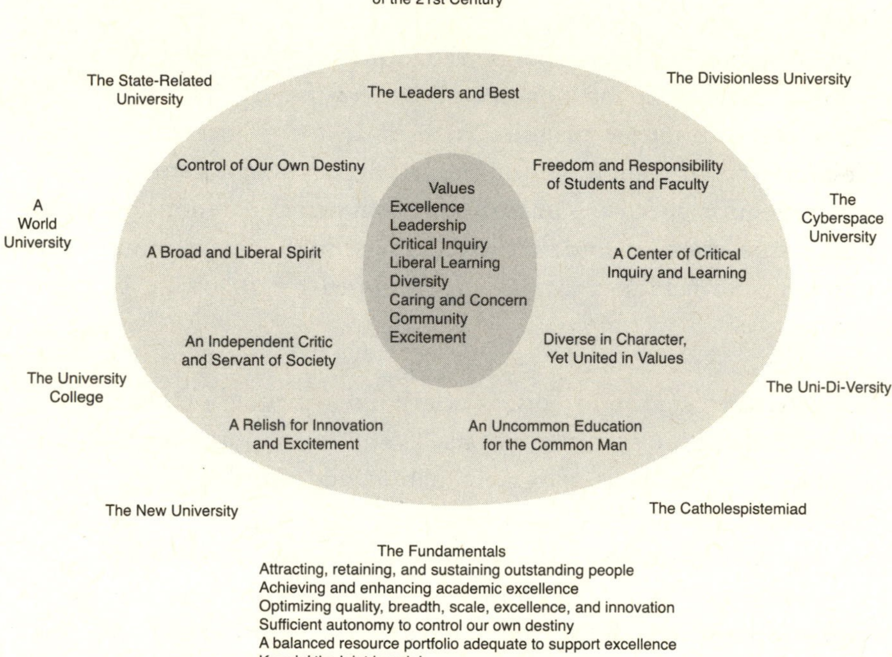

Goal 2: To provide these people with the resources, environment, and encouragement to push to the limits of their abilities and their dreams

Goal 3: To build a university culture and spirit that values adventure, excitement, and risk taking; leadership; excellence; diversity; and social values, such as community, caring, and compassion

Goal 4: To develop the flexibility and ability to focus resources necessary to serve a changing society and a changing world

Although simply stated, these four goals were profound in their implications and challenging in their execution. For example, while Michigan had always sought to attract high-quality students and faculty to the university, it tended to recruit those who conformed to more traditional measures of excellence. If we were to go after "paradigm breakers," other criteria—such as creativity, intellectual span, and the ability to lead—would become important. The university needed to acquire the resources necessary to sustain excellence, a challenge at a time when public support was dwindling. Yet this goal suggested something beyond that: we needed to focus resources on our most creative people and programs. We also needed to acquire the flexibility in resource allocation to respond to new opportunities and initiatives.

While most people would agree with the values set out in our third goal of cultural change, many would not assign such a high priority to striving for adventure, excitement, and risk taking. However, if the university was to become a leader in defining the nature of higher education in the century ahead, this type of culture was essential. Developing the capacity for change, while an obvious goal, would be both challenging and controversial. We needed to discard the status quo as a viable option (to challenge existing premises, policies, and mind-sets) and to empower our best people to drive the evolution—or revolution—of the university.

The transformation agenda we proposed, like the university itself, was unusually broad and multifaceted. Part of the challenge lay in directing the attention of members of the university community and its multiple constituencies toward those aspects of the agenda most appropriate for their talents. For example, we believed that faculty should focus primarily on the issues of educational and intellectual transformation and the evolving nature of the academy itself. The regents, because of their unusual responsibility for policy and fiscal matters, should play key roles in the financial and organizational restructuring of the university. Faculty and staff with strong entrepreneurial interests and skills should be asked to guide the development of new markets of the knowledge-based services of the university.

It is hard to persuade existing programs within an organization to change to meet changing circumstances. This is particularly the case in a university, in which top-down hierarchical management has limited impact in the face of the creative anarchy of academic culture. One approach is to identify and then support islands of entrepreneurialism, those activities within the university that are already adapting to a rapidly changing environment. Another approach is to launch new or greenfield initiatives that are designed to build in the necessary elements for change. If these initiatives are provided with adequate resources and incentives, faculty, staff, and students can be drawn into the new activities. Those initiatives that prove successful will grow rapidly and, if designed properly, will pull resources away from existing activities resistant to change. Greenfield approaches create a Darwinian process in which the successful new initiatives devour older, obsolete efforts, while unsuccessful initiatives are unable to compete with ongoing activities capable of sustaining their relevance during a period of rapid change.

Institutional transformation requires a clear and compelling articulation of the need to change and a strong vision of where the change process will lead. While the debate over specific elements of the transformation process should involve broad elements of the university community and its constituents, the vision itself should come—indeed, must come—from the president. My administration made the case for transformation and both short- and long-range visions (Vision 2000 and Vision 2017) in a series of documents intended to serve as the foundation for the effort. Further, these documents summarized the ongoing planning effort, developed a scheme to measure progress toward goals, and sketched a plan for transforming the university.[4]

Beyond this task, I served, as president, not only as the leader of the transformation effort but also as its principal evangelist. In an academic institution, the role of the president is in many ways like that of a teacher, explaining to various campus and external constituencies the need for transformation and setting out an exciting and compelling vision of where the transformation process will lead. In almost every address I gave during my presidency, in every available forum, I stressed two recurring themes: leadership and change. Each of my annual State of the University addresses during my latter years as president focused on different aspects of required change and on the challenges and opportunities these presented to the university—for example, diversity, intellectual change, and renegotiating the social contract between the public university and society. Each of these presentations stressed that the University of Michigan had a long heritage of providing leadership to higher education during periods of change and that it was positioned to do the same in the twenty-first century. As my administrative team's efforts moved into high gear, we televised roundtable discussions among students and faculty on key strategic issues, such as diversity, undergraduate education, and multidisciplinary scholarship. These discussions, moderated by myself, were videotaped and shown both on the university's internal closed-circuit broadcasting network and on the community-access channels on Ann Arbor's cable television network.

When we launched the transformation effort in 1993, we held dozens of meetings with various groups on campus (much as we had done with the Michigan Mandate), both to explain the importance of the transformation effort and to seek input and engagement. Over the course of the next two years, I managed to meet not only with the faculties of each of our major schools and colleges and larger departments but also with several dozen staff groups in such areas as business, finance, and facilities. The final element of communication and engagement was to launch a series of presidential commissions composed of leading faculty members, to study particular issues and develop recommendations for university actions. These commissions were chaired by several of our most distinguished and influential faculty and populated with change agents. Among the topics included in their studies were the organization of the university; recruiting and retaining the extraordinary (students, faculty); streamlining processes, procedures, and policies; the faculty contract (i.e., tenure); and developing new paradigms for undergraduate education within the environment of a research university. A more complete description and analysis of the UM experience in strategic planning and institutional transformation during the 1990s is provided in the Internet document *Positioning the University of Michigan for the New Millennium.*[5]

EXPERIMENTS AND VENTURES

As the various elements of Michigan's transformation agenda came into place, our philosophy also began to shift. We came to the conclusion that in a world of such rapid and profound change, as we faced a future of such uncertainty, the most realistic near-term approach was to explore possible futures of the university through experimentation and discovery. Rather than continue to contemplate possibilities for the future through abstract study and debate, it seemed a more productive course to build several prototypes of future learning institutions as working experiments. In this way, the university could actively explore possible paths to the future.

Some experiments had actually been launched during the Vision 2000 positioning phase. One example was our exploration of the possible future of becoming a privately supported but publicly committed university by completely restructuring our financing, raising over $1.4 billion in a major campaign, increasing tuition levels, dramatically increasing sponsored research support to the highest in the nation, and increasing our endowment tenfold. Another early experiment was exploring the theme of a "diverse university" through such efforts as the Michigan Mandate and the Michigan Agenda for Women.

There were also new experiments. The university established campuses in Europe, Asia, and Latin America, linking them with robust information technology, to understand better the implications of becoming a "world university." Michigan played leadership roles in the building and management of first the Internet and then its successor, Internet2, to explore the "cyberspace university" theme. We also launched the Michigan Virtual University as such an experiment.

Of course, not all of our experiments were successful. Some crashed in flames—in some cases, spectacularly. My administration explored the possibility of spinning off our academic health center, merging it with another large hospital system in Michigan to form an independent health care system. But our regents resisted this strongly, concerned that we would be giving away a valuable asset (even though we would have netted well over $1 billion in the transaction and avoided an anticipated $100 million in annual operating losses as managed care swept across Michigan). Although eventually the Michigan Supreme Court ruled that the intrusive nature of the state's sunshine laws interfered with the regents' responsibilities for selecting presidents, we ran into a brick wall when attempting to restructure how our governing board was selected and operated. And the university attempted to confront its own version of Tyrannosaurus Rex by challenging the Athletic Department to better align its athletic activities with academic priorities—for example, by recruiting real students, reshaping competitive schedules, throttling back commercialism, and even appointing a real educator (a former dean) as athletic director. Yet the university is now poised to spend over $250 million on skyboxes for Michigan Stadium after expanding stadium capacity in the 1990s to over 110,000 and raising ticket prices to over $150 per game.

Nevertheless, in most of these cases, at least we learned something—if only about our own ineffectiveness in dealing with such cosmic forces as college sports. More specifically, all of these efforts were driven by the grassroots interests, abilities, and enthusiasm of faculty and students. While such an exploratory approach was disconcerting to some and frustrating to others, there were fortunately many on our campus and beyond who viewed this phase as an exciting adventure. All of these initiatives were important in understanding better the possible futures facing our university. All have influenced the evolution of our university.

MORE LESSONS LEARNED: THE CHALLENGES OF TRANSFORMATION

The experience of the University of Michigan during the 1990s suggests the importance of several factors in achieving successful transformation. First, it is important that any transformation effort always begin with the basics, by launching a careful reconsideration of the key roles and values that should be protected and preserved during a period of change. The history of the university in America is that of a social institution created and shaped by public needs, public policy, and public investment to serve a growing nation. Yet in few places within the academy, at the level of governing boards, or in government higher education policy does there appear to be a serious and sustained discussion (at a time when it is so desperately needed) of the fundamental values so necessary to the nature and role of the university.[6] It is the role of the president to stimulate this dialogue by raising the most fundamental issues involving institutional values.

It is critical that the senior leadership of the university buy into the transformation process and fully support it—or else step off the train before it leaves the station. This is required not only of executive officers and deans but of key faculty leaders as well. It is also essential that the governing board of the university be supportive—or at least not resist—the transformation effort. External advisory bodies are useful to provide alternative perspectives and credibility to the effort. In fact, it is the duty of the governing board to charge a president with the responsibility to develop a plan for the future of the university (setting goals and developing the means to achieve them), if it is to have a framework for assessing presidential performance.

Mechanisms for active debate concerning the transformation objectives and process must be provided to the campus community. At Michigan, we launched a series of presidential commissions on such key issues as the organization of the university, recruiting outstanding faculty and students, and streamlining administrative processes. Each of our schools and colleges was also encouraged to identify key issues of concern and interest. Effective communication throughout the campus community is absolutely critical for the success of the transformation process.

Efforts should be made to identify individuals—at all levels and in various units of the university—who will buy into the transformation process and become active agents on its behalf. In some cases, these will be the institution's most influential faculty and staff. In others, it will be a group of junior faculty or perhaps key administrators. Every opportunity should be used to put in place leaders at all levels of the university—executive officers, deans and directors, chairs and managers—who not only understand the profound nature of the transformations that must occur in higher education in the years ahead but are effective in leading such transformation efforts.

Clearly, significant resources are required to fuel the transformation process, probably at the level of 5 to 10 percent of the academic budget. During a period of limited new funding, it takes considerable creativity (and courage) to generate these resources. As I noted earlier in considering financial issues, the only sources of funding at the levels required for such major transformation are usually tuition, private support, and auxiliary activity revenues, so reallocation must play an important role.

Large organizations will resist change. They will try to wear leaders down or wait them out (under the assumption "This, too, shall pass"). Administrators must give leaders throughout the institution every opportunity to consider carefully the issues compelling change and must encourage them to climb on board the transformation train. For change to occur, administrators need to strike a delicate balance between the forces that make change inevitable (whether threats or opportunities) and a certain sense of stability and confidence that allows people to take risks. For example, how do administrators simultaneously establish sufficient confidence in the long-term support and vitality of the institution and make a compelling case for the importance of the transformation process?

Leading the transformation of a highly decentralized organization is a quite different task than leading strategic efforts that align with long-accepted goals. Unlike traditional strategic activities, where methodical planning and incremental execution can be effective, transformational leadership must risk driving an organization into a state of instability in order to achieve dramatic change. Timing is everything, and the biggest mistake can be agonizing too long over difficult decisions, since the longer an institution remains in an unstable state, the higher the risks of a catastrophic result can be. It is important to minimize the duration of such instability, since the longer it lasts, the more likely it is that the system will move off in an unintended direction or sustain permanent damage. Those who hesitate are lost.

I had learned from my days as dean of the College of Engineering that during the early stages of transformative leadership, you can make a great deal of progress simply because most people do not take you very seriously, while those who do are usually supportive. However, as it becomes more apparent not only that you mean what you say but that you can deliver the goods, resistance begins to build from those moored to the status quo. I sensed that I was becoming increasingly dangerous to those who feared change.

As we broke our thinking out of the box, pushing the envelope further and further, I worried that it was increasingly awkward and perhaps even hazardous for the president to be carrying the message all the time. As my awareness grew about just how profound the changes occurring in our world were becoming, my own speculation about the future of higher education was beginning to approach what some might consider the lunatic fringe. I worried that my own capacity to lead could well be undermined by my own provocative thinking on many of these issues. There were times when I wondered if it was time for the president to stop simply posing public questions (and taking behind-the-scenes actions) and instead begin to provide candid assessments of how we were changing and where we were headed. Or perhaps it was time to set aside the restrictive mantle of university leadership and instead join with others who were actually inventing this future.

Yet university leaders should approach issues and decisions concerning transformation not as threats but, rather, as opportunities. It is true that the status quo may no longer be an option. However, once one accepts that change is inevitable, it can be used as a strategic opportunity to shape the destiny of an institution, while preserving the most important of its values and traditions.

PART III

The University President: An Endangered Species?

10

LIFE AS A UNIVERSITY PRESIDENT

Many people would probably regard a university presidency as the ideal career, where one is highly admired, heavily pampered, and leads a life of luxury comparable to that of an English lord. To be sure, university presidents have many exciting experiences and meet some fascinating people. However, those contemplating such careers for the perks and luxuries should take caution, because not only are these few and far between, but they are accompanied by some serious drawbacks.

True, a university president may live in a large mansion, but for many presidents, this is more a place of work than a pleasant residence. With the increased public scrutiny of such roles, many presidential families have found themselves assuming roles of caretakers and even servants in the presidential residence, in addition to their responsibilities as hosts for university events. What about all of those perks like a box at the football games and center-row orchestra seats at concerts and theatrical events? To the president, an athletic event is a working assignment with the primary objective of raising money from donors or lobbying politicians for the university's interests. My wife, Anne, and I would generally entertain several hundred guests before each game and then invite several dozen guests to our box for the game itself. Who had the time to watch the game while entertaining, persuading, and cajoling potential donors or lobbying politicians? Since we were usually at events most nights of the week (when we were in town), there was little time to attend concerts, unless, of course, we were cultivating donors in the process. Usually, we just gave our tickets away to students.

Now don't get me wrong. A university presidency can be a very satisfying assignment. You get to meet lots of interesting people, and you are working on behalf of an important social institution. But the presidency is certainly not a lifestyle for the rich and famous, as this chapter will demonstrate.

THE PRESIDENT'S SPOUSE

Although unwritten in the university contract for a president, there has long been an expectation that the president's spouse will be a full participant in presidential activities. Much like the presidency of the United States or the governorship of a state, a university presidency is really a two-person job, although generally only one partner gets paid and recognized in an employment sense. At many universities, such as Michigan, the First Lady of the university is expected to play an important role not only as the symbolic host of presidential events—and perhaps also as the symbolic mom of the student body—but in actually planning and managing a complex array of events, facilities, and staff. These responsibilities include hosting dignitaries visiting the campus; organizing almost daily events for faculty, students, and staff; and managing entertainment facilities, such as the President's House or the hospitality areas of the football stadium.

Throughout the University of Michigan's history, the spouse of the president has played an important role. Julia Tappan provided strong leadership for the frontier community of Ann Arbor and was affectionately called "Mrs. Chancellor." Sarah Angell was strongly supportive of women on campus and was instrumental in launching the Women's League. Nina Burton started the Faculty Women's Club and served as its first president. Florence Ruthven, Anne Hatcher, and Sally Fleming all played key roles in building a sense of community on campus—hosting students, faculty, and visitors. In addition to her role as a faculty member in the School of Social Work,

Vivian Shapiro provided important leadership for the university's fund-raising activities, taking the lead in raising funds to expand Tappan Hall.

This partnership nature of the university presidency continues to be important in today's era of big-time fund-raising, political influence, and campus community building. Yet the spouse's role is rarely recognized formally in terms of appointment or compensation—at least in public universities—although participation by the spouse is clearly expected by governing boards and university communities alike (just as the American public expects of the spouse in the Washington White House). The role of the presidential spouse is an archaic form of indentured servitude that goes with the territory at most universities.

Looking across the higher education landscape, there are several approaches that presidential spouses can take to this challenge. Perhaps the simplest approach is a passive one—to just sit back and enjoy life as royalty. Here, the idea is to simply show up when you are supposed to, smile politely at guests, and let the staff take care of all the details, while you enjoy the accoutrements of the position. Of course, since the perks of today's university presidency are few and far between, such a royal lifestyle has become a bit threadbare on many campuses. Moreover, giving the staff total control over presidential events can sometimes lead to embarrassment, if not disaster. But the laissez-faire approach is certainly one option.

The other extreme would be a take-charge approach, in which presidential spouses decide that rather than accept a merely symbolic role (with their calendar and activities determined by staff), they will become a more active partner with the president. Not only do these spouses assume major responsibility for planning, managing, and hosting presidential events, but they also sometimes become important participants in institution-wide strategy development in such areas as fund-raising and building the campus community.

A third approach that is increasingly common today is simply to reject any involvement whatsoever in presidential activities (as if to say, "A pox on you! I'm not a 'first' anything!") and pursue an independent career. Although this is understandable in an era of dual-career families, it also can be awkward at times in view of the long tradition of university presidencies. In reality, many spouses with professional careers do double duty, participating fully in the presidency while attempting to maintain their careers, at considerable personal sacrifice. This may be particularly true, for example, of a First Gentleman, since many universities are now led by women. While many male spouses have independent careers, some have joined in partnerships with their presidential mates in advancing the interests of their university.

Fortunately, in our case, Anne and I had long approached university leadership positions—whether as dean, provost, or president—as true partnerships. To be sure, Anne faced a formidable challenge when she was thrust into the role as the university's First Lady, responsible for the myriad of events, facilities, and staff associated with the president's role in institutional development. Beyond the responsibility for creating, designing, managing, and hosting the hundreds of presidential events each year, Anne also managed several major facilities—the President's House; Inglis House, a large estate used for university development activities; and the reception and hosting areas at Michigan Stadium—as well as a talented staff. Fortunately, her earlier university experiences as president of the Michigan Faculty Women's Club and through my roles as dean and provost had prepared her well for such a role. Through these efforts, she had developed considerable experience in designing, organizing, and conducting events and gained an intimate knowledge of both university facilities and staff. She also had developed a keen sense of just what one could accomplish in terms of quality and efficiency within the very real budget constraints faced by a public university.

Anne believed that since the image of the university—as well as the president—would be influenced by the quality of an event, it was important that the hosts (i.e., the president and First Lady) be involved in key details of planning the event. Furthermore, she realized that running these many events on automatic pilot would inevitably lead to significant deterioration in quality over time, a rubber-chicken syndrome. She also realized that by raising the expectations for quality at the presidential level, there would likely be a cascade effect in which other events throughout the university would be driven to develop higher quality standards. The challenge was to do this while simultaneously reducing costs. In effect, Anne launched one of the university's early total quality management efforts in the arena of presidential events. While she was able to recruit and lead a talented staff, she also participated in all aspects of the activities, from planning to arrangements, from working with caterers to designing seating plans, from welcoming guests to cleaning up afterward. No job was too large or too small, and her very high standards were applied to all.

While Anne's direct involvement in all aspects of presidential events was perhaps unusual, there is nevertheless an expectation that the presidential spouse will be a partner in advancing the interests of the university. There is a certain inequity in the expectation of such uncompensated spousal service, and this expectation is an additional constraint placed on those seeking to serve as university presidents. But it is important to understand that even in these times of dual careers and the ascendancy of women to leadership roles, the university presidency remains a two-person job.

THE HIRED HELP

Legend has it that in the good old days, university presidents were treated as royalty: they were provided with presidential mansions staffed with cooks and servants and were driven about by chauffeurs in limousines; they traveled to exotic locations and spent their summers golfing, reading, and relaxing in their comfortable summer homes. While there are presumably still a few presidents of private universities who enjoy such perquisites (although this, too, may be a myth), the lives of today's public university presidents are far more austere. Particularly in these days of concern about the rising costs of a college education, university presidents can be swept away by public perceptions of luxury or privilege. The list of presidential casualties from excessive expenditures on residences, offices, entertainment, or stadium boxes continues to lengthen. Because Anne and I were bathed in a public spotlight in which the local newspaper routinely led attacks on the president for excessive salary, it was clear that we needed to be creative in how we handled our personal lives. Far from being pampered residents, we served more in the roles of the butler, maid, and cook.

Like many universities, Michigan requires its president to live in the President's House. This ancient facility, located in the center of the Michigan campus, is the oldest building on the university campus, built in 1840 as a home for professors and later enlarged and modified over the years by each of Michigan's presidents, until it became one of the largest and most distinguished-looking houses in Ann Arbor. Like most residents of Ann Arbor, Anne and I used to drive by the stately Italianate structure at 815 South University and wonder what it must be like to live there. From the outside, it looked elegant, tranquil, and exactly like what one would expect as the home for the university's First Family—the "White House" for Ann Arbor.

Yet as we were soon to learn after accepting the Michigan presidency, the external appearance of the house was deceptive, to say the least. Our first visit to the house after being named as president was during the course of a massive renovation project. The front yard looked like a battlefield, with trenches all around. As we entered the house, we noticed a large toilet sitting quite prominently in the middle of the dining room. The interior of the house had a rather threadbare look. The plaster walls were cracked and stained by the not-infrequent leaks in the plumbing. The carpet, drapes, and furniture dated from the 1950s. The wallpaper was taped together in many places. While earlier presidents had decorated the house with some of their own art and furniture, this had been largely replaced by rented furniture during the interregnum between presidencies. The age of the President's House posed a particular challenge, since rare was the day when something did not malfunction or break down. This disruption by repair projects turned out to be a perpetual characteristic of living and working in a house designed for the mid-nineteenth century but used as if it were a modern conference center.

There was one positive result to the extensive work done in the house prior to my presidency. Since much of the house was torn up for mechanical and fire protection equipment (an absolute necessity for a 150-year-old facility), the university had budgeted funds to patch things back together again after the heavy construction. By the time I assumed the presidency, the university's interior decorating staff was already having a field day, picking out new carpets and expensive ornamental items, such as silver tea services and custom fireplace screens. At this point, Anne stepped in and brought the restoration project to an abrupt halt—out of concern both for the details of the restoration plan and for the dangers that might evolve from any appearance of inappropriate expenditures. Since she had a strong interest in historic preservation, she wanted to first assess the opportunities to return the house to a more elegant and timeless design.

Actually, this turned into one of those teachable moments that educators so enjoy. First, it provided a case study in how university staffs relate to the first family. "Don't you worry about these things. We've maintained the President's House for decades and we knew just how it should look. So why don't you folks take a long trip someplace, and when you return it will all look just like new?" Well-intentioned paternalism, coupled with a good dose of "Well, I told you so . . ." and "The new president is not going to get his way with our house!"

However, it also gave us an opportunity to demonstrate the Duderstadt style. "Just because it isn't broken doesn't mean that it's right! Humor us. Let us try it a different way and see if we can improve things." With the help of some of the Plant Department people—the carpenters, electricians, painters, and plumbers who were to become some of our best friends through their frequent visits to the house—Anne stripped off the old carpets and wallpaper and exposed the true majesty of the house. Original quarter-sawed oak floors. Hand-crafted trim and molding. Donations of furniture were sought from several of Michigan's fine old companies. When the work was completed, and the dust settled, the house had been restored to its earlier elegance, while the total cost of the restoration project was actually less than the amount budgeted originally simply to replace the carpeting in the house ($100,000).

This experience demonstrates a very important lesson for university presidents. While the efforts of staff to serve the president are usually very well intentioned, they can become very dangerous when accepted with benign neglect, particularly in public institutions. Expenditures on ceremonial facilities—such as the president's home, football box, or office—should always involve the approval of the trustees and ongoing review by the president, since the president must eventually bear the burden of public scrutiny for these expenditures.

A closely related issue concerns the staffing of presidential activities. While there was no shortage of staffing, there were serious concerns both about quality and cost. Anne inherited a staffing cadre of over a dozen people, including an assistant to the president for special events, a secretary to the First Lady, a facilities and grounds manager, cooks and housekeepers for both the President's House and Inglis House, and a crew of gardeners. It was clear, however, that in an era of budget pressures and public accountability, considerable restructuring was necessary. By merging the management of the President's House, Inglis House, and presidential events, Anne reduced the number of staff by half and the operating budget even further. Key in this strategy was the use of local caterers to handle most presidential events. By developing close working relationships with the best caterers in Ann Arbor, then having them compete against one another in terms of quality and price, Anne and her team were able to get exceptionally high quality at highly competitive costs.

Although it took several years of natural attrition and job redefinition, Anne managed to build an outstanding team of talented and creative staff who were hardworking and dedicated. Not only did the quality of presidential events rise sharply, but these standards soon propagated to other activities for the university's advancement. This result would prove critically important to the upcoming fund-raising campaign.

Still, these efforts were not enough. We soon realized that the only way we could walk the tightrope between cost containment and quality of events was to accept personal responsibility for many of the roles that in earlier years had been handled by staff. We shopped for our own groceries and cooked our own meals, so that we could dispense with a cook. We did our own laundry and cleaned our living areas in the President's House, so we could reduce housekeeping expenses. We used our own furniture for those areas where we lived, and we augmented university furniture in public areas of the house with our own items, to make the house a home. We drove our personal car for most of our trips. Recalling the legend about Michigan State University's John Hannah (see chapter 7), I stopped using the university driver for trips about the state and began to drive myself about in one of the oldest Fords in the university fleet. We even paid for our own moving expenses, both when we moved into the President's House and when we moved out eight years later.

Needless to say, this parsimonious style imposed additional time, labor, and personal financial burdens. It also led to a rather strange life, in which we lived alone and largely responsible for a gigantic house (14,000 square feet) that had been maintained throughout most of its existence by professional staff—a manager, cook, housekeepers, gardeners, and so on. Yet we managed to reduce very significantly the operating expenses of the President's House. Perhaps more important, we removed any possibility that we could be targeted for living a life of luxury at the expense of the public, although that did not stop the local newspaper from trying to create the false impression that we did.

Security was another particular challenge. Since the house was so visible (similar to the White House in Washington), people with an ax to grind with the university or just mad at the world in general would be drawn to the house as a symbol of whatever angered them. All too frequently, those showing up at the house posed some security risk. Since we were usually alone in the house, we had to be very careful in how we handled access. We were advised by campus security not to answer the door during the evening, unless we were expecting someone or could determine who was at the door.

While protesting students rarely targeted the house directly, there were occasions when demonstrations against one tyranny or another would show up on the doorstep. Since many of the protests would march down the street passing right in front of the house, it was common for groups to stop to give the president a few blasts as well. Perhaps the most annoying such incident occurred during the protests over establishing a campus police force and a student disciplinary policy. (Michigan came quite late to these common university practices.) Several hundred students chanting "No cops, no code, no guns!" marched up to the front porch, installed a podium with a sound system, and began a series of speeches about how the president was trampling all over student rights. The students then decided to demonstrate their anguish by symbolically burying students' rights in the front yard, digging graves and placing crosses. Finally, as night approached, about one hundred students set up tents on the lawn and spent the night.

Fortunately, we decided early in the presidency to keep our own house as a refuge for those times when we needed an escape from the headaches of living in the President's House. We not only kept our house fully furnished and operational, but we actually maintained it as our official residence (for mail delivery and such) throughout our tenure in the presidency. The peace and quiet and simplicity of our old home was very reassuring—and only ten minutes away.

Certainly one of the most disconcerting aspects of a major university presidency—particularly a university located in a small town—is the intensely public life one must lead. To Ann Arborites, the residents of the President's House were every bit as much public figures as those in Washington's White House. Every aspect of the presidential family's lives was subject to public scrutiny, particularly by the local media. While we eventually got used to this public visibility in Ann Arbor, it frequently was disconcerting when folks would come up to us elsewhere (e.g., in California or Washington or London or Paris) and ask, "Aren't you the president of the University of Michigan?" While I was hosting an alumni group on a trip one fall to Egypt, a young man approached me in front of the Sphinx to exclaim, "Hey, it's President Duderstadt! Mr. President, do you know who won the Michigan-Illinois game yesterday?" (I did. We didn't.)

It is little wonder that many of today's university presidents believe that the stresses of the modern presidency are simply too intense to add the burden of requiring the president and family to live in a ceremonial university house and therefore be on duty 24 hours a day, seven days a week. Some universities are moving away from requiring presidents to live in a president's house and are instead allowing them to purchase—and, in some cases, actually helping them to finance—their own home a short distance from the campus. This gives the president's family some measure of privacy. It also allows them to maintain equity in rapidly inflating real estate marketplaces.[1]

During my tenure as president, however, we were required to make the President's House our home, and so we did for the eight-year term of my presidency. While we never really felt at home in the house, we did everything we could to restore and maintain the elegance of the facility. When we finally moved out of the house on July 1, 1996, we made certain that it was left in spotless condition for the next president. Despite the inevitable repair projects that would continue, we were confident that we had left the President's House in perhaps the finest condition of its long history (just as we hoped we had left the university).

A TURN ABOUT THE UNIVERSITY CALENDAR

Just as does the university itself, the life of a university president revolves around the calendar, changing with the seasons. After the hot, humid doldrums of a Midwestern summer, excitement begins to build in late August, as students begin to return to campus. The fall is a time of beginning and renewal, as new students and faculty arrive on campus, bringing the excitement of new beginnings. The energy and activity level are high, with community celebrations such as football weekends, alumni reunions, Homecoming, and fall traditions such as apple picking and trips to the local cider mills.

As Labor Day approaches, streets become crowded, parking disappears, and one of the most traumatic moments in a college education begins: the "Great Dropoff." Parents bring their young students to the university, moving them into residence halls and away from home for the first time. I always made it a point to speak to the parents of new students, to reassure them that their sons and daughters were academically talented and would be carefully nurtured by the university. Both Anne and I would participate in welcoming activities, such as hosting a Good Humor ice cream wagon in front of the dorms as tired parents moved in their excited students, presenting a freshman convocation to convey to new students a few words of advice (usually ignored, of course), and holding an array of welcoming events for new graduate students and new faculty. I always used to tell parents that there was only one college event more traumatic than the Great Dropoff. It was that moment, following commencement, when, just as parents swell with pride, their graduating students happen to mention their intent to move back home until deciding what to do next.

Universities are places where tradition is important, and there are always many traditions during the beginning of a new academic year. During my years as dean and provost, Anne and I had long been accustomed to hosting a fall kickoff event to get the new academic year under way. Anne had been particularly creative in designing novel ways and interesting venues to get the new academic year off to a good start—a dinner hosted on the stage of one of our theaters or in a gallery of our art museum, "Dining with the Deans and the Dinosaurs" at our museum of natural history, and even a brunch in our new solid state electronics facility (complete with clean-room suits). In our presidential role, we felt such events were extremely important to build the necessary spirit of teamwork among deans and executive officers.

The spectacle of college football is a celebration of the joys of fall. A football Saturday is a community experience, drawing tens of thousands together in a festival designed to celebrate more the wonders of a fall weekend than the game itself. While most of those attending the game probably draw some excitement from the game, many are probably not fans, at least in the intense sense that one finds in such sports as basketball and hockey. Some come to enjoy the spectacle, the tailgate parties, the bands, and the crowds. Some have a more social interest in seeing friends. Still others are there simply because it is the thing to do on a fall weekend. After all, how else can they participate in conversations later in the week if they have missed the game?

Everything was always too busy in the fall, particularly for the Office of the President. Activities that had been suspended for the summer would come alive once again, demanding time and attention. No matter how much time one spent getting ready for the new term, it never seemed enough to cope with the demands and the challenges. Although it usually took several weeks for the first crisis to develop, sometimes it was earlier. Perhaps the endgame of the summer state budget process in Lansing would have gone amiss, requiring days of follow-up effort with state government to repair the damage through supplemental appropriations. Sometimes Washington would spring a new surprise on the university—for example, a new scheme for cutting the amount of research grant support or a congressional inquiry. With new students came new issues that could rapidly dominate the agenda for campus activism. Even the regents would occasionally pitch in, returning to their first meeting after the August recess with new demands or accusations, particularly in an election year when positions on the board were at stake.

Even with all of the activity, fall is a pleasant time at the university. Michigan falls are glorious, with bright blue skies, the color of the turning leaves, and moderate temperatures. There is always a sense of optimism, the excitement of returning students and faculty, the hope of a winning football season (since Michigan usually does well during its early, nonconference season), the enthusiasm of returning alumni and friends.

However, as the skies turn gray and the leaves disappear, more serious matters begin to take hold. Student activists have defined their agendas and developed their strategies, and campus demonstrations begin. One can always depend on a crisis developing in one academic unit or another—a faculty revolt against a dean, the raid of an outstanding scholar by a competing university, a serious budget problem. The local newspapers run out of national or regional news to report and turn their attention to stirring up controversy about (or within) the university. Perhaps most demoralizing of all, the football team would sometimes be upset by Michigan State or Ohio State.

Winters in Michigan can be rugged. The temperature usually drops below freezing by Thanksgiving, where it remains until late March. An Alberta clipper sweeping across the Great Lakes can be ferocious. But more typically, a Michigan winter is wet and overcast. The phrase "good, gray Michigan" is apt. It is just the kind of season when one wants to stay home, curled up in front of a warm fire.

The focus during winter at Michigan is on serious matters: classes, research, politics, and student protests. Yet there are also basketball, hockey, and a number of other indoor sports. And, on not infrequent occasions, there is the joy of a holiday season concluding in the warm sunshine of a New Year's Day in Pasadena.

During my presidency, Anne and I, like many other members of the central administration, were ready to collapse by the time the Christmas holidays approached. Yet even during the holiday season, we had little respite. From Thanksgiving to Christmas was the season of holiday events and receptions. Anne was always particularly busy, since she was responsible for numerous activities associated with the holiday season. She first had to decorate both the President's House and Inglis House for the countless events scheduled for the month of December. Here, Anne had to steer a careful course between creating an appropriate spirit of the season and yet not having the season labeled as any particular religious experience. She was finally reduced to explaining that trees and wreaths were, in reality, pagan symbols of the winter solstice from prehistoric times (although my electric train under the tree in the President's House was a pagan rite of more recent origin).

However, the real impact of winter on life at the university sets in when students and faculty return after New Year's. Since Michigan is high in latitude and on the western edge of the eastern time zone, not only are the days short, but darkness falls by midafternoon. Although Michigan's proximity to the Great Lakes prevents long periods of subzero weather, it is usually wet, and the skies are always overcast. Winter sports provide some distraction, but trudging through the snow to a basketball game or hockey match on a bitterly cold night is a challenge.

Not surprisingly, after a few weeks, there are the first signs of cabin fever—or perhaps sunlight-deficiency syndrome. People become more irritable. The frequency of complaints increases. The newspapers become more hostile. And much of this eventually finds its way to the Office of the President. During my presidency, I found that one could be certain that February and March would also be the peak times for student activism. Usually, it took several weeks for campus politics to regain momentum after the holidays. But by February, protest leaders would have created a fever pitch of concerns—although, of course, the issues would change every year. This fever would generally peak during the February regents' meeting, which usually provided the opportunity for maximum public visibility. Fortunately, the week of spring break would follow in early March. But after break, even though the weather was not quite as bitterly cold, Michigan remained in winter's grip, the campus remained irritable, and protest movements could be easily reignited.

There were usually several distractions that kept such politics from coalescing into a crescendo. First, if the basketball or hockey team was nationally ranked, students could look forward to the NCAA tournaments, March Madness, the Final Four, or the Frozen Four. Second, Michigan's unusually short winter term left very few weeks for building major political movements before the period of final exams and commencement. It is sometimes rumored that the reason the university shifted in the 1960s to a trimester system in which the term ends by May 1 is that the faculty wanted to get students out of town before warm weather brought the potential for real disruptions. While this is not true, it also is not a bad idea.

In contrast to the rest of society, the university approaches spring with mixed enthusiasm. Certainly, the end of winter and the transition from gray slush to green growth is welcome. Yet spring also signals the approaching end of the academic calendar, commencement, and the departure of students and faculty. Academic administrators turn to the serious business of budgets and state politics.

Spring is a very brief season in Michigan. In late April, the thermometer finally moves above freezing. It then keeps right on going into the seventies and eighties, so that by early May, summer has arrived. The tulips bloom, leaves appear on the trees, and students graduate and leave—all in the space of a few weeks. Hence, my spring memories as president of the university are few and brief: the blooming of the peony garden in the Arboretum, the May Festival when the Philadelphia Orchestra spent a week performing at the university, spring commencement—that is about it.

Summer is a strange time on university campuses, with most students and faculty gone, many campus facilities closed, and campus life in a dormant state. For most university faculty members and students, summer is a welcome break from the hectic pace of the academic year. Many faculty scatter to the winds, traveling about the globe, combining scholarly work and traveling vacations. Even those who stay in Ann Arbor to work on their research generally slow their pace a bit and try to take a few weeks of pure vacation.

Long ago, or so I am told, summertime was also a time of rest and relaxation for university presidents. Many had summer places, to which they would retreat to read, write, and relax during the summer months. It was also a time to travel abroad, to fly the university flag in far-flung locales and be wined and dined by local alumni. Michigan president Harlan Hatcher once boasted to me that he had played golf in every city where the university had an alumni club.

But from my perspective in the 1990s, it was hard to imagine that such peaceful summers had ever existed for university presidents. In the fast-paced world of state and federal politics, summertime in the 1980s and 1990s was the time when the critical phase of the budget process occurred. May, June, and July involved nonstop negotiations—with governors, legislators, and regents—to pin down university funding and determine how it would be distributed. During times of limited resources, this period was particularly stressful. Many were the long days I spent in Lansing pleading the university's case for an adequate appropriation or attempting to persuade contrarian regents about the importance of charging adequate tuition levels to sustain the quality of the institution. The Detroit-to-Washington shuttle also became a familiar experience for me as Congress and the administration worked their way through appropriations bills with major implications for leading research universities, such as Michigan.

This political period required intense effort, involving long hours and seven-day workweeks. It also required constant vigilance, since a slight shift in a vote from a legislative conference committee or an inane comment to the press by a maverick regent could blow the strategy apart. As a result, by the time the July regents' meeting was completed, the executive officers were usually on the verge of collapse and looked toward the month of August for a well-deserved break—usually as far away from Ann Arbor as they could get. Unfortunately, the same was not true for the president.

August was always a traumatic month for me as president, since I was frequently left quite alone to protect the university from the slings and arrows of outrageous fortune. For example, early in my presidency, the challenge was an ongoing political struggle to prevent the governor from eroding the university's autonomy by attempting to control its tuition levels. As chair of the President's Council of the State Universities of Michigan, it was my role to lead a bitter yet successful struggle to resist the governor's efforts to control tuition. This fight usually came to a head in August, following the state legislature's approval of the appropriation bill, when the governor's staff would begin to pressure the presidents and governing boards to roll back tuition increases. Hence, I would spend much of my time in August on the phone coordinating the efforts of the other universities to stand up to this intimidation. Much of the time, I was the only one left in the fort to carry on the fight, while others were on vacation. This was a lonely battle, but one in which defeat would have seriously damaged the university. In the end, Michigan managed to win each time—much to the consternation of the governor and his staff.

LIFESTYLES OF THE RICH AND FAMOUS

One of the most fascinating aspects of a major university presidency involves the people that one meets and hosts on behalf of the university. During our presidency, Anne and I hosted several presidents, numerous distinguished guests from the academy, corporate leaders, celebrities, and even a god. Several examples illustrate the entertainment of the rich and famous.

Although she was just recovering from bronchitis, Anne organized a reception at the President's House for Leonard Bernstein following his concert with the Vienna Philharmonic in honor of his seventieth birthday. The guests, mostly students from the School of Music's conducting program, began to arrive around 11:00 p.m., but Bernstein did not arrive until 12:30. After a couple of large scotches, he warmed up to the students (who were drinking nonalcoholic punch, of course). At one point, he went to the piano and began to play some of his Broadway compositions, singing along with lyrics a bit more bawdy than one is used to hearing. At about 2:30, Bernstein decided to go out on the town, and off he went, followed by a dozen students, looking for a bar.

The evening before Michigan retired Gerald Ford's football jersey number, we hosted a formal dinner for him and Mrs. Ford, attended by Governor John Engler and the real celebrities, Bo Schembechler and Steve Fisher. President Ford suggested that Michigan's retirement of his football number meant almost as much to him as being president.

Many celebrities were key volunteers for the Campaign for Michigan. Mike Wallace agreed to be one of the cochairs of the campaign and played a critical role not only in the New York fund-raising efforts but also in hosting the campaign's major kickoff events. He also made an important contribution to fund the facility housing the Michigan Journalism Fellows Program, named the Mike and Mary Wallace House.

In 1994, the university had the privilege of hosting Dr. Jonas Salk, in recognition of the fortieth anniversary of the announcement of the successful tests of the Salk vaccine. Many of Salk's former collaborators and a large number of polio survivors visited the campus for the event, which was sponsored in part by the March of Dimes.

One of the most interesting events hosted in the President's House was a reception for the Dalai Lama, who was visiting the campus to receive the Wallenberg Medal. Of course, the Dalai Lama is the most revered figure in Tibetan Buddhism, regarded by the faithful as the fourteenth reincarnation of Siddhārtha and as a living god. The visit itself required some careful planning, since the Dalai Lama does not eat or drink after noon. Anne arranged for a small tea ceremony using hot water, so that we could first meet and chat with His Holiness for several minutes before introducing him to the many guests. He was charming, and the discussions ranged from theoretical physics to Tibetan flowers. He presented the guests with traditional Tibetan silk scarves. Then, after a receiving line, we rode with him over to Crisler Arena for the Wallenberg Lecture. It was quite an occasion.

Because of Michigan's prominence as an institution, not a year passed without numerous command performance events. Many of these involved commencements in which the university awarded honorary degrees to distinguished visitors. On some occasions, these took on national importance, such as when the university gave honorary degrees to President George Bush and Barbara Bush and to First Lady Hillary Clinton. In both cases, the honorees actually spent only a short time on campus, arriving just before and leaving just after the commencement ceremony. However, preparing even for these short visits was a Herculean task.

ON THE ROAD

There are times in a university president's life when one begins to feel as if the drill for each morning is to be handed an airline ticket and told that the car to the airport is waiting. Travel is no stranger to university presidents and their spouses. Whether it is fund-raising, visiting alumni, attending meetings, lobbying, or simply flying the university flag, the life of a president is always on the go. I once developed a hypothesis that there were, in reality, only about 500 people in the nation who traveled all the time and that most of these were university presidents. We always ran into each other at airports. One good measure of travel mileage is elite customer status with airlines, generally requiring 75,000 miles or more each year. I once earned this status simply by traveling back and forth to Washington (on about 75 round-trips) for National Science Board meetings.

Compounding the calendar complexity of leading a university are a number of other commitments. It is customary for presidents of major universities to serve on a variety of public and private boards. Not only do such service activities benefit a university through the contributions their leaders make to such efforts, but they also add to the experience and influence of the president.

During my presidency, I participated in many such activities: the Big Ten Conference, the executive committees of such higher education organizations as the Association of American Universities and the National Association of State Universities and Land-Grant Colleges, the Presidents Council of the State Universities of Michigan, the executive council of the National Academy of Engineering, and so on. I also served as a director of two major corporations. However, my most significant and demanding service activity was on the National Science Board, a national body consisting of 24 leading scientists and engineers appointed by the U.S. president and confirmed by the Senate to be responsible for both the National Science Foundation and the development of broader national science policy. Appointed to consecutive six-year terms by Presidents Reagan and Bush, I was elected chairman of the National Science Board during the early 1990s. In this role, I was responsible not only for the operation of the board and the oversight of the NSF but also for the supervision of a staff of roughly two dozen professionals. In a very real sense, I had a second demanding chief executive job in national science policy, beyond the myriad responsibilities of the Michigan presidency. It was always an interesting mental transition to shift gears from the issues swirling about the campus or Lansing when I set aside my Michigan president's hat and donned my federal hat to worry about congressional committees or White House policy or international relations.

Yet another demanding responsibility that I held during my UM presidency involved the Big Ten Conference. During the early phase of my presidency, my primary role was just protecting the university from conference actions, since I did not yet have sufficient seniority to be in a leadership role. In later years, my seniority increased to the point where I became a member of the executive committee of the Big Ten Conference, first as chair of its finance committee and then finally as chair of the board of directors. In these latter roles, I found myself spending a great deal of time on conference matters—for example, restructuring the NCAA from an association into a federation, representing the Big Ten during its centennial year, and negotiating with the Pac Ten Conference over the Rose Bowl relations. Although the day-to-day management of conference activities rested with the conference commissioner, I, as chair, had the executive responsibility to keep on top of matters. This was another job-related overload unseen and certainly unappreciated by most.

The president and his or her spouse also serve as the official representatives of the university in numerous organizations. Since the University of Michigan is generally regarded as a leader of public higher education in America, Anne and I were expected to play a significant leadership role in many of these organizations. While this provided us with many opportunities, it also imposed very significant responsibilities and time commitments on the president.

The Association of American Universities (AAU) is the most important of the higher education associations for a Michigan president to be involved in, since it is a presidents/spouses-only organization representing the top research universities in the United States and Canada. Since both presidents and spouses are involved together in its activities, it is also a very important mechanism in building personal relationships among the leaders of various universities. While the AAU meetings held during my presidency did deal with some important issues, their real value was to provide an opportunity for informal discussions of higher education and to build a network among the presidents. Perhaps the only disconcerting aspect of the

AAU was its tradition of publishing each year the names of the 60 presidents, ranked by longevity. The turnover in this group was quite extraordinary. By the time I stepped down, I ranked eighth in seniority among the AAU presidents. Furthermore, there were only three presidents left on the list who had served more than 10 years.

There were numerous other organizations that met on a regular basis and required presidential participation. They included, to name only a few, the National Association of State Universities and Land-Grant Colleges, the American Council on Education, the Council of Presidents and associated Committee on Institutional Cooperation of the Big Ten universities, the Business–Higher Education Forum, and the Presidents Council of the State Universities of Michigan. Needless to say, the meetings of these and similar organizations kept the calendar full and the travel load heavy.

Probably the most interesting and enjoyable higher education gathering was the least visible: the Tanner Group. This group consisted of the presidents and spouses of the leading universities in the world: Harvard University, the University of Michigan, the University of California, Stanford University, Yale University, Princeton University, Oxford University, Cambridge University, and the University of Utah (which was the home institution of the benefactor, O. C. Tanner). The presidents and spouses served formally as trustees of the Tanner Trust, which sponsored the Tanner Lectures on Human Values at each of the institutions. They met for several days in late June, at either university campuses or world-class resorts. Beyond the enjoyment of the surroundings, participation in the Tanner Group offered one of the few opportunities not only to build friendships with presidents of other institutions but to discuss in a candid and confidential way the trials and tribulations of university leadership.

Needless to say, the time available for rest, relaxation, and recreation was limited. Anne and I used what little spare time we had available to balance the wear and tear of the presidency with physical exercise. We had both become dependent on jogging for maintaining both physical condition and sanity. In other university roles, we had been able to set aside convenient times during the day for this activity. However, the time demands of the presidency forced our exercise earlier and earlier in the day, until eventually we were up well before dawn and over at the varsity track (or the indoor track) to work out at 6 a.m. or so. We became familiar companions to various other early birds: the "Dawn Patrol" of wounded football players doing their obligatory mile, the ROTC students, and various other masochists.

A MATTER OF STYLE

Each presidency is characterized by a distinctive style that, over time, tends to affect—or infect—the rest of the institution. Contributing to this style are the way the president approaches the challenge of leadership; the nature of the president's working relationships with students, faculty, and staff; the spirit of teamwork the president inspires among other university leaders; and even the character of university events. Since both Anne and I had grown up in a small, Midwestern farm town, we generally tended to approach our roles in an informal, unpretentious, and straightforward fashion. We both realized that we came from peasant stock, and we viewed ourselves very much as commoners thrust for a time into the complex and demanding roles of public leadership.

Of course, we brought our own quirks and patterns to our roles. I tend to be one of those folks who always has to have lots of balls in the air, although I will drop a few from time to time. Perhaps a more appropriate circus metaphor for my management style is the juggler who starts a whole series of plates spinning on sticks, jumping quickly from plate to plate to keep them spinning together. As UM president, I would launch a series of activities, assigning the responsibility for each to a member of my leadership team. For example, I might initiate a project to secure capital outlay funding from state government or an effort to better integrate academic learning with student housing or a scheme to go after a major federal research laboratory. Once each project was launched, I would generally move ahead to another activity, only checking back from time to time to see how things were going. I rarely strove for perfection in any particular venture. Rather, I felt that, at least for such a large, diverse, and complex institution as Michigan, it was better to keep lots of things going on than to focus on any one agenda.

By contrast, Anne is a detail person. She focuses her attention on only a few matters at a time and is not satisfied until they have met her standards of excellence. Whether her concern as First Lady at Michigan was a major renovation project (e.g., the President's House or the Inglis House), the photographic book she helped design for the university, or a special fund-raising event, Anne's standards were very high. Just as my spinning-plate style kept the university in high gear, Anne's insistence on excellence rapidly propagated across the campus.

ALWAYS SOME DOUBTS

Sometimes Anne and I would wonder whether we had taken on too much, whether there was any way to reduce the number of our commitments, whether we could streamline our presidential calendar. In the end, we concluded that streamlining was probably impossible, as much due to the nature of the presidential position as to our own personalities. Over time, a university president accumulates roles and responsibilities much like a ship accumulates barnacles. As one becomes more visible as a university leader, opportunities arise that simply must be accepted as a matter of responsibility. Our experience was that the number of new roles put before us always seemed to outnumber the number of old roles that we managed to complete.

Perhaps this is one of the reasons why the tenure of the modern university president has become so short. The inevitable accumulation of the barnacles of multiple roles so weights down the presidential ship that it eventually sinks. Eventually, it must be replaced by a fresh president, a clean ship, unencumbered as a relative unknown by the array of obligations and duties that build up over years of service.

During my ten years in the central administration as provost and president, Anne and I never really had a true vacation. We did manage to get away on several university trips—more precisely, expeditions—to exotic places, such as China and Eastern Europe. But even on these trips, we were representing the institution and usually working on its agendas. Although the times made it impossible for us to ever take an extended vacation during our presidency as had our predecessors, we sometimes were able to escape for a few days. But we were never more than a phone call or an e-mail message away from the demands of the university. Many were the times when I had to fly back to handle a quick emergency. Even when we were able to get several days' distance away, the time was frequently filled with phone calls, e-mail messages, and faxes. Rare indeed was the day when we could set aside university problems or demands. This inability to decouple from the university, to regain our strength, eventually played a key role in our decision to step down from the presidency

So, what was the personal life of a university president like? Once, after a long discussion of the past year's wear and tear by the presidents of the Tanner Group, Neal Rudenstine of Harvard passed me a note with a quote from Robert Frost that perhaps best expresses it: "Happiness makes up in height for what it lacks in length." Both of us were coming off rough years.

11

TILTING WITH WINDMILLS

In any book concerning an American university presidency, it seems most appropriate to include several examples of failed agendas, to complement those that have actually succeeded. After all, university presidents, like other leaders, need to remember that one usually does not win a war without losing a few battles along the way. There are times when presidents almost feel on a quixotic quest, tilting with one windmill after another on behalf of an apparently hopeless cause. Yet perseverance is an important trait for successful presidencies.

Twenty years of making the case for the importance of a rational civilian nuclear power program in the United States had taught me well the importance—and yet also the frustration—of fighting what seem to be endless and sometimes losing battles. There were times when many of the causes I was called on to defend as president—academic freedom, diversity, tenure, and tuition—seemed almost as difficult to explain to regents, legislators, and the press as nuclear fission chain reactions and radioactive waste disposal. While careful planning, skillful execution, and determined persistency helped me to accomplish a great deal, there were some issues that defied all our efforts. This chapter considers three of the most intractable: (1) the increasingly "private" reality of the public research university, (2) the threat posed to the university by the increasing commercialization and corruption of college sports, and (3) the hapless and seriously outdated nature of university governance.

WINDMILL NO. 1: THE PRIVATELY SUPPORTED PUBLIC UNIVERSITY

Here, the issue is simple enough to state, even if intractable to address. The experience of the past two decades and a bit of demographic forecasting suggest that an aging population is unlikely to regard higher education as a high priority for its tax dollars when compared to its more urgent needs, such as health care, retirement, protection from crime, homeland security, and tax relief. Hence, if America's public universities—particularly the flagship public research universities—are to sustain their quality and capacity to serve both present and future generations, they have no choice but to function more similarly to a private university, drawing an increasing fraction of their support from the marketplace (through student tuition, private gifts, and sponsored research) and weaning themselves from dependence on declining state appropriations. Whether this takes the form of explicit public policy to create a new class of public-private hybrid institutions, such as "charter" or "enterprise" universities, or whether a natural evolutionary trend eventually leads to the body politic's acceptance of the institutional reality that the state has become a small, minority shareholder in the public university, the consequence is the same: for all effective purposes, the best of America's public research universities will inevitably become, to use a phrase suggested by Frank Rhodes, predominantly "privately financed but publicly committed" institutions,[1] albeit with strong public purpose and public accountability.

The challenge, then, becomes one of educating the public and its elected government officials and persuading them that until higher education rises higher on the priority list for public tax support, it is in the best interests of society to turn the public research university loose, to allow it to compete in a fiercely competitive marketplace for resources, students, faculty, and reputation, albeit with some agreement on how it will be held accountable for serving the public interest. Yet it is easier to persuade the environmental movement that nuclear power is the key to mitigating global climate change driven by fossil fuel combustion than to persuade governors and state legislatures that if they are unable to adequately support their flagship public research universities, they should allow their institutions to compete in the marketplace and thereby attain the agility and autonomy necessary to preserve their quality and their capacity to serve.

There is a deeper principle at stake here. For at least three decades, both the public and its elected leaders have been telling us, through actions and rhetoric, that a college education should be viewed less as a public good and more as a personal benefit for individual college students, as measured by future earning capacity and quality of life attributable to a college degree. They have reflected this shifting perspective both in declining tax support of public higher education compared to other social priorities (e.g., health care and prisons) and through an array of state and federal financial aid policies that increasingly benefit the students from middle- and upper-income families rather than those with serious financial needs.

Today, even as the needs of society for postsecondary education intensify, we find an erosion in the perception of education as a public good deserving of strong societal support. Our society seems to have forgotten the broader purposes and benefits of the university as a place where both the young and the experienced can acquire not only knowledge and skills but the values and discipline of an educated mind, so essential to a democracy; where we defend and propagate our cultural and intellectual heritage, even while challenging our norms and beliefs; where we develop the leaders of our governments, commerce, and professions; and where new knowledge is created through research and scholarship and applied through social engagement to serve society.[2] Whether a deliberate or unconscious response to the tightening tax constraints and changing priorities for public funds, along with the escalating value of a college education in the knowledge economy, the new message is that education has become a private good that should be paid for by the individuals who benefit most directly: students, patients, business, and other patrons from the private sector. Government policies such as the Bayh-Dole Act that not only enable but intensify the capacity of universities to capture and market the commercial value of the intellectual products of research and instruction represent additional steps down this slippery slope.

As a consequence, we need to question the viability of the long-standing public principle that because of the broader benefit to all of society, education in public universities should be primarily supported through tax dollars rather than student fees. The traditional model of financing public higher education, relying on large state appropriations to enable nominal tuition levels, coupled with modest need-based student grants and loans from the federal government, looks increasingly fragile.[3] If interpreted primarily as individual benefit, the concept of low-tuition public universities amounts to a highly regressive social policy, particularly at flagship public research universities, since it taxes the poor to subsidize the educational opportunities available only to middle- and upper-class families. Put another way, low tuition at public research universities amounts to welfare for the rich at the expense of educational opportunity for low-income students.

Let me illustrate this by describing the current situation at the University of Michigan. For some time, our state legislature has adopted a policy (at least in rhetoric) that state tax dollars should only be used to support Michigan residents. For that reason, the University of Michigan sets the tuition levels for nonresidents at essentially private university levels—$30,000 dollars for 2006–7, which also happens to be roughly the university's estimate of actual instructional costs for undergraduates. For Michigan residents, this tuition is discounted to $10,000. The current state appropriation ($320 million) for the university amounts to about $12,000 per Michigan student. Hence, you see that even if the university were to apply the full appropriation to the subsidy of Michigan residents (ignoring the use of these funds for other state-mandated activities, such as public service, health care, etc.), $8,000 ($30,000 – $10,000 – $12,000) of the discount from actual costs would remain to be covered from other sources. In reality, this funding gap must be covered from the same discretionary funds (from private gifts and endowment income) that the university would use for student financial aid programs. The policy implications of this reality become even more apparent when it is noted that the average student family income for Michigan undergraduates is now in excess of $120,000. It is clear that for the University of Michigan and many other flagship public research universities, maintaining in-state tuition levels far below the discount funded by state appropriations is coming at the expense of student financial aid. Low in-state tuitions represent a very substantial subsidy of the costs of a college education for the affluent at the expense of the educational opportunities of those from less fortunate economic circumstances. Inadequate state support coupled with political constraints on tuition are not only threatening the quality of the university; they are transforming Michigan into a university of the rich.

To survive with quality intact in this brave new world of constrained state support, a situation likely to last for at least a generation, many of the best public universities have begun to move toward policies of high tuition and increased financial aid. State support is becoming correctly viewed as a tax-supported discount of the price of education, a discount that should be more equitably distributed to those with true need. With the continuation of this trend, the leading public universities will increasingly resemble private universities in the way they are financed and managed. To replace declining state appropriations, they will use their reputation—developed and sustained during earlier times of more generous state support—to attract the resources they need from federal and private sources. Many institutions will embrace a strategy to become increasingly privately financed, even as they strive to retain their public character.

This privatization of support for public higher education actually began more than three decades ago, when inadequate state appropriations forced public institutions to begin to charge significant tuition. It intensified with major fund-raising and financial independence, including spin-off operations, of medical centers and law and business schools. Ironically (though perhaps not surprisingly, in view of the nature of politics), even as public universities became less dependent on state support, state governments attempted to tighten the reins of state control with even more regulations and bureaucracy in the name of public accountability. It is little wonder that in many states, public universities are now moving into a new phase of privatization by seeking to free themselves from state control, since taxpayers now pay for such a small share of their overall operations—typically less than 20 percent for most flagship state universities. Public university leaders are increasingly reluctant to cede control of their activities to state governments. Many institutions are even bargaining for more autonomy from state control as an alternative to growth in state support, arguing that if granted more control over their own destiny, they can better protect their capacity to serve the public.[4]

It is instructive to return again to the Michigan case study. Throughout much of the twentieth century, the University of Michigan benefited from generous state support. At the time, a booming automobile industry made the Michigan economy unusually prosperous, and the University of Michigan was the only major university in the state. However, by the 1970s, the energy crisis and foreign competition weakened Michigan's industrial economy. Furthermore, regional needs, ambitious leadership, and sympathetic political forces allowed a number of other public colleges in Michigan to grow into comprehensive universities, thereby competing directly with the University of Michigan for limited state appropriations.

As state support dropped throughout the last decades of the twentieth century, the University of Michigan became, in effect, a privately financed university, supported by a broad array of constituencies at the national—indeed, international—level, albeit with a strong mission focused on state needs. Today, the state of Michigan has become the smallest shareholder in the university, contributing less than 7 percent of its total support (compared to 16 percent from student tuition, 18 percent from research grants and contracts, 10 percent from private gifts, and 49 percent from auxiliary income). Just as a private university, the University of Michigan must today earn the majority of its support in the competitive marketplace. It allocates and manages its resources in much the same way as private universities. It still retains a public character, however, committed to serving the people whose ancestors created it two centuries earlier.

Yet as the Michigan president who had the task of selling this vision of Michigan's future (or perhaps the reality of the university's present), I can attest to the difficulty of explaining this fact of life. The people of the state continued to hold tight to the persistent belief that they not only owned the University of Michigan but paid for the campus and supported most of its activities through their taxes. State government, the press, and the public at large demonstrated little awareness that the state had become the smallest shareholder in the university.[5] Motivated by this point of view, the state legislature frequently passed legislation that intruded on university operations. It attempted to dictate whom the university admitted, how much tuition students were charged, what they were taught, and even who taught them. At the same time, Michigan, like most flagship institutions, had long been plagued by the populist view that what was good enough for regional, predominantly undergraduate colleges was good enough for the University of Michigan. This view ignored almost entirely Michigan's broader role in performing the research that drove economic growth and operating the leading hospital system in the state.

My administrative team attempted to develop a strategy to respond to this public perception. The early effort was aimed at getting citizens to understand the multiplicity of ways that the university was vital to the state. Beyond simply providing a place to send their kids to college, we hoped to convince them of the broad impact of the university in such areas as health care, economic development, the training of professionals, the arts, and mass entertainment (the Michigan Wolverines). In meeting after meeting with citizens groups, editorial boards, legislators, and leaders of Michigan industry, I would make the case for the broader impact of the university as an important national and global resource, which leveraged the small subvention from the state's taxpayers into very considerable impact on Michigan citizens. We could demonstrate that every $1 of Michigan tax revenue invested in the university generated over $10 of additional institutional support and roughly $30 of related economic activity. We stressed that in a state that ranked forty-ninth in the nation in the return of federal tax dollars, the university's ranking as the nation's leading research university was key to getting Michigan's fair share of federal support through research grants. Furthermore, we sought to shift the public perception of the university from a consumer of state resources to an institution that attracted and stimulated very considerable economic growth in Michigan, creating new companies, new jobs, and economic prosperity.

However, as these arguments frequently fell on deaf or unsympathetic ears, we considered more pragmatic strategies. One cynical approach would be aptly described by the saying "You get what you pay for." Our sophisticated information systems could determine the real costs of all of the university's services, including undergraduate education, professional education, and public service. Hence, we considered shifting from our current political stance of begging the state legislature for our appropriation each year to instead offering to sell the state our services. For example, offering 20,000 undergraduate student positions at a cost of $30,000 but priced at $10,000 tuition would present the state a bill of $400 million a year. I imagined presenting the state with a menu that contained both services and prices, then inviting it to purchase whatever it wished—making for a very interesting appropriations hearing. Today, this approach, known as *performance contracting,* is becoming more popular in some states.

Some consideration was given to possible legislation that might set the University of Michigan apart as a more independent university or that would at least relax the state's web of controls to a level more commensurate with our increasingly limited state support. We already had been given such autonomy in the state's constitution, but it was vested in a politically elected board of regents. Achieving true autonomy and flexibility would have required that we either persuade the elected regents to go against the wishes of the body politic or restructure the way the board itself was selected. Needless to say, neither approach was well accepted by the board members or their political parties. In the end, we concluded that such efforts would be unrealistic in view of the current political environment and the constitutional nature of our university's charter. Of particular concern here was a state referendum that imposed term limits on members of our state legislature, eliminating not only much of the experience so necessary to state government but any sense of continuity and perspective. Hence, our concerns about the eroding autonomy of the university remained unaddressed.

At least we managed to get the key issues on the table and into public discourse. In the face of the priorities of an aging baby boomer population, how can a state responsibly and effectively maintain public institutions—such as the University of Michigan—that are distinctive in terms of their mission to provide the highest quality advanced graduate and professional education and research? Can it simultaneously sustain these universities' comprehensiveness in terms of student body, programs, and statewide responsibility? What happens when the state becomes a truly minority shareholder in the university, contributing 10 percent or less of its resources or capital facilities? Do state taxpayers then deserve to own the university and dictate its role, character, and quality? Will such privately supported public universities have the necessary autonomy, integrity, freedom from political interference, and bureaucratic controls? Or will the centrifugal forces of political and educational regionalism, the tempting but destructive urge to involve higher education in partisan politics, prevail, allowing the distinctive role of the public research university to deteriorate and pulling down the quality of all public higher education in a state?

It must be acknowledged that without some form of accountability to the body politic, the public purpose of the university is at risk. If the states and the nation are to balance the importance of values and public purpose in the face of the market-driven priorities of profit, leaders need to get the issues on the table for public consideration. But this will not happen until public leaders recognize, first, that they must allow higher education to adapt to the demands of the marketplace (e.g., by acknowledging the inevitability of high-tuition/high-financial-aid models for public research universities) and to recognize further that they have the capacity to influence these markets to value once again the public purpose and social engagement of public research institutions. They must strive for a better balance between autonomy and accountability, at least for flagship public research universities, or else the marketplace will sweep over them, eroding away their quality and capacity to serve, which were established long ago, during more prosperous—and enlightened—times.

WINDMILL NO. 2: COLLEGE SPORTS

Mention Ann Arbor, and the first images that probably come to mind are those of a crisp, brilliant weekend in the fall; walking across campus through the falling leaves to Michigan Stadium; gathering at tailgate parties before the big game; and the excitement of walking into that magnificent stadium—the "Big House"—with 110,000 fans thrilling to the Michigan Marching Band as they step onto the field playing "Hail to the Victors." Intercollegiate athletics at Michigan are not only an important tradition at the university, but they also attract as much public visibility as any other university activity. They are also a critical part of a university president's portfolio of responsibilities. As any leader of an NCAA Division I-A institution will tell you, a university president ignores intercollegiate athletics only at great peril—both institutional and personal. As a result, whether they like it or not, most presidents learn quickly that they must become both knowledgeable about and actively involved in their athletic programs.[6]

If you corner any major university president in a candid moment, he or she will admit that many of the problems they have with the various internal and external constituencies of the university stem from athletics. The concerns are many: program integrity, a booster-driven pressure for team success, the insatiable appetite of ambitious athletic directors for more revenue and larger stadiums, media pressure to fire a coach, or overinvolvement by trustees. All can place the university president in harm's way because of the excesses of intercollegiate athletics.

The role of the president in Michigan athletics has been complex and varied. Although the president of the university has always had an array of formal, visible roles associated with athletics (e.g., entertaining visitors at football games and representing the university at such key events as bowl games), there are other far more significant roles necessary to protect the integrity of the institution. The concerns about scandals in college sports have led to a fundamental principle of institutional control—at both the conference and the NCAA level—in which university presidents are expected to have ultimate responsibility and final authority over athletic programs. Although previously there had usually been a formal reporting relationship of the athletic department to the president, in many cases powerful athletic directors had kept the president and the institution at arm's length.

Although Michigan had long had a reputation for successful programs with high integrity, there were warnings as early as the 1960s about systemic flaws in its Athletic Department. Perhaps most serious was the strong autonomy of the department, which used its proclaimed financial independence to skirt the usual regulations and policies of the university (concerning personnel, finances, conflicts of interest, etc.) and operate according to its own rules and objectives, usually out of sight and out of mind of the university administration. The "Michigan model," in which the revenues from the football program—due primarily to the gate receipts generated by the gigantic Michigan Stadium—would support all other athletic programs, would eventually collapse, as the need to add additional programs (e.g., women's sports), coupled with an unwillingness to control expenditures, led to financial disaster by the late 1990s. But perhaps a more serious threat to institutional integrity was a shift in recruiting philosophy during the 1960s, away from recruiting students who were outstanding athletes to recruiting, instead, outstanding athletes with marginal academic ability, athletes who would "major in eligibility" so that they could compete. While this generated winning programs, particularly in football and basketball, it would eventually erode the integrity of the department and lead to scandal in later years.

By the 1980s, it became clear that the days of the czar athletic director and the independent Athletic Department were coming to an end. Athletics activities are simply too visible and have too great an impact on the university to be left entirely to the direction of the athletics establishment, its values, and its culture. Both Harold Shapiro and I faced the challenge of reining in the excesses of the Athletic Department during the days of two particularly powerful figures, athletic director Don Canham and football coach Bo Schembechler, both of whom were media celebrities adept at building booster and press support for their personal agendas. Despite considerable resistance, Shapiro successfully negotiated Canham's retirement. As provost, I reestablished control of admissions and academic eligibility for student athletes. But the high visibility of Michigan athletics and the myth of its financial wealth and autonomy would continue to haunt the university for years to come.

An additional complication arose from the incorporation of the Big Ten Conference during the 1980s, with the university presidents serving as its board of directors. This new corporate conference structure demanded both policy and fiduciary oversight by the presidents, frequently in direct conflict with the athletic directors. It also demanded a great deal of time and effort, since the operations of the Big Ten Conference are more extensive than those of the professional athletic leagues. Many were the lonely, invisible battles I fought for the university on such issues as sharing football gate revenue, conference expansion, and gender equity. Some were won. Some were lost. But most battles were unseen, unrecognized, and certainly unappreciated.

It also frequently falls to the president to protect the Athletic Department from inappropriate intrusion by alumni and boosters, the media, and occasionally even the regents. I believed it critical to stand solidly behind each of my athletic directors, particularly when they were faced with difficult decisions or challenges. Actually, there were some occasions when I even had to stand solidly in front of them to protect them from the criticism and attacks launched by others.

This is not to say that a university president should become involved in the details of running the athletic department beyond hiring the athletic director—a task that frequently proves difficult enough because of the governing board's strong interest and not infrequent interference—and handling institution-level issues at the conference or NCAA level. The hiring and firing of coaches, decisions to add athletic programs, and the general management of the finances and facilities of the athletic department are the responsibility of the athletic director, and the president should become involved only when the interests of the broader university are at stake. However, I also firmly believe that the athletic department should be treated in all matters precisely the same as any other administrative or academic unit, subject to the same policies and controls in financial, personnel, and academic matters. The days of regarding athletics as an independent, auxiliary entertainment business of the university are or should be over.

Most concerns about college sports today derive from the fact that the culture and values of intercollegiate athletics have drifted far away from the educational principles and values of their host universities. Today's athletic departments embrace commercial values driven by the perception that the primary purpose of athletic competition is mass entertainment. There is ample evidence that the detachment of intercollegiate athletics from the rest of the university—its mission and values, its policies and practices—has led to the exploitation of students and has damaged institutional reputation to an unacceptable degree.

While the defense of truth, justice, and the Michigan way in intercollegiate athletics was a necessary role for the president, it was never a very pleasant or easy one. Over time, it took its toll. But it also provided a vivid education concerning what I gradually came to view as one of the most serious threats to the contemporary American university: the extraordinary commercialization and corruption of big-time college sports.

Over four decades as a faculty member, provost, and president of the University of Michigan and a member and chair of the Council of Presidents of the Big Ten Conference have brought me to several conclusions. First, while most of intercollegiate athletics are both valuable and appropriate activities for universities, big-time college football and basketball stand apart, since they have clearly become commercial entertainment businesses. Today, they have little, if any, relevance to the academic mission of the university. Furthermore, they are based on a culture—a set of values—that, while perhaps appropriate for show business, are viewed as highly corrupt by the academy and deemed corrosive to our academic mission. Second, although one can make a case for the relevance of college sports to our educational mission to the extent that they provide a participatory activity for our students, I find no compelling reason why American universities should conduct intercollegiate athletic programs at the current, highly commercialized, professionalized level of big-time college football and basketball simply for the entertainment of the American public; the financial benefit of coaches, athletic directors, conference commissioners, and NCAA executives; and the profit of television networks, sponsors, and manufacturers of sports apparel. Of course, these two statements are nothing new. Many have voiced them, including most American university faculties. But beyond that, I have reached a third conclusion: that big-time college sports do far more damage to the university—its students and faculty, its leadership, and its reputation and credibility—than most people realize or are willing to admit.

The examples are numerous. Far too many university athletic programs exploit young people, recruiting them with the promise of a college education or a lucrative professional career, only to have the majority of Division I-A football and basketball players achieve neither. Scandals in intercollegiate athletics have damaged the reputations of many U.S. colleges and universities (e.g., the University of Colorado and Duke University). Big-time college football and basketball have put inappropriate pressure on university governance, as boosters, politicians, and the media attempt to influence governing boards and university leadership. The impact of intercollegiate athletics on university culture and values has been damaging, with inappropriate behavior of both athletes and coaches all too frequently tolerated and excused. The commercial culture of the entertainment industry that characterizes college football and basketball is not only orthogonal to academic values but corrosive and corruptive to the academic enterprise. Ambitious athletic directors and coaches have insatiable appetites for excessive expenditures—on programs, facilities, and themselves—that drive unbridled growth in athletic budgets and facilities, both distorting university priorities and burdening the university with considerable financial risk (much as do out-of-control university medical centers).

Clearly it is important for all of higher education to set firm principles for the conduct of intercollegiate athletics. This involves prioritizing student welfare, institutional welfare, and the dominance of academic values over competitive or commercial objectives. But this is not enough. University leaders must go further and translate these into strong actions that both reform and regain academic control of big-time college sports.

As it became increasingly clear that the autonomous nature of the UM Athletic Department, driven increasingly by commercial profits rather than student or even institutional welfare, was putting the university at ever greater and unacceptable risk, my administrative team began to take steps to rein in its independence. Perhaps most important was the effort to appoint athletic directors who had a deeper understanding and appreciation for the purpose of a university than characterizes most coaches. Working with these leaders, we attempted to establish a concern for students as the Athletic Department's top priority, rather than the determination of celebrity coaches to build winning programs. We rapidly expanded the opportunities for varsity competition for women, becoming the first major university to achieve true gender equity. Numerous programs were put in place to deal with student concerns, ranging from academic support to substance abuse. The Athletic Department developed a more systemic approach to compliance with the complex rules governing intercollegiate athletics, including my annual meeting with the coaches when I would stress that there was only one way to conduct our programs, the right way, in complete compliance with university, conference, and NCAA rules. I also attempted to use Michigan's influence to slow efforts by the Big Ten Conference and the NCAA to commercialize college sports even further—for example, opposing postseason conference tournaments and a national football championship playoff system.

Yet despite these efforts, Michigan continued to be plagued by all of the usual problems facing big-time college sports: the intense pressure on coaches to win, the tendency to recruit talented athletes with limited academic ability or interests, the behind-the-scenes efforts of the old guard—past coaches and athletic directors—to manipulate the program through booster groups or even political influence. Despite our best efforts, we were unable to avoid scandals. The most serious involved star basketball player Chris Webber's acceptance of secret loans from a long-standing Detroit basketball booster—although this activity did not become known until several years after I had left the presidency. Within a short time after I had stepped down from the presidency, the old guard had again taken over the university's athletic programs, influencing athletic directors and refocusing the Athletic Department once again on the dominance of Michigan's football program.

Of course, my administration's failure in achieving permanent reform at Michigan should not have been surprising. After all, a century of efforts to reform college sports have been largely ineffective. I finally came to the conclusion that working through athletic organizations (e.g., the NCAA, the conferences, or the athletic departments) is futile. These are led or influenced by those who have the most to gain from the further commercialization of college sports. It is my belief that university leaders will never achieve true reform or control through these organizations, where the foxes are in firm control of the hen house. Instead, reform efforts might more effectively proceed through academic organizations, characterized by the academic interests of higher education rather than the commercial values of the entertainment industry. Hence, the key to reform is to reconnect college sports to the academic enterprise by stopping the treatment of athletic departments, coaches, and student athletes as special members of the university community, subject to different rules, procedures, policies, and practices than the rest of the university. To achieve this, the academy must simply demand that athletic programs and their participants be mainstreamed back into the university in three key areas: financial management, personnel policies, and educational practices.

Athletic departments should be subject to the same financial controls, policies, and procedures as other university units. Their financial operations should report directly to the chief financial officer of the university and be subject to rigorous internal and external audit requirements and full public disclosure as an independent (rather than consolidated) financial unit. All external financial arrangements, including those with athletic organizations (e.g., conferences and the NCAA), commercial concerns (e.g., licensing, broadcasting, endorsements), and foundation or booster organizations, should be under the strict control of the university's chief financial official rather than the athletic director. In that regard, I would even suggest that we take the Sarbanes-Oxley approach (designed to eliminate abuses in the financial operations of publicly held corporations), by requiring the athletic director, president, and chair of the governing board to sign annual financial and NCAA compliance statements and holding them accountable should these later be found to be fraudulent.

All athletic department staff (including coaches) should be subject to the same conflict-of-interest policies that apply to other university staff and faculty. For example, coaches should no longer be allowed to exploit the reputation of the university for personal gain through endorsements or special arrangements with commercial vendors (e.g., sports apparel companies, broadcasters, automobile dealers). Employment agreements for coaches should conform with those characterizing other staff and should be subject to review by university financial and personnel units. Personnel searches for coaches should comply fully with the policies and practices characterizing other staff searches (e.g., equal opportunity).

Athletic programs should not be allowed to interfere with or undermine academic policies and principles. For example, the admission of student athletes, their academic standing, and their eligibility for athletic competition must be controlled by the faculty. There should be a ban on special academic support activities that isolate athletes from the rest of the student body and the university, such as special academic support centers or counseling services under the control of the athletic department. Universities must insist that athletic schedules are compatible with the academic calendar, even if this has significant revenue implications.

But how could one accomplish such an agenda? Although one might first turn to presidents' organizations, such as the Association of American Universities or the American Council on Education, I have become increasingly skeptical that university presidents are capable of taking the lead in the reform of college sports. Most university presidents are usually trapped between a rock and a hard place: on the one hand is a public demanding high-quality entertainment from the commercial college sports industry they are paying for; on the other are governing boards that have the capacity (and all too frequently the inclination) to fire presidents who rock the university boat too strenuously. It should be clear that few contemporary university presidents have the capacity, the will, or the appetite to lead a true reform movement in college sports.

There is an important ally that could challenge the mad rush of college sports toward the cliff of commercialism: the university faculty. In the end, it is the governing faculty that is responsible for the academic integrity of a university. Faculty members have been given the ultimate protection, tenure, to enable them to confront the forces of darkness that would savage academic values. The serious nature of the threats posed to the university and its educational values by the commercialization and corruption of big-time college sports has been firmly established in recent years. It is time to challenge university faculties (through their elected bodies, such as faculty senates) to step up to their responsibility to defend the academic integrity of their institutions, by demanding substantive reform of intercollegiate athletics.

To their credit, several faculty groups have already responded well to this challenge and stepped forward to propose a set of principles for the athletic programs conducted by their institutions. Beginning first with a small group of faculty known as the Drake Group, then in the Pacific Ten Conference universities, propagating to the Big Ten Conference and Atlantic Coast Conference, and most recently considered and adopted by the American Association of University Professors, such principles provide a firm foundation for true reform in college sports.[7]

Unfortunately, however, examples of faculty concern and commitment are few and far between. Most faculty members regard college sports as an aberration that long ago was torn away from academic controls by commercial interests. While they deplore the exploitation of student athletes and the corruption of academic values, they feel helpless to challenge the status quo in the face of pressures from coaches, athletic directors, and boosters—not to mention the benign neglect by presidents and trustees.

Therefore, while I must acknowledge my own distaste for government interference, I have concluded that it is time for Congress to step in, at least in a limited way, to challenge several of the current anomalies in federal tax policy that actually fuel the commercial juggernaut of big-time college sports. Today, much of the expansion of the commercialization of college sports is financed by IRS tax policies that treat as charitable contributions the payment of leasing fees for stadium skyboxes and the "seat taxes" required to purchase season tickets at many universities. Of course, there is nothing charitable about these mandatory fees for commercial services. Furthermore, these fees would normally be classified as unrelated business income and hence subject to further tax as are other university activities unrelated to academic programs. It is my belief that a congressional challenge to these IRS loopholes could attack the Achilles' heel of big-time colleges sports, drying up the revenue stream that currently fuels much of the excess.

In the longer run, however, I continue to believe that the permanent cure for this commercial infection of the academy will only occur when faculties challenge university trustees, who in the end must be held accountable for the integrity of their institutions.[8] To be sure, there will always be some trustees who are more beholding to the football coach than to academic values. But most university trustees are dedicated volunteers with deep commitments to their institutions and to the educational mission of the university. Furthermore, while some governing boards may inhibit the efforts of university presidents willing to challenge the sports establishment, few governing boards can withstand a concerted effort by their faculty to hold them accountable for the integrity of their institution. As trustees come to understand and accept their stewardship for the welfare of their institutions, they will recognize that their financial, legal, and public accountability compels them to listen and respond to the challenge of academic integrity from their faculties. The American university is simply too important to the future of the nation to be threatened by the ever-increasing commercialization, professionalization, and corruption of intercollegiate athletics.

WINDMILL NO. 3: UNIVERSITY GOVERNANCE

If one asks any group of university presidents about the greatest challenges to university leadership, the issue of university governance rapidly emerges, whether the concerns are internal (the shared governance of lay governing boards and faculty senates) or external (the complex web of political and regulatory forces exerted on universities by state and federal governments). Despite dramatic changes in the nature of scholarship, pedagogy, and service to society, American universities today are organized, managed, and governed in a manner little different from the far simpler colleges of a century ago. They continue to embrace—indeed, enshrine—the concept of shared governance involving public oversight and trusteeship by governing boards of lay citizens, elected faculty governance, and inexperienced (generally short-term and usually amateur) administrative leadership. Today, however, the pace of change in American society and the growing complexity and accountability of American universities are exposing the flaws in this traditional approach to university governance.

Of course, from a legal perspective, "shared governance" is a misnomer. By law or by charter, essentially all of the legal powers of the university are held by its governing board, although they are generally delegated to and exercised by the administration and the faculty, particularly in academic matters. When it works well, shared governance delegates academic decisions (e.g., criteria for student admissions, faculty hiring and promotion, curriculum development, awarding degrees) to the faculty and administrative decisions (e.g., acquiring resources and planning expenditures, designing, building, and operating facilities) to the administration, leaving the governing board to focus on public policy and accountability (e.g., compliance with federal, state, and local laws; fiduciary responsibilities; and selecting key leadership, such as the president). In short, shared governance allocates public accountability and stewardship to the governing board, academic matters to the faculty, and the tasks of leading and managing the institution to the administration.

The University of Michigan is certainly no exception in facing the multiple challenges of university governance. To be sure, Michigan is an anomalous institution in certain respects. For example, it is one of the very few American research universities whose governing board is determined through statewide popular election, involving partisan candidates nominated by political parties. With two of its eight regents up for election every two years, the frequently changing political stripes of Michigan's governing board present a particular challenge to both the university and its president.

To some degree this anomaly in the selection of the university's governing board is balanced by another unusual feature of the university's governance. The Michigan state constitution grants the university an extraordinary degree of autonomy as a "coordinate branch of state government," by giving its regents full powers over all university matters. More specifically, the constitution authorizes the board to "have the general supervision of the university and the direction and control of all expenditures from university funds." But the constitution also directs the board to elect a president who should preside, without vote, at all their meetings. This latter detail is very important, since it clearly identifies the president as both "chief executive officer" and "chairman of the board" (at least at their meetings), a stature held by few other university presidents, who generally attend governing board meetings only as observers. It allows the president both to determine the agenda and to orchestrate the activities of the governing board. Through this mechanism, the state constitution deftly relieves the regents of the ability to administer the university. In theory, at least, they need only to determine policy—and, of course, hire and fire the president.

Unfortunately, the political nature of a board determined by partisan nomination and popular election sometimes gives the Michigan governing board more the character of a legislative committee—with a prime objective of making certain that the university serves the body politic—than the character of a trustee body committed primarily to institutional welfare. The political variability of an elected board, its inability to agree on many politically controversial issues, and its tendency to circle the wagons and protect even the most outrageous behavior of its occasionally maverick members can erode the board's credibility. University administrators are always concerned that the regents not only will fail to support them but actually might attack them publicly on one agenda or another that advances a political purpose—a not infrequent occurrence.[9]

Faculty governance is also a challenge at Michigan. To be sure, the university has a long tradition of strong faculty governance at the level of individual academic units such as departments or schools, through faculty executive committees. Here, clearly identified responsibilities (hiring, promotion, tenure, budget priorities) attract the participation of strong faculty and provide effective faculty governance. But at the university-wide level, the limited authority of the faculty senate all too frequently transforms it into a debating society more concerned with "p" issues (e.g., pay, parking, and the plant department) than with strategic academic issues facing the university.

Like many other university presidents, I gradually reached the conclusion that the complexity of the contemporary university and the forces acting on it had outstripped the ability of the current shared governance system of lay boards, elected faculty bodies, and inexperienced academic administrators to govern, lead, and manage these important institutions. Many of the most formidable forces shaping the future of American universities have become political in nature—from governments, governing boards, public opinion, and, at times, even faculty governing bodies—rather than reflecting both the long-standing academic values and traditions that have sustained American institutions and the changing needs of the society they were created to serve. To be sure, most of the citizens and faculty members serving on various governing bodies do so with the best of intentions, loyal to the institution and committed to its welfare and capacity to serve. Yet all too frequently, they do so within an awkward structure of shared governance that allows political forces to inhibit access to both adequate information and communication. It is also a structure that can easily be hijacked by those with strong personal or political agendas that could harm the university.

As such concerns grew, my administration set out on a dangerous course to attempt to improve the quality of our governance. We attempted to restructure the meetings of our governing board to allow more discussion of key strategic issues facing the university and to prevent the agenda from being dominated by the usual flow of routine business decisions. We tried to help the board develop internal leadership and discipline so that the occasional antics of maverick board members would not hold it hostage. Although we explored with state government the possibility of modifying the laws requiring popular (and partisan) election of regents, their constitutional nature finally proved too difficult to amend, and we instead focused our attention on using our political contacts (particularly alumni) to improve the quality of candidates nominated by the political parties, although this approach ran the risk of retaliation by some of the current board members.

A similar effort was directed at improving faculty governance. We encouraged the deans to urge their faculties to nominate strong candidates for the university's faculty senate. My executive officers and I met regularly and frequently with the leadership of the faculty senate and most faculty advisory committees. We attempted to engage the executive committees of the university's schools and colleges in university-wide strategic issues. To facilitate interactions with faculty, we brought former leaders of faculty governance into the Office of the President, to serve as liaison and secretary of the university.

Yet it seemed that each painful step forward would quickly be followed by two steps backward. An incumbent regent would become irritated and attempt to retaliate against our alumni association's efforts to encourage interested alumni to stand as candidates for regent. The local newspapers would become attracted to our strategic discussions and attempt to use the state's sunshine laws to pry into more sensitive areas, such as business strategies or property acquisitions. A cabal of discontented faculty members in a particular department would engineer a coup to take over the faculty senate in an effort to push their personal agendas.

Looking back over my decade of leadership as provost and president, I have concluded that one of my most significant failures was my inability to improve the quality of governance at the university at any level—faculty, governing board, state, or federal. I took some consolation that I was not alone in this. Many other presidents, both at the University of Michigan and elsewhere in the state, including some of our most distinguished leaders (Tappan at the University of Michigan, Hannah at Michigan State University), had broken their pickax on governance issues. Yet it was still frustrating to look back on such exhausting efforts resulting in so little progress.

More generally, it is important to recognize that shared governance is, in reality, an ever-changing balance of forces involving faculty, trustees, and administration.[10] It represents the effort to achieve a balance among academic priorities, public purpose, and operating imperatives, such as financial solvency, institutional reputation, and public accountability. Different universities achieve this balance in quite different ways. For example, at the University of California, a strong tradition of campus and system-wide faculty governance is occasionally called on to counter the political forces characterizing the governing board, examples being the loyalty oath controversy of the 1950s, the Reagan takeover of the board of regents in the 1960s, and the debates over the use of affirmative action in student admission during the 1990s.

In contrast, at the University of Michigan, campus-wide, elected faculty governance has historically been rather weak, at least compared to faculty influence through executive committee structures at the department, school, and college level. Hence, the tradition has been to develop a strong cadre of deans—both through aggressive recruiting and through the decentralization of considerable authority to the university's schools and colleges—and then depend on these academic leaders to counter the inevitable political tendencies of the university's regents from time to time. When the deans are strong, this checks-and-balances system works well. When they are weak or myopically focused on their own academic units, the university becomes vulnerable to more sinister political forces.

Where is the influence of the university administration—particularly the president—in this balancing act? It is usually out of sight or perhaps out of mind. After all, senior administrators, including the president, serve at the pleasure of the governing board. They are also mindful of faculty support, since they may be only one vote of no confidence away from receiving their walking papers—a long-standing academic tradition recently reestablished by Harvard and several other universities. While it has always been necessary for the American university president to champion the needs of the academic community to the board and the broader society while playing a role in ensuring that the academic community is in touch with society's interests and needs, it is not surprising that the administration is usually quite reluctant to get caught publicly in skirmishes between the governing board and the faculty.

The danger of such a bilateral balance of power arises when one party or the other is weakened. When the faculty senate loses the capacity to attract the participation of distinguished faculty members or when a series of poor appointments at the level of deans, executive officers, or president weakens the administration, a governing board with a strong political agenda can move into the power vacuum. Of course, there have also been numerous examples of the other extreme, in which a weakened governing board caved in to unrealistic faculty demands—for example, by replacing merit salary programs with cost-of-living adjustments or extending faculty voting privileges to part-time teaching staff in such as way as to threaten faculty quality.

Part of the difficulty with shared governance is its ambiguity. The lines of authority and responsibility are blurred, sometimes intentionally. Although most members of the university community understand that the fundamental principals of shared governance rest on the delegation of authority from the governing board to the faculty in academic matters and to the administration in operational management, the devil in the details can lead to confusion and misunderstanding. Turf problems abound. One of the key challenges to effective university governance is to make certain that all of the constituencies of shared governance—governing boards, administrations, and faculty—understand clearly their roles and responsibilities.

Nothing is more critical to the future success of higher education than improving the quality and performance of boards of trustees. Today, during an era of rapid change, colleges and universities deserve governing boards comprised of members selected for their expertise and experience, members who are capable of governing the university in ways that serve both the long-term welfare of the institution and the more immediate interests of the various constituencies it serves. Trustees should be challenged to focus on policy development rather than intruding into management issues. Their role is to provide strategic, supportive, and critical stewardship for their institution and to be held clearly publicly, legally, and financially accountable for their performance and the welfare of their institution.

For public boards, the need is particularly urgent. As long as the members of the governing boards of public universities continue to be determined through primarily political mechanisms (without careful consideration or independent review of qualifications or institutional commitment) and are allowed to pursue political or personal agendas (without concern for the welfare of their institution or its service to broader society), the public university will find itself increasingly unable to adapt to the needs of a rapidly changing society. Every effort should be made to convince leaders of state government that politics and patronage have no place in the selection of university governing boards or in efforts to determine their administrative leadership. Quality universities require quality leadership and governance. Even as public university governing boards have become increasingly political and hence sensitive to special interests, they have also become increasingly isolated from accountability with respect to their quality and effectiveness. Not only should all university governance be subject to regular and public review, but the quality and effectiveness of governing boards should also be an important aspect of institutional accreditation.

As the contemporary university becomes more complex and accountable, it may even be time to set aside the quaint American practice of governing universities with boards comprised of lay citizens (with their limited expertise and all too frequently political character) and to shift instead to true boards of directors similar to those used in the private sector. Although it may sound strange in these times of scandal and corruption in corporate management, it is nevertheless my belief that university governing boards should function with a structure and a process that reflects the best practices of corporate boards. Corporate board members are selected for their particular expertise in such areas as business practices, finance, or legal matters. They are held accountable to the shareholders for the performance of the corporation. Their performance is reviewed at regular intervals, both within the board itself and through more external measures, such as company financial performance. Clearly, directors can be removed either through action of the board or by shareholder vote. Furthermore, they can be held legally and financially liable for the quality of their decisions—a far cry from the limited accountability of the members of most governing boards for public universities.

Perhaps the simplest approach to identifying possible reforms in faculty governance is to examine where it seems to work well and why. From my own experience—as a faculty member, a former member of faculty governance at both the academic unit and university level, and a has-been university president—faculty governance seems to work best when focused on academic matters, such as faculty searches, promotion and tenure decisions, and curriculum decisions. This is because rank-and-file faculty members understand clearly not only that they have the authority and integrity to make these decisions but that these decisions are important to their academic departments and likely to affect their own teaching and research activities. As a result, the very best faculty members (i.e., those with the strongest reputations and influence) are drawn into the academic governance process—either through formal election or appointment to key committees (hiring, promotion, tenure, curriculum, executive)—or are at least consulted for influential opinions in their role as department mandarins.

In sharp contrast, most active faculty members view university-wide faculty governance bodies, such as faculty senates, primarily as debating societies, whose opinions are invariably taken as advisory—and frequently ignored—by the administration and the governing board. Hence, rare is the case when a distinguished faculty member spares time from productive scholarship, teaching, or department matters for such university service. Of course, there are exceptions, but more common is the squeaky wheel syndrome, where those outspoken faculty members with an ax to grind are drawn to faculty politics, frequently distracting faculty governance from substantive issues, to focus it instead on their pet agendas.

Hence, a key to effective faculty governance is to provide faculty bodies with executive, rather than merely advisory, authority, thereby earning the active participation of the university's leading faculty members. Advisory bodies, paid only lip service by the administration or the board of trustees, rarely attract the attention or the participation of those faculty most actively engaged in scholarship and teaching. The faculty should become true participants in the academic decision process rather than simply watchdogs on the administration or defenders of the status quo. Faculty governance should focus on those issues of most direct concern to academic programs, and faculty members should be held accountable for their decisions. Faculties also need to accept and acknowledge that strong leadership, whether from chairs, deans, or presidents, is important if their institution is to flourish, particularly during a time of rapid social change.

One controversial proposal would be to provide faculty with a stronger voice in true university governance by appointing faculty representatives as members of the governing board. This would be similar to the practice in many other nations of governing universities with unicameral bodies consisting of a balanced composition of lay citizens, faculty members, administrators, and perhaps even students. It may be time to explore this approach in American colleges and universities.

The contemporary American university presidency also merits a candid reappraisal and probably a thorough overhaul. The presidency of the university may indeed be one of the more anemic in our society, because of the imbalance between responsibility and authority, the cumbersome process used to select university leaders, and the increasing isolation of "professional" academic administrators from the core teaching and scholarship activities of the university.[11] Yet it is nevertheless a position of great importance, particularly from the perspective of the long-term impact a president can have on an institution.

Universities have a style of governance that is more adept at protecting the past than preparing for the future. All too often, shared governance tends to protect the status quo or perhaps even a nostalgic view of some idyllic past, thereby preventing a serious consideration of the future. During an era characterized by dramatic change, university leaders must find ways to cut through the Gordian knot of shared governance, of indecision and inaction, to allow our colleges and universities to better serve our society. Not only must our institutions develop a tolerance for strong leadership; they should demand such leadership.

The complexity of the contemporary university and the forces acting on it have outstripped the ability of the current shared governance system of lay boards, elected faculty bodies, and inexperienced academic administrators to govern, lead, and manage. It is simply unrealistic to expect that the governance mechanisms developed decades or even centuries ago can serve well either the contemporary university or the society it serves. To blind ourselves to these realities is to perpetuate a disservice to those whom we serve, both present and future generations.

THE IMPORTANCE OF FIGHTING LOSING BATTLES

Clearly, the windmills described in this chapter—the privatization of the public university, the corruption of intercollegiate athletics, and the obsolescence of university governance—are neither unique to my years as president nor to my institution. Most flagship public universities have always battled to achieve sufficient autonomy to ride out the inevitable ebb and flow of state support. So, too, many institutions have fought to counter the exploitation of student athletes and the corruption of academic values by the commercialization of big-time college sports. And the principle of shared governance has always represented a very delicate balance of powerful forces from constituencies with vastly different values and objectives.

Like most university presidents, I felt it necessary to pick up my sword and fight these battles, even knowing that sooner or later I was likely to lose, just as had my predecessors at Michigan and my colleagues elsewhere in higher education. Fighting battles you know you are likely to lose is frustrating, to be sure. But it is also very important. A president cannot give up the fight and walk away, since then things are likely to get worse—usually much worse, in fact.

In such battles, consistency and persistence can be as important as creativity and political acumen. It is essential to stay on message to both internal constituencies (e.g., the faculty) and external patrons (e.g., government, industry, and alumni). Any uncertainty or wavering will rapidly erode support for your efforts. Besides, you might actually be able to make things better. Many apparently hopeless causes have been won. Sometimes, the key to progress is to continue to beat your head against the wall, until a window of opportunity is suddenly jarred open in what appears to be an immovable barrier.

12

THE ENDGAME

Sooner or later, several facts of life begin to dawn on most university presidents. They become increasingly aware of just how much of their time is spent doing things they do not really like to do, such as stroking potential donors for gifts, lobbying politicians, pampering governing board members, and flying the flag at numerous events—football games, building dedications, political rallies—that eventually become rather boring. This is particularly true for those who come from academic ranks, since these are just the kind of activities that most faculty members avoid like the plague. Presidents also begin to notice how much of their time is spent with people that most faculty members would choose to avoid, including politicians, reporters, and bureaucrats of various persuasions. Finally, they realize how much of their role has become that of a lobbyist, a huckster, or, worse, a sayer of things they know to be exaggerations, intentionally confusing, or even (for some) mildly false.

These are all warning signs that a university president is outgrowing the job—or at least growing weary of its trials and tribulations. This realization soon leads one to a critical decision: determining when and how to step down (aside or elsewhere). Note that there are two concerns here: when and how. In many ways, knowing when to hold and when to fold is far more straightforward a decision than figuring out how to do it, particularly in public universities. The challenge is analogous to dismounting a bucking bronco without getting trampled in the process.

Of course, one approach is to simply accept a job elsewhere and leave. Some presidents move like gypsies from one university to another, typically staying five years or so at each before moving on to the next. Sometimes, their progression is upward, through institutions of higher and higher distinction. But just as frequently, the transition is sideways or even downward, leading one to suspect, in many cases, that the president has left just before the fall of the ax. Other presidents move into retirement, although this is becoming more of a rarity as presidents end their service at ever-younger ages. Some—although few and far between—return to active faculty roles, although very rarely in the institution they have led.

In private universities, presidents usually are allowed to step down with honor, grace, and dignity and return to the faculty or retire completely from academic life. In sharp contrast, many public university presidents these days end their tenure by stepping on a political land mine. Sometimes, they run afoul of their governing board or faculty discontent or even the intrusion of a powerful political figure, such as a governor determined to control the state's public universities. Occasionally there is a triggering event, such as a financial crisis or an athletic scandal. But more frequently, it is the continued wear and tear of university leadership that eventually leads to a personal decision that enough is enough, that the further sacrifice of health and good humor is simply not worth it. Whatever the reason, many presidents who have served their institutions well, with deep commitment, loyalty, and considerable accomplishment, all too frequently leave bitter and disappointed. One of the greatest fears of many presidents, particularly those leading public universities, is that they will not be able to control the endgame of their presidency and will be savaged by hostile political forces and perhaps even severed from the very institution on whose behalf they have worked so hard and sacrificed so much.

The history of presidents at the University of Michigan provides examples of each endgame strategy. Several Michigan presidents—including Angell, Hutchins, Ruthven, Hatcher, and Fleming—retired after many years of service. Since Angell had served for 38 years, until the age of 80, the regents gave him the honorific title of chancellor and allowed him to continue to live in the President's House until his death. One Michigan president, Marion Burton, died in office, after a very brief but productive five-year tenure. Several have moved on to university presidencies in private institutions (Erastus Haven to Northwestern University and Syracuse University, Harold Shapiro to Princeton University, and Lee Bollinger to Columbia University), suggesting that the grass may indeed be greener on the other side of the fence between public and private universities. Two of Michigan's presidents left under more difficult circumstances: Tappan, regarded by some as Michigan's most influential and visionary president, was fired by a lame-duck board of regents; C. C. Little, Michigan's youngest president, lasted only a brief four years before being driven out by faculty discontent. One Michigan president—and only one—has managed to return successfully to the Michigan faculty in an active role as a teacher and a scholar: me.

It is also interesting to note that most Michigan presidents have ended their presidencies on a sour note. Tappan was understandably bitter at the capricious actions leading to his dismissal and wrote an incendiary letter lambasting all of those among the regents and faculty who had undermined his presidency. His successor, Erastus Haven, also became frustrated at what he viewed as lack of support. Haven's papers indicate that he felt he had accomplished little as Michigan's president, while being subject to unfair criticism: "I started with an unfair sentiment against me and can never secure impartiality. Why should I work all my life to sustain a cause at a dead lift? Nothing whatever would, or should, induce me to remain here but a belief that I can do more for truth and good than anywhere else."[1]

Harry Hutchins was effective in sustaining Angell's legacy, but he was eventually worn down by the stresses of World War I on the university. Burton remained upbeat and energetic throughout his very brief presidency, but he was the only Michigan president to have died in office. C. C. Little left Michigan after a brief four-year period, frustrated with the faculty's unwillingness to accept his proposals for reshaping the university's programs to more closely resemble those of the Eastern colleges, his personal life in turmoil.[2]

Although highly successful as president, Alexander Ruthven was weary after his two-decade-long tenure and called his decision to accept the presidency "the greatest regret of my life": "I find now that I get little satisfaction in looking back over the years. I have only done what my conscience dictated but in driving ahead, I have failed to make friends and to enjoy life. The job has been a lonesome one."[3] Harlan Hatcher had a similarly long and successful tenure, but in his latter years, it became clear that the university would require a different style of leadership to cope with growing student activism and campus disruption. The Hatchers disengaged from the university after his retirement, and it was only during my presidency, two decades later, that my wife, Anne, and I were able to reinvolve them in the university community—much to our delight and the university's benefit.

Robben Fleming was one of the few Michigan presidents who stepped down on a high note, leaving to assume the presidency of the Corporation for Public Broadcasting and then returning to the campus several years later as president emeritus. Perhaps because of Fleming's personality and achievements in leading the university during the difficult period of the 1960s and 1970s, he and his wife, Sally, remained highly engaged in the university, with Fleming serving as a confidant of later presidents and regents. Harold Shapiro left Michigan after a highly successful tenure as a faculty member, provost, and president. Although he had accomplished a great deal as president—and would continue to provide strong leadership at Princeton University—his last years at Michigan were made difficult by a marked deterioration in the quality of the board of regents and by attacks directed at his leadership by student activists and intrusive legislators. As for me, well, this chapter is intended to reveal the endgame period of my Michigan leadership experience. Like most of my Michigan predecessors, I also did not have the opportunity to ride off peacefully into the sunset.

SURVIVAL INSTINCT

Michigan scores! The hockey fans begin to point at the visiting goalie and chant: "It's all your fault! It's all your fault! It's all your fault!"

Perhaps out of reflex, I find myself slinking down into my seat, trying to hide.

"It's all your fault!" is perhaps the most common invective tossed at a university president, because the presidency of a major university is one of those rare leadership roles in which anything good that happens is generally due to someone else, but anything bad is always the president's fault. Or so students, faculty, trustees, and the media like to believe. The governor cuts a sweetheart deal to slip a few extra million to his alma mater, Michigan State University—my fault. A racist flyer is taped to the door of a minority faculty member in the Law School—my fault. As the stock market drops 100 points, the value of the university endowment loses a few hundred million dollars, at least temporarily—my fault again. A congressman interested in publicity attacks the university for "political correctness" (I have always marveled at how Congress always seems to know what is politically correct and what is not)—again, the president's fault. When the Colorado quarterback Cordell Stewart faded back and tossed a 70-yard bomb to beat Michigan as the clock expired, whose fault was it? Well, the president did not call Michigan's prevent defense, but since I was at the game, it was probably my fault. Ditto for Chris Webber's illegal time-out in the closing seconds of the NCAA basketball championship game against North Carolina.

One of my Michigan predecessors, Robben Fleming, put it best: "Anyone in public office, or a position like a university president, is subject to the continual expression of unkind, unfair, inaccurate, and sometimes vicious criticism which we have to accept as the price of a society in which we place so high a value on freedom of expression."[4] It is characteristic of the university presidency, as of many in leadership positions, that one acquires a sense of personal responsibility for everything bad that happens in the institution, even though most of these events are clearly beyond the president's control. Furthermore, although most rational people understand this, someone has to take the blame. The president is usually the most convenient scapegoat.

As a consequence, a strange personality transformation occurs during the years of a university presidency. Successful presidents—or shall we say, surviving presidents—develop a sixth sense, a primitive instinct that keeps them always on the alert for danger, almost as if they were hunted animals. And well they should, since today's university presidents seem increasingly under attack by politicians, governing boards, and even their own faculties. Understandably, university presidents must develop not only an unusually thick skin but also an acute instinct to sense danger.

Anne and I had the good fortune of entering the Michigan presidency with a great deal of knowledge about the university from many years on the faculty, as members of the campus community, and in service in key leadership positions, including dean and provost. We already knew where most of the snakes nested about the campus and where most of the bodies were buried. But even with this advance forewarning, we were probably not prepared for the onslaught that accompanies public life.

Like other public figures, university presidents are frequently targets for those—both on and off campus—who are mad at the administration, at the university, or simply at life itself. This long list might include faculty members with particularly political or personal agendas, student activists, regents (including the inevitable mavericks on the board), the media (always on the lookout for a provocative story), politicians (local, state, and federal), and the usual list of obsessed or disturbed folks for whom the university president is simply a convenient target for their personal angst. Of course, one might add to this list the usual practitioners of court politics, particularly within the administration.

To some degree, this aggravation just goes with the territory characterizing any public leadership position. Following the meeting in which the Michigan Regents elected me as the eleventh president of the university, Robben Fleming pulled me aside for some advice. He suggested that a public university president should never regard the slings and arrows launched by others as personal attacks. Rather, he argued, most critics were simply angry at the institution, not the president. But he also acknowledged that university presidents made a most convenient target for taking out frustrations and that such attacks could not only hurt but cause fatal injury.

Some degree of paranoia is both appropriate and advisable. There are always those who believe that their personal agendas can be advanced by attacking the president. There are numerous examples (including the overthrow of Michigan's first president, Henry Tappan) where even the most successful presidents have been toppled and universities have been torn apart by individuals or special interest groups whose causes seem minor in the broader scheme of university priorities but whose ability to destabilize the institution—particularly its governing board—was seriously underestimated. After years of enduring such attacks, one develops a survival instinct, a tendency to look under every rock and behind every tree, to question everything and everyone. It is little wonder that some presidents eventually self-destruct and that others surround themselves with mildly paranoid staff to serve as canaries in the mine shaft.

PUTTING IT ALL ON THE LINE

I received another piece of well-heeded advice from Robben Fleming: "A university president must develop the capacity to tolerate risk as a necessary characteristic of the position. If you do not occasionally face critical moments when you must put your job on the line in defending or advancing the institution, then you are likely not doing your job well."[5] Well, if living dangerously is a measure of a successful president, my experience must rank high, since my list of tightrope walks is long indeed. After a particularly frustrating day late in my presidency, I went back over my calendar and tried to identify some of the times when the interests of the university required me to confront powerful forces that posed significant risks to my presidency. Several examples from that list illustrate the point well:

1. Building and leading a statewide coalition of university presidents and influential alumni to block a governor's efforts to control public university tuition
2. Launching and leading the Michigan Mandate and Michigan Agenda for Women, to diversify the campus
3. Modifying the university's nondiscrimination policies to include gays and lesbians, then extending staff benefits to same-sex couples
4. Putting into place a new student disciplinary policy against strong student opposition (and regent lobbying)

5. Creating a campus police force—the first in the university's history—to protect the campus
6. Insisting on academic control of the admission and academic progress of student athletes—much to the ire of power coaches in our football and basketball programs
7. Restructuring the formula for sharing football gate receipts within the Big Ten Conference—an objective that required a not-too-subtle threat to withdraw Michigan from the Big Ten but resulted in a 40 percent increase in Athletic Department revenues
8. Standing up to and surviving an attack on the university by a powerful congressional investigative committee attempting to exploit a preliminary indirect cost audit, which, on later review, actually substantiated the university's integrity
9. Challenging the leadership of Michigan's fraternities and threatening strong action if they did not address serious disciplinary behavior that was threatening both the university and the Ann Arbor community
10. Publicly challenging the UM athletic booster clubs' tradition of excluding women
11. Creating and leading a statewide effort to build stronger support for public higher education in the midst of a close gubernatorial election campaign
12. Year after year, persuading, pressuring, and pleading with the regents to support adequate increases in student tuition and fees to sustain quality and provide adequate need-based financial aid
13. Attempting to improve the quality of university governing boards in Michigan by working with alumni and the media, thereby earning the great ire of several Michigan regents who believed this matter should be left to incumbent board members
14. Challenging city government to stop beating on the university for its tax-exempt status and instead support a city income tax that would generate adequate tax revenue, which would be paid in large measure by university employees
15. Challenging state government to recognize that a tax structure from the 1950s, based on a manufacturing economy, would lead

to disaster as the state's economy was increasingly dominated by knowledge-intensive services that were excluded from the tax base—a warning that would prove all too true by the end of the 1990s

16. Persuading the regents to adopt new (and occasionally high-risk) strategies for financing highly needed academic facilities on campus
17. Using the bully pulpit of the Michigan presidency to take on important national issues such as diversity, K–12 education, post–cold war national priorities, the regressive nature of public policies for supporting public higher education, global change, and so on
18. Threatening sacred cows by publicly raising the possibility of spinning off major auxiliary activities—such as the university's hospitals and semiprofessional athletic programs (football and basketball)—or by suggesting that Michigan was evolving into a "privately supported public university"
19. Making difficult personnel changes, particularly when they involved replacing highly visible or regent-popular staff
20. When necessary, standing up to individual regents over issues important to the university or the community, including gay rights, supporting a Holocaust monument on campus, retired faculty housing, minority admissions, and personal behavioral issues (e.g., conflict of interest, "perk-itis," and abusive treatment of staff)

And the list goes on and on and on.

Not surprisingly, I used to worry about this frequency of putting it all on the line time after time. While it was true that this high-risk style led to quite remarkable progress for the university, it also put considerable strain on Anne and me, while sometimes putting the university administration at some risk. I wondered about the wisdom of always putting the president out front to fight these battles when others, such as executive officers or senior staff, were far less vulnerable. Yet putting someone else in front was not my style—after all, my position in college football was tackle, always first into battle.

Perhaps it is not surprising, in retrospect, that while these high-risk actions were some of the most difficult and important tasks the president performed for the university, few folks—particularly among the faculty—were aware of them. Instead of sympathy and support, it was more common to encounter the attitude expressed in the phrase "So what have you done for us lately?" While tentativeness has never been one of my character traits, I must confess a growing weariness that arises from fighting battle after battle to keep the university moving ahead, with little understanding and appreciation and even less support. It is hard to keep fighting the good fight when those you are trying to protect keep pecking away at your rear flank.

WEAR AND TEAR

The presidency of a major university is a 24-hour-a-day, 365-day-a-year job—both for the president and the spouse. Needless to say, the wear and tear can be considerable. Today's modern university runs year-round, around the clock, as do the various elements of society that depend on and influence it. While faculty can look toward summertime as a more relaxed period for rest and travel, June and July are usually the time when key budget decisions are made both in state legislatures and Congress, and when legislative bodies are in session, no one and no public institutions are safe, particularly public universities, such as the University of Michigan.

Modern telecommunications has made it even more difficult to decouple from the stresses and strains of presidential leadership. Associated with its early years in building and managing national computer networks, Michigan benefited from an exceptionally advanced e-mail and computer conferencing system that permeated the university. On a typical day as president, I would receive and respond to literally hundreds of e-mail messages from staff, faculty, students, and others, both on and off the campus, nationwide and worldwide. Wherever I went, my laptop computer and cell phone were constant companions. Like most of the senior officers of the university, I also carried a pager that could download brief e-mail messages anyplace in North America—the precursor to today's Blackberry device. Hence, this electronic umbilical cord—computer, phone, and pager—kept me constantly in touch with the university and kept it constantly in touch with me.

I do not doubt that many would seriously question the wisdom of this real-time connectivity. Yet my experience with leading such a complex institution in a continually changing environment convinced me that beyond carefully developed strategies, much of the advancement of the institution occurred through unanticipated opportunities—being in the right place at the right time. So too, many of the greatest threats to the institution ignited rapidly and would reach the explosive stage if prompt effective action were not taken. Hence, while the personal toll was great, I was convinced that the times required this style of leadership. I always had to be prepared for the unexpected.

THE TWO-MINUTE WARNING

There were many factors that eventually persuaded me that it was time to step aside as president. Since I had served both as acting president during Harold Shapiro's sabbatical and then as provost and "president-in-waiting" for roughly two years prior to being inaugurated as president in 1988, I was approaching the 10-year point in my leadership of the university. I was already second in seniority among Big Ten presidents (serving as chairman of the Big Ten Conference) and sixth in longevity among the 60 AAU presidents. Hence, as Anne and I approached a new academic year in 1995, we felt it was time to take stock of how far the university had come and what the road ahead looked like.

Looking back, I would identify three quite separate phases in my presidency. The early phase involved setting the themes of challenge, opportunity, responsibility, and excitement and developing a vision for the future of the university. During this phase, much of my time was spent meeting with various constituencies both on and off campus, listening to their aspirations and concerns, challenging and encouraging them, harvesting their ideas and wisdom, and attempting to build a sense of excitement and optimism about the future of the university. This period marks the establishment of some of my administration's most important strategic directions for the university: for example, the Michigan Mandate, financial restructuring, the Campaign for Michigan, the Undergraduate Initiative Fund, NSFnet and the Internet, and numerous international activities. This bottom-up visioning process was assisted by numerous small groups of faculty and staff, some formal, some ad hoc.

The second phase of my leadership, while not so public, was equally substantive, since it involved developing and executing an action plan to move toward the vision. Key were a series of strategic initiatives designed to position the university for the leadership role proposed in Vision 2000, described in chapter 9. These ranged from the appointment of key leaders at the level of executive officers, deans, and directors, to setting new standards for academic and administrative quality, to rebuilding our campuses, to a bold financial restructuring of Michigan as the nation's first privately supported public university. Largely as a result of these efforts, the university grew rapidly in strength, quality, and diversity during the early 1990s. One by one, each of the goals of Vision 2000 was achieved.

By the mid-1990s, my administration began to shift the university into a third phase, shifting from a positioning effort to a transformation agenda. I had become convinced that we were entering an era of great challenge and opportunity for higher education, characterized by a rapid and profound transformation into a global knowledge society. I realized that the task of transforming the university to better serve society and to move toward a new vision for the century ahead would be challenging. Perhaps the greatest challenge of all would be the university's very success. It would be difficult to convince those who had worked so hard to build a leading public university of the twentieth century, that they could not rest on their laurels, that the old paradigms would no longer work. The challenge of the 1990s would be to reinvent the university to serve a new world in a new century.

It was clear that the transformation agenda of the university would require wisdom, commitment, perseverance, and considerable courage. It would require teamwork. It would also require an energy level, a "go for it" spirit, and a sense of adventure. But all of these features had characterized the university during its past eras of change, opportunity, and leadership. These were, in fact, important elements of the institutional saga of the University of Michigan.

During this final phase, my administration launched a series of initiatives aimed at providing the university with the capacity to transform itself to better serve a changing world. Several of these initiatives were highly controversial, such as the launch of several cutting-edge academic programs (e.g., the Center for Molecular Medicine and the School of Information), a new system for decentralized budgeting that transferred to individual units the responsibility for both generating revenues and meeting costs, and a new approach to academic outreach involving the Internet (leading to the creation of the Michigan Virtual University). Hence, it was important that, as president, I returned once again to a more visible role. In a series of addresses and publications, I challenged the university community, stressing the importance of not only adapting to but relishing the excitement and opportunity characterizing a time of change.

During this decade-long effort, begun with Harold Shapiro during my provost years, the university made remarkable progress. Due to the extraordinary talents, commitment, and depth of the leadership team (not to mention a great deal of luck), we had been able to accomplish essentially everything we had originally set out as goals. The institution had been restructured financially and was now as strong as any university in the nation. The Campaign for Michigan, with over a year yet to go, had surpassed its original goal of $1 billion. The endowment had passed $2 billion, almost 10 times the amount we began with. Minority enrollments and faculty representation had doubled as a result of the Michigan Mandate. Michigan had surpassed MIT and Stanford University in research volume, to become the nation's leading research university. The massive $2 billion effort to rebuild the university's campuses was approaching completion, with over a dozen new building dedications already scheduled in the year ahead. Not only was our senior leadership team—executive officers, deans, and administrative directors—highly regarded as one of the strongest in the nation, but talent ran deep throughout the university administration and staff. Furthermore, most of our enemies in state and federal government had either been vanquished or had long since moved on, leaving us with relatively strong support among various external constituencies—including, for a change, even the state's media.

The more difficult transformation effort, Vision 2017, was also well under way, with the key strategic initiatives in place, important planning teams and faculty commissions up and running, and extensive communications efforts continuing to both educate and engage on-campus and off-campus constituencies. Many of our most important experiments were launched and coming up to speed, such as the effort to improve undergraduate education, the new School of Information, the creation of a new university health care system, and the Big Ten academic alliance. New facilities, such as the Media Union and the School of Social Work, were nearing completion. Furthermore, we were grooming the next generation of leaders and had begun the search effort for several key positions, including provost, dean of graduate studies, and executive vice president for medical affairs.

Hence, there was every reason to feel satisfied as Anne and I walked amid the construction cranes on campus in the summer of 1995, with yet another academic year soon upon us. But I hinted at my deeper concerns in a passage contained in several of my speeches to the campus community and various alumni groups during the spring of 1995:

> I believe the UM is as strong as it has ever been right now, . . . better, stronger, more exciting. That is due to the efforts of an enormous number of people, obviously. I inherited the fruits of the financial wisdom of Harold Shapiro, the diplomatic-political skills of Robben Fleming, and an enormous number of talented faculty and executive officers that brought us to this point. Yet while Michigan is very strong right now, it is also a time when institutions of higher education are being asked to change very dramatically to serve a changing world, just as other social institutions are. And leading an institution during a time of change, during a time of transformation, puts an additional stress on the entire system.

I had become increasingly convinced that the university needed to undergo a further series of profound transformations and that this period would require sustained leadership for many years. Both Anne and I were increasingly concerned about whether we would be able to sustain the energy and drive necessary to lead Michigan through such an extended period.

Another related consideration was the very nature of the activities I saw as necessary for the university in the years ahead. In part because our progress had been so rapid, I began to look farther ahead—five years, a decade, even a generation or more into the future. I became more interested in blockbuster goals than in the incremental and opportunistic approach of our earlier efforts. I sought larger agendas than those that could be addressed by Michigan alone, agendas that would require new coalitions at the national and even international level.

Although I had a personal vision for the future of the University of Michigan, I also realized that there were many questions involving the evolution of higher education that remained unanswered. As a scientist, I preferred to look at the decade ahead as a time of experimentation, in which leading universities, such as Michigan, had both an unusual opportunity and a responsibility to explore new paradigms of the university. Looking through my notes from that period, it is clear today that my sense of the challenges and opportunities facing higher education in general and the University of Michigan in particular were moving ever farther beyond the perceptions of my colleagues.

Although I had a very strong interest in leading progressive efforts, I began to question whether I could do so in my role as president. The ongoing roles of the presidency must continue—as chief executive officer for the institution; its lead promoter and fund-raiser; the shepherd tending its many flocks; and defender of its values, missions, and quality. I became increasingly concerned about whether I could build sufficient regental understanding and support for this bolder agenda, particularly when the board was becoming increasingly divided. Although many faculty and staff in the university were excited and energized by the boldness of the transformation agenda, many others were threatened. Hence, awareness began to build that my next stage of leadership for higher education might best be accomplished from elsewhere, far from the politics of the presidency and the glare of the media. It was becoming increasingly clear that as I challenged the university to change in more profound ways to serve a changing world, I would gradually exhaust my political capital.

Ironically, Anne and I were forced to think a bit more seriously about our future when two regents of the University of California flew out to visit us over a Memorial Day weekend to discuss the possibility of the UC system presidency. This was probably the only leadership position in the nation more complex than Michigan, with nine major campuses and three national laboratories. This, combined with our earlier experiences in California, compelled us to at least consider the possibility of the UC presidency. The University of California had looked earlier to Michigan for its leadership, tapping UM provost Roger Heyns for chancellor of the University of California, Berkeley, in the 1960s and approaching Robben Fleming about the UC presidency in the 1970s.

But for us, there were serious drawbacks to the UC presidency, not the least of which was the intent of the UC regents to pass a motion to ban the use of affirmative action in admissions (a decision later reinforced by California's Proposition 209). Such a policy would have placed me in almost immediate conflict with both the UC governing board and the state of California, in view of my successful efforts through the Michigan Mandate to build diversity at Michigan. But more significantly, Anne and I also realized that we had invested far too much in serving the University of Michigan to simply walk away.

Yet perhaps it was in this effort to take stock of what we had accomplished and what remained that we began to think more seriously about just how much longer we could serve. Early in the fall of 1995, as Anne and I walked through the campus and saw all the new buildings and landscaping and went to events to meet the new faculty, we had an increasing sense that our job might be complete. After all, we were entering our eighth year in the presidency, a term comparable in length to the terms of our predecessors and longer than average for public university presidents.

As fate would have it, another factor became the straw that broke the camel's back, pushing us to a decision to step down after 10 years at the helm: this was the deteriorating support provided by the university's board of regents. As a result of the 1994 elections, the board of regents had become badly fragmented—in political beliefs (it was composed of four conservative Republicans and four labor-left Democrats), in generation (four young regents resisted the leadership of more senior members of the board), and in relations with the university (four regents who were Ann Arbor residents were regularly lobbied by students, faculty, and staff on various agendas). But more seriously, the long-standing senior leadership of the board, its chair and vice-chair, were defeated in the 1994 elections. The four-to-four political division of the newly elected board made it difficult for members to agree on new leadership. Several regents soon reached the conclusion that the board would remain dysfunctional until a new political majority could be reestablished. One regent even stressed to me that my role must become that of protecting the university from its governing board during this stalemate. As a sign of the difficulties to come, the board finally assigned its most senior member, ironically the board's true maverick (in whom they had little confidence), with the task of being the primary interface with the president and administration—a decision perhaps meant to send a signal of the eroding support of some members of the new board.

As a result, the executive officer team was forced to deal with a governing board without any internal structure whatsoever—no chair or even party caucus leadership. Although I, as president, had constitutional authority to preside over the meetings of the board, I did so without a vote. Hence, with a four-to-four political split, it became increasingly time-consuming to obtain the additional vote to achieve a majority on matters of importance, such as setting tuition or approving property acquisitions, and to avoid getting a majority vote on issues that could harm the university, such as the rejection of the Michigan Mandate diversity agenda or our student disciplinary policy. The political divisions on the board, its inability to agree on many issues, and its instability made the executive officers increasingly tentative, always concerned that the regents might fail to support them or even attack them publicly on one agenda or another.

A badly divided governing board can take a considerable toll on the executive officers, the university, and the president. Roughly one-third of my time was spent dealing one-on-one with various regents because of their inability to trust one another. Regent intrusion into such areas as finance, personnel, state politics, and athletics was particularly excessive, placing added pressure on the executive officers responsible for these areas.

It soon became apparent that the changing character of the board not only had put our transformation strategy at risk but was also increasingly threatening the university. The executive officer team eventually concluded that we had no choice but to narrow our transformation agenda, stressing only those efforts we believed could be completed over the next year or two and lashing down the wheel to prepare for the stormy seas ahead. Since it was also becoming increasingly clear that my own tenure might be shortened considerably by an intrusive governing board, we began to lock in place a series of key actions—for example, developing the responsibility center management structure and endowment investment strategy and protecting university financial reserves—and moved even more aggressively to decentralize authority to the unit level. Needless to say, developing and executing this doomsday strategy was depressing at times, particularly in view of the extraordinary progress that the university had made over the past decade. But in the end, we became convinced that our responsibility to the institution and to those it would serve in the future demanded such downside strategies.

This was the atmosphere surrounding the university administration as I approached my last year in the Michigan presidency. It was the calm before the storm, characterized by both a sense of satisfaction about remarkable accomplishments of the past decade and a growing dread of the damage that, despite the best efforts of several regents to heal divisions among their colleagues, an increasingly divided governing board was capable of inflicting on the institution as some members pursued their political and personal whims.

Finally, following a particularly difficult week in early fall, when several of the regents undercut my efforts to recruit a new provost, I realized that the oscillations of the board were becoming increasingly volatile and dysfunctional. Hence, I concluded that the only way to stabilize the board, regain control of the agenda, and refocus the university on academic issues once again was to use the visibility of my resignation and a year as lame duck to regain command. This was not an easy decision (at least as far as timing was concerned), but sometimes the general has to fall on his sword to save his army.

My decision was announced simultaneously to the regents, the university community, and the world (via the Internet). By carefully designing both the tone of the announcement and its broad release, I tried to take the high ground and set the right context for the decision as the key paragraph in my letter to the board indicates.

> After considerable thought, Anne and I have decided that the university, the board, and the two of us would be best served if I was to retire from the presidency at the end of the current academic year (June 30, 1996). This would provide the Regents with both the opportunity and the time to conduct a search for a new president. It would also allow me to keep the university on course, hold together a stable leadership team, and prepare for a graceful transition back to the faculty. We ask only for the respect, honor, and dignity that our efforts and accomplishments merit through service both as president and as dedicated members of the university for the past 27 years.[6]

Unfortunately, Michigan's governor at the time, John Engler, ever the political opportunist, used my announcement to blast the Michigan regents, in an effort to make the case for shifting from elected to appointed governing boards. While his criticism was valid in principle, his attacks were far too strident, too blatantly political, and without any follow-through. This unleashed a torrent of criticism by the media,[7] with most calling for a new process for selecting university governing boards and condemning the behavior of the Michigan board. Anne and I were deluged by hundreds of letters of support and thanks, which were reassuring, but we now faced the challenge of repairing the damage the governor had inflicted on the board. Fortunately, the regents' new role in searching for and selecting a successor soon smoothed the waters, while most people close to us understood and accepted our decision. Over the course of the next several months, the many constituencies we had served throughout the university arranged events to both honor and thank us.

TAKING STOCK

I mentioned earlier that one of the most important guidelines for a university president is to make certain that you pass the institution along to your successor in better shape than you received it. In 1996, Anne and I handed off a university that not only benefited from the highest academic program rankings in its history but had become regarded nationwide as a leader and an innovator. Michigan led the nation in the magnitude of its research activities. It had the most successful medical center in the nation. It had achieved national leadership in information technology, playing a key role in building the Internet. It had become the strongest public university in the nation in a financial sense, as evidenced by the fact that Wall Street gave it its highest credit rating, Aaa, in 1996 (along with the University of Texas, the only two public universities in the nation to receive this rating). A *CBS News* segment on the University of Michigan in 1995 observed, "While America has a number of world-class universities, Michigan truly stands in a class by itself."

More specifically, by the time I stepped down, Michigan's endowment had surpassed $2.5 billion, an increase of almost tenfold. The Campaign for Michigan was nearing completion, raising over $1.4 billion, 40 percent beyond its original goal. The university's portfolio of resources was far more balanced, with tuition revenue increasing to over $450 million per year, and private support (gifts received plus endowment payout) had passed $260 million per year, clearly on track to surpass my administration's goal of exceeding state support by the end of the decade.

The campus environment for teaching and research had been improved significantly. All of the university's campuses—Ann Arbor, Dearborn, and Flint—were essentially rebuilt, with over $2 billion of new construction and renovation. The campuses had also been relandscaped, and new master plans had been not only adopted but achieved. As the quality of the campus was improved, a new sense of pride appeared within the campus communities (particularly among the students), resulting in a dramatic decrease in littering and other activities that defaced the environment.

There was also a significant change in the quality and style of university events and facilities. Both the President's House and Inglis House had been completely renovated. There was a new level of quality achieved in university advancement events. The university had also begun to reconnect itself with its remarkable past, developing a new sense of understanding and appreciation for its history and traditions and restoring historically important facilities, such as the Detroit Observatory.

The student body was characterized by a new spirit of leadership and cooperation. Such programs as Leadership 2017 attracted a new generation of leaders, and fraternities and sororities accepted a new sense of responsibility for their activities. Although initially difficult to implement, the student code and campus police had become valuable contributions to the quality of campus life. This was augmented by a major effort to improve campus safety, including the improvement of lighting, transportation, and security.

Michigan athletics had evolved far beyond its football-dominated history, to achieve leadership across a broad range of men's and women's sports. Furthermore, Michigan became the first major university in America to achieve full gender equity in varsity opportunities. The Michigan Mandate and Michigan Agenda for Women had a dramatic impact on the campus, doubling the number of underrepresented minorities among Michigan's students, faculty, staff, and leadership; breaking through the glass ceiling to appoint women to senior leadership positions; and creating a new appreciation for the importance of a diverse campus community.

The external relations of the university were back on track. There were strong teams in place in Lansing, Washington, development, and alumni relations. The university also benefited from what was regarded as one of the strongest leadership teams in the nation at the level of executive officers, deans, and senior administrative staff—although, unfortunately, many of these were to leave early in the tenure of the next president.

Not to say that there were no remaining problems. The regents still suffered from a political selection process that posed a gauntlet to many qualified candidates. The state's sunshine laws had become increasingly intrusive and were clearly hampering the operations of the university. A scandal was uncovered in the men's basketball program that would plague future presidents. Prospects for the restoration of adequate state support continued to look dim.

Yet in assessing the decade of leadership from 1986 to 1996, it is clear that the university made remarkable progress. It approached the twenty-first century better, stronger, more diverse, and more exciting than ever, clearly positioned as one of the leading universities in the world. During this decade, the University of Michigan completed the ascension in academic quality launched years earlier by Harold Shapiro. Its quality and impact across all academic disciplines and professional programs ranked it among the most distinguished public and private universities in the world.

As the strategic focus of my administration shifted from building a great twentieth-century university to transforming Michigan into a twenty-first-century institution, a series of key initiatives were launched that were intended as seeds for a university of the future. Certainly, highly visible efforts, such as the Michigan Mandate and financial restructuring, were components of this effort. However, beyond these were numerous exciting initiatives led by many of our most distinguished faculty members and designed to explore new paradigms for higher education. These included the Institute for the Humanities, the School of Information, the Global Change Program, the Molecular Medicine Institute, and the Media Union.

Each Michigan president seems to have filled a particular leadership role for the university, perhaps less because of how they were selected than the degree to which the institution and its needs shaped their presidency. Which earlier presidency most resembled my administration? There were probably some faculty members who initially regarded me as the barbarian from the North Campus, an engineer rather than a scholar. To be sure, I was a builder, like Burton, leading a successful $2 billion construction effort to rebuild all of the university's campuses. While bricks and mortar do not make a great university, it was difficult to conduct high-quality teaching and scholarship in the dismal facilities that housed many of Michigan's programs prior to my presidency.

Some on the faculty regarded me as a corporate type, a CEO president, who completed Harold Shapiro's effort to financially restructure the university. Driving the $1.4 billion Campaign for Michigan, increasing endowment from $250 million to $2.5 billion, fighting the political battles to build Michigan's tuition base to compensate for the loss of state support, providing the environment and incentives to make Michigan the nation's leading research university, and reducing costs through such efforts as Total Quality Management and decentralized budgeting were all components of a strategy to preserve and enhance the quality of the university despite the serious erosion in state support, which I believed was likely to continue for the foreseeable future. It was certainly true that I was a driver, with a relentless commitment to completing the ascension on academic quality launched during the Shapiro years. Like Shapiro, my academic roots were with institutions committed to the highest academic standards—Yale and Caltech—and I was determined that Michigan should strive for similar quality. Hence, the aspiration for excellence was pervasive throughout all of our efforts.

It was probably not surprising that a scientist as president would develop, articulate, and achieve a strategic vision for the university that would provide it with great financial strength, rebuild its campus, and position it as the leading research university in the nation. But many were surprised by my deep commitment to diversifying the university through such initiatives as the Michigan Mandate, the Michigan Agenda for Women, and the revision of Regental Bylaw 14.06 to prevent discrimination based on sexual orientation. Furthermore, my broad effort to improve undergraduate education and campus life were far beyond what one might have expected from one who had spent his academic career in graduate education and research.

If, however, I were to choose my own descriptor to characterize my tenure, it would be that of providing leadership during a time of change. In a sense, I aimed at serving as both a prophet and a force for change, recognizing that to serve a rapidly changing world, the university itself would have to change dramatically. In my view, the most important contribution of my decade of leadership was building the recognition that to serve a rapidly changing world, the university itself would have to change dramatically.

Fortunately, in 1996, as I approached the end of my presidency, the state of Michigan and America were entering what would become the most prosperous time for higher education in decades. State support was relatively generous, and a booming equity market stimulated strong private giving and endowment growth. The university coffers were filled. A strong leadership team of executive officers, deans, and administrative staff were in place, and numerous important initiatives were running in high gear. Hence, when I stepped down from the presidency, the future of the university seemed secure—at least for the moment.

FADING AWAY

During my last, lame-duck year in the presidency, the pace certainly did not slow down. The transformation effort moved ahead, as did other major efforts, such as various academic initiatives, the fund-raising campaign, the major capital facilities projects, and the effort to strengthen support of the university from both state and federal government. The effort to appoint a new provost was put on hold, to preserve the prerogative of the next president. Fortunately, we were able to entice one of our senior deans, Bernie Machen, dean of dentistry, to serve in the interim role. Bernie was highly respected by the deans and executive officers, and although my successor, Lee Bollinger, would look elsewhere for his provost, Bernie went on to highly successful presidencies at the University of Utah and then the University of Florida.

Anne turned much of her personal attention to providing encouragement and support to the deans and executive officers during the transition. As I mentioned earlier, unlike Harold Shapiro, I found that my power, responsibility, and accountability continued undiminished, with major decisions put on my desk up to my final day as president in the summer of 1996. Since people realized that Anne and I fully intended to remain at the university as active members of the faculty and community, they trusted us to do what was best for the institution up until the very end of our tenure.

This decision to remain at the university was rather unusual. As I noted in an earlier chapter, most university presidential searches today end up selecting candidates from outside. While these individuals bring new ideas and experience, they usually do not have the emotional attachment that comes from years of service on the faculty or within the campus community. Hence, when they step down from their presidency, they usually do not remain as part of the university community but, rather, move on to another institution or retire from higher education entirely.

Anne and I were somewhat unusual in higher education, since we had spent our careers at the same institution that I would lead in the presidency. We had many opportunities to go elsewhere. Yet we turned away these approaches by saying, each time, that our job was not yet complete at Michigan. Our commitment to finish what we had started was firm. We did give some thought to life after the presidency, as all presidents should—particularly in a public university with a political governing board. In the negotiation associated with my decision to continue for several more years of service following my first five years as president, I followed a pattern set by Harold Shapiro and negotiated a path to return to my role as an active professor, but reporting to the provost rather than to a particular academic unit. To indicate the university-wide character of the appointment, the regents approved the title "university professor of science and engineering," noting it was comparable to an endowed chair. I was given a small suite of offices in one of the last buildings constructed on the university's North Campus during my presidency, the Media Union (eight years later to be renamed the James and Anne Duderstadt Center). I was able to marshal sufficient funds for a small staff and several student assistants for a research project called the Millennium Project, aimed at exploring over-the-horizon topics involving the impact of technology on society.

However, remaining at the institution where one had served as president—even when this had been preceded by decades as a faculty member and a member of the university community—was, in itself, a rather stressful experience. I remember well the "good news–bad news" advice given me by a colleague who had also returned to the faculty after long service as the leader of his campus. First the bad news: He warned that life would be difficult under my first successor, since in public universities, there is a tendency for new presidents to obliterate any evidence of the existence of their predecessors—"The king is dead, long live the king!" A retiring president will frequently be ignored—if not buried and paved over. He noted that loyal staff would be replaced and that programs would be dismantled as the new leader tried to establish his or her own agenda and steer the university in a different direction. However, my colleague also had some good news. First, he suggested that my first successor would not last very long, since, like an ocean liner, a university is very hard to turn about, and efforts to attempt this usually end in failure. Second, he believed that life could be quite enjoyable under my second successor, who no longer would have any need to discount the accomplishments of earlier predecessors and hence could welcome them back once again as valued members of the university community.

TEN YEARS AFTER A DECADE AT THE HELM

What has life been like as a president emeritus? Fortunately, my post-presidency agreement with the regents provided me both the position (with a university-wide faculty appointment) and the platform (as director of a small research center) to reenter the professoriat—an important lesson for those university presidents considering a faculty position in the presidential afterlife. To be sure, there have been occasional frustrations beyond those of suddenly becoming powerless during a period when valued colleagues are replaced and programs are dismantled. The first jarring transition is the loss of the strong support staff so necessary for the hectic life of a university president. In the transition back to the faculty, it soon becomes apparent that execution becomes more important than delegation, as one must learn once again how to make travel arrangements, maintain a filing system, use the copy machine, and make the coffee.

Calendar management also becomes a new challenge. Although has-been presidents are expected to be ghosts on their campuses, the former leadership of such a prominent university as Michigan still retains some visibility and credibility on the national stage. The invitations to speak or participate in various activities are quite numerous. The challenge, of course, is to prioritize these opportunities into a coherent pattern. Otherwise, one soon finds the calendar filled with too many such commitments, leaving little time for other activities, including the normal faculty pursuits of teaching and research. In my own case, this overload of opportunities was compounded by my continued involvement with numerous state and national agencies, including the National Science Board, the National Science Foundation, the Department of Energy, and the National Academies. Beyond this, I faced the very pragmatic challenge of seeking longer-term funding for my own research interests, since grantsmanship is a requirement for any productive faculty role in science and engineering.

It soon became apparent that beyond acquiring the usual speaking and writing roles characterizing the afterlife of a university president, I had become, in effect, a "professional chairman," because of the numerous requests to chair various committees and task forces. Here, I suppose that chairing an elected board of regents for many years had prepared me for almost any chair assignment. The assignments ranged from chairing a wide range of National Academy groups on such topics as national science policy, information technology, and science education to advisory committees for federal agencies on such topics as nuclear energy research and space exploration. Michigan's governor asked me to launch a new Internet-based university, the Michigan Virtual Automotive College—later renamed the Michigan Virtual University—so I was once again a university president, if only in a virtual sense.

Many of my speaking engagements were at the invitation of my colleagues who were still sitting in the saddle as active presidents. I used to refer to my role in such engagements as that of a "professional two-by-four," recalling the old Missouri adage that, sometimes, to get a mule to move, one has to first whack it over the head with a two-by-four to get its attention. I would be invited to a campus to meet with trustees, the faculty, or even governors and legislators, to help them read the writing on the wall about the future of higher education and to raise such issues as tuition, tenure, and college sports, which were dangerous territory for a sitting president.

Fortunately, as I became more adept at calendar management, I was soon able to define my own priorities and began to resume my prepresidency activities as an author, although this time on subjects of current interest, such as the future of the university, public higher education, and intercollegiate athletics, rather than, as in my past efforts, on such archaic subjects as nuclear engineering and mathematical physics.[8] I launched a series of projects under the umbrella of my research center, the Millennium Project, including exploring the impact of rapidly evolving digital technologies on learning, the development of strategies for assisting regions in evolving into knowledge economies, and the future of engineering education.

Since I had considerable freedom in my teaching activities, I arranged with the deans to develop and teach an array of new courses scattered across the university, depending on my interests of the moment. These ranged from new undergraduate courses in engineering to a history course developed for last-term seniors in our liberal arts college to graduate-level courses on information technology, nuclear technology, science policy, and higher education. Finally, after Lee Bollinger had left for Columbia and Mary Sue Coleman had arrived as Michigan's new president, it became politically acceptable once again for the president to ask me to take on various assignments within the university, including building a new program in science, technology, and public policy within our Gerald R. Ford School of Public Policy; leading a university-wide effort to build a major effort in energy research; and helping the university develop a strategy for information technology.

Ironically, however, perhaps of most lasting value to the university was my and Anne's effort to better capture and articulate Michigan's remarkable history. This effort was really stimulated by Anne. During my presidency, she developed a strong interest in historical preservation and documentation, stimulating the creation of a university-wide History and Traditions Committee and launching numerous projects involving the renovation and preservation of facilities of major historical importance, such as the University's historic Detroit Observatory. Hence, one of the major activities within the Millennium Project has become an effort to document the history—and hence the institutional saga—of the University of Michigan. This has resulted in a growing series of books on the history of the university.[9] In addition, we were able to utilize the unique resources of the Duderstadt Center to develop new ways to present this history, including three-dimensional virtual reality simulations of the Michigan campus in various eras, a highly detailed computer model of the historical evolution of the campus, and a historical Web site designed as a research tool for scholars (see http://umhistory.org.)

Hence, 10 years after the conclusion of my presidential service, I can confirm that there can indeed be an active life after a university presidency. To be sure, there are particular challenges when one decides to return to faculty life at the same campus one has led, not the least of which is reentering faculty life as a ghost—or in my and Anne's case, I suppose guardian angels would be a more appropriate analogy. Furthermore, it is possible to have considerable impact built on the experience and external visibility gained during a presidency. It is even possible to have greater influence and impact after serving as a university president than during the actual leadership period, at least beyond the campus, since as a faculty member, one not only has more time to think but, perhaps more significantly, fewer constraints on one's activities. Put another way, as a faculty member, one regains those valuable prerogatives frequently absent in a university presidency: academic freedom, freedom of expression, and freedom to think.

WHENCE AND WHITHER THE UNIVERSITY

It is hard for those of us who have spent much of our lives as academics to look objectively at the university, with its tradition and obvious social value, and accept the possibility that it might change in dramatic ways. But although its roots are millennia old, the university has changed before. In the seventeenth and eighteenth centuries, scholasticism slowly gave way to the scientific method as the way of knowing truth. In the early nineteenth century, universities embraced the notion of secular, liberal education and began to include scholarship and advanced degrees as integral parts of their mission. After World War II, in return for federally funded research, they accepted an implied responsibility for national security, economic prosperity, and public health. Although the effects of these changes have been assimilated and now seem natural, the changes involved profound contemporary reassessment of the mission and structure of the university as an institution.

Of course, this ever-changing nature of the university is part of the challenge, since it gives rise to not only an extraordinary diversity of institutions but also a great diversity in perspectives. What is a university? Is it a "college," in the sense of the heritage of the colonial colleges (and, before that, the English boarding schools)? Is it the twentieth-century image of university life—football, fraternities, Joe College, protests? Is it Clark Kerr's multiversity, accumulating ever more missions in response to social needs—health care, economic development, entertainment, and technology transfer. Or is the true university something more intellectual: a community of masters and scholars (*universitas magistorium et scholarium*) or a school of universal learning? What is the core of its university activities: student development; creating, curating, archiving, transmitting, and applying knowledge; or serving society, responding to its contemporary needs—health care, economic development, national defense, homeland security, entertainment (e.g., athletics)? What is its core value: critical, rigorous thinking (e.g., "the life of the mind"); academic freedom; or individual achievement (with the contemporary organization of the university designed to enable individuals to strive to their full potential as students, faculty, and even as athletes)?

With the university having much the character of the proverbial elephant being felt by the blind men, it is not surprising that discussions involving the future of the university can be difficult. It is particularly difficult to ignite such discussions among university presidents, who generally fall back on a famous observation by Clark Kerr: "About 85 institutions in the Western World established by 1520 still exist in recognizable forms, with similar functions and with unbroken histories, including the Catholic Church, the Parliaments of the Isle of Man, of Iceland, and of Great Britain, several Swiss cantons, and . . . 70 universities."[10] In contrast, during a recent workshops for university presidents and provosts, Susanne Lohmann, of the University of California, Los Angeles, noted that in a single generation following the Civil War, higher education in America changed quite radically.[11] There was a shift from the colonial colleges to the Humboldtian research university, with the Land Grant Acts creating the great public universities with strong service missions. Enrollments went from hundreds to thousands of students, and empowerment shifted to the faculty. Everything that could change about the university did change during this brief period. The consensus in several of our workshops has been that we are well along in a similar period of dramatic change in higher education. Some academic leaders have even been willing to put on the table the most disturbing question of all: will the university, at least as we know it today, even exist a generation from now?

Today, we live in a time of great change, an increasingly global society, knitted together by pervasive communications and transportation technologies and driven by the exponential growth of new knowledge. It is a time of challenge and contradiction, as an ever-increasing human population threatens global sustainability; a global, knowledge-driven economy places a new premium on workforce skills through such phenomena as off-shoring; governments place increasing confidence in market forces to reflect public priorities even as new paradigms, such as open source technologies, challenge conventional free-market philosophies; and shifting geopolitical tensions are driven by the great disparity in wealth and power about the globe, national security, and terrorism. Yet it is also a time of unusual opportunity and reason for optimism, as these same technologies enable the formation of new communities and social institutions, better able to address the needs of our society. Not surprisingly, we have also entered a period of significant change in higher education, as our universities attempt to respond to the challenges, opportunities, and responsibilities before them. Much of this change will be driven by market forces (by a limited resource base, changing societal needs, new technologies, and new competitors), although we must remember that higher education has a public purpose and a public obligation.

It is likely that the university as we know it today—or, rather, the current constellation of diverse institutions that comprise the higher education enterprise—will change in profound ways to serve a changing world. But this is just as the university has done so many times in the past. From this perspective, it is important to understand that the most critical challenge facing most institutions will be the development of the capacity for change. Universities must seek to remove the constraints that prevent them from responding to the needs of a rapidly changing society. They should strive to challenge, excite, and embolden their campus communities and diverse stakeholders to embark on what should be a great adventure for higher education.

What might we anticipate as possible future forms of the university? The monastic character of the ivory tower is certainly lost forever. Many important features of the campus environment suggest that most universities will continue to exist as physical places, at least for the near term. But as digital technology makes it increasingly possible to emulate human interaction with arbitrarily high fidelity, perhaps we should not bind teaching and scholarship too tightly to buildings and grounds. Certainly, both learning and scholarship will continue to depend heavily on the existence of communities, since they are, after all, highly social enterprises. Yet as these communities are increasingly global in extent, detached from the constraints of space and time, we should not assume that the scholarly communities of our times would necessarily dictate the future of our universities. For the longer term, who can predict the impact of rapidly evolving technologies on social institutions—including universities, corporations, and governments—as they continue to multiply in power by the thousands, millions, or billions?

What are university leaders and stakeholders to do as their institutions are buffetted by such powerful forces of change and in the face of unpredictable futures? I certainly can claim no particular wisdom on this issue, but my decade of leading a major university transformation effort does suggest some possibilities. First, it is important to always begin with the basics, by considering carefully those key roles and values that should be protected and preserved during a period of transformation. For example, how would an institution prioritize among such roles as educating the young (e.g., undergraduate education), preserving and transmitting our culture (e.g., libraries, visual and performing arts), basic research and scholarship, and serving as a responsible critic of society? Similarly, what are the most important values to protect? Clearly academic freedom, an openness to new ideas, a commitment to rigorous study, and an aspiration to the achievement of excellence would be on the list for most institutions. But what about such values and practices as shared governance and tenure? Should these be preserved, and at what expense?

Of course, all academic leaders aspire to excellence, but just how do we set our goals? There is an increasing sense that the paradigm characterizing many elite institutions, which simply focuses more and more resources on fewer and fewer people, does not serve the broader needs of our society. Rather, the future premium will be on the development of unique missions for each of our institutions, missions that reflect not only their tradition and their unique roles in serving society but also their core competency. If such differentiation occurs, far greater emphasis should be placed on building alliances with other institutions that will allow universities to focus on core competencies while relying on alliances to address the broader and diverse needs of society.

In a rapidly changing world characterized by unpredictable futures, perhaps experimentation will become more important. Perhaps more emphasis should be placed on exploring possible futures of the university through experimentation and discovery. Rather than continuing to contemplate or debate possibilities for the future, perhaps academic leaders might embark on a more productive course if we build several prototypes of future learning institutions as working experiments. In this way, we could actively explore possible paths to the future.

Finally, it is important for university leaders to approach issues and decisions concerning institutional transformation not as threats but, rather, as opportunities. True, the status quo is no longer an option. However, once we accept that change is inevitable, we can use it as a strategic opportunity to control our destiny, while preserving the most important of our values and our traditions. Creative, visionary leaders can tap the energy created by such threats as the emerging for-profit marketplace and technology, to engage their campuses and to lead their institutions in new directions that will reinforce and enhance their most important roles and values.

SOME FINAL THOUGHTS ON THE UNIVERSITY PRESIDENCY

The importance of the university in our society demands experienced, enlightened, visionary, and committed leadership. It is my belief that the most appropriate training ground for a university presidency remains the traditional academic path, where one first establishes a solid record as a teacher and a scholar before climbing the academic leadership ladder. I also remain convinced that the best university presidents are those who have progressed through the ranks of academic leadership, assuming positions of increasing responsibility and accountability and developing a strong, intuitive understanding of university values and academic excellence in institutions of quality comparable to those they will serve as president.

To be sure, a university president has many responsibilities that simply have no counterpart in academic life: working with governing boards, influencing governors and state legislatures, fund-raising, and intercollegiate athletics. There may indeed be a need to augment the academic experience of potential university leaders with additional training, similar to that given through executive management education by business schools. But it is my belief that without an understanding of the fundamental purpose, values, and traditions of the university and a sense of academic intuition that understands what excellence is all about and how to achieve it, a university president can rarely be effective. This understanding can only be gained by toiling in the vineyards of teaching and scholarship. For a lay governing board to select a president with little experience or understanding of academic institutions is to perpetuate the fallacy of the blind leading the blind.

Part of the reason that the university presidency has become less attractive and less capable of attracting talented candidates is due to the wearisome and distasteful nature of many presidential duties. Fund-raising, political lobbying, pampering governing board members and prima donna faculty, scrapping with other presidents over such trivia as the sharing of football gate receipts, and enduring endless committee meetings and rubber-chicken banquets and water-sogged shrimp receptions eventually becomes quite tiresome. To repeat an earlier epiphany, when presidents realize that most of their activities involve things they do not like to do, with people they do not enjoy being with, and saying things they do not believe, it is probably time to look for other employment.

There are many other frustrating aspects of the job. Many find the mismatch between responsibility and authority disturbing; most grow weary of being responsible and accountable for everything that happens in the university, whether they could influence it or even know about it. The distraction of the current and urgent from the strategic and important is an ongoing annoyance. Yet when a trustee calls (or a governor or a donor or a football coach), everything stops until his or her matter is handled.

For true academics, perhaps the greatest frustration of the position is the all-consuming nature of the responsibilities and duties, leaving precious little time to think deeply about substantive issues. Many presidents fall into a "rip and read" practice where they reach for the script from a speechwriter as they head out the door for their next meeting (or, rather, performance). The time for careful consideration and reflection vanishes during a presidency, at least if one wants to keep on top of university matters. While I actually enjoyed the spinning-plate trick—that is, keeping lots of activities moving ahead with only a nudge from time to time—many others have difficulty partitioning their brains to handle such massively parallel processing. Even in my case, a plate would occasionally spin out of control and crash to the floor.

In reading over an early version of the manuscript of this book, one of my colleagues remarked about how depressing it made the life of a university president appear, observing, "You make it sound like you were continually beaten with whips." In looking back over that period, it could well be that the memory of frustration and occasional failure lingered longer than the joys from success. Yet whenever I hear university presidents proclaim publicly how much they enjoy the position, I must question their candor, their sanity, or perhaps their effectiveness. It is my belief that, like so many leadership roles in our society, a successful university presidency requires great personal sacrifice. It is the kind of job one enjoys most afterward, looking back with a sense of satisfaction in serving an important institution or community, but decidedly not because of personal enjoyment or reward while in the role.

There is one very positive aspect of the hectic pace of a presidency, however. One does meet some interesting people and has the opportunity to enjoy (or endure) some fascinating experiences, creating a storehouse of memories (or, more accurately, notes) that can be digested later, long after a president finally gains the understanding and wisdom to see the true path. There might even be enough material to write a book.

Shortly after announcing my intention to leave academic administration and return to the faculty, after a decade of leading the University of Michigan as provost, acting president, and president, one of my colleagues slipped me a scrap of paper with the following well-known quote from Machiavelli:

> There is no more delicate matter to take in hand, nor more dangerous to conduct, nor more doubtful of success, than to step up as a leader in the introduction of change. For he who innovates will have for his enemies all those who are well off under the existing order of things, and only lukewarm support in those who might be better off under the new.[12]

To this, I could only respond, "Amen!" Leading in the introduction of change can be a challenging and risky proposition. The resistance can be intense, the political backlash threatening. As one who has attempted to illuminate the handwriting on the wall and to lead an institution in transformation, I can attest to the lonely, hazardous, and usually frustrating life led by an agent of change.

The times clearly call for such leadership. Today, our society faces a crossroads, as a global knowledge economy demands a new level of knowledge, skills, and abilities on the part of our citizens. We have entered an era in which educated people and the knowledge and innovation they possess and produce have become the keys to economic prosperity, public health, national security, and social well-being. Sustaining the strength, prosperity, and leadership of our nation will demand a highly educated citizenry and hence a world-class system of higher education.

This educational goal faces many challenges, including an increasing stratification of access to (and success in) quality higher education, based on socioeconomic status, questionable achievement of acceptable student learning outcomes (including critical thinking ability, moral reasoning, communication skills, and quantitative literacy), and cost containment and productivity. Equally challenging is the ability of our colleges and universities to adapt to changes demanded by the emerging knowledge services economy, globalization, rapidly evolving technologies, an increasingly diverse and aging population, and an evolving marketplace characterized by new needs (e.g., lifelong learning), new providers (e.g., for-profit, cyber, and global universities), and new paradigms (e.g., competency-based educational paradigms, distance learning, open source/open content educational resources).

In particular, higher education today faces the challenge of complacency. This was captured by an observation of a senior member of Congress, who portrayed the typical message from today's academic leaders as: American higher education is the best in the world, so give us the money we ask for and leave us alone! It has become increasingly clear that higher education must do more than change and become more innovative to meet the changing needs of the nation. If it is to play the role it must in our future, it must strive to rebuild a far greater sense of trust and confidence on the part of the American public and its elected leaders.

In part, the lack of confidence that American higher education can adapt to the imperatives of a changing world has occurred because of a leadership vacuum among university presidents, governing boards, and faculties. In the face of formidable resistance to change, many presidents have resigned themselves to becoming more "representatives" than "leaders" of their institutions. There is ample evidence today that few lay governing boards offer presidents the degree of support necessary for courageous or visionary leadership. Boards are increasingly detached from their institutions, in both experience and understanding, and are hence more likely to withdraw support at the slightest sign of concern from within (e.g., from the faculty) or from without (e.g., from politicians, donors, and the media).

There is an even more fundamental reason for the leadership vacuum in American higher education. We have allowed the contemporary university presidency to drift ever farther from the academy and the academic mission of the university, redefining it as a separate profession in and of itself, more similar to the professions of corporate executives or government leaders than to academic leadership. To some degree, this has been a consequence of the marching orders many presidents receive to focus their energy on external activities, such as fund-raising or political persuasion. It has also occasionally arisen from lay boards whose deep suspicion of the academy motivates them to bring in leadership with little experience with the academic activities of the university.

Today, there is an urgent need to reconnect the university presidency with the academic values and public purposes of higher education, to link university presidents tightly to the institutional saga that animates and shapes the evolution of their institutions. The pace and nature of change affecting the higher education enterprise both in America and worldwide in the years ahead will require such strong, informed, and courageous leadership. True, it is sometimes difficult to act for the future when the demands of the present can be so powerful and the traditions of the past so difficult to challenge. Yet such academic leadership will be the most important role of the university president in the years ahead, as we navigate our institutions through the stormy seas of a changing world.

NOTES

PREFACE

1. A. Bartlett Giamatti, *A Free and Ordered Space: The Real World of the University* (New York, NY: W. W. Norton and Company, 1988), 17.

2. Ironically, this austere and detached fortress of a building was named after one of Michigan's most respected presidents, Robben Fleming, and his wife, Sally, who used extraordinary diplomatic skill and a strong sympathy for student concerns to calm the campus disruptions of the 1960s and 1970s.

CHAPTER I

1. Burton R. Clark, *The Distinctive College: Antioch, Reed, and Swarthmore* (Chicago: Aldine, 1970), 235.

2. Clark, *Distinctive College,* 235.

3. Also deserving of mention here are a bevy of candidates, including Gary Hart, Jerry Brown, Paul Tsongas, Dick Cheney, Joe Lieberman, Howard Dean, and John Kerry. See also Warren Goldstein, "The Yale Candidates," *Yale Alumni Magazine,* May/June 2004, 46–53.

4. Roger Heyns, private communication with the author, 1992.

5. Clark, *Distinctive College,* 235.

6. Northwest Ordinance, Article 3., printed in F. N. Thorpe, ed., *The Federal and State Constitutions, Colonial Charters, and Other Organic Laws* (Washington, DC: U.S. Government Printing Office, 1909), 957.

7. Richard Rees Price, "The University of Michigan: Its Origin and Development," *Harvard Bulletin in Education* 3 (January 1923).

8. The majority of the university's students were from out of state until the baby boom surge in Michigan enrollments following World War II. After a brief

rise in the proportion of in-state students during the early 1980s, the university today has returned to its more traditional ratio of 40 percent of undergraduate and 70 percent of graduate and professional students drawn from out of state.

9. Howard H. Peckham, *The Making of the University of Michigan 1817–1992,* ed. and updated by Margaret L. Steneck and Nicholas H. Steneck (Ann Arbor: University of Michigan Bentley Historical Library, 1994), 37.

10. Andrew D. White later became the founding president of Cornell University. Charles Adams also served as president of Cornell, as have three other members of the Michigan faculty (Ezra Day, Frank Rhodes, and Jeffrey Lehmann).

11. Peckham, *Making of the University of Michigan,* 39.

12. The *Harper's* article continued: "Students are allowed the widest freedom consistent with sound scholarship in pursuing the studies of their choice; they are held to no minute police regulation, but are treated as persons with high and definite aims from which they are not easily to be diverted. No religious tests are imposed, but devotional exercises are held at stated times, which no one is compelled to attend against his choice, though all are welcome. Women are admitted to all departments on equal terms with men; the doors of the University are open to all applicants who are properly qualified, from whatever part of the world they may come" (*Harper's Weekly,* July 1887, quoted in Peckham, *Making of the University of Michigan,* 95).

13. Clark Kerr, *Troubled Times for American Higher Education: The 1990s and Beyond,* SUNY Series, Frontiers in Education (Albany, NY: SUNY Press, 1993), 173.

14. Peckham, 96.

15. Frederick Rudolph, *The American College and University: A History* (Athens: University of Georgia Press, 1962), 277.

16. Rudolph, 269.

17. Peckham, 53.

18. Technically, John Monteith, a Scottish Presbyterian minister, was selected as Michigan's first president in 1817, when the territorial government formed the Catholespistemead or University of Michigania. But since this was, in reality, a system of public education in which college-level instruction would not occur for another two decades, it is understandable that Tappan would be regarded as Michigan's first true president.

19. Paul E. Lingenfelter, "The Firing of Henry Philip Tappan, University Builder" (master's thesis, University of Michigan, 1970), 8.

20. Peckham, *Making of the University of Michigan,* 56.

21. Rudolph, *American College and University,* 282–83.

22. Charles M. Perry, *Henry Philip Tappan: Philosopher and University President* (Ann Arbor: University of Michigan Press, 1933), 274.

23. Peckham, *Making of the University of Michigan,* 85.

24. Walter Byers, *Unsportsmanlike Conduct: Exploiting College Athletes* (Ann Arbor: University of Michigan Press, 1998), 37.

25. Rudolph, *American College and University,* 269.
26. Peckham, *Making of the University of Michigan,* 155.
27. Peckham, *Making of the University of Michigan,* 193.
28. Peckham, *Making of the University of Michigan,* 323.
29. Derek Bok, private communication with the author, 1985.
30. This distinction among the frontier analogies of trailblazer, pioneer, and settler was taken from a presentation by Dr. Cherry Pancake concerning the future of cyberinfrastructure in scientific research at the National Science Foundation in 2004.

CHAPTER 2

1. In the state of Texas, however, the campus CEO is called "president" and the system CEO "chancellor."
2. Stephen James Nelson, *Leaders in the Crucible: The Moral Voice of College Presidents* (Westport, CT: Bergin and Garvey, 2000)
3. Perhaps because of the high-tech nature of California's economy, eight of that state's nine leaders of research universities in the Association of American Universities come with backgrounds in science or engineering.
4. As Michigan president, I would later lead five Michigan expeditions to the Rose Bowl. I used to be introduced at Pasadena Rose Bowl functions as "Caltech's ultimate Rose Bowl prank," a former Caltech student who would later lead doomed football teams from the Big Ten into battle in Pasadena. (Actually my record was two wins versus three losses—not bad for those days.)
5. The Academic Affairs Advisory Committee of the Senate Assembly was sometimes known as the "little aaac" to distinguish it from the Academic Affairs Advisory Council (the big "AAAC") comprised of the deans. Much later, this confusion was rectified by renaming the committee the Provost's Advisory Group, or PAG. However, to keep things simple, I use "AAAC" in this book.
6. James J. Duderstadt, *On the Move: A Personal History of the University of Michigan's College of Engineering* (Ann Arbor: University of Michigan, Millennium Project, 2003), 50–53.
7. Larry Downs and Chunka Mui, *Killer App* (Cambridge, MA: Harvard Business School Press, 1998).
8. Thomas S. Kuhn, *The Nature of Scientific Revolution* (Chicago: University of Chicago Press, 1962).
9. Although Michigan had never selected an engineer for a university leadership position, it is interesting to note that President Angell had practiced civil engineering early in his career. Brown University actually offered him a choice of an appointment in civil engineering or literature; he chose the latter.

CHAPTER 3

1. Peter T. Flawn, *A Primer for University Presidents: Managing the Modern University* (Austin: University of Texas Press, 1990), 23.

2. Michigan's longest-serving president, James Angell, received a letter from the secretary of the board of regents advising that he was their second choice and that should their first choice decline the offer, he would be invited to be president.

3. Vartan Gregorian, *The Road to Home: My Life and Times* (New York: Simon and Schuster, 2003), 308–9.

4. It is amusing to note that my persistent stress on these themes would predate by almost two decades the high visibility given to them by such recent books as Thomas L. Friedman's *The World Is Flat: A Brief History of the Twenty-First Century* (New York: Farrar, Straus, and Giroux, 2005) and the National Academies' *Rising above the Gathering Storm: Energizing and Employing America for a Brighter Economic Future* (Washington, DC: National Academies Press, 2005)—perhaps another sign of being too far ahead of one's time.

5. "A Chronicle Survey: What Presidents Think," *Chronicle of Higher Education,* Special Report, November 4, 2005, A26.

6. Here, I would define a university president as a "pro" if he or she has served as leader of three or more university campuses.

7. Derek Bok, "Are Huge Presidential Salaries Bad for Colleges?" *Chronicle of Higher Education,* November 22, 2002. See also Derek Bok, *Universities in the Marketplace: The Commercialization of Higher Education* (Princeton, NJ: Princeton University Press, 2003).

CHAPTER 4

1. Nannerl O. Keohane, "More Power to the President?" in *The Presidency* (Washington, DC: American Council on Education, 1998), 12–18.

2. K. E. Weick, "Educational Organizations as Loosely Coupled Systems," *Administrative Science Quarterly* 21 (1976): 1–19.

3. Lao Tzu, *Tao Ten Ching,* trans. John C. H. Wu (New York: St. John's University Press, 1961).

4. *AGB Task Force on the State of the Presidency in American Higher Education, The Leadership Imperative* (Washington, DC: Association of Governing Boards, 2006).

5. Flawn, *Primer for University Presidents,* 23.

6. Theodore Roosevelt, *The Strenuous Life: Essays and Addresses* (New York: Kessing Publishers, 1904), 2–3.

7. Donald Kennedy, "Making Choices in the Research University," *Daedelus* 122, no. 4 (1993): 127–56; Robert Birnbaum, *How Academic Leadership Works: Understanding Success and Failure in the College Presidency* (San Francisco: Jossey-Bass, 1992); Keohane, "More Power to the President?"

CHAPTER 5

1. There is an old saying at Michigan that each president is allowed only three provosts, after which he or she must step down as well. This experience

seems to have held for many years (at least for each of the presidents serving during the last half of the twentieth century, through Fleming, Shapiro, me, and Bollinger).

2. One of the signs of the strength of this leadership philosophy of attracting the best people, providing them with the encouragement and support to push to the limits of their ability, and then getting out of their way is the number of Michigan executive officers and deans who went on to university presidencies. The Michigan offspring who served in the administration during my decade as university provost and president illustrates this "school for presidents" tradition:

Niara Sudarkasa, president, Lincoln University
Linda Wilson, president, Radcliffe College
Jim Crowfoot, president, Antioch College
Chuck Vest, president, Massachusetts Institute of Technology
Bernie Machen, president, University of Utah at University of Florida
Walt Harrison, president, University of Hartford
Maureen Hartford, president, Meredith College
Blenda Wilson, chancellor, California State University at Northridge
Jim Renick, chancellor, North Carolina Agricultural and Technical State University
Nancy Cantor, chancellor, University of Illinois and Syracuse University
Jeff Lehmann, president, Cornell University
Lee Bollinger, president, University of Michigan and Columbia University
Joe White, president, University of Illinois
Robert Weisbuch, president, Drew University

3. Harold T. Shapiro, "University Presidents—Then and Now," in *Universities and Their Leadership,* ed. William G. Bowen and Harold T. Shapiro (Princeton, NJ: Princeton University Press, 1998), 70.

4. For an important case study, consider the difficulties that the University of California experienced over executive compensation during 2005–6, which brought the institution to a crisis point; "Report of the Task Force on UC Compensation, Accountability, and Transparency" (Oakland: University of California Board of Regents, 2006).

5. We contemplated an even more ambitious goal to build endowment to a level such that endowment income would exceed our state appropriation by 2010. This $10 billion target seemed formidable but well within reach, considering that we had increased endowment from $250 million to $2.5 billion from 1988 to 1996. Although the dot-com collapse of the late 1990s and a loss of momentum in university fund-raising in the late 1990s slowed the growth of endowment temporar-

ily, recent efforts by Mary Sue Coleman and her development team have put the university back on track to achieve this goal by 2010.

6. Winston Churchill, Speech to House of Commons, October 28, 1943.

7. This is Pentagon parlance for "Defense Condition 3," a serious level of preparation for defense against a thermonuclear attack.

8. For example, at Michigan, presidents attempting to reorganize the Medical Center have usually encountered a firestorm of opposition from those schools that might be threatened by new reporting arrangements (e.g., medicine, nursing, dentistry, public health, and pharmacy). Here, I offer an important word to the wise: always beware of regents just after their annual physical checkup at the university medical center.

CHAPTER 6

1. Howard H. Peckham, *The Making of the University of Michigan, 1817–1992* (Ann Arbor: University of Michigan Press, 1994), 40.

2. Edward A. Krug, ed., *Charles W. Eliot and Popular Education,* Classics in Education, vol. 8 (New York: Teachers College, Columbia University, 1961).

3. John Henry Newman, *The Idea of a University* (New Haven, CT: Yale University Press, 1996; 1st ed., New York: Longman, Green, 1899); Henry Philip Tappan, *University Education* (New York: George P. Putnam, 1851).

4. Faculty soon began to refer to the funding directed toward rebuilding the strength of the sciences at Michigan as "duder-dollars."

5. While president, I once joined with my colleagues from Stanford University and Columbia University to meet with James Fallows, then editor of *U.S. News and World Report,* to point out the many fallacies in the rankings. He agreed, but he also acknowledged that the importance of the rankings to the magazine's financial bottom line made it highly unlikely that they would disappear.

6. I later learned that the Medical School had a full-time clerk whose sole assignment was to crank out their promotion casebooks, with the belief that if they were not approved the first time through, they certainly would be on a subsequent try.

7. Memorandum from Provost to Dean of Medicine, February 15, 1987.

8. Burton R. Clark, *Creating Entrepreneurial Universities: Organizational Pathways of Transformation* (Surrey: Pergamon, 1998).

9. R. S. Lowen, *Creating the Cold War University: The Transformation of Stanford* (Berkeley: University of California Press, 1997).

10. In this spirit, the deans gave the name *Leonardo's* to the coffee shop on the university's North Campus.

CHAPTER 7

1. A. Bartlett Giamatti, *A Free and Ordered Space.*

2. In 2000, after a redistricting led by the Republican legislature, Congress-

man Dingell found himself representing a district containing Ann Arbor, a very sharp contrast to the labor-dominated district that he had represented for over 40 years. To his credit, he has worked quite hard to understand the bizarre politics of a university town and continues to be the senior member of the House.

3. During my presidency, I insisted that this silly practice be terminated.

4. Gary Owens, former Speaker of the Michigan House of Representatives, private communication with the author, 1992.

5. This team included the late Richard Kennedy (long-standing vice president for state relations), Ralph Nichols (who tragically passed away early in my tenure), Keith Molin, and Roberta Palmer.

6. Each fall, one of Ann Arbor's mayors, Ingrid Sheldon, and I would have a pie-baking contest in which we would exchange apple pies we produced.

7. John Immerwahr, *The Price of Admission: The Growing Importance of Higher Education* (Washington, DC: National Center for Public Policy and Higher Education, 1998).

8. John Immerwahr, *Taking Responsibility: Leaders' Expectations of Higher Education* (Washington, DC: National Center for Public Policy and Higher Education, 1999).

9. Shapiro, "University Presidents," 67.

10. Richard T. Ingram, *Transforming Public Trusteeship,* Public Policy Paper Series (Washington, DC: Association of Governing Boards of Universities and Colleges, 1998).

CHAPTER 8

1. Nelson, *Leaders in the Crucible,* 9–11.

2. William H. Honan, "At the Top of the Ivory Tower the Watchword Is Silence," *New York Times,* July 24, 1994.

3. Nelson, *Leaders in the Crucible,* 28–29.

4. Actually, the earliest name for the effort was "The Michigan Plan." But before this name became public, a new chancellor at the University of Wisconsin, Donna Shalala, announced "The Madison Plan," a far less ambitious effort that was aggressively promoted.

5. James J. Duderstadt, *A University for the 21st Century* (Ann Arbor: University of Michigan Press, 2001), 206.

6. James J. Duderstadt Papers (1963–97), Bentley Historical Library, University of Michigan, http://www.hti.umich.edu/cgi/f/findaid/findaid-idx?c=bhlead&idno=umich-bhl-9811. See also President (University of Michigan) Records (1967–), Bentley Historical Library, University of Michigan, http://www.hti.umich.edu/cgi/f/findaid/findaid-idx?c=bhlead&idno=umich-bhl-87274.

7. *Gratz v. Bollinger,* Docket 02–516, 539 U.S. 244 (2003), Decision: June 23, 2003; *Grutter v. Bollinger,* Docket 02–241, 539 U.S. 306 (2003), Decision: June 23, 2003.

8. Jeffrey Selingo, "Michigan: Who Really Won?" *Chronicle of Higher Education,* January 14, 2005.

9. Richard Atkinson, "Opportunity in a Democratic Society: A National Agenda," Nancy Cantor Distinguished Lectureship on Intellectual Diversity, University of Michigan, May 18, 2005.

10. James J. Duderstadt, State of the University address, University of Michigan, Ann Arbor, October 15, 1991.

11. The absence of a student disciplinary policy and process left the university with only one recourse to address serious student incidents: for the president to act directly using presidential authority (according to Regental Bylaw 2.03) to sanction the student. I was forced to do this in particularly serious cases, such as when I suspended one of our hockey players after he went into a violent rage and destroyed the furniture in his girlfriend's sorority house (just before the playoffs for the national championship, much to the chagrin of our hockey coach). But with 36,000 students, it made for an extremely awkward system.

12. Stephen Burd, "Bush's Next Target?" *Chronicle of Higher Education,* July 11, 2003.

13. Carl Cohen, an eminent university professor of philosophy (and, because of deeply held convictions about the inequity of "racial preference" in admissions, one of the early litigants against the university's affirmative action policies), put it this way: "President James Duderstadt is a gracious and eloquent representative of the UM. No one who knows him or has occasion to differ with him will deny that he is invariably patient and courteous, that he listens carefully, reasons well, and presents balanced arguments with restraint and grace." Letter to the Editor, *Ann Arbor News,* March 19, 1996.

14. However, I quickly followed these statements by saying, "I must hasten to add here that they are also run for their students and their society as well!" "The Challenge of Change," The Presidential Inauguration Address of James Johnson Duderstadt, University of Michigan, Ann Arbor, October 4, 1988.

CHAPTER 9

1. R. C. Heterick, Jr., and C. A. Twigg, "Interpolating the Future," *Educom Review* 32, no. 1 (1997).

2. Eamon Kelly, presentation to the American Association of Universities, Indiana University, October 24, 1994.

3. C. K. Prahalad and Gary Hamel, *Competing for the Future* (Cambridge, MA: Harvard Business School Press, 1996).

4. The transformation documents can be found on the Millennium Project Web site, http://milproj.dc.umich.edu.

5. James J. Duderstadt, *A Case Study in University Transformation: Positioning the University of Michigan for the New Millennium* (Ann Arbor: University of Michigan, Millennium Project, 1999), http://milproj.dc.umich.edu/publications/strategy.

6. Robert Zemsky and Gregory Wegner, "A Very Public Agenda," *Policy Perspectives* 8, no. 2 (1998).

CHAPTER 10

1. At Yale University, Rick and Jane Levin took the brilliant step of "giving" the President's House back to the university for full-time entertaining, noting that while people want to be entertained in the facility, some are irritated that the president should live in such a mansion. Hence, the Levins live in their own house and are perceived as visitors to the President's House for the events they host. This arrangement has apparently been well received by the Yale community.

CHAPTER 11

1. Frank H. T. Rhodes, *The Creation of the Future: The Role of the American University* (Ithaca, NY: Cornell University Press, 2001), 137–39. Rhodes is the former president of the first of the nation's truly public-private hybrids, Cornell University.

2. Werner Z. Hirsch and Luc E. Weber, eds., *Challenges Facing Higher Education at the Millennium* (Phoenix: Oryx Press, 1999), 177–82.

3. Thomas J. Kane and Peter R. Orzag, "Funding Restrictions at Public Universities: Effects and Policy Implications" (working paper, Brookings Institution, Washington, DC, September 2003).

4. David Breneman, *Are the States and Public Higher Education Striking a New Bargain?* Public Policy Paper Series (Washington, DC: Association of Governing Boards and Colleges, 2005).

5. At Michigan, as at most public universities, both legislators and the public at large have little understanding of just who pays for the operation of public universities. One of my colleagues, the president of a major public university, once told me that in a legislative hearing, the chairman of the higher education appropriations committee suggested that the university's football team was generating so much income that surely it could pick up some of the support of the academic programs during hard times. He was incredulous when the president pointed out that the entire revenue of the athletic program was less than 2 percent of the university's operating budget.

6. For considerably more detail on this frustrating subject, see James J. Duderstadt, *Intercollegiate Athletics and the American University: A University President's Perspective* (Ann Arbor: University of Michigan Press, 2000).

7. Bill Pennington, "Unusual Alliance Forming to Rein in College Sports," *New York Times,* January 17, 2003, C21–C24.

8. Julie Basinger and Welch Suggs, "Trustee Group Plans to Join with Faculty Senates in Bid to Change College Sports," *Chronicle of Higher Education,* January 31, 2003.

9. In a confidential survey of UM deans and executive officers in the 1990s,

there was a unanimous consensus that the most serious challenge facing the university was the increasing politicization of its board of regents. They further suggested that the primary responsibility of the president and the executive officers must become that of protecting the university from its own governing board. This same view characterized many other public universities throughout the state. In a meeting with the senior editor of one of the state's leading newspapers early in my presidency, I was warned that my most difficult challenge would be that of preventing politics of the board from harming the university.

10. Keohane, "More Power to the President?"

11. National Commission on the Academic Presidency, *Renewing the Academic Presidency: Stronger Leadership for Tougher Times* (Washington, DC: Association of Governing Boards of Colleges and Universities, 1996; reprint, 2006).

CHAPTER 12

1. Wilfred B. Shaw, ed., *The University of Michigan: An Encyclopedic Survey,* vol. 1 (Ann Arbor: University of Michigan Press, 1942), 57–58.

2. It is worth noting here that his wife had refused to accompany him to Michigan. Little eventually hired a Michigan regent to act as his attorney in suing her for 14 years of desertion.

3. Peter E. VandeWater, *Alexander Grant Ruthven: Biography of a University President* (Grand Rapids, MI: Wm. B. Eerdman Publishing, 1977), 243.

4. Robben Fleming, private communication with the author, 1988.

5. Ibid.

6. James J. Duderstadt, confidential letter to the Board of Regents of the University of Michigan, September 28, 1995.

7. One of the more thoughtful editorials was that of noted historian Jim Tobin, then a reporter for the *Detroit News:* "In a sense, Duderstadt was a major corporate executive, juggling a multibillion dollar budget and overseeing a gigantic work force. Yet unlike CEOs, he had to answer to many masters, university regents, state legislators, powerful alumni, even deans and faculty. That frustration—enormous pressures combined with limited authority—may be the toughest burden university presidents bear according to experts in higher education. Governor Engler maintained, 'It became an issue of Jim Duderstadt not getting a passing grade in the care and feeding of regents—everything from which box they get at University of Michigan football games to how they're being recognized at university events to how much stature they can have as regents'"; James Tobin, "Duderstadt Kept a Frantic Pace," *Detroit News,* September 29, 1995.

8. J. Duderstadt, *University for the 21st Century;* J. Duderstadt, *Intercollegiate Athletics and the American University;* J. Duderstadt, *Positioning the University of Michigan;* James J. Duderstadt and Farris W. Womack, *The Future of the Public University in America: Beyond the Crossroads* (Baltimore, MD: Johns Hopkins University Press, 2002); James J. Duderstadt, Daniel E. Atkins, and Douglas Van

Houweling, *Higher Education Faces the Digital Age: Technology Issues and Strategies for American Colleges and Universities* (Westport, CT: Praeger Publishers; Washington, DC: American Council on Education, 2002); James J. Duderstadt and Luc E. Weber, eds., *Reinventing the Research University* (London: Economica, 2004).

9. Anne Duderstadt, *A Pictorial History of the College of Engineering of the University of Michigan* (Ann Arbor: University of Michigan, Millennium Project, 2003); J. Duderstadt, *On the Move;* Anne Duderstadt, *The Michigan Saga: A Pictorial History* (Ann Arbor: University of Michigan, Millennium Project, 2006).

10. Clark Kerr, *The Uses of the University,* 5th ed. (Cambridge: Harvard University Press, 2001), 115.

11. Susanne Lohmann, Meeting of the National Academics IT Forum with the Provosts of the Association of American Universities, Beckman Center, Irvine, CA, September 9, 2003.

12. Niccolo Machiavelli, *The Prince: Utopia, Ninety-Five Theses,* Harvard Classics, Part 36, ed. Charles W. Eliot (New York: P. F. Collier and Sons, 1910), 53.

INDEX